Critical Practices in International Theory

D1756360

Critical Practices in International Theory brings together for the first time the essays of the leading IR theorist, James Der Derian. The essays cover a variety of issues central to Der Derian's work including diplomacy, alienation, terrorism, intelligence, national security, new forms of warfare, the role of information technology in international relations, poststructuralist theory, and the military-entertainment-media matrix.

The book includes a framing introduction written for this volume in which Der Derian provides historical and theoretical context for a diverse body of work. Discussing his own influences and reflecting upon the development of international theory, he advocates a critical pluralist approach to the most pressing problems of world politics.

Written in the eloquent style that marks out Der Derian as one of the most provocative and innovative thinkers in international relations, this collection is essential reading for scholars and students interested in the past, present, and future of international relations.

James Der Derian is a Watson Institute research professor of international studies at Brown University, where he directs the Global Security Program and the Global Media Project. He is the author of many articles and books, including the highly acclaimed *Virtuous War* (2001, 2009).

University of Edinburgh

30150   024926732

Critical Practices in International Theory
Selected essays

James Der Derian

Routledge
Taylor & Francis Group

LONDON AND NEW YORK

First published 2009
by Routledge
2 Park Square, Milton Park, Abingdon, Oxon, OX14 4RN

Simultaneously published in the USA and Canada
by Routledge
270 Madison Avenue, New York, NY 10016

*Routledge is an imprint of the Taylor & Francis Group,
an informa business*

Typeset in Times New Roman by Keyword Group Ltd
Printed and bound in Great Britain by CPI Antony Rowe, Chippenham, Wiltshire

British Library Cataloguing in Publication Data
A catalogue record for this book is available from the British Library

Library of Congress Cataloging in Publication Data

Library of Congress Cataloging-in-Publication Data

Der Derian, James.
Critical practices in international theory : selected essays /
James Der Derian.
    p. cm.
    ISBN 978-0-415-77240-2 – ISBN 978-0-415-77241-9 –
    ISBN 978-0-203-88263-4   1. International relations–Philosophy.
    2. International relations. I. Title.
    JZ1318.D464 2009
    327.101–dc22   2008033851

ISBN 13: 978-0-415-77240-2 (hbk)
ISBN 13: 978-0-415-77241-9 (pbk)
ISBN 13: 978-0-203-88263-4 (ebk)

ISBN 10: 0-415-77240-0 (hbk)
ISBN 10: 0-415-77241-9 (pbk)
ISBN 10: 0-203-88263-6 (ebk)

Contents

Preface

Nicholas Rengger

Over the last twenty years, James Der Derian has established himself as one of the most provocative, ingenious, stimulating and prescient interpreters of the vicissitudes and dissonances of the international political condition. In three books, one enormously influential edited book, to say nothing of many commercially commissioned articles, several documentaries and dozens of powerful and influential essays – many of them collected in the present volume – he has developed a rich and extraordinarily fruitful alliance of the 'classical approach' to international relations – the historical and philosophical assumptions so beloved of his teacher Hedley Bull – with the powerful and sinuous strategies and articulations of contemporary continental thought that he first read under Charles Taylor's tutelage at McGill. He has forged a powerful set of assumptions drawn from this twin heritage to illuminate and disturb the categories of world politics increasingly bundled together by what he calls (in his introduction to the present volume) 'the increasing acceleration, complexity and interconnectivity of everything'. He is, in particular, widely, and rightly, seen as one of the most inventive and acute analysts of the emerging constellations of military, media, governmental and intellectual assumptions that have emerged in the aftermath of 9/11 and the technological shifts and developments – I do not say advances – of the last twenty or so years, and which are continuing to evolve and multiply at an ever accelerating rate.

Given this, it was not clear (at least not to me) that there was anything that I could add, by way of a preface to this collection that did not consist simply in saying – in as professional prose as I could manage – 'well done, James, keep up the good work'. But that seemed a rather poor preface for a book as richly provocative and illuminatingly heterodox as this one. Since James is one of my oldest friends and intellectual sparring partners in 'IR' proper (my own background and graduate work being in political philosophy and intellectual history), it would also be decidedly poor payment for twenty years of spirited and engaging conversation.

As luck would have it, however, an anniversary that by chance falls this year provides me with an opportunity to do better. Twenty-one years ago, the academic journal *Millennium* sent me a book to review. Then, as now, *Millennium* was one of the leading journals in IR that seeks to develop and explore new theoretical departures – perhaps because its editors are graduate students and thus rather less set in their ways than we tend to become when professional responsibility has set about hardening our intellectual arteries. This was important for me since it was the first book in IR I had been asked to review (I had reviewed some in political theory previously). The review was duly published in the summer 1988 issue of *Millennium,* thus exactly twenty years ago, as I write this preface. The book in question was *On Diplomacy: A Genealogy of Estrangement*, by James Der Derian. Ironically enough, James and I first met at the December 1987 British International Studies Conference at Aberystwyth, after the review had been written, but before it had appeared. The substance of the review thus became the subject of our first conversation. It goes without saying that I liked and admired the book (I still do) and wrote an appropriately positive review, though not without dissenting from some aspects of the argument. But on reading the review after twenty years, two particular observations I made then seem worth emphasising in the light of the collection of essays gathered together here.

The first point is that the review refers to Der Derian's 'scholarly range and philosophical sureness of touch', and emphasised how unusual that was in the literature of IR. We might hope – and indeed I think we could generally claim – that philosophical sureness of touch is much less rare in theoretical reflections on IR today than it was twenty years ago, and inasmuch as it is less rare, much of the credit should go to those like James whose work so clearly blazed this particular trail. But I also want to suggest that in the essays gathered here, this range and sureness of touch are superbly well displayed. From the opening essay, very much part of that first book, through the historically and philosophically acute readings of Hobbes, Marx, Nietzsche and Baudrillard on security, to the superbly effective job of deflation he does on Kissinger's *Diplomacy* and on to the final essay on Hedley Bull and the case for a post-classical approach, the essays all point up James' astonishing range and ability to bring the philosophical and empirical together to inform our understandings of the shifts and ruptures that make, and remake, contemporary world politics.

The second point I drew attention to in the review, was Der Derian's prose. He has always written with a panache and a sense of style that marked him out in a field where, let us be honest, stylish prose stands out, to use a phrase of Martin Wight's, like Roman masonry in a London suburb. Indeed, I closed the review by remarking that 'David Hume once divided the republic of letters into two worlds: the learned and the conversable. On the evidence of this book, Der Derian has a foot in both'. I would now make even more of this than I did then. I think Der Derian's prose style has in fact always been one of his chief tools to disturb and disrupt established practices in international relations, both academic and non-academic. Allusive, playful, witty, ironic, at times drawing on the languages and tropes of popular culture but also gently undercutting them, it is a subtle and powerful tool of critique by itself.

But there is a further sense in which Der Derian has a foot in both the learned and the conversable worlds, to which he himself alludes in his introduction and which is especially visible in the essays collected here. This is simply his sense that, without disavowing his contribution to the theoretical debates of the late 1980s and early 1990s in IR, he wanted to move on; to interrogate the 'critical issues of global politics', as he saw them. This trajectory, while present, I think from his first book, has become much more marked from the mid 1990s onwards. It shapes his account of MIMENET in *Virtuous War*, his ongoing research agenda at Brown (where he is currently research professor), is central to the profusion of media through which he disseminates his work (as his discussion in the introduction makes plain) and is very visible in many of the essays collected here. In particular, the interpenetration of what in his introduction he refers to as 'the relationship of global media, global security and global governance' is becoming the nexus of his critical inquiries towards the end of the first decade of the twenty-first century. The 'conversable world' is increasingly a wired world and in charting the manner and the matter of the wiring and its multiple significances for global politics, Der Derian is mapping the new terrain that we all need to pay attention to, whether we agree with Der Derian's take on it or not.

In short, then, the essays collected here mark various way stations on one of the most interesting and thoughtful intellectual trajectories in contemporary IR. And, indeed – I would say – in contemporary social theory more generally. His future critical inquiries will, I have no doubt at all, leave us even further in his debt than we already are but we have been given a great deal already. So how to end? Well, I suppose, 'Well done, James, keep up the good work' (and that's another pint you owe me …).

NJR
St Andrews, July 2008.

Acknowledgements

The work in this collection has been published previously in a variety of different forms. I would like to thank the publishers for granting permission to use copyright material.

Der Derian, James. 'Mediating Estrangement: A Theory for Diplomacy' April 1987 pp. 91–110, *Review of International Studies*, Cambridge University Press.

Der Derian, James. 'Arms, Hostages and the Importance of Shredding in Earnest: Reading the National Security Culture', *Social Text* (Spring, 1989), 22, pp. 79–91. © 1989 by Duke University Press.

Der Derian, James. 'The (S)pace of International Relations: Simulation, Surveillance and Speed', *International Studies Quarterly* (September 1990) pp. 295–310, Wiley-Blackwell.

Der Derian, James. 'S/N: International Theory, Balkanisation, and the New World Order', *Millennium Journal for International Studies* (Winter 1991), vol. 20, no. 3, pp. 485–506 (permission kindly granted by Sage UK).

Der Derian, James. 'The C.I.A., Hollywood, and Sovereign Conspiracies', *Queen's Quarterly* (Summer 1993), vol. 100, no. 2, pp. 329–347. Reproduced with permission of Queen's Quarterly.

Der Derian, James. "ACT IV: Fathers (and Sons), Mother Courage (and Her Children), and the Dog, the Cave, and the Beef", in *Global Voices: Dialogues in International Relations*, pp. 83–96 © 1993 ed. James N. Rosenau (Boulder, CO and Oxford, UK: Westview Press, 1993), and published by Westview Press, a member of the Perseus Books Group. All rights reserved.

Der Derian, James. "Great Men, Monumental History, and Not-So-Grand Theory: A Meta-Review of Henry Kissinger's *Diplomacy*", Forum review article, *Mershon International Studies Review* (April 1995), vol. 39, no. 1, pp. 173–180, Wiley-Blackwell.

Der Derian, James. 'Post-Theory: The Eternal Return of Ethics in International Relations' Taken from the book: *New Thinking in International Relations Theory*, © 1997 eds Michael Doyle and John Ikenberry and published by Westview Press, a member of the Perseus Books Group. All rights reserved.

James Der Derian, 'Global Swarming, Virtual Security, and Bosnia', *The Washington Quarterly*, 19:3 (Summer, 1996), pp. 45–56. © 1996 by the Center for Strategic and International Studies (CSIS) and the Massachusetts Institute of Technology.

James Der Derian, 'Virtuous War and Hollywood', *The Nation*, 3rd April 2000 pp. 41–44.

Der Derian, James. 'Virtuous War/Virtual Theory', *International Affairs* (Fall, 2000) pp. 771–788 Wiley-Blackwell.

Der Derian, James. 'The Illusion of a Grand Strategy', Op-ed, this article first appeared in *The New York Times* on May 25, 2001.

Der Derian, James. 'In Terrorem: Before and After 9/11', pp. 101–116 in *Worlds in Collision*, eds. Ken Booth and Tim Dunne, 2002, Palgrave Macmillan. Reproduced with permission of Palgrave Macmillan.

Der Derian, James. 'The Question of Information Technology in International Relations', *Millennium Journal of International Studies* (vol. 32, no. 3, 2003), pp. 441–456 (permission kindly granted by Sage UK).

Der Derian, James. 'Hedley Bull and the Case for a Post-Classical Approach', Millennium: Journal of International Studies. This article first appeared in *International Relations at LSE: A History of 75 Years* pp. 61–87 eds Harry Bauer and Elisabetta Brighi (London: Millenium Publishing House, 2003) and is reproduced with the permission of the publisher.

James Der Derian.

Introduction

I have done my best over the course of a chequered academic career not to force a logical order upon a resistant past or to trim my ideas to fit a disciplinary conformity. Having now collected a diverse mix of journal articles, magazine essays, op-ed pieces, a book review and a one-act play, to be published under the pretense that works produced over the course of two decades might possibly add up to a coherent whole, I cannot help but feel complicit in a literary felony – and compelled to provide a defense.

Adequate justification is hampered by the need to explain why these essays were written in the first place, entailing a shot-gun marriage of retrospection and introspection that I fear, like dream interpretation, would be much more convincing to the dreamer than the interpreter. It would just as likely produce dubious rationales for past decisions. Did I go to the archives in Paris to find that key aide-mémoire on revolutionary diplomatic practices, or was it to escape one more college hall dinner featuring mashed Brussels sprouts? Did I go to the local mall to watch another bad spy film in search of further symptoms of Cold War pathologies, or was it to escape the hot weather that day? Did I go to the Mojave Desert once more to figure out why the military were so intent on making a game of war, or was it just an excuse to play soldier?

From an intellectual and chronological distance it is safer, but no more or less truthful, to say that my primary motivation was to make international theory worthy of global practices, in the manner of Gilles Deleuze, who appreciated how the significance as well as the ethical import of the event was shaped by the character and efficacy of our theoretical interventions. For me, this meant using international theory to disturb, dismantle, and disabuse the contradictions, assumptions, and outright myths of International Relations (IR), in the hope of imagining, enabling, perhaps even enacting more non-violent, democratic and equitable practices in international politics. These essays are theoretically informed, historically bounded, and policy-oriented interpretations of diplomatic practices, violent conflicts, and global events. They were not written in pursuit of self-evident or timeless truths. My intention was to alert readers to what I considered to be clear and present dangers, because and in spite of the fact that they were not showing up on the radar screens of conventional politics nor in the mainstream offerings of international relations theory.

My abiding concern was the increasing acceleration, complexity, and interconnectivity of *everything*, which meant that I put a premium on finding fast yet effective styles, methods, and mediums of communication. My use of pluralist approaches, diverse publishing venues, and multiple media was only reinforced by the auto immune response to 9/11, the 'long war' on terrorism, and the fiasco in Iraq. In an era of mediated terror, symbolic violence, and preemptive war, getting up to speed took on whole new meaning as an intellectual and ethical imperative. Hence my early preference for the short essay over the long monograph; the defamiliarizing concept over the testable theory; the fractal montage over the linear narrative; the commercial over the university press; the online website over the journal article; and, as technology made it feasible, the video documentary over the written treatise. If there is to be any redemption for once more inflicting these writings upon the reading public, I hope it can be found in a life-long effort to represent the greatest dangers of world politics without pretending to 'make sense' of one of its most persistent and repugnant practices: the use of organized (and, increasingly, disorganized) violence not just to continue political differences by other (and, increasingly, mediated) means, but to magnify and multiply those differences into permanent states of war.

This book is an arbitrary selection of work that coheres no more than the world that it 'records'. But therein lies my secondary defense, drawn from a critique of one of the lowest form of rhetorics, mimesis, which underpins of one of the most powerful schools of IR, realism. This collection does not seek to mimic reality; on the contrary, it reflects the resistance of global events, from the end of the Cold War to the beginnings of the war on terror, to be temporized and theorized into recurrent, predictable and therefore safer patterns of behavior. Theories and concepts are developed to illuminate and to understand critical practices, including diplomacy, espionage, terrorism, information technology, and global media, but with a self-reflexive awareness of how both theory and practice are shaped by acts of perception, comprehension, and ethical intervention. Rather than surveying the field from static levels of analysis (in the Waltzian manner, of man, state, and system, which curiously persists after powerful poststructuralist and feminist critiques), these essays explore rapid phase-shifts of global power in which human, national, international, and global actors oscillate in significance as global events are elevated by the media into an international crisis one moment, only to be disappeared the next.

Caveats aside, I am very grateful for the opportunity to present in a single volume critical interventions on what I considered to be the most important theoretical and political concerns of the day. I will leave it to others to assess the aptness of the collection (I owe Nicholas Rengger yet another pint for taking first crack in the Preface, as well as Craig Fowlie and Nicola Parkin from Routledge for making it possible). Instead, I wish to provide a few warning signs and mileposts for readers who might be less familiar with the issues and debates that generated these essays. By title and intent, this collection critically explores how practice informs theory and theory enables practice in world politics. My main mentors as an undergraduate at McGill University, Charles Taylor in political philosophy and

Peter Gourevitch in international relations, exposed me to heavy doses of German and French continental philosophy, making it impossible to extricate theory from practice. Critical theory gave me essential tools for understanding how the most pathological politics and most powerful technologies can combine to produce recurring crises of insecurity. Indeed, Walter Benjamin, the most brilliant outlier of the Frankfurt School, provided me with what became my four mantras of late modernity:[1]

- 'There is no document of civilization which is not at the same time a document of barbarism'.
- 'The history that showed things "as they really were" was the strongest narcotic of the century'.
- 'History decays into images, not into stories'.
- 'In times of terror, when everyone is something of a conspirator, everybody will be in a situation where he has to play detective'.

Of equal influence has been an array of French structuralist and poststructuralist thinkers, beginning with Roland Barthes, who traced the practice of literary critique back to the etymology of 'crisis', in the sense of 'calling into question' the most dangerous truths and practices of the day. Recognizing that the power of truth most effectively circulates through opaque discursive practices, Barthes believed that a critical investigation must necessarily disturb language itself. This can be a dangerous activity, in more ways than one. Barthes' experience in French literary circles in the 1960s is not unlike what many critical international theorists faced in the 1980s:

> Discourse reflecting upon discourse is the object of a special vigilance on the part of institutions, which normally contain it within the limits of a strict code: in the literary State, criticism must be controlled as much as a police force is: to free the one would be quite as 'dangerous' as democratizing the other: it would be to threaten the power of power, the language of language.[2]

But probably my most profound (and most unresolved) anxiety of influence remains the 'classical approach' or 'English School' of IR, primarily gleaned from Hedley Bull, my tutor, supervisor and mentor while I was a graduate student at Oxford. As I elaborate in the final chapter (which circles back to my intellectual origins), my understanding of how theory produces and is sustained by power might differ in vernacular but is not wholly alien to the classical approach espoused by Martin Wight (who coined the term, 'international theory') or Hedley Bull (who defined it as 'the leading ideas that have governed and do govern our thinking about International Relations').[3]

Critical, poststructuralist, and classical theories fuse in this collection, producing what I first referred to in the 1980s as a 'post-classical approach', in recognition of a drawing upon but going beyond the 'English School' through a critical engagement with continental philosophy, genealogical history and pluralist ethics.

This approach interprets international politics as in a constant process of construction – and destruction – through discursive and performative acts of diplomacy, statecraft, trade, war, and other global activities. Conversely, international theory is considered to be inseparable from the historical production of sovereignty, the state, and the citizen-subject. Unsurprisingly, many of the self-appointed guardians of International Relations, dedicated to theory/practice, fact/value and normative/empirical distinctions sought to check such foreign thoughts at the borders of the discipline. Most of us did not mind too much, sharing an affinity – perhaps too much so – with the view of that other critical Marxist, Groucho, who found considerable pleasure in refusing to join any club that would have him as a member. Much less frequently quoted was Groucho's more belligerent turn of the phrase – 'I have a mind to join a club and beat you over the head with it' – which, given the tendency of an intellectual insurgency to become the next academic hegemony, is no less of a danger (something I witnessed firsthand while participating in 2007 in an ESRC/BISA Benchmark Review of the top Politics and International Studies Departments in the UK).

I have also sought, by pairing practice with theory, to move beyond the scholastic debates and intra-disciplinary squabbles that seem to have a life of their own in International Relations. I still consider myself fortunate to have been in exile in Great Britain during the not-so-great debate between the neorealists and neoidealists as well as the conceptual wars between the relative and absolute gainsayers. However, I wish to temper my criticisms – past and present – with the confession that some of us, after we found the keys to the cabinet of continental philosophy, did get a little drunk on theory in the late 1980s and early 1990s. But long before the band Devo sang of 'post-postmodern man' or Baudrillard's work showed up in *The Matrix*, I cautioned (indeed, in the preface of my first book in 1987) against the strategic use of such terms like postmodernism and others that enjoyed the curious utility of transparent meaning for some and utter meaninglessness for others. At some point – probably the same one that Foucault identifies, where each new form of resistance produces a new form of power – I decided to leave the theory wars behind, so as to shift my focus to what I considered the critical issues of global politics.

In my most recent writings I turn to new threats and vulnerabilities that defy mainstream theoretical approaches as well as traditional modes of governance. With the fixities of boundaries and identities threatened by increased flows of information and capital, pollutants and drugs, viruses and weapons, after a 'global war on terrorism' becomes the primary security issue of the most powerful state in the international order, and when global media is not simply a conveyor or catalyst of change but a powerful actor, a central modality, and the main battlefield of global politics, I think it is time for International Relations to retool. Post-Cold War, post-9/11, we have witnessed the emergence of competing sources and mediations of power: what I call the *new global heteropolarity*, in which different actors are able to produce profound global effects through interconnectivity. Varying in identity, interests and strength, ranging from fundamentalist terrorists to peace activists, new global actors gain advantage through the broad bandwidth of information technology rather than through the narrow stovepipe of territorially based sovereign governments. Enhanced by global media, non-state actors have become super-empowered players in international politics. If we are ever to get beyond terror and begin to adequately address other neglected, no less pressing global issues – the fear of pandemic, the apprehension of famine, the resentments of resource conflicts, the slow anxiety of global warming – we need to undertake a critical inquiry into the relationship of global media, global security, and global governance. The product of that investigation will more likely be streamed to your iPhone than published in a book, so please do enjoy this artefact of knowledge while you can.

Notes

1 Walter Benjamin, *Theses on the Philosophy of History,* in *Illuminations*, ed. Harry Zohn (New York: Shocken, 1977), p. 260; *The Arcades Project*, trans. Howard Eiland and Kevin McLaughlin (Cambridge: MA: Belknap Press, 1999), pp. 463 and 476; Walter Benjamin, *Charles Baudelaire: A Lyric Poet in the Era of High Capitalism* (London and New York: Verso, 1973), p. 40.
2 Roland Barthes, *Criticism and Truth*, trans. K. Keuneman (Minneapolis: University of Minnesota Press, 1987), pp. 32–33.
3 See Chapter 21, p. 292–294.

1 Mediating estrangement

A theory for diplomacy

Source: *Review of International Studies* (April, 1987), 13, pp. 91–110.

> How does one live according to reason if the *other*, the *alien*, the *foreigner*, whether remote or nearby, may burst into one's world at any moment?
>
> Raymond Aron, *Peace and War*

Diplomacy has been particularly resistant to theory. What knowledge we do have of the practice and principles of diplomacy is largely drawn from the works of former diplomatists like Abraham de Wicquefort's *L'Ambassadeur et ses Fonctions* (1681), François de Callières' *De la Maniere de Négocier avec les Souverains* (1716), Ernest Satow's *Guide to Diplomatic Practice* (1917) and Harold Nicolson's *Diplomacy* (1939).[1] Conveying a view of diplomacy as a specialized skill of negotiation, these works seek to 'maximize' that skill for the benefit of novices entering the profession. Understandably, their histories of diplomacy tend to be sketchy and rather anecdotal, and their theories of diplomacy, when they do exist, usually consist of underdeveloped and implicit propositions. Moreover, since the authors were serving governments at the apogee of imperial power, they were not interested in looking too widely and too deeply into a past which might undermine the foundations of skilful negotiation—order, continuity and 'common sense'.

Neither is there to be found a substantial theoretical work on the subject in the contemporary literature of international relations.[2] Usually intending rationally to order the present or to prepare decision-makers for the future, the behaviouralist or 'scientific' school has shown itself to be preoccupied (for the most part methodologically) with the more empirical, policy-oriented side of diplomacy. The 'classical' or traditionalist approach in international relations offers a richer, more historical vein to mine. Its strength lies in the recognition that the origins and development of diplomacy, along with international law and a balance of power, were essential to the emergence of the European states system. A section on diplomacy can be found in almost all of the larger general texts.[3] However, the strength of the classicists often contains a hidden analytical weakness. By considering diplomacy chiefly as an exchange of accredited envoys by states, and as a valuable norm for the international order, they have demonstrated a conservative preference for the status quo in international politics.[4]

Equally, they often have attributed an 'essence' or 'nature' to diplomacy which bears this preference, the best example being Nicolson's repeated claim that 'common sense is the essence of diplomacy'.[5] To be fair, this is not so much a weakness as it is a normative evaluation of diplomacy, or, as Martin Wight says, 'a statement of belief about the way international politics ought to go'.[6] The problem, however, is that as often as not the normative element of the classical works is implicitly and uncritically supportive of a teleological view of diplomacy. Left unexplored are the dynamic forces which originally created the need for diplomacy and defined purposes often antithetical to the traditional teleology. This is yet another reason why a theoretical enquiry is needed, to dig deeper into the past, to offer an account of the *pre-history* of diplomacy which the classical school has neglected.

It could well be that diplomacy has suffered from theoretical neglect to the extent that power politics has profited—in theory and practice. When diplomacy is construed as a continuation of war by other means, as is often the *realpolitik* case, then little intellectual energy needs to be wasted on the illumination of power's shadow. However, I would argue that it is possible to recognize the paramountcy of the power relation in human affairs, *and to* assert the need for a theory of diplomacy. Like Hans Morgenthau and the other realists who have followed him, I believe that an analysis of power is necessary for understanding diplomacy. However, power alone is not sufficient to explain the origins and conduct of diplomacy. Martin Wight provides an important reason

> Powers have qualitative differences as well as quantitative, and their attraction and influence is not exactly correlated to mass and weight. For men possess not only territories, raw materials and weapons but also beliefs and opinions. It is true that beliefs do not prevail in international politics unless they are associated with power ... But it is equally true that power varies very much in effectiveness according to the strength of the beliefs that inspire its use.[7]

Diplomatic theory is needed if we are to understand the relationship between power and diplomacy, to investigate how this relationship has been historically manifested in the attempt to govern the ungovernable—the anarchical society— through discursive and cultural practices. Hedley Bull broached this terrain, the question of how international diplomacy, in the absence of a sovereign power, constituted and was sustained by a *diplomatic culture*, which he defined narrowly as 'the common stock of ideas and values possessed by the official representatives'.[8] What he and others from the classical school have not explored in any depth is how this diplomatic culture was formed and transformed, and how its power of normalization in a Leviathan-less world has been reproduced. The need for a theory of diplomacy points, I believe, toward the need for a neo- or post-classical approach.

There are, of course, other reasons for diplomacy's resistance to philosophical comprehension, probably as many reasons as there are approaches to the study of international relations. The dominance of the power political approach can account for only one dimension of the theoretical lacunae in diplomacy. But if power cannot provide the conceptual, let alone theoretical sufficiency to explain the origins, transformations, and current state of diplomacy, what can? Taking into account the complexity and breadth of the subject, I cannot pretend that any one concept or theory is sufficient. I will argue, however, that there is a ready-made theory which has suffered from neglect in the field of international relations. I refer to the theory of alienation, as elaborated by Hegel, Feuerbach, Marx, Sartre, and others.

On what grounds can we justify its application to the study of diplomacy? First, alienation theory is highly suited for a *historical* analysis. It seeks to explain man's alienation from an 'original' state of solidarity: as a result of certain causes, new forms of alienation develop which manifest themselves in a historical framework. In Hegel, it is the self-consciousness which is alienated 'to put itself in the position of something universal'; in Feuerbach, man alienates his essential humanity to religion, in the desire to find in heaven what he cannot find on earth; and in Marx, man is alienated from his 'productive activity' which leads to man's alienation from nature, himself, his product, and other men.[9] Thus, alienation has been interpreted as a ubiquitous spiritual, religious, or social process which has always been active in history. Second, the primeval alienation of man gave rise to estranged relations which required a *mediation*. In the most general sense, the form this mediation takes, as estranged relations change, constitutes a theoretical and historical base for the study of diplomacy. Third, alienation theory is well-equipped to explain the emergence and transformations of diplomatic relations, because it is a 'systems' theory. It attempts to explain a system by studying the genesis of its internal relations, which are seen as expressions of alienated *powers*. Hence, instead of the conventional micro/macro dichotomy or bifurcated level of analysis, the mediation of estrangement on pre-intra- and inter-state levels can be interpreted as the basis of the diplomatic system.

Finally, I believe that the interpretative dimension of alienation has something to offer to the classical approach to international relations. Because its history is usually back-tracked only to Marx, alienation's rich intellectual tradition as a concept in law history, and philosophy has been forgotten or neglected. In the course of this essay I will use alienation theory to present some overlooked 'classics' which I hope might conceptually and textually stimulate the traditionalist ruminations.

Definitions?

Not only the theories but some of the terms I will use are relatively new to the study of international relations. Equally, some familiar words will be used in unfamiliar ways. The most notable case is the term 'diplomacy'. Although the word does not become current in its modern sense, as the conduct or management of international relations until the late eighteenth century, I will use it for lack of a better one to represent the earliest manifestations of diplomacy. In this enquiry

I will offer a general working definition of diplomacy as a mediation between estranged individuals, groups of entities, which will be defended and become more specific in due course.[10] The word 'mediation' will be used in two senses. First, in the conventional sense (which emerges coevally with the modern meaning of diplomacy), mediation means a connecting link or, for the purpose of reconciling, an intervention between two or more individuals or entities. By utilizing this term, I admit to an interpretation which emphasizes the interdependent and reconciliatory nature of diplomacy yet acknowledges the necessity for interventions. The other sense of the term is derived from the theory of alienation itself, as drawn from the writings of Hegel and Marx.[11] There are two types or orders of mediation. The first is between man (his powers) and nature (his needs). In this subject-object relationship, mediation refers to an activity, manual or intellectual, which brings man's powers and needs together; at the most basic level an example would be one which enables man's hunger to be fulfilled by eating. The second order of mediation is a historically specific one made necessary when man's activity, or the product of his activity, is alienated from him. Examples taken from Feuerbach, Hegel and Marx, of mediatories acting between man and his alienated needs, would include God, the state, and money. All these mediations are essential to the authors' explanations of religion, politics, and economics to the extent that they are related to alienation. A mediation can also be alienated as instanced by Marx's analysis of the origins of money: acting as the necessary mediator between man and his wants, it comes to *be* what he wants. Marx describes this second type of mediation as 'an alienated mediation', and also as the 'mediation of a mediation'.[12] An example of how this type of mediation might be adapted to diplomatic theory would be to explain the passage of diplomacy from its early mythological phase to its first historical phases when one of the earliest Western mediations, Christendom (founded on man's estrangement from an original state of solidarity) is supplanted by the 'alienated mediations' of states (following their mutual estrangement from Christendom's institutionalized representatives, the papal state).

Of course, such an explanation would involve an extensive historical investigation—which is not the purpose of this essay. Not is its purpose to explain all aspects of diplomacy: otherwise it would include an account of its multifarious functions as a system of communication, negotiation, and information. Rather, the intention of this essay is to provide a theoretical foundation for an enquiry into a neglected area of diplomacy: its origins and transformations which are related to conditions of alienation, and the attempt to mediate those conditions through systems of thought, law, and power.

The alienation of theory

The premise of this essay is that diplomacy is demarcated by alienation. To determine fully whether or not this has been the case from the inception of diplomacy would require a sifting through of the historical evidence. The task at hand, however, is to reconstruct alienation as an archaeological tool, that is, to consider changes in the nature of alienation and changes in theories of alienation which might enhance our understanding of diplomacy. This involves, I believe, four preliminary levels of comprehension: (1) demonstrate the validity of the idea of alienation for diplomacy; (2) provide definitions for 'alienation' and 'estrangement'; (3) give a short history of how the concept changed according to different relations of otherness; and (4) present the theories of alienation which can be used to investigate the development of diplomacy.

While the words 'alienation' and 'estrangement' are frequently heard in the discourse of international relations, the concept itself is for the most part a stranger to the discipline. In an utterly unscientific study of the media from 1981 to date I have noticed a resurgence of the terms, particularly in reference to international affairs. Understandably, they appear frequently in journalistic reports on areas of tension and hostility, like the Middle-East. For instance, a headline in the *International Herald Tribune* of 5 May 1982 reads 'Diplomats say Assad risks alienating Allies that oppose Teheran'. The London *Observer* reports on 4 July 1982 that if diplomatic sources are right, 'King Fahad's telephone call contributed to the estrangement between the President and the Secretary of State which led to Alexander Haig's resignation'. More recently, the *New York Times* of 14 February 1984 notes that 'The most agonizing decision the President faces is whether to sign the May 17 security accord with Israel. Signing it would alienate Syria; voiding it would alienate Israel.' However, it is the *International Herald Tribune* of 20 July 1982 which earns top honours for cramming the key terms into one short paragraph

> Schultz passed one essential test in diplomacy: *alienate* no one without a purpose. The next test is to convince America, its *estranged* allies—and its adversaries, that the Reagan administration can operate with increased coherence in the world with its second Secretary of State.

What these terms mean in such contexts will be discussed in the following pages.

At one level, perhaps the highest level of international relations, alienation is not a stranger. It has, with some irregularity, visited the domain of international law. In the *Dictionnaire de la Terminologie du Droit International* it is defined

> Terme désignant pour un Etat le fait de renoncer a un droit, à une competence, d'ordinaire en faveur d'un autre Etat ou d'une institution internationale. Terme employé surtout dans l'expression 'aliénation territoriale' pour désigner le fait pour un Etat de renoncer en faveur d'un autre Etat à sa souveraineté sur un territoire déterminé.[13]

It is also in this capacity, as a transfer of rights or power, that we shall examine the important historical and theoretical uses of alienation which have attracted little modern attention.[14]

At the level of disciplinary debates, it is hardly remarkable that the thinkers of international relations—including the diplomatic theorists—have ignored or avoided the theories of alienation and left the concept for sociologists and psychologists to (ab)use. 'Value-laden' and politically suspect, the concept might be considered by international political 'scientists' to be unsuitable for the precise quantification, and verification through statistical analysis, which are the hallmarks of their school. Equally, alienation might seem too vague, or even worse, too much in vogue, for the 'classicists' of international relations theory. Although the term was anointed by their noted forerunner, Thucydides,[15] it has yet to penetrate the *conceptual* framework of the modern classicists. The term does crop up in the writings of the British classicists like Martin Wight, Hedley Bull, Maurice Keens-Soper, and Adam Watson quite often in the context of diplomatic matters, but no effort has been made to reconceptualize or theorize about alienation or estrangement in reference to international relations.[16]

Other theorists who do not fit into the rather arbitrary categories of numerates and literates could legitimately transfer their criticisms of power—particularly its susceptibility to reductionism—to similar applications of alienation. Often stretched beyond its conceptual capacity, alienation has acquired a mystique which can express but not explain the mechanics of the real world. Also mystifying to realists would be the utopian assumptions of a pre-existing, or a teleological, state of non-alienation. And conversely, the meliorists or idealists might take issue with the bleak outlook alienation attaches to global interdependence.

Are these sufficient reasons to take another path, straw constructions to blow away, or just worthy criticisms to keep in mind? Some of each, but all, I would argue over-ridden by the fact that theorizing itself is a process of alienation: we must 'make strange', as did the Russian formalists with literature, our habitual ways of seeing diplomacy. The process takes different forms; it can involve a distancing of ourselves from the events or a defamiliarization of the evidence in order to present them to ourselves—and to others—in new and edifying ways. For Hegel, rationality requires that this distancing step be taken

> Quite generally, the familiar, just because it is familiar, is not cognitively understood. The commonest way in which we deceive either ourselves or others about understanding is by assuming something as familiar, and accepting it on that account; with all its pros and cons, such knowing never gets anywhere, and it knows not why.[17]

Although Marx offers his thoughts on alienation as a critique of Hegel, there are noted similarities in his view of its relationship to theory, as demonstrated by his often quoted remark that 'The philosopher, himself an abstract form of alienated man, sets himself up as the measure of the alienated world'.[18] Similarly, the type of theorization I am suggesting entails scrutiny of a form of alienation, that is, alienation immanent in diplomacy. In effect, then, we are in diplomatic theory prepared to alienate ourselves from a form of alienation. We shall see in our study of the alienation theories of Hegel and Marx how they considered this process, which they called the 'alienation of the alienation', an essential step in making the real philosophically intelligible. For the moment, I shall simply say that alienation theories can provide a better understanding of diplomatic theory, or a meta-theory of diplomacy.

At other, less abstract—or at least more conventional—levels, we can find evidence of alienation to justify a meta-theoretical approach. First, there is the nature of the discipline of international relations. It is relatively young, and estrangement is an essential part of growing up. In other words, developing a self-identity involves a willed detachment from one's environment (that is, the other social sciences). When it comes to the specific state of *theory* in the discipline, there is probably little agreement on this point and the differing views probably line up with the differing intra-disciplinary schools of thought.

On a second, perhaps safer level, there is the etymological nature of theory itself. It comes from the Greek *thea*, meaning 'outward look' and *horao*, that is, 'to look at something attentively'. Originally an Orphic word, it has been interpreted by Cornford to signify a 'passionate sympathetic contemplation', in which 'the spectator is identified with the suffering god, dies in his death, and rises again in his new birth.[19] In this early use of theory it expresses man's primal alienation from nature: experiencing a Feuerbachian alienation, man seeks in heaven what he cannot find or understand on earth. This view is supported by Walter Kaufmann, who believes the alienation of theory goes back to the great classical thinkers: 'Plato and Aristotle remarked that philosophy begins in wonder or perplexity. We could also say that it begins when something suddenly strikes us as strange—or that philosophy is born of estrangement.'[20]

This use of theory is 'modernized', meaning that it is linked to the Judeo–Christian tradition, by Plotinus and, later, Augustine, who considered theory to constitute a spiritual understanding of the world, in contrast to the discursive thinking that posed as knowledge in the earthly city.[21] Theory can be said, both in its archaic and modern forms, only to accommodate that which is strange to us. However the renewed, often eclectic (some might risk opprobrium to say *post*-modern) interest in alienation as a theoretical approach, beginning with Nietzsche and the Russian formalists and continuing with Derrida, Foucault, Barthes and others, hinges on a reversed framework: to theorize, we must make strange what we have accommodated ourselves to.[22] And, as I stated before, that can include ourselves.

This brings us to the third aspect, the non-theoretical alienation of the theorists. As noted by Stanley Hoffmann, some of the greatest contributions to modern theories of international relations have come from strangers who have found themselves writing in a strange land before and after the Second World War.[23] Included in the foreign pantheon would be Arnold Wolfers, Klaus Knorr, Karl Deutsch, Ernst Haas, George Liska, and Hans Morgenthau. Later came Henry Kissinger and Zbigniew Brzezinski. A partial, perhaps exaggerated, explanation of this phenomenon can be found in their collective caricature, Dr Strangelove. Estranged from the twin European catastrophes of power gone soft (appeasement) and power gone mad (Hitlerism), Strangelove in turn converts the innocents with his sophisticated argument for the 'flexible use' of the ultimate expression and instrument of alienation, The Bomb. To put the arguments more soberly, it is probable that the dialectic operating between the fear of and the desire for power has shaped more than one thinker's thoughts. We have a string of aphorisms as evidence, that knowledge is power, that power corrupts knowledge, in Cambridge, Washington, Hollywood, wherever. What is needed is an analysis of how alienated power, be it pedagogical, political or popular, produces and is sustained by theories of diplomacy.

The terminology of alienation

The ultimate root of the English word 'alienation' is the Latin *alius*, meaning 'other' (as an adjective) and 'another' (as a noun).[24] It developed into *alienare*, which means to make something another's, to take away or remove. It was used as a noun, *alienato*, in the early writings of Seneca and Cicero to denote the sale of a commodity and the transfer of rights appertaining to property. The juridical tradition of the term was continued in Middle English; Adam Smith notes that in this period 'the vassal could not alienate without the consent of his superior'.[25] The appropriation of this usage by the social contract writers and the resulting conceptualization of the word to explain *transfers* of power will be examined below.

Also prevalent in Middle English was the use of the phrase *alienatio mentalis* to describe a medical or psychiatric condition in which one is 'aliened of mind or understanding; or aliened and turned from reason'.[26] This meaning crossed or met in the mid-Channel around this period, since, according to Michel Foucault in *Histoire de la folie, alienation mentale* was also in vogue in eighteenth- and nineteenth-century France. Its usage to denote psychological conditions continued into the early twentieth century, and in some countries, court psychiatrists kept the nomenclature of 'alienists'.

The *interpersonal* nature of alienation is already significant in the first volume of the *Oxford English Dictionary* (1888). It firmly established the standard definition: 'To convert into an alien or stranger ... to turn away in feelings or affection, to make averse or hostile, or unwelcome.'[27] Here we see one of the modern meanings of alienation, a relationship marked by separation, which will figure largely in a genealogy of diplomacy. The English term has expanded to include, among the meanings, the separation between individuals; between individuals and society, supernatural beings, and states of mind; between peoples; and more importantly for this enquiry, *between states.*

The central role of alienation in the thought of modern German writers makes a brief exposition of its German origins useful. The Grimms' *Wörterbuch*, tracing the term *enfremden* back to the late Middle Ages, defines it as 'to make alien, to rob, to take, to strip of'.[28] Here we can already detect an intermingling of the positive juridical and negative social connotations found in the English term. However, there exists another German term which was usually identified with the transfer or relinquishment of property: *Entäussering*. Possibly one can make a terminological distinction between the words to find an English equivalent: the root *fremd* or 'strange' better corresponds to 'estrangement' and *aussen* or 'outside' with alienation. However, the conceptual distinction is even less clear-cut. As we shall see, philosophers often dip in and out of the multiple meanings of alienation.

The conceptualization of alienation

In his magisterial work *Peace and War* Raymond Aron states that the 'ambiguity in "international relations" is not to be imputed to the inadequacy of our concepts: it is an integral part of reality itself'.[29] His statement can equally be applied to alienation, to explain partially some of the conceptual confusion which attends its use. Second, as alienation's conceptual use has multiplied, in social, economic and political theory, and philosophy and psychology, we can better understand why confusion has increased. Third, the meaning of alienation has from the outset been refracted by its see-saw history of evaluation and devaluation by Lutheran dogmatists, Soviet apologists, neo-Marxists and others. It is possible that the term carried this potential within it from the start. Nonetheless, the purpose of this summary and partial *Wortgeschichte* is to draw as wide as possible boundaries for alienation, and to allow a broad enquiry into diplomacy to situate the concept in its historical and theoretical context.

We have seen that alienation in the sense of an economic or juridical transfer had a neutral connotation in the feudal epoch. Resting on the firm foundation of Roman civil and agrarian law, the concept fits in well with a hierarchical order where everything had its proper place. With the transition from feudalism to capitalism, however, we witness alienation being employed in a manner somewhat like a rearguard action. The change is gradual, from the description of an arrangement whereby the vassal could not alienate without his lord's consent, to the thirteenth century sanctions that 'Le bourgeois ne peut pas aliéner la chose de la commune sans le commendement de roi'; and 'Chascun peut le rien donner et aliéner par sa volenté'.[30] The transition foretells the appropriation of this particular meaning by Enlightenment thinkers, who would use it in their critique of economic and social conditions. But generally, the concept in this period is relatively neutral on the value spectrum.

The same cannot be said about its related theological use. To avoid the dense area of religious origins, we will take the biblical account of alienation at face value for the present. The main idea conveyed by alienation is separation from God. In Ephesians 4:18, Paul says of the Gentiles that 'they are darkened in their understanding, alienated from the life of God because of the ignorance that is in them, due to the hardness of their heart'. Here alienation clearly has a negative connotation which is repeated frequently in the theology of Augustine. In fact, alienation is central to his idea of two cities in opposition. Augustine states in the *City of God* that his purpose was to

> … write about the origin, the development, and the destined ends of the two cities. One of these is the City of God, the other the city of this world, and

> God's City lives in this world's city as far as the human element is concerned, but it lives there as an alien sojourner.[31]

Protestant theologians, such as Luther and Calvin, continued this tradition and some commentators go so far as to claim that Hegel 'imbibed the concept of alienation' from them.[32] However, theoretical evidence points to another influence—the social contract writers.

But first, what was the nature of the concept before they grasped hold of it? To aid comprehension, it might be pictured as a coin: on one side a neutrally-valued idea of a transfer of property; on the other, a negatively charged meaning of an imbalanced separation between man and God. As agents and products of the Enlightenment, the social contract writers secularized the religious sense to attack old and accommodate new forms of social estrangements. In the process, they evaluated the juridical sense to explain and justify the free (and sometimes equal) alienation of rights and power. In their hands, the coin would undergo a radical revaluation.

Hugo Grotius has long been recognized as 'the father of international law', and more than one theorist of international relations has honoured him with his own paradigm, the 'Grotian', to categorize thinkers who considered the relations between states to constitute a legalistic-moralistic society in which 'Machiavellian' conflict was attenuated by 'Kantian' co-operation.[33] However, his seminal writings on social contract writing, particularly his original application of alienation to contract theory, have earned him hardly a second-cousin status in international theory.

The title of the sixth chapter in Grotius' *De Jure Belli ac Pacis* shows, in shorthand, the central role he ascribed to alienation in the relationship between property and sovereignty: 'Of acquisition derivative, by the act of man; and herein of the alienation of the sovereignty and its accompaniments'.[34] Grotius acknowledges that it is now (in the seventeenth century) considered natural that things shall be acquired and transferred from one person to another. When such an action is expressive of a rational will, it requires an external 'sign', that is, natural, civil, or 'international' law. Which form of law depends on what level the transfer takes place, and on what series of rights and obligations have been engendered. In this context, we see alienation giving rise to social sanctions.

Taking quite a leap from his precursors, and in the logic of his argument, Grotius then asserts that this basic alienation be instrumental to the erection of a political authority:

> As other things may be alienated, so may sovereign authority by him who is really the owner, that is as we have said above, ... by the king, if the authority is patrimonial: otherwise, by the people, but with the consent of the king; because he too has his right, as tenant for life, which is not to be taken away against his will.

Alienation appears to be a two-way street between the ruled and the ruler; but Grotius, an actor in and an observer of the tumultuous seventeenth century, is not prepared to take up this claim to challenge the 'imperial dignity' (as sovereignty was then known). Grotius' notions of a social contract and his use of the organic analogy would have radical international implications when future thinkers used them to assert 'inalienable' rights. But Grotius is cautious:

> In the alienation of a part of the sovereignty, it is also required that the part which is to be alienated consent to the act. For those who unite to form a state, *contract* a certain *perpetual* and *immortal* society, in virtue of their being integrant parts of the same, whence it follows that these parts are not under the body in such a way as the parts of a natural body which cannot live without the life of the body. The body of which we speak is of another kind, namely a voluntary combination: and this must not be supposed to have been such that the body should have the right of cutting off parts from itself and giving them into the authority of another.[35]

Grotius' movement towards a theory of popular sovereignty is a careful and tenuous one. To a democratic firebrand like Rousseau, Grotius' timidity was reprehensible:

> Grotius denies that all human power is established in favour of the governed, and quotes slavery as an example. His usual method of reasoning is constantly to establish right by fact. It would be possible to employ a more logical method, but none could be more favourable to tyrants.[36]

Grotius' position and purpose is understandable. Writing at the time of the Thirty Years' War, and anxious, perhaps even nostalgic, for the lost unity of Christendom, he was more interested in buttressing than tearing down the evolving society of absolutist states. Hence, it was only natural that he should place the concept of alienation in the service of *order*.[37] In contrast, Rousseau's priorities of equality and liberty necessitated a radical interpretation of alienation. As well, he thought Grotius' circumstances were to be deplored, not excused:

> Grotius, a refugee in France, ill content with his own country, and desirous of paying his court to Louis XIII to whom his book is dedicated, spares no pains to rob the people of their rights and invest kings with them by every conceivable artifice.[38]

Hobbes, another contract writer who incurred Rousseau's wrath, proffered rigid prescriptions for acts of alienation which would strengthen the hand of a Leviathan outwardly facing a state of perpetual war. Hobbes never uses 'alienation' *per se* in the *Leviathan*, but he does make extensive use of the idea to refine Grotius' argument, albeit with more brutal interpretations of the international order. In Chapter XIV, 'Of the first and second natural laws, and of contract', he states 'to *lay down* a man's *right* to any thing, is to *divest* himself of the liberty, of hindering another of the benefit of his own right to do the same'.[39] He distinguishes the *renunciation* of rights from *transferring* rights: the former entails no necessary reciprocation in the form of obligations while the latter does. The ultimate end of this renouncing or transferring is in itself an *inalienable* right, namely, security 'of a man's person, in his life, and in the means of so preserving life, as not be weary of it'.[40]

The means of a mutual transference of rights is by contract, or, if it involves a deferral of an obligation (that is, promise), by covenant. In Part II 'Of Commonwealth', this basic contractual scheme is elevated to justify the establishment of the 'Leviathan' as sovereign power. It should be noted that estrangement is the major reason that men erect a sovereign power 'as may be able to defend them from the invasion of foreigners'.[41] The Hobbesian renunciation of liberty for security, although mutual and revocable among individuals, is perpetual and decidedly one-sided between men and the Leviathan. The question Rousseau directs to Grotius in the fifth chapter of the *The Social Contract*, 'Slavery', could also be levelled at Hobbes: 'If an individual says Grotius, can alienate his liberty and make himself the slave of a master, why could not a whole people do the same and make itself subject to a king?'[42]

Rousseau's answer relies on alienation—and its sometimes intentionally ambiguous use—to ridicule the possibility:

> There are in this passage plenty of ambiguous words which would need explaining; but let us confine ourselves to the word *alienate*. To alienate is to give or sell. Now, a man who becomes the slave of another does not give himself. He sells himself, at least for his subsistence; but for what does a people sell itself?[43]

Rousseau concedes that the despot may provide 'civil tranquillity'. But, he asks, what good is that if it comes at the price of wars and conflict brought about by the unchecked ambition and greed of the king and his courtiers? Rousseau mixes common sense and nonsense to make his point:

> A king is so far from furnishing his subjects with their subsistence that he gets his own only from them and according to Rabelais, kings do not live on nothing. Do subjects then give their persons on condition that the king takes their goods also? I fail to see what they have left to preserve.[44]

The solution Rousseau found in the social contract and the general will is familiar enough. Let it be sufficient to highlight the central role of alienation in his scheme with a significant excerpt from Chapter VI, 'The Social Compact':

> These clauses, properly understood, may be reduced to one—the total alienation of each associate together with all his rights, to the whole community; for in the first place, as each gives himself absolutely, the conditions are the same for all; and, this being so, no one has any interest in making them burdensome to others.[45]

The last point I wish to make about the Rousseauian use of alienation is an important one for the future of the concept. Above all, Rousseau is responsible for 'socializing' the concept, and in the process, giving it a bi-valency. In the sense outlined above, Rousseau has further extended the originally neutral economic meaning of the term to incorporate social transactions essential to liberty. *La volonté générale* (that is, free sociability) replaces Hobbes' *raison d'état* (that is, endangered viability) as the ultimate need and justification for alienation. The second sense is found more frequently in the *Discourses* and might be considered proto-Marxian in character. First, he suggests 'it is impossible to conceive how property can come from anything but manual labour'.[46] Then he asserts that alienated (that is, transferred) property becomes *estranged*. Reinforcing his link to early theorists of international relations, Rousseau cites the jurist Pufendorf to make his case:

> Pufendorf says that we may divest ourselves of our liberty in favour of other men, just as we transfer our property from one to another by contracts and agreements. But this seems a very weak argument. For in the first place, the property I alienate becomes quite foreign to me, nor can I suffer from the abuse of it, but it very nearly concerns me that my liberty should not be abused and that I cannot without incurring the guilt of the crimes I may be compelled to commit, expose myself to become an instrument of crime.[47]

Of course, Marx would claim, in contrast to Rousseau, that property as alienated labour can become estranged just as life and liberty can. But the point not to be overlooked is that Rousseau has linked (though in a rudimentary way) the economic and juridical sense of alienation (transference or relinquishment) to the early political and religious sense (estrangement or separation), with the innovative product being a socially critical concept. It was to be turned against St. Pierre's irenist writings, to influence Kant's cosmopolitan arguments for the constitution of a perpetual peace, and—most importantly—to resurface in Hegel's and Marx's theories of alienation.

The theorization of alienation

In summary, and in the most general terms, the historical and conceptual path of alienation was an *ascent* from the state of nature (economic) to the nature of the state (juridical), and a *descent* from the heavens (theological and religious) to earth (philosophical and sociological). It should be clear from this exposition that the modern theory of alienation did not spring full-blown from the massive brow of Karl Marx. It is impossible to identify and trace all of the social phenomena and intellectual influences which converged to make a theory of alienation, as Marx would say, possible and necessary. And besides, it is probably more profitable in such matters to analyse the germ rather than study intensively who caught it from whom, especially since neither human nor international relations is a controlled experiment. Nonetheless, some names may be given of those who were, so to speak, exposed. Others before Hegel and Marx who were concerned with the economic or juridical aspects of alienation were James Harrington,[48] John Locke,[49] James and J. S. Mill,[50] and Adam Smith.[51] And some of the more prominent theologians and philosophers who have entered at least the margins of the alienation discourse are Thomas Aquinas and Meister Eckhart,[52] the protestant theologians Thomas Munzer, Calvin, and Luther,[53] and the German philosophers, Fichte, Schelling, and Schiller.[54]

Kant

I have omitted Kant's name intentionally because he warrants a brief word on his own, not just because he plays the role of foil (as did Grotius for Rousseau) for much of Hegel's work on alienation. In an international context, Kant expresses hopes that power might eventually be constitutionally alienable, and be transferred by treaty from states to a confederated power which could secure an eternal peace.[35] In the domestic context, Kant offers a more complex interpretation of alienation, relating it to his moral radicalism, and considering it to be a necessary action with sometimes reprehensible effects. In the standard usage, he states 'the transference of one's property to someone else is its alienation'.[56] But he adds a moral clause born seemingly out of changing social conditions. Hitherto, when people and labour were part of a static cosmic order, only *dead* property was alienated. But as capitalism made inroads into this feudal fixity, both people and their labour became 'freely' alienable (as was also true of property which was now considered a product of labour). In this process of alienation, Kant believed that this 'living' property became 'deadened', or 'converted into a thing' (*Verdingung*).[57] Here Kant is crudely forging a link between alienation and reification, one which imputes a value-judgement on the process of economic transfers. These rudimentary ideas of objectification reappear in the writings of Hegel and Marx—but as a system rather than a fragment of thought.

Hegel

How can we account for Hegel's radical reformulation of alienation into a system of thought? A partial answer can be found in the circumstances in which Hegel found himself, that is, the political and social fragmentation of Germany. Some evidence of this is to be found in his early writings. In *Fragment of a System*, he says that 'disunity is the source of the *need* for philosophy and as the culture (*Bildung*) of the age it is its unfree, predetermined aspect'.[58] And Hegel believes the responsibility for this state of affairs can be traced to the foreign European powers. 'In the Peace of Westphalia', says Hegel, 'this statelessness of Germany was organised ... Germany renounced establishing itself as a secure state power and surrendered to the good will of its members.'[59] However, always the dialectician, Hegel thought this situation would eventually produce a stronger, unalienated, Germany. As goes the Spirit, so too would the state: 'a mind estranged from its age reproduces itself in scientific form'.[60] Intellectually brash where Kant was timid, certain that his systemization of knowledge was reciprocally related to the formation of a German system of power, Hegel, in effect, was as dogmatic as Bacon in the belief that 'knowledge is power'.

Interpreting Hegel has been likened by Charles Taylor to the classic drama of hugging the shoreline and staying safely within reach of shallow conventional language, or of risking the open sea, where Hegel's linguistic whirlpools await the unwary. The number and complexity of Hegel's works make any lengthy exegesis of Hegel impracticable. Instead, I will rely mainly on Hegel's *Phenomenology of Spirit* to present a theory of alienation which will, I hope, make up in heuristic value for what it lacks in inclusiveness.

Alienation operates at two levels in the development of the human spirit. At the gnomic level, Hegel uses it to plot the individual's emergence from an unreflective psychic unity to a bifurcated subjective consciousness moving toward reunification with its objectified consciousness. At the historical level the *Phenomenology* is a study first of the Spirit's path from the original harmony of classical Greece to the imperfect unity of Christendom and subsequent discord, and second, of the Spirit's potential for reunification in the wake of the French Revolution. At both levels, alienation is the driving-wheel. The Spirit can be conceived as an empty universal which only takes on specific content through its externalizations as something other than itself, and in turn, its overcoming of that otherness. In Hegel's terminology it is a 'mediation' which is 'nothing beyond self-moving selfsameness'.[61] Through the negation of this negation, an estranged self-identity emerges from the spirit. In other words, through the mediation of particular alienated self-consciousnesses, the reunification takes place of the universal Spirit.

A concrete example of alienation in action, particularly one of significance for international relations can help elucidate matters: this would be Hegel's account of Lordship and Bondage in the section 'Independence and Dependence of Self-Consciousness' (also known as the 'master-slave' relation). The opening sentence is a key one: 'Self-consciousness exists in and for itself when, and by the fact, that it so exists for another; that is, it exists only in being acknowledged.'[62] Introduced here is what John Torrance refers to as the 'struggle for recognition': each individual, treating the other as an object of his need, is involved in a life-and-death struggle for independent self-consciousness.[63] Death, however, can only be the reified life of the subordinate ego. Otherwise the essential mirror for the dominant ego would be shattered. But how is it that one ego becomes dominant ('recognized') and the other subordinate ('recognizing')? Cannot the recognition be mutual *and* equal? Hegel does not preclude the possibility—but only in 'pure Notion' can we speculate about this possibility. Although the style may be convoluted it is worth repeating Hegel here, for the passage bears special significance for the transformation from suzerain to states system and the emergence of a secular diplomatic culture. Hegel says

> Each is for the other the middle term through which each mediates itself; and
> each is for itself, and for the other, an immediate being on its own accord,

which at the same time is such only through this mediation. They recognize themselves as mutually recognizing one another.[64]

The import and the language of Hegel's claim becomes clearer in the following passage where he states that the individual who is not willing 'to stake his life' in the recognitional 'trial by death' is the one who 'is simply to live or to be for another'.[65] It seems, then, that the individual who risks his life in the death struggle proves his autonomy from determinate objects. Interesting parallels could be made with the nature of the mutual recognition of states, and with the distinctions later made by Treitschke and Ranke between great powers and lesser powers. Or, as Martin Wight has remarked, 'A great power does not die in bed'.[66]

As well, parallel patterns of imperial decline and 'the Third World revolt' can be detected in the next stage of the lord-bondsman relationship, when the 'irony of history'—or dialectic—comes into play. The lord is still dependent upon the bondsman for recognition because full autonomy would constitute self-negation. But the bondsman is now thing-like, an instrument of the lord's purposes in both the spiritual and physical sense. Thus, the lord's self-consciousness comes to develop, because it is a reflection of a reified consciousness. The bondsman, however, possesses an alternative means to self-realization: his *work*. Moreover, his hostility to the power of the lord, internalized as fear, compels him to shape his own consciousness through the alien product of his own labour, rather than through the alien will of the lord. The outcome of his 'rediscovery of himself by himself, says Hegel, is that 'the bondsman realizes that it is precisely in his work wherein he seemed to have only an alienated existence that he acquires a mind of his own'.[67]

In summary, we note the dialectical movement Hegel has evinced from alienation. First, in his philosophical usage: the positive alienation of Spirit for self-consciousness; its negative estrangement from the discord which follows; and a positive alienation of self-consciousness for a consensual social existence. Second, in his innovative systematic and sociological application: a negative intrapersonal estrangement created by the positive alienation of self-consciousness which can potentially be overcome by the positive estrangement of labour. Do these expositions of alienation have some heuristic value for the study of diplomacy? At the entrance to the archives, I can only assert that Hegel's philosophical account of alienation can be used to explain two critical moments in the history, when the *mutual* estrangement *of* states *from* western Christendom gives rise to an international diplomatic system; and when the Third World's revolt against western 'Lordship' precipitates the transformation of diplomacy into a truly global system.

Feuerbach

Before we acknowledge the contribution of the thinker who is most closely identified with the theory of alienation—Karl Marx, we must give Ludwig Feuerbach his due, for it was Feuerbach who put Hegel's feet firmly back on the ground and prepared the terrain for Marx's 'anthropological' theory of alienation. Marx willingly and frequently acknowledges his debt to Feuerbach. In his 'Critique of Hegel's Dialectic', Marx writes

> Feuerbach's great achievement is to have shown that philosophy is nothing more than religion brought into thought and developed by thought, and that it is loudly to be condemned as another form and mode of existence of human alienation.[68]

An enormous enthusiasm greeted the publication of Feuerbach's *The Essence of Christianity* in 1841, and its main thesis—that man alienating his essential attributes created God—generated a great deal of criticism. Regretfully, it is not possible here to reproduce Feuerbach's arguments on religious alienation; but I would argue that it provides an analytical framework for understanding the heavily mythologized prehistory of diplomacy which, for the most part, the traditional writers have neglected. From the representatives of the Amphictyonic league of the Greeks to the *missi* of the Carolingian empire, from the early papal legations to the mediatory role of the Pope today, we can find evidence of the role mythology has played in mediating the intractable, even preternatural problems that diplomats have perpetually faced. In particular, we could point to the early Middle Ages when the immunity of proto-diplomats, according to Gentili, was as much dependent upon a mythic relation to God's messengers, angels, as it was upon reciprocal interests.

Marx

For the moment, I wish only to note the extent to which Marx's idea of alienation is similar to Feuerbach's: it is polemical, critical, secular, and above all, historical. But in Marx, the history of alienation begins with 'political economy', which only a theory of alienation can explain. First, says Marx, this is true because 'political economy starts with the fact of private property'; and second, because 'private property is the material and sensuous expression of estranged human life'.[69] Marx's critique, then, entails an evaluation of the economic–juridical meaning of alienation which he confronted in the works of the classical English economists and philosophers (James Stewart, James and J. S. Mill, and David Ricardo). This was possible because the theological meaning of estrangement had been 'brought down to earth'. Thus, when Marx states that 'estrangement (*Entfremding*) forms the real interest of … alienation (*Entäusserung*)', he is not giving way to tautology; rather he is outlining his synthesis of alienation, that is the separation of man by the surrender of his labour.[70]

This separation is a social relationship, but it can arise from several forms of alienation. The individual can be estranged from: (1) his product; (2) the process of labour; (3) the means of labour; (4) the species; and (5) other individuals. This is not to say that *all* forms of labour constitute estrangement. According to Marx, the satisfaction of needs by productive activity is essential for human consciousness and a sensuous awareness of nature. Labour becomes estranged when it is *coerced* and 'merely a *means* to satisfy needs external to it'.[71] Under the control of another, it becomes a hostile alien force. Marx falls back on Feuerbachian metaphysics to describe the *zero-sum* relationship which develops:

> For on this premise it is clear that the more the worker spends himself, the more powerful becomes the alien world of objects which he creates over and against himself, the power he himself—his inner world—becomes ... It is the same in religion. The more man puts into God, the less he retains in himself.[72]

But man's collective self-alienation has found a new elevated expression. Since the 'political emancipation' of man (that is, Enlightenment and French Revolution), religion has been supplanted by the 'spirit of *civil society' (bürgerliche Gesellschaft)* which Marx describes in his essay 'On the Jewish Question' as 'the sphere of egoism, of the *bellum omnium contra omnes* ... no longer the essence of *community* but the essence of *differentiation*'.[73] Security becomes the civil society's paramount value: with each individual existing as a means for the other, he seeks political and legal guarantees for his self-preservation, his rights, and his property. But Marx denigrates this elevated concept, which in our time has been fetishized as the national security state: 'The concept of security is not enough to raise civil society above its egoism. Security is, rather, the *assurance* of its egoism.'[74]

Like Hegel, Marx considers the formation of the state to be necessitated by alienated particular interests both within and outside of civil society. And Marx sees its supposed universality to be as 'spiritual' (that is, mythical) as Hegel's abstract idea of the absolute Spirit. In short, particular *material* interests pose as universal abstract interests in the bourgeois state.

Therefore, the teleology of the Marxian concept of alienation is not aimed, as is Hegel's, toward some perfect Prussian state, but towards the ideal of statelessness. Marx is purposely vague about this non-alienated after-life, except to make it sound like a world of bucolic bliss where cows are milked in the morning and philosophy discussed after dinner. As Marx became more scientific and 'class' conscious in his later writings, his use of alienation as a concept diminished significantly, as did his ruminations on a mythical world of non-alienated individuals and communities. But the eschatology immanent in the Marxian concept of alienation flourished and certainly added to its appeal for later theorists in the social sciences. One subsequent side-effect has been to neglect the religious, juridical and philosophical expressions of alienation—the pre-history of the theory—in favour of a sociological orientation. Also left unexplored has been the systemic hermeneutic of alienation which might help explain the link between *intra-* and *inter*-state estrangement, that is, the dynamic of how the conduct of diplomacy under revolutionary regimes shifts from the mediation of particular states to the mediation of the universal alienation of humanity. It is hoped that this schematic summary redresses this neglect.

Sartre

An overview of the theories of alienation is incomplete without mentioning a modern writer on alienation who stands out from all the rest: Jean-Paul Sartre. He deserves a hearing, not just because he has been neglected in international relations theory, but also because of his enormous effort comprehensively to understand history and technology at (alienated) work; and because he is an archetype of Hegel's and Marx's 'estranged philosopher' (being at one time or another alienated from the State and the Party, and the East and the West). His major philosophical work, the *Critique of Dialectical Reason*, is notorious for its density and neologisms. Its labyrinthine structure and Sartre's adaptation of Hegelian concepts present a challenge to the reader. But all of the difficulties and obfuscations are attenuated by one truth: even his blindspots illuminate areas of international relations theory which have been overshadowed by the empirical *Realpolitikers*. This is especially true in the case of terrorism, for which I believe Sartre offers more insights on the history, motivations, and consequences than all of the present pundits engaged in learned repetition at the proliferating institutes of terrorist studies.

On the abstract personal level, Sartre's concept of alienation resembles Hegel's and Marx's positive views of labour as self-objectification. However, self-objectification in an historical context is an alienating activity because *scarcity* rules all human relations. Sartre presents scarcity as a given. This leads to 'a domination of man by matter and the domination of matter by man'.[75] It is clearly within a Marxian framework that Sartre considers economic alienation, which is characterized as 'a mediated relation to the other and to objects of labour'.[76] However, Sartre does not confine its negative value or explanatory value to capitalism, as did Marx. Since all types of praxis are alienable, and potentially hostile, the concept of alienation is expanded by Sartre to include other forms of domination through alienation. This means that there are multiple, often overlapping mediations at work in all sectors of society, including the international society. For instance, Sartre observes and analyses alienation in a bus queue, the family, and, significantly, in the East as well. He also finds states of non-alienation in some odd places, such as in a soccer team and a serial group of terrorists. As global surveillance and communications becomes the linchpin of modern diplomacy, Sartre's elaborate interpretation of the power of the other's gaze is of particular significance; and in general, his rigorous extension of alienation to new areas makes, I believe, his work a valuable theoretical aid to the study of diplomacy.

A meta-theory of alienation?

In the preface to the English edition of *Das Kapital*, Engels makes an apology to the reader:

> There is, however, one difficulty we could not spare the reader: the use of certain terms in a sense different from what they have, not only in common life,

but in ordinary Political Economy. But this was unavoidable. Every new aspect of a science involves a revolution in the technical terms of that science.[77]

The study of international relations is relatively new, but it certainly does not constitute a science. Nor, for that matter, is the use of alienation in the context of international relations 'a revolution in technical terms'. Its use is quite common. What is missing is the *theoretical recognition* of that fact, a text for the preface, so to speak.

I have already given my reasons for undertaking an exposition of alienation. High among them was the proposition that new tools of analysis might assist the valuable classicist approach. Thus, some familiarization of theoretical instruments alien to international relations was necessary. That done, it is now possible to indicate some of the basic features of alienation which might further our understanding of the development of diplomacy.

First, we have noted the transformations of the concept. The direction of these historical transformations might be viewed as vertical and bilateral. In the form of 'alienation' (that is, transfer or relinquishment) it has ascended from an economic to a juridical meaning. In the form of 'estrangement' (that is, separation marked by indifference to hostility) it has descended from theological and religious to 'anthropological' (in the sense Feuerbach and Marx used the term) and political meanings. The two concepts were then conflated, to some extent by Rousseau and Hegel, but most significantly by Marx when he related both concepts to the 'political economy' of industrializing Europe. In the case of the concept's evaluative transformations, we have seen how the relationship of the thinkers to the reality they wish to describe or explain through the use of alienation determines the critical, subjective nature of the concept. For instance, Grotius makes use of the concept in pursuing his purpose of preserving and peacefully reforming what was left of a disintegrating Christendom. By the time of Rousseau and Hegel, this prospect had diminished, and we see the rise of particularist interests accompanied by a radical change in the meaning of the concept, to signify a dialectical relation of estrangement. Within states the debate was entered over which rights were 'inalienable'; and between states the overriding question was how best to secure and to manage the powers alienated from Christendom. The question was then raised by Kant and other Utopian writers how power and rights might be alienated by individual states to create a confederation or union of states. And in Hegel and Marx, the subjectivity of alienation becomes theoretically fixed by their professed political ends: for Hegel the state, for Marx the end of the state.

In the belief that the history of diplomacy is the history of the mediation of estrangement, I have attempted to provide a theoretical foundation for a historical enquiry into diplomacy. Only the first step has been taken in this exposition of alienation. What lies ahead is a journey to the archives, with the concepts and theories of alienation in hand. But I do wish to reiterate that alienation is not a philosopher's stone. It cannot provide laws of development for diplomacy, nor can it explain everything there is to know about diplomacy. I do not believe, however, that the neglected terrain of diplomacy's origins and transformations can be fully illuminated without the rich history, conceptual variations, and theories of alienation.

References and notes

1 A. de Wicquefort, *L'Ambassadeur et ses Fonctions* (Amsterdam, 1730); F. de Callières, *On the Manner of Negotiating with Princes*, A. Whyte (trans.), (Notre Dame, Ind., 1963); E. Satow, *Guide to Diplomatic Practice* (London, 1979); H. Nicolson, *Diplomacy* (London, 1963).

2 However, an admirable sequel to Nicolson's work has recently appeared, Adam Watson's *Diplomacy: The Dialogue between States* (London, 1982). Watson's work is also valuable because it investigates early *non*-Western views of diplomacy (such as Kautilya's *Arthashastra)*, an area which will be peripheral to our enquiry into the form of diplomacy that spread to become the dominant *global* system, *Western* diplomacy.

3 See Hedley Bull, *The Anarchical Society* (London, 1977); F. S. Northedge, *The International Political System* (London, 1976); Martin Wight, *Power Politics* H. Bull and C. Holbraad (eds.), (Harmondsworth, 1979); and *Systems of States*, H. Bull (ed.), (Leicester, 1977).

4 This is not to imply that the behaviouralist approach is inherently less conservative. Interesting (but certainly not sufficient) evidence of this is provided by its nominal origins. Seeking to avoid any objections from corporate trustees, the Ford Foundation changed a 'social' (too close to 'socialism') science research proposal to a 'behavioural' (thought to be more neutral in connotation) science proposal. See K. Deutsch, 'Problem Solving: The Behavioral Approach', in A. Hoffman (ed.). *International Communication and the New Diplomacy* (Bloomington, 1968), p. 75.

5 Nicolson, *Diplomacy*, pp. 20, 24.

6 Wight, *Power Politics*, p. 94.

7 Ibid., p. 81.

8 See Bull, *Anarchical Society*, pp. 173–83, on diplomatic culture and Nicolson, *Diplomacy*, p. 16, for a general discussion of diplomatic theory ('the generally accepted idea of the principles and methods of international conduct and negotiation').

9 Hegel, 'Spirit in Self-Estrangement', *Phenomenology of the Mind*, quoted in Marx, *The Economic and Philosophic Manuscripts of 1844*, Dir Struik (ed.), (New York, 1967), p. 38; L. Feuerbach, *The Essence of Christianity*, George Eliot (trans.), (New York, 1957); and Marx, *Economic and Philosophic Manuscripts.*

10 This enquiry shuns narrow definitions of terms. If I were to pretend that a single definition could capture the essence of diplomacy, then there would be no purpose for an enquiry. In fact, it would *negate* an enquiry, for its very rationale is to question the existence of a defining essence. Moreover, the high level of ambiguity inherent in international relations can render the attempt for exactitude in definition a specious activity. Specificity of terms should, of course, be expected from any historical investigation that would apply alienation theories.

11 See Bertell Oilman, *Alienation* (Cambridge, 1971).

12 Marx, 'Comments on James Mills Elements of Political Economy', MEWE, Suppl. vol. I, p. 463, quoted by I. Mészáros, *Marx's Theory of Alienation* (London, 1970), p. 91; and *Writings of Young Marx*, pp. 176, 229.

13 One example of a test-case states: 'L'idée que suggère tout naturellement le mot "aliener" est celle de transmission d'un sujet a un autre: il semble toutefois que ce mot peut aussi j'en signifier "perdre volontairement se défaire de, renoncer, etc"'. *Dictionnaire de la Terminologie du Droit International* (Paris, 1959).

14 See also H. Smit, *et al., International Law, Cases and Materials* (St. Paul, Minn., 1980), pp. 175–7, for a modern use of the term in the treaty of 1931 which established a customs

union between Germany and Austria and 'imposed a duty on Austria not to alienate her independence without the consent of the council of the League of Nations'.

15 For instance, see the address of the representatives of Corcyra to the assembled Athenian and Corinthian representatives on the question of gaining support from Athens against the threat of a Corinthian naval rearmament: 'If the Corinthians say that you have no right to receive one of their colonies into your alliance, they should be told that every colony, if it is treated properly, honours its mother city, and only becomes *estranged* (emphasis added) when it has been treated badly. Colonists are not sent abroad to be the slaves of those who remain behind, but to be their equals.' Thucydides, *The Peloponnesian War*, R. Warner, (trans.), (Harmondsworth, 1954), p. 56.

16 For instance: Bull, *Anarchical Society*, pp. 308–9 (The Third World is alienated from the Western states not simply because of the latters' lack of high-mindedness but because of their overwhelming power ...'); Keens-Soper, 'The Liberal Disposition of Diplomacy', *International Relations*, v (1973), p. 913 ('Here the issue is the sense of alienation with which newcomers from several different traditions of civility confront the predominantly European character of diplomacy.'); Wight, *Power Politics*, p. 32 ('Alien societies had different principles of existence from Europe ...'); Watson, *Diplomacy*, p. 15 ('initially diplomacy appears as a sporadic communication between very separate states ... /some/ states remained alien to the cultural and historical assumptions which engendered the rules and conventions of European diplomacy').

17 Hegel, *Phenomenology of the Spirit* (Oxford, 1979), p. 18.

18 Marx, 'Critique of Hegel's Dialectic', E. Fromm, (ed.), *Marx's Concept of Man* (New York, 1966), p. 174.

19 F. M. Cornford, *From Religion to Philosophy*, p. 201, quoted by Bertrand Russell, *History of Western Philosophy* (London, 1961), p. 52.

20 W. Kaufmann, 'The Inevitability of Alienation' in Preface to R. Schacht, *Alienation* (New York, 1970), p. xxvii. Kaufmann also notes that many of the great classical thinkers were estranged from societies which highly valued harmony and unity. He also asserts that many of the great modern philosophers suffered psychological or societal estrangement. He adduces the fact that Descartes, Spinoza, Liebnitz, Pascal, Hume, Rousseau, Kant, Hegel, Nietzsche, Russell and Sartre lost one, in some instances both, parents when young.

21 P. Ludz, 'A Forgotten Intellectual Tradition of the Alienation Concept' in R. F. Geyer and p. Schweitzer (eds.), *Alienation: Problems of Theory and Method* (London, 1981), pp. 24–5.

22 For an excellent synopsis of structuralist and post-structuralist approaches, see T. Eagleton, *Literary Theory* (Minneapolis, 1983).

23 See S. Hoffmann's valuable appraisal of the discipline, 'An American Social Science: International Relations', *Daedalus*, cvi (1977), pp. 41–60.

24 These definitions were compiled from the following books on alienation from which more detailed histories of the term and the concept can be found: Geyer and Schweitzer, *Alienation: Problems of Theory and Method*, pp. 21–33, 38–40, 68–70; I. Mészáros, *Marx's Theory of Alienation*, pp. 27–65; Schacht, *Alienation*, pp. 9–37; John Torrance, *Estrangement, Alienation and Exploitation: A Sociological Approach to Historical Materialism* (London, 1977), pp. xi–xvi, 3–20.

25 A. Smith, *An Inquiry into the Nature And Causes of The Wealth of Nations* (London n.d.), vol. II, p. 342, quoted by Mészáros, p. 34.

26 H. Kirath and S. Kuhn (eds.), *Middle English Dictionary* (Ann Arbor, Mich., 1956), quoted in Schacht, *Alienation*, p. 10.

27 J. Murray (ed.), *New English Dictionary on Historical Principles* (Oxford, 1888), quoted by Schacht, *Alienation*, p. 11.

28 J. and W. Grimm, *Deutsches Wörterbuch* (Leipzig, 1862), quoted in Schacht, *Alienation*, p. 8.

29 R. Aron, *Peace and War: A Theory of International Relations* (London, 1962), p. 7.

30 P. N. Rapetti (ed.), *Livre de justice et de plait* (Paris, 1850), p. 47; and A. A. Beugnot (ed.), *Assises de Jérusalem* (Paris, 1841), vol. I, p. 183, quoted in Mészáros, *Marx's Theory of Alienation*, p. 34.

31 Augustine, *City of God*, H. Bettenson (trans.), (Harmondsworth, 1972), p. 761.

32 Lewis Feuer, 'What is Alienation? The Career of a Concept', *New Politics*, I (1962), p. 117.

33 See Bull, 'Martin Wight and the Theory of International Relations', *British Journal of International Studies*, 2 (1976), pp. 104–8.

34 H. Grotius, *De Jure Belli ac Pacis*, W. Whewell (trans.), (London, 1853), pp. 340–50.

35 Ibid., pp. 342–3.

36 J.-J. Rousseau, *The Social Contract and Discourses*, F. P. H. Cole (trans.), (London, 1966), p. 4.

37 Contract and justice form the twin legal pillars of the Grotian order. Since alienation is given a central role in the formulation of both, it is an important conceptual foundation of that order. For further evidence see *De Jure Belli*, vol. I, chapter XX 'Of Promises', pp. 33–5: vol. II, chapter XII, 'Of Contracts', pp. 55–8.

38 Rousseau, *The Social Contract*, p. 22.

39 T. Hobbes, *Leviathan*, M. Oakeshott (ed.), (Oxford, n.d.), p. 85.

40 Ibid., p. 87.

41 Ibid., p. 112.

42 Rousseau, *The Social Contract*, p. 7.

43 Ibid.

44 Ibid.

45 Ibid., p. 12. See Book II, Chapter I, 'That Sovereignty is Inalienable', for the relationship between sovereignty, the general will and alienation. Here is one example: 'I hold then that sovereignty, being nothing less than the exercise of the general will, can never be alienated, and that the sovereign, who is no less than a collective being, cannot be represented except by himself: the power indeed may be transmitted but not the will', p. 20.

46 Ibid., p. 201.

47 Ibid., p. 211.

48 See C. B. MacPherson, *The Political Theory of Possessive Individualism: Hobbes to Locke* (Oxford, 1962), pp. 41, 163–91.

49 See J. Locke, *Two Treatises of Civil Government*, Peter Laslett (ed.), (Cambridge, 1960), Part II, sect. 26, 36, 173, 323.

50 See Torrance, *Estrangement*, pp. 92, 143, 241.

51 See A. Smith, *Wealth of Nations*, II, p. 342.

52 See Ludz, 'A Forgotten Intellectual Tradition', p. 25.

53 See Feuer, 'What is Alienation?' p. 117; Mészáros, *Marx's Theory of Alienation*, pp. 33; Schacht, *Alienation*, pp. 15–16.

54 See Ludz, 'A Forgotten Intellectual Tradition', pp. 26–7; Mészáros, *Marx's Theory of Alienation*, pp. 60–1; Schacht, *Alienation*, pp. 21–5, 30.

55 See I. Kant, *Perpetual Peace and other essays*, T. Humphrey (trans.), (Ind., 1983), pp. 108–10, and 115–18. Kant also believed a 'spirit of commerce' might provide the opportunity for a natural alienation of power by states, leading to a treaty for perpetual peace (pp. 122–5).

56 I. Kant, *Werke* (Berlin: Akademishe Ausgabe, 1902), vol. vi, p. 271, quoted and trans. by Mészáros, p. 34.

57 Ibid., p. 315.

58 G. Hegel, *Fragment of a System*, quoted by G. Lukasc, *The Young Hegel: Studies in The Relation between Dialectics and Economics*, R. Livingstone (trans.), (London, 1975), p. 263. This work is actually a collection of notes to which Herman Nohl gave the title

Systemfragment. Hegel's quote on disunity as the source of philosophy also appears in *Difference between the Philosophical Systems of Fichte and Schelling* (1801) See F. Copleston, *A History of Philosophy*, vol. 7, part 1 (New York, 1965), pp. 201–3.

59 Hegel, *Erste Druckschriften*, p. 219, quoted by Lukásc, p. 307.

60 Ibid., p. 91 in Lukásc, p. 267. The same idea is more poetically expressed in the famous 1820 'preface' to *The Philosophy of Right:* 'The owl of Minerva spreads its wings only with the falling of dusk'.

61 G. Hegel, *The Phenomenology of Spirit*, A. V. Miller (trans.), (Oxford, 1977), p. 11.

62 Ibid., p. 111.

63 Torrance, *Estrangement*, pp. 24–5.

64 Ibid.

65 Hegel, p. 112.

66 Wight, *Power Politics*, p. 48.

67 Hegel, pp. 118–19.

68 Marx, *The Critique of Hegel's Philosophy of Right*, in Bottomore, Early Writings, p. 44.

69 Marx, *1844 Manuscripts*, p. 106. and p. 137.

70 Ibid., p. 175. The phrasing of 'separation through surrender' is derived from Richard Schacht's lucid account of Marxian alienation. See Schacht, *Alienation*, p. 120.

71 Ibid., p. 11.

72 Ibid., p. 108.

73 Marx, 'On the Jewish Question', in *Early Writings*, p. 25.

74 Ibid., p. 26.

75 J.-P. Sartre, *Critique of Dialectical Reason*, A. S. Smith (trans.), (London, 1976), p. 152.

76 Sartre, quoted by Schacht, *Alienation*, p. 236.

77 F. Engels, 'Preface to the English Edition' in K. Marx, *Capital*, vol. I (Moscow, 1974), p. 14. Unfortunately, Engels did not live long enough to witness the ironic decision of a Russian censor to allow the entry of *Capital*, not because it wasn't subversive but because he thought it too difficult for the general public.

2 Arms, hostages, and the importance of shredding in earnest

Reading the national security culture (II)*

Source: *Social Text* (Spring, 1989), 22, pp. 79–91.

> The social intervention of a text (not necessarily achieved at the time the text appears) is measured not by the popularity of its audience or by the fidelity of the socioeconomic reflection it contains or projects to a few eager sociologists, but rather by the violence that enables it to exceed the laws that a society, an ideology, a philosophy establish for themselves in order to agree among themselves in a fine surge of historical intelligibility. This excess is called: writing.
>
> Roland Barthes, *Sade/Fourier/Loyola*

Deciphering the contemporary culture of the state requires excessive writing, to offset academic silences and to reclaim the subject from the official scribes, but also to overcome prevailing problems of estrangement. How do we define what defines us, what separates Us from Them, what draws symbolic boundaries between order and disorder, what distinguishes meaning from meaninglessness in international relations? There is the temptation to ape traditional diplomatic history, that is, to sift through the archival accretions which define and constitute a national culture. But if the reader/writer travels to the borders of the national *security* culture, instead of definitions, they find fences of arcane classifications surrounding the most significant archives. And when they finally gain entry through freedom of information actions or by public disclosures, worse news awaits them:

> "When did you shred them, sir?"
>
> "My answer, Mr. Nields, is that I started shredding documents in earnest, after a discussion with Director Casey in early October ... Director Casey and I had a lengthy discussion about the fact that this whole thing was coming unraveled and that things ought to be cleaned up. And I started cleaning things up."[1]

Thus on the first day of his testimony at the Iran-contra hearings, Lieutenant Colonel Oliver North informed the American people of the importance of shredding in earnest, of sanitizing the messy margins of the national security culture. Perched on the edge of this culture, Oliver North offers a special perspective on its most significant and deconstructive activity: terrorism. He first dogged President Reagan's heels when he carried the "football" containing the codes for launching nuclear terror; in 1981 he was brought into the National Security Council "to handle easels and carry the charts" (according to Richard Allen, the first of President Reagan's five national security advisers); and he eventually worked his way up to the post of Assistant Deputy Director for Political-Military Affairs at the NSC, from which he directed U.S. counterterrorism policy while secretly managing the aid program for the contras and the negotiation with Iran of arms for hostages.

In this shadowy corner of the state, North is our compass point, a guide to traverse the terrorist-etched boundaries of the national security culture. This is not to say that the "nature" of this "culture" would be revealed if the "truth" about North's story could be pasted or "pastiched" together again; nor is it to claim that he represents or is the incarnation of the national security culture. These were the faulty presuppositions of many members of the media and of the House and Senate Select Committee investigating the exploits of North; they also acted as impediments to any politically meaningful revelations, because the true North—magnified and globally projected by television—proved to be the magnetic North. In this sense, North was the living simulacrum of a national security culture: more real than the reality the Committee sought to uncover, more seductive than anything the polymorphous, acephalous Committee could reconstruct. North's truth was like the CIA outside the CIA that he and William Casey sought to create—an "off-the-shelf, self-sustaining, stand-alone entity"—the perfect agent for constructing and combatting a hyperreal terrorism.[2]

This means that a cultural reading of terrorism requires much more than an inquiry into the state's archival accretions: we must seek out its most sensitive *secretions.* The way in which they leak out and then reappear as public narratives in the news, fiction, and film, provides us with a map of a particular *cultural economy*, by which I mean a flow and exchange of valorized symbols. But once obtained, how might we read the archive of the "high" (political) culture of the national security state, that is, the official currency of discursive practices which circulates, accumulates, *piles up* around the great power, with the techno-bureaucrats of the state on one side, the deconstructive forces of terrorism on the other, and in the moat between, Oliver North and his crypto-military? The penumbra of the Iran-contra case certainly provides some immediate material, but our "first" hostage crisis in Iran illuminated, and in the process revealed chinks in the modern national security culture. Some artful investigative techniques were generated by, among others, the Iranian Revolutionary Guard who used ancient weaving techniques to create politically sensitive tapestries from the shredded documents of our embassy in Teheran, and then published them as a fifty-four volume set of the Great Satan's hitherto unknown sayings.[3] Now, however, the most relevant and revealing archives of the NSC are pulverized or cross-cut (rather than linguini-shredded) and burnt. The only recourse for a critical inquiry, it would seem, would be an epiphenomenology of terrorism, a study of the smoke rising from the "burn bags" of the executive branch.

But let us pretend for a dialogical moment that Marx was on epistemologically solid ground when he wrote in the *Preface to the Critique of Political Economy* that "mankind always sets itself only such tasks as it can solve, since it will always be found that the task itself arises only when the material conditions for its solution already exist or are at least in the process of formation." Lt. Colonel North shredded in earnest and retyped letters with a doctored IBM golf ball; Ms. Fawn Hall surreptitiously removed documents and erased incriminating floppy disks with a vengeance; Director of Central Intelligence William Casey conveniently died with his secrets, yet an electronic archive was preserved and discovered, for the magnetic tracks of the now infamous PROF notes lived on in the memory of the computers. As all hackers know, you must *overwrite* a file to obliterate it.

The problem confronting all inscriptive readers and semio-critical writers of this story is how are we, armed with this resurrected data, excessively to reinscribe this story of arms, hostages, and terrorism without overwriting the disorder which gave rise to it?[4] This is not just a figurative concern, for the media transformation of violence into a news event has magnified and distorted the terrorist threat, further reducing the possibility of any meta-critical *and* ethico-political response to it. From a safe distance the commentator might condemn terrorism, but the camera zooms in to fascinate us with the fear and spectacle of death which usually attend acts of terrorism.[5] Further complicating the problem of media reinscription is the proliferation of terrorist "experts" who appear ad nauseam in the media: we hang on the words of national security "consultants" who speak and write to compensate for the fact that we cannot hang the international terrorist (or more reasonably, *deter* through internationally legalized homicide); nations cannot agree to a common definition of terrorism, let alone a common power to enforce sanctions against it. That would require the discipline of a universal law and order, and there can be no law where there is no sovereign, as Thomas Hobbes said and Oliver North pleonastically embellished: "it is very important for the American people to understand that this is a dangerous world, that we live at risk and that this nation is at risk in a dangerous world."[6]

It would seem that outside the cultural economy of national security the non-military options for responding to terrorism are severely limited—semantically, epistemologically, ethically, practically. Is it possible to write/read about terrorism without a teleology, without trying, self-consciously or unself-consciously, to make terrorism "safe"—safe for definition, criminalization, or even legitimation? Or is the only other option to remain silent/blind, as we do in the face of "natural" disasters like Armenian earthquakes, Bangladeshi floods, and Ethiopian famines, when no rational explanation or response can possibly encompass the meaninglessness and contingency of catastrophic deaths?[7]

Wandering in intertextual and international relations, between post-modernity in thought and what looks like a neo-medievalism in practice, I can make no privileged claims for an explanatory or analytical reading of terrorism and the national security culture. The best I can offer—and the best I believe the material will provide—is a *de-scripting*. In effect, this means a melding of the reconstructive technology of the Iran-contra hearings with the palimpsest technique of the Middle Ages. It is only the first step—I believe a necessary step—for an inquiry into the national security culture behind the official documents, inside the "erased" electronic files, within the sub-texts of violent hyperrealism, all of which maintain the immaculate esplanade between the dark wood and the castle, terrorism, and counter-terrorism.[8]

Fact, factoids, and the factotum of terrorism

Just as Nietzsche alleged the precession of meaning to facts, North—the factotum of terror and counter-terror—preceded the factoids of terrorism. To be sure, there are some commonly accepted "facts" about international terrorism. A selection of Rand corporation documents on international terrorism reveals the following: over the last ten years terrorists have seized over fifty embassies and consulates, held the oil ministers of eleven states hostage; kidnapped hundreds of diplomats, businessmen and journalists; made several hundred million dollars in ransom money; assassinated Lord Mountbatten, President Sadat, and the former premier of Italy, attempted to assassinate the president of France, the Pope, and Alexander Haig (a near miss with a rocket launcher when he was supreme allied commander of NATO). Terrorist incidents and their severity *have* increased over the last ten years, but most terrorist actions involve few or no casualties: they are symbolic acts of violence. Compared to the ruthlessness and destructiveness of states, or even to natural disasters, terrorism is a mere nuisance. Yet it is cause for crises of state, media spasms on a seismic scale, and the hyper-production of institutes, conferences, and books on terrorism.

Why is this? International terrorism does represent a crisis, but *not* in terms of body-counts or a revolutionary threat to the states-system. On a political level, the simulacrum of terrorism, that is, the production of a hyperreal threat of violence, anticipates a crisis of legitimation.[9] What this means is that international terrorism is not a symptom or a cause or an effect of this systemic crisis: it has become a spectacular, micro-cosmic simulation. International terrorism simulates a legitimation crisis of the international order. Conversely, counter-terrorism is a counter-simulation, an attempt to engender a new disciplinary order which can save the dominant legitimacy principle of international relations.[10] On a representational level, the spectacle of terrorism displaces—and distracts us from—the signs of a pervading international disorder. As a result, much of what is read and written of terrorism displays a superficiality of reasoning and a corruption of language which effects truths about terrorism without any sense of how these truths are produced by, and help to sustain official discourses of international relations. This was repeatedly evidenced by the proceedings and documents of the Iran-Contra hearings, in which our reason of state was exposed as ideological expediency and redressed as principled policy.

If the reader of terrorism is to break out of the dominant cultural economy, in which each of us acts as a factotum of factoids, that is, a transmitter of official truths, then some critical interpretive skills must be deployed. Along with an empirical study of the salient sources of disorder around us, we need a genealogy of our knowledge of international terrorism and legitimacy, of how consumers in this cultural economy arrive at some shared assumptions about the exchange-value of both. One goal, then, of a cultural reading is to reach a better understanding of whether these assumptions or constructions of terrorism and legitimation serve to preserve principles and practices beneficial to the international order, or whether they forestall the knowledge necessary to deal effectively with an increasing fragmentation, a diffusion of power, and a sustained challenge to the sovereign state's once-natural monopoly of force: in short, the neo-medievalism alluded to earlier.

What this entails—and what this essay attempts—is a critical preface to a text that each reader of terrorism must "write." Having asserted the procession of meaning in terrorism, I do, however, recognize the need to address the definitional factoids of terrorism. Some originally useful but now obfuscating distinctions have been made between state terrorism and non-state terrorism; but the forces of the conservative status quo have won out, with Jeane Kirkpatrick (formerly at the U.N.), and Claire Sterling (of the *New York Times)* leading the definitional battle for the expropriation of the phrase, state terrorism, to the West. The linguistic annexation has been made official through lists published annually by the State Department which inform us which states are or sponsor terrorists. Unsurprisingly, and in spite of our sponsorship of terrorist activities in Central America, the Middle East, and elsewhere, the U.S. does not appear on that list: Libya, North Korea, Iran, and a shifting group of other pariah states do.

But as noted, confusion over definitions arises not just because of terrorism's multiple sponsors and forms, but because of the cultural efforts to tame its arbitrary nature, unpredictability, and chimeric character. Rigorous or rigid, sloppy or broad, definitions are in themselves an important discursive practice of the terrorism industry. Often they appear to be yet another weapon in the vast arsenal of counter-terrorism, aiming to re-establish order and meaning in international relations practice and discourse at a time when both are undergoing extensive and intensive assaults.

Is it possible to recognize the battlefield of contending definitions without getting bogged down by it, to stand at the edge of the political fray, to launch "truth"-seeking missives which might clear the ground for a new reading of terrorism? Probably not. In the Age of Surveillance and Speed, the ultimate strategic power of terrorism and counter-terrrorism is not the quantity and secure *siting* of weapons/targets, that is, geo-politics, but the velocity and timely *sighting* of them, that is, chrono-politics.[11] In other words, a different strategic game requiring a different cultural analysis is being played out: to match the opacity rendered by Stealth technologies, the transparency achieved by satellites and ELINT (Electronic Intelligence), the targeting ("illuminating") power of radar and laser, a new cultural reading is needed. Hence, the best I can offer is a deterrent description rather than a pre-emptive definition, a view of the boundaries of the national security culture drawn by terrorism from two elevations which might yield a parallax advantage over the conventional one-dimensional definitions. In high orbit and at low resolution, I see terrorism as does the social critic Jean Baudrillard, historically "initiated by the taking of hostages and the game of postponed death"; but in a lower orbit, at higher resolution on the screen, I view it as do others—as a televisual strategic simulation of choreographed violence staged for a fearful, captive global audience.[12]

A possible text for the preface

So far, I have established some of the important problems of reading/writing about terrorism. First, the question of legitimacy: how we signify statements and discursive practices in international relations as reasonable, justifiable, verifiable, or authorized determines in part who are the victims and agents of terrorism, the legitimate and pariah state and non-state actors.[13]

Second, this signification is difficult enough within the borders and security of the state, but outside the state, with no sovereign authority (in both the juristic and linguistic senses) to rule on legitimacy, we cannot establish facts which will bring an end to terrorism.

Third, there is a historiographical problem to contend with. Histories of terrorism are rare: rarer yet is a history of how terrorism has been read, or interpreted.[14] What usually stands in for a history of terrorism is a televised factive, sometimes fictive narration of thirty seconds to three minutes. Of course, there is always the option of acquiring information from the proliferating Institutes of Terrorist Studies. For the most part, though, what they provide is simply learned repetition of what can be heard on ABC's "Nightline."[15]

Fourth, this is not so much a crisis in the legitimation process as it is a crisis of representation, in which the once-dominant state's construction of legitimate political violence, now competing with terrorism's fragmentation of power and globalization by the media, is reduced to a pure simulation of terrorism and counter-terrorism.[16]

Fifth, this evokes an ethical and political dilemma: How do we reconstruct a reading of terrorism which critiques the maintenance of an order favorable to the dominant interests of the superpowers while recognizing the imperative of assuring the internal and external security of citizens who face natural and "artificial" disasters in an international, quasi-anarchical society?

There is the temptation, prompted by the practices of post-structuralist theory, to end with this summation and critical interrogation, to leave it to the reader to construct an alternative history of terrorism out of the "fragged" remains of the bodypolitic. But this would highlight the worst aspects of post-structuralism, its propensity for the extremes of gaming or despairing when confronted by the seemingly implacable problems of modernity. In international theory we must demonstrate something more than what Nietzsche referred to as "the strength to forget the past," by which he meant forgetting the kind of history that neatly adds up past events to rationalize our present condition. Otherwise, we leave a void, a vacuum of knowledge and power in which others engaged in a different kind of "positive forgetting"—most notably political leaders who preside over the past through a process of selective senility—can install metaphysical visions of terrorism. For counter-terrorism, then, I suggest a counter-history: Instead of the flash-bang grenades of anti-terrorist rhetoric which have blinded and deafened us to past struggles of international political violence and legitimacy, we need a study of the relevant archives, in the Foucauldian sense of the "play of rules which determines within a culture the appearance and disappearance of statements."[17]

The sanitation of terror: from the making of pledges to the taking of hostages

The cultural archive of terrorism eternally recurs with the making and breaking of pledges: the loyalty oath of feudal warriors, the first contracts of the traders, the compact for a commonwealth, the *pacta sunt servanda* of the fledgling system of states; all founded on promises—some kept and many broken—to move from anarchic terror to a ruled order.[18] A skimming of some of the exemplary thinkers of the rationalist episteme discloses the anti-terrorist role of the pledge in reason and history. Although Thomas Hobbes' prescription of a one-sided pledge to the Leviathan for security in the permanent "war of all against all" has dominated modern thinking about international relations, there have been significant challengers to his realist paradigm, like Hugo Grotius and Samuel Pufendorf, the foremost jurists of the seventeenth century who saw in the promise a cultural mechanism through which natural law and a mutual alienation of interests could provide rules for an international society.[19] In the grip of realist and neo-realist paradigms, we have "forgotten" how the pledge/promise acted as a vehicle for ordering societies, juristically and discursively, but also theoretically through social contracts (Rousseau), the confederation of states (Kant), the universalization of Spirit (Hegel), and the solidarity of a class (Marx). But now, in a society fragmented and nuclearized by terrorism and the balance of terror, there are no authors, no subjects, only hostages—actual and potential— for the international pledge. The anonymity of mutual asssured destruction, the indiscriminate exchange of hostages by terrorism, the requisite secrecy of counter-terrorism, each act as ellipses in international relations. Held hostage to a pledge which is significant for everyone but signed by no one, inscribed by a death sentence that makes no juristic or grammatical sense outside of the official context, the subject is predicated—"disappeared"—by the terrorist ellipsis.

In the Iran-Contra hearings Oliver North filled the ellipsis and became a "heroic" subject to the extent that he was able to assert a pure identity (the counter-terrorist/victim) against an evil difference (the terrorist/criminal). In contrast to the threats of master-terrorist Abu Nidal, Iranian fanatics, and "totalitarian Sandinistas," the issues of a free security systems for his home, missing travelers' checks, and Swiss bank accounts seemed insignificant. For North, moving from his rule-less world of counter-terrorism to the litigious stage of the hearings, the only pledge of importance became the one against perjury:

Sullivan: Well, what is your question, counsel?
Nields: Have you forgotten the question?
Sullivan: Well I have and I have to make objections, so you ask it again and I'll—
Nields: You did and it was overruled and the question stands. I'd like the witness to answer it, if he remembers it.
Sullivan: Could we—he obviously doesn't remember it, he just asked you to repeat it. May we have—
Nields: You did, you did, he did not Sir, do you remember the question?
North: My memory has been shredded. If you would be so kind as to repeat the question.

A modernist attempt to resurrect the historical relationship between the pledge and security, terror and freedom, is made by Jean-Paul Sartre in his much-maligned but rarely read *Critique of Dialectical Reason.* His theoretical distillation of the pledge and alienated group dynamics offers an interpretive conduit for plotting the historical transformations of the modern national security culture:

> But *this* is precisely what a pledge is: namely the common production, through mediated reciprocity, of a statute of violence; once the pledge has been made, in fact, the group has to guarantee everyone's freedom against necessity, even at the cost of his life and in the name of freely sworn faith. Everyone's freedom demands the violence of all against it and against that of any third party as its defence against itself (as a free power of secession and alienation). To swear is to say, as a common individual: you must kill me if I secede. And this demand has no other aim than to install Terror within myself as a free defence against the fear of the enemy (at the same time as reassuring me about the third party who will be confined by the same Terror). At this level the pledge becomes a material operation.[20]

How would a history of the "material operation" of the pledge read? There is no text to turn to, really only fragments, but the best pieces come, I believe, from the erudite writings of Martin Wight, the British "classical" international theorist.[21] Wight's sweeping inquiry into the development of principles of international legitimacy offers a panoramic view of how violence was made safe for the society of states. This story of the sanitation of political violence, what could be called "the hygienics of terror," begins with the establishment of the dynastic principle and ends with the popular principle of legitimacy.[22] It is a long story, which cannot be retold here, of the formation of hierarchies and rituals of power in Latin Christendom (the Holy Roman Empire, papacy, national monarchs, fiefdoms, principalities, and city-states) based on precedence and prescriptive rights. What concerns this inquiry is a counter-plot, how a series of challenges in the seventeenth and eighteenth centuries to the dynastic principle of legitimacy—the republicanism of the Dutch revolt, the theories of political and social contract, and the English, American, and French Revolutions—shifted pledge-making from dynastic rulers to popular politics; and how from the American revolution to the imperialism of the French revolution the principle of legitimacy underwent a sea-change, from all men are created equal and have inalienable rights to the idea of *national* self-determination. "The rights of man," says Wight, "gave way to the rights of nations."[23] With this alienation of obligations, the nation-state takes on the pledge, or contract, of security. But it is the sub-plot of the counter-plot which informs this modern reading of terrorism: that is, the emergence of a neo-medieval hostage-taking to enforce, and increasingly displace, a newly challenged national security pledge.

For those more materially or neorealistically inclined in their global analysis, these may seem like "paper" issues in a *kapitalpolitik* world where trade and microchips, if no longer blood and iron, seem to rule. But from the first chanceries of the early Middle Ages to the modern national security archives, the "text" has always preceded the state. It is the chancellor, or *cancellarius*, "keeper of the barrier," who by his accumulation of official diplomas inscribed the first boundaries of the early Holy Roman Empire that Charlemagne only fleetingly and tenuously secured by sword. It is the statutory power of the National Security Act of 1947, "to perform such other functions and duties related to intelligence affecting the national security as the National Security Council may from time to time direct," that so effectively redrew the reach of the American Empire after its military troops had come home.

To be sure, war, the *ultima ratio* of the state, still counts, but in nuclear and cybernetic times it counts for less. It was the *sign* of war—the uniform, the silver and bronze stars, and purple hearts, the ramrod posture—that protected North from the media glare and committee probings. North took a hostage—our concept of patriotism. And it is the war of signs, not a presidential pardon or judicial prestidigitation, that will probably determine North's future. Having subpoenaed the president, president-elect, and other high government officials, and having demanded over 30,000 classified documents, North has taken the ultimate hostage: the secret archive of the national security state.

We probably will never learn of the pledges (let alone their legality) made and broken in this particular campaign of terror and counter-terror because we— or some counterfeit "we" that bought into the cultural economy of the national security state—pledged not to. We can, however, use this reconstruction of the relationship between the pledge and terror to ask broader, critical questions about the future of the international order. Will the fragmentation of state-power, the pervasiveness of the nuclear and chemical terror, the rise of a new international disorder void the international contracts of the dominant powers and once again "legitimate" the taking of hostages? Are we returning to a practice institutionalized when Europe was evolving from a suzerain system to a states-system, where only a physical pledge was sufficient to maintain order? At best, can we hope for a recur-rence of the mutual exchange of elite hostages as a commitment to keep a pledge, as Spain and France exchanged hostages—one of them William of Orange—to enforce the Treaty of Cateau-Cambresis in 1559? For control of nuclear terror, should we be prepared to offer the Soviets Abraham Sofaer (legal advisor to the Department of State) as insurance for maintaining the "narrow" interpretation of the Anti-Ballistic Missile Treaty? When intermediate (and if theater) nuclear weapons are removed from Europe, will American troops be sufficient hostages for NATO? And could more extreme hostage-takings be institutionalized, such as guaranteed air-time on ABC's "Nightline" for the year's most popular terrorist and counter-terrorist—Abu Nidal and Oliver North in split-screen?

Penultimatum

For now, I will leave it to more historicist others to argue whether modern terrorism, the breakdown of the pledge, and the taking of hostages are harbingers of a new medievalism, or morbid symptoms of a Gramscian moment where the old is dying and the new cannot yet be born. My final speculation returns instead to the critical link between international terrorism and the balance of terror, where everyone, combatants and non-combatants alike, are conceivable hostages. At the polemical level, the most effective anti-terror tactic would be to attack the stasis of a global insecurity that presently privileges superpowers and marginalizes lesser powers, that perpetually postpones a negotiated settlement in the Middle East, that assures an opportunistic rather than serious commitment to disarmament. But this begs an expanded interpretation of the international cultural economy which might allow us to reinscribe broader, looser borders to the national security culture, to deconstruct institutions like the balance of terror which we have created but seem beyond our control, and of no lesser importance, to be less earnest when reading/writing/shredding the archive of terrorism.

Notes

* This essay is revised from a paper given at the Rand Corporation which was published as "Arms, Hostages, and the Importance of Shredding in Earnest: Reading the National Security Culture and Terrorism," in *Cultural Politics in Contemporary America*, eds. Ian Angus and Sut Jhally (Routledge Press, 1988). I would like to thank Ruth Abbey, Kiaran Honderich, John Santos, and Anders Stephanson for their criticisms.

1 *Taking the Stand: The Testimony of Lieutenant Colonel Oliver North* (New York: Pocket Books, 1987), pp. 26–27.

2 "Abstraction today is no longer that of the map, the double, the mirror or the concept Simulation is no longer that of a territory, a referential being or a substance. It is the generation by models of a real without origin or reality: a hyperreal." From J. Baudrillard, *Simulations* (New York: Semiotext(e), 1983), p. 2.

3 Entitled *Documents From the U.S. Espionage Den* (not readily available at $248.00, but selected volumes can be found at the National Intelligence Book Center and the National Security Archive in Washington, D.C.), the collected work contains intelligence reports on Iran, Pakistan, Kuwait, Turkey, the Soviet Union, and other near and Middle-Eastern countries. Of special interest is a 170-page study of international terrorism which shows that Syria "sponsored" many of the incidents of Middle-Eastern terrorism in the 1970s.

4 "Hence, there exists today a new perspective of reflection—common, I insist, to literature and to linguistics, to the creator and the critic, whose tasks, hitherto absolutely self-contained, are beginning to communicate, perhaps even to converge, at least on the level of the writer, whose action can increasingly be defined as a critique of language … This new conjunction of literature and linguistics, which I have just mentioned, might provisionally be called, for lack of a better name, *semio-criticism*, since it implies that writing is a system of signs." From Roland Barthes, "To Write: An Intransitive Verb?", in *The Rustle of Language*, trans. by R. Howard (New York: Hill and Wang, 1986), pp. 11–12.

5 "Is it the media which induce fascination in the masses, or is it the masses which divert the media into spectacle? Mogadishu Stammheim: the media are made the vehicle of the moral condemnation of terrorism and of the exploitation of fear for political ends, but, simultaneously, in the most total ambiguity, they propagate the brutal fascination of the terrorist act." From Jean Baudrillard, "The Implosion of Meaning in the Media", in *In the Shadow of the Silent Majority* (New York: Semiotext(e), 1983), pp. 105–6.

6 *Taking the Stand*, p. 12.

7 Two provocative studies of how cultures of terror subvert order and meaning, and how disasters compel silence or dissimulation, are Michael Taussig's *Shamanism, Colonialism, and the Wild Man: A Study in Terror and Healing* (Chicago and London: The University of Chicago Press, 1987), and Maurice Blanchot's *The Writing of the Disaster* (Lincoln and London: University of Nebraska Press, 1986).

8 "There is no distinction possible between the spectacular and the symbolic, no distinction possible between the "crime" and the "repression." It is this uncontrollable eruption of reversibility that is the true victory of terrorism." From J. Baudrillard, "Our Theater of Cruelty", in *In the Shadow of the Silent Majorities*, pp. 115–6.

9 See Jean-Francois Lyotard's *The Postmodern Condition: A Report on Knowledge* (Minneapolis: University of Minnesota Press, 1984), particularly the foreword by Frederic Jameson, pp. vii–xxi. Two seminal writings which anticipate Baudrillard's study of simulation and hyperrealism as legitimating forces for political order—one on the "culture of distraction" and the other on the "society of the spectacle"—are Siegfried Kracauer's *Das Ornament der Masse* (Frankfurt a.M.: Suhrkamp Verlag, 1963), forthcoming as *The Mass Ornament*, translated and edited by Thomas Y. Levin (Cambridge: Harvard University Press); and Guy Debord's *Society of the Spectacle* (Detroit, MI: Black and Red, 1983).

10 See P. Virilio, *Pure War* (NewYork: Semiotext(e):1983), and *Speed and Politics* (New York: Semiotext(e): 1986); and J. Der Derian, chapter eight on "Techno-diplomacy" in *On Diplomacy: A Genealogy of Western Estrangement* (Oxford: Basil Blackwell, 1987), and "Spy vs. Spy: Intertextual Power in the Literature of International Intrigue", in *International/Intertextual Relations*, eds. J. Der Derian and M. Shapiro (Lexington, MA: Lexington Press, 1988).

11 Baudrillard supplies the theoretical base for this definition, and the major networks' production standards for coverage of terrorism provide an empirical foundation.

12 These questions presuppose if not confim a legitimacy crisis in international relations; or it would appear so, if we share a view of inquiry into legitimacy with "the owl of Minerva", whose wings stretch from Hegel to Habermas to Frederic Jameson who says soothly in the Foreword to Lyotard's Postmodem Condition that "legitimation becomes visible as a problem and an object of study only at the point in which it is called into question" (p. viii).

13 For its narrative style and absence of scientific pretensions, Walter Laqueur's *Terrorism* (and his anthology on terrorism) stands out as an exception to the ruling policy-oriented material on the subject. See in particular his preface to the Abacus Edition, where he states that "the failure of political scientists to come to terms with the terrorist phenomenon cannot possibly be a matter of legitimate dispute …Historical experience,

it is said, cannot teach us much about terrorism; but what else can?" From *Terrorism* (London: Sphere Books, 1978), pp. 7–8.

14 I wonder, after watching some of these pundits (like Michael Ledeen) who are wheeled out as impartial commentators on terrorism, whether the best counter-terrorism action would be a surgical airstrike on some of those institutes (but then again, it might miss and hit the Institute of Policy Studies).

15 For the transformation of political representation into simulation, see Baudrillard's *Simulations*, pp. 11–13 ("Whereas representation tries to absorb simulation by interpreting it as false representation, simulation envelops the whole edifice of representation as itself a simulacrum."); and for its elision through the balance of terror into a "mutual simulation", see Virilio's *Pure War*, op. cit., 159–172.

16 M. Foucault, "Response au cercle d'epistemologie", *Cahiers pour l' analyse*, 9 (Summer 1968). This is of course only a sketch of Foucault's historiographical technique. On the difficult task of plumbing our own archive, "the general system of the formation and tranformation of statements," see the introduction and chapter 5 of Foucault's *The Archaelogy of Knowledge* (London: Tavistock Publications, 1972); and on his recuperation of the genealogical approach, "gray, meticulous, and patiently documentary", see his seminal essay, "Nietzsche, Genealogy, History", in *Language, Counter-Memory, Practice: Selected Essays and Interviews*, ed. D.F. Bouchard (Ithaca: Cornell University Press, 1977).

17 For a related view on the function of the promise in both the domestic and international order, see chapters 1 and 2 of Hedley Bull's *The Anarchical Society* (London: Macmillan, 1977).

18 See T. Hobbes, *Leviathan*, ed. M. Oakeshott (Oxford: Blackwell), pp. 85–87 and 112; H. Grotius, "Of Promises," in *De jure belli ac pacis*, trans. W. Whewell (London: John Parker, 1835), vol II, pp. 35–36; S. Pufendorf, "Of the Nature of Promises and Pacts in General," in *Of the Law of Nature and Nations* (Oxford: Clarendon, 1935), pp. 390–401; and I. Kant, "Second Section Which Contains the Definitive Articles for Perpetual Peace Among Nations", in *Perpetual Peace and Other Essays* (Indianapolis: Hackett Publishing, 1983), p. 111.

19 *New York Times*, 8 July 1987, p. 8.

20 For Sartre, then, terror is not an anomalous feature of modem society, but fundamental, as is scarcity, to the formation of societies: 'The origin of the pledge, in effect, is fear (both of the third party and of my self)… Terror…is common freedom violating necessity, in so far as necessity exists only through the alienation of some freedom" *Critique of Dialectical Reason*, Verso: London, pp. 430–431.

21 See M. Wight, *Systems of States* (Leicester: Leicester University Press, 1977); and *Power Politics* (Middlesex: Penguin, 1979).

22 "By international legitimacy I mean the collective judgment of international society about rightful membership of the family of nations; how sovereignty may be transferred; and how state succession is to be regulated, when large states break up into smaller, or several states combine into one. Until the French Revolution, the principle of international legitimacy was *dynastic*, being concerned with the status and claims of rulers. Since then, dynasticism has been superseded by a *popular* principle, concerned with the claims and consent of the governed." From Wight, *System of States*, p. 153.

23 Ibid., p. 160.

3   The (s)pace of international relations

Simulation, surveillance, and speed

Source: *International Studies Quarterly* (September 1990), pp. 295–310.

Against the neorealist claim that the "reflectivist" or postmodernist approach is a dead-end unless it merges with the "rationalist" conception of research programs, this chapter argues that new technological and representational practices in world politics require not synthesis but theoretical heterogeneity to comprehend the rise of chronopolitics over geopolitics. The theoretical approaches of Baudrillard, Foucault, and Virilio are drawn upon to investigate three global forces in particular: simulation, surveillance, and speed. They have eluded the traditional and re-formed delimitations of the international relations field—the geopolitics of realism, structural political economy of neorealism, and neoliberal institutionalism—because their power is more "real" in time than space, it comes from an exchange of signs rather than goods, and it is transparent and diffuse rather than material and discrete. This chapter offers an alternative, poststructuralist map to plot how these and other new forces are transforming the traditional boundaries in international relations between self and other, domestic and international, war and peace.

Introduction

In his 1988 presidential address to the International Studies Association, Robert Keohane gave notice of a new approach to the study of international relations. He labeled it "reflective," in the sense of reflecting, for the most part critically, on how institutions are thought and written about in international relations. In an edited version of the address that appeared in the International Studies Quarterly, Keohane went on to criticize the reflective approach for failing to research the empirical reality of institutions. Within the criticism lies an implicit imprecation: if one is to find a "genuine research program" it is better to take the enlightened road of rationalist reflection than the benighted wood of poststructuralist reflexivity (Keohane, 1988). There is, moreover, a metaphoric power in Keohane's choice of terms which insinuates a kind of generic passivity in the reflectivist camp. It would seem that the reflectivist, by definition, prefers or has little choice but to reflect others' thoughts and actions rather than to engage in the more productive work of empirically testing hypotheses. Then, after dazzling the reflective creature on this familiar road of the enlightenment tradition with an impressive pair of twin high-beams—rationalist theory and empirical research—Keohane concludes that "eventually, we may hope for a synthesis between the rationalistic and reflective approaches" (Keohane, 1989: 393).

I have reflected on Keohane's well-traveled road. I have weighed its quite reasonable rules against the historical evidence, the international events born out of both accidental (famine, flood, earthquake) and intentional (war, terrorism, genocide) disasters that have taken place on this road. I have considered Keohane's destination, the higher "normative grounds" of "international cooperation," and found it to be laudable, and indeed shared by many of the reflective routes. But his conclusion makes the unbeaten track seem more appealing if not necessary: it is not in synthesis but by learning to live with irreconcilable differences and multiple identities—in high theory and in everyday practices—that we might find our best hope for international relations. I think here Keohane might agree: unless we are willing now and then to head the big American car of international relations theory off in untried, untestable, even unreasonable directions, the only perpetual peace—to update Kant—will be that of the roadside kill.[1]

This essay is not a polemic against Keohane's rationalist institutionalism, nor is it a theoretical defense of poststructuralism. They are no longer needed, for each side has begun to recognize the legitimacy of the dialogue if not the epistemological claims of the other.[2] Judging, however, from critical comments that have arisen as much from confusion as from disagreement, a few prefatory points are in order about some differences between rationalists and poststructuralists that resist synthesis.

First, poststructuralism is a semio-critical *activity*, ever searching for and seeking to dismantle the empirico-rational *positions* where power fixes meaning.[3] Second, post-structuralism does not hold that reflectivists *or* rationalists reflect the field of international relations. Both use and are used by language, by the tropes, rhetoric, narratives and grammar that make up an array of ambiguous and indeterminate signifying practices. It is this heterological nature of discourse that dominant powers, in a demonstrative, hegemonic act, always dream of fixing, reducing, subjecting to a single, monological meaning. Third, the rationalists demonstrate this power play when they construct a transcendental, privileged space to make truth-claims about international relations (like those made by game and rational choice theory from the supposed high-point of scientific progress). Alternatively—and Keohane deserves credit for now making it less of an alternative—the rationalists might simply ignore the problem of discourse, in the vain hope that it will ignore them. But the poststructuralists are always aware of—and always irritating others by demonstrating—the stickiness of the web of meaning.

Perhaps they are too irritatingly aware and demonstrative, which is why I intend to de-script some criticisms of Keohane and others. I will do so not by metatheoretically arguing against them (for this has been done elsewhere—see Walker, 1990), nor by piling up empirical evidence (as I am sure numerous latter-day encyclopedists of international relations will soon be doing on Keohane's other, hyper-rationalist flank), but by reading poststructuralism or "reflectivism" as a powerful epistemological activity which can help us understand something that cannot be fully understood: the impact of an array of new technological practices that have proven to be resistant if not invisible to traditional methods of analysis. These (post)modern practices are elusive because they are more "real" in time than space, their power is evidenced through the exchange of signs not goods, and their effects are transparent and pervasive rather than material and discrete. They do not fit and therefore they elude the traditional and the re-formed delimitations of the international relations field: the geopolitics of realism, the structural political economy of neorealism, the possessive institutionalism of neoliberalism. In contrast, I believe that poststructuralism can grasp—but never fully capture—the significance of these new forces for international relations.

In this essay I will examine three forces that stand out for their discursive power and shared problematic. Their discursive power is *chronopolitical* and *technostrategic*, and they have generated a postmodern problematic for a system of states which increasingly seems resistant to comprehension by traditional systems of thought. To clarify: they are "chronopolitical" in the sense that they elevate chronology over geography, pace over space, in their political effects;[4] they are "technostrategic" in the sense that they use and are used by technology for the purpose of war (see Clausewitz, 1976: 128, 177; Der Derian, 1987: Ch. 9; Klein, 1989); they have a discursive power in that they produce and are sustained by historically transient statements which mediate our relations with empirical events (Foucault, 1972: 21–39, 46–47, 181–184); and the problematic is postmodern because it defies the grand theories or definitive structures which impose rationalist identities or binary oppositions to explain international relations (Der Derian, 1988: 189). Hence, a poststructuralist analysis of discourse is called for to show how these new technological practices mediate and often dominate our relations with other states, but also to demonstrate their relationship to ourselves, that is, how their power is manifested in the boundaries they establish for what can be said and who can say it with authority in international theory.

The three new forces in international relations that I will examine are *simulation, surveillance*, and *speed*. The problematic they have generated can be simply put: the closer technology and scientific discourse bring us to the "other"—that is, the more the model is congruent with the reality, the image resembles the object, the medium becomes the message—the less we see of ourselves in the other. Back to the big American car: reflection loses out to reification.

This can be simply expressed but not fully explained. Why is this so? A full answer would surely lead to an ontological bog, so instead this article offers a partial explanation—and a provocation that might prompt others to lead the way on the ontotheological question that I have begged. I imagine that many of our leaders and scholars, like earlier estranged tribes who sought in heaven what they could not find on earth, have given up on peace on earth and now seek peace of mind through the worship of new techno-deities. They look up to the surveillance satellite, deep into the entrails of electronic micro-circuitry, and from behind Stealth protection to find the omniscient machines and incontrovertible signs that can help us see and, if state reason necessitates, evade or destroy the other. And should one pause too long to reflect skeptically on this reification of technical reason, one is consigned to the ranks of the dissident other, as infidels who refuse to believe that there can be a single power or sovereign truth that can dispel or control the insecurities, indeterminacies, and ambiguities that make up international relations.[5]

The three sections that follow investigate the impact of simulation, surveillance, and speed on international relations by providing: (1) an introduction to the relevant work of poststructuralist authors who have grappled with these issues; (2) an intertextual (as opposed to a content) analysis of samples drawn from documents, interviews, and periodicals; and (3) some foreign policy implications for the superpowers. This article outlines a larger project on the antidiplomatic discourses which have emerged with these new technostrategic practices.[6] It acts as a preface to establish that these new forces, in their theorization and practical application, respond better to interpretation than verification. Examples will follow, of how the radar operator on the *U.S.S. Vincennes* based his interpretation of data about an approaching Iranian aircraft on training simulations, how a former head of Air Force Intelligence found in surveillance photographs and computerized data evidence of systematic violations of arms control agreements while the head of the CIA saw an occasional misdemeanor, and how speed as the essence of modern warfare has radically changed the image of battle. And for those rationalists who might concede that what follows constitutes a sufficient body of empirical evidence but not proof unless it is scientifically tested, a model sits on my desk, constructed from a kit for a Stealth fighter-bomber three years before it officially existed, demonstrating that credible proof in national security matters is as much a function of hegemonic power as it is the product of visible knowledge.

Simulation: from realism to hyperrealism

Writing for the *Frankfurter Zeitung* in 1926, marveling at the immense popularity of the newly constructed picture palaces in Berlin, Siegfried Kracauer chronicled the emergence of a "cult of distraction." It is in these new "optical fairylands," he wrote, that "distraction—which is meaningful only as improvisation, as reflection of the uncontrolled anarchy of the world—is festooned with drapes and forced back into a unity that no longer exists."[7] In Kracauer's view the picture palaces served as a kind of Hegelian asylum from Weimar disorder, ornate spaces where the alienated Berliner could seek reunification through a new, totally imaginary, cinematic (yet organic) *Zeitgeist.*

Surveying the rise of a consumer society, anticipating the failure of conventional, radical, *spatial* politics in 1968, Guy Debord, editor of the journal *Internationale Situationniste*, opened his book Society of the Spectacle with a provocative claim: "In societies where modern conditions of production prevail, all of life presents itself as an immense accumulation of *spectacles.* Everything that was directly lived has moved away into a representation" (1983: 1).[8] At the root of this new form of representation was the specialization of power, with the spectacle coming to speak for all other forms of power, becoming in effect "the diplomatic representation of hierarchic society to itself, where all other expression is banned" (1983: 23).

After analyzing the political economy of the sign and visiting Disneyland, Jean Baudrillard, the French master of edifying hyperbole, notified the inhabitants of advanced mediacracies that they were no longer distracted by the technical reproduction of reality, or alienated and repressed by their over-consumption of its spectacular representation. Unable to recover the "original" and seduced by the simulation, they had lost the ability to distinguish between the model and the real: "Abstraction today is no longer that of the map, the double, the mirror or the concept. Simulation is no longer that of a territory, a referential being or a substance. It is the generation by models of a real without origin or reality: a hyperreal" (1983a: 2).

Baudrillard exceeds Nietzsche in his interpretation of the death of god and the inability of rational man to fill the resulting value-void with stable distinctions between the real and the apparent, the true and the false, the good and the evil. In the excessive, often nihilistic vision of Baudrillard, the task of modernity is no longer to demystify or disenchant illusion—for "with the real world we have also abolished the apparent world" (see Nietzsche, 1968: 40–41; Der Derian, 1987: Ch. 9) —but to save a principle that has lost its object:

> Disneyland is presented as imaginary in order to make us believe that the rest is real, when in fact all of Los Angeles and the America surrounding it are no longer real, but of the order of the hyperreal and of simulation. It is no longer a question of false representation of reality (ideology), but of concealing the fact that the real is no longer real, and thus of saving the reality principle (1983a: 25).[9]

The representation of international relations is not immune to this development. In a very short period the field has oscillated: from *realist* representation, in which world-historical figures meant what they said and said what they meant, and diplomatic historians recorded it as such in Rankean fashion ("wie es eigentlich gewesen ist"); to *neorealist*, in which structures did what they did, and we did what they made us do, except of course when neorealists revealed in journals like the *International Studies Quarterly* and *International Organization* what they "really" did; to *hyperrealist*, in which the model of the real becomes more real than the reality it models, and we become confused.[10]

What is the reality principle that international relations theory in general seeks to save? For the hard-core realist, it is the sovereign state acting in an anarchical order to maintain and if possible expand its security and power in the face of penetrating, de-centering forces such as the ICBM, military (and now civilian) surveillance satellites, the international terrorist, the telecommunications web, environmental movements, transnational human rights conventions, to name a few of the more obvious. For the soft-core neorealist and peace-research modeler, it is the prevailing pattern of systemic power which provides stable structures, regime constraints, and predictable behavior for states under assault by similar forces of fragmentation.

Before we consider how simulations in particular "work" to save the reality principle, we should note the multiple forms that these simulations take in international relations. From the earliest *Kriegspiel* (war-play) of the Prussian military staff in the 1830s, to the annual "Global Game" at the Naval War College in Newport, Rhode Island, simulations have been staged to prepare nation states for future wars; by doing so, as many players would claim, they help keep the peace: *qui desiderat pacem, praeparet bellum*. Simulations are used at other defense colleges, such as the strategic and counterterrorist games played at the National Defense University or the more tactically oriented computerized "Janus" game perfected at the Army War College.[11] Then there are the early academic models, like Harold Guetzkow's seminal InterNation Simulation (INS), which spawned a host of second- and third-generation models: SIPER (Simulated International Processes), GLOBUS (Generating Long-term Options by Using Simulation), and SIMPEST (Simulation of Military, Political, Economic, and Strategic Interactions).[12] Many simulations are now commercially available: the popular *realpolitik* computer game *Balance of Power;* the remarkably sophisticated video games modeled on *Top Gun*, the Iranian hostage rescue mission, and other historical military conflicts; and the film/video *WarGames*, in which a hacker taps into an Air Force and nearly starts World War III. And then there are the ubiquitous think-tank games, like those at the Rand Corporation, that model everything from domestic crime to nuclear war, as well as the made-to-order macro-strategic games, like the war game between Iraq and Iran that the private consulting company BDM International sold to Iraq (the highest bidder?).

It may grate on the ears of some of the players to hear "gaming," "modeling," and "simulation" used interchangeably.[13] Yet in the literature and during interviews I found users using all three terms to describe practices that could be broadly defined as *the continuation of war by means of verisimilitude* (Allen, 1987: 6–7). Conventionally, a game uses broad descriptive strokes and a minimum of mathematical abstraction to make generalizations about the behavior of actors, while simulation uses algorithms and computer power to analyze the amount of technical detail considered necessary to predict events and the behavior of actors. Judging from the shift in the early 1980s by the military and think-tanks to mainly computerized games—reflected in the change of the Joint Chiefs of Staff gaming organization from SAGA (Studies, Analysis, and Gaming Agency) to JAD (Joint Analysis Directorate)—it would seem that simulation is becoming the preferred "sponge" term in international relations. "Simulation" also has the obvious advantage of sounding more serious than "gaming" and of carrying more of a high-tech, scientific connotation than "modeling."

The object of this inquiry is not to conduct an internal critique of the simulation industry, nor to claim some privileged grounds for disproving its conclusions.[14] Rather, the intent is to show how, in the construction of a realm of meaning that has minimal contact with historically specific events or actors, simulations have demonstrated the power to displace the "reality" of international relations they purport to represent. Simulations have created a new space in international relations where actors act, things happen, and the consequences have no origins except the artificial cyberspace of the simulations themselves.

Over the last four years I have collected numerous examples of this new phenomenon; I will share two of them here.[15] The first is the case of the *U.S.S. Vincennes* which shot down an Iranian civilian airliner on July 3, 1988, in the mistaken belief that it was a military aircraft. The *Vincennes* was equipped with the most sophisticated U.S. naval radar system, the Aegis, which according to a later military investigation functioned perfectly.[16] It recorded that the Iranian Airbus was on course and flying level at 12,000 feet, not descending towards the *Vincennes* as the radar operator, the tactical information coordinator, and one other officer reported at the time. Somehow, between machine and man, a tragic misreading took place which resulted in the death of 290 people. One possible cause is stress: the *Vincennes* and its crew had never been in combat and were engaged with Iranian speedboats when the Airbus was first detected. Yet stress has many origins, and the military shows signs of ignoring the most serious one. The *Vincennes* trained for nine months before it went into the Persian Gulf. That training relied heavily on tapes that simulate battle situations, none of which included overflights by civilian airliners—a common occurrence in the Gulf.[17]

To be sure, much more was involved in the decision to fire at the Airbus, not least the memory of the *U.S.S. Stark* which was nearly destroyed in the Persian Gulf by an Exocet missile from an Iraqi warplane. But I would like to suggest that the reality of the nine months of simulated battles displaced, overrode, absorbed the reality of the Airbus. The Airbus disappeared before the missile struck: it faded from an airliner full of civilians to an electronic representation on a radar screen to a simulated target. The simulation overpowered a reality which did not conform to it.

Let us look at another case, an exemplary intertext of simulation: the work of Tom Clancy. Clancy saves U.S. hegemony in *The Hunt for the Red October* when a Soviet commander of a nuclear submarine defects *with* the submarine which contains advanced technology, more advanced than the silencing technology that the U.S. four years later penalized Toshiba (and jeopardized relations with Japan) for transferring to the Soviets. Clancy, whose *Red October* dustjacket sports a hyperbolic blurb from Reagan, supplied one in kind for Thomas Allen's book on strategic simulations, *War Games Today:* "Totally fascinating," Clancy wrote, "his book will be the standard work on the subject for the next ten years." Clancy's *Patriot Games* received a laudatory review from Secretary of Defense Caspar Weinberger in the *Wall Street Journal*, which was then reprinted in the *Friday Review of Defense Literature* of the Pentagon's *Current News* for the edification of the 7,000-odd Defense and State Department officials who make up its readership (*Current News* 7 August 1987: 6). Clancy's *Red Storm Rising*, inspired by war gaming, was cited by Vice-Presidential candidate Dan Quayle in a foreign policy speech to prove that the U.S. needs an anti-satellite capability.[18] In *Patriot Games*, Clancy magnifies the threat of terrorism to prove that the state's ultimate power, military counter-terror, still has utility. In a later novel, *The Cardinal of the*

Kremlin, Clancy plots the revelations of a mole in the Kremlin to affirm the need to reconstruct with Star Wars the impermeable borders of the sovereign state. Taken together, Clancy's novels stand as strategic simulations: jammed with technical detail and seductive ordnance, devoid of recognizable human characters, and obliquely linked to historical events, they have become the perfect free-floating intertext for saving the realist principle of the national security state.

What policy implications are raised by these proliferating simulations? In the military arena we soon could see life copying the hyperreal art of *Aliens*, where the Colonial Marines are buffeted as they enter the planet's atmosphere and Ripley asks the obviously anxious Lieutenant how many drops this is for him. He replies "Thirty-eight," pauses, and then adds "Simulated." He quickly proves incapable of responding to situations that do not follow his simulation training. In interviews I conducted with fast-track lieutenant colonels attending the U.S. Army War College, where a state-of-the-art, multi-million dollar simulation center is currently under construction, I learned that simulations are becoming the preferred teaching tool. And at the Foreign Service Institute simulations like the "Crisis in Al Jazira" are being used to train junior-level diplomats in the art of crisis management and counterterrorism (see Redecker, 1986).

This is not to issue a blanket condemnation of simulations. Their proliferation can, from another perspective, be seen as symptomatic of a "neither war nor peace" situation that may be fraught with dangers but is certainly preferred to a shooting war. Properly executed, simulations can play an edifying role in alerting individuals to the horrors of war. It has been said that Ronald Reagan's participation in a DEFCON alert simulation, which included an evacuation from Washington, D.C., noticeably altered his attitude toward strategic issues and arms control.

However, there is evidence of a *simulation syndrome* creeping into strategic discourse. I have provided some examples, but perhaps the best evidence is, suitably, metaphoric. Just as Army, Navy, and Marine Corps have become alarmed by the sharp increase in instances of "simulator sickness"—a condition in which users of flight simulators, especially those that provide the most realistic motions and graphic representations of flight, experience flashbacks, visual distortions, and physical disorientation[19]—we should be on the alert against a similar simulation syndrome appearing in the ranks of military and diplomatic officials as well as the international relations specialists who create and promote the simulations.

Surveillance: from panopticism to TECHINT

Within the utopian dream of the Enlightenment for the expansion of the social contract into a universal eternal peace, there lies a darker shadow, one that the rationalists of international relations rarely note in their exaltations of modernity's promise. It is the perpetual dream of power to have its way without the visible exercise of will that would produce resistance. Readers of Gramsci have found evidence of a similar form of hegemonic power operating in international relations, but their focus has usually been limited to the state and class origins of this power.

To understand the technostrategic origins of this pervasive power in international relations, one must turn to the rupture point of the Enlightenment, the French Revolution, as does Michel Foucault, who sees in it ample evidence that modern politics would progress as war by other means: "Historians of ideas usually attribute the dream of a perfect society to the philosophers and jurists of the eighteenth century: but there was also a military dream of society; its fundamental reference was not to the state of nature, but to the meticulously subordinated cogs of a machine, not to the primal social contract, but to permanent coercions, not to fundamental rights, but to indefinitely progressive forms of training, not to general will but to automatic docility" (1977: 169).

The French Revolution embodied both aspects of the Enlightenment: the high ideals of the Declaration of the Rights of Man coexisted with the power of terror, and both were promulgated by revolutionary wars that quickly took on imperial aims with the rise of Napoleon. These revolutionary tensions yielded changes over the battlefield, in the workplace, and in military institutions. In April 1794, for the first time, a company of *aerostiers* successfully used a balloon to observe the battle of Fleurus in Belgium; throughout the early 1790s "manufactories" were built according to principles found in the *Encyclopédie*, which called for close observation rather than coercion of the workforce; and in military schools, barracks, and hospitals a new architecture was developing, based on a monastic model of spatial distribution.[20] Looking first like a progressive, scientific reform, then playing a repressive, militarized role in the years of the *ancien régime*, and eventually flourishing in modern societies as a positive, benign form of social control and penal correction, a new power took hold which now pervades modernity: a disciplinary power based on surveillance.

The same Bentham who coined the name that graces our discipline provided a name and a blueprint for the architecture of the new disciplinary regime: the "panopticon." By now almost everyone in the social sciences is familar with the concept of the panopticon, an annular structure with a tower in the center which contains—or might not contain—a guard to observe and through this observation indirectly, nonviolently control the behavior of prisoners, schoolchildren, hospital patients, military trainees, whomever is on the other side of the one-way gaze. In the final chapter of *Discipline and Punish*, after a detailed, critical historiography of the panopticon, Foucault elaborates a theory of "panopticism." The prison is merely the extreme version, the most graphic model, the ultimate "pen" of our disciplinary society which inscribes the difference between normal and abnormal behavior, the good citizen and the delinquent. It is the ultimate sign of modernity's twin powers of normalization and surveillance. Put bluntly by the literary critic Maurice Blanchot: "If it weren't for prisons, we would know that we are all already in prison" (1986: 66).

Foucault does not take his acute analysis of modernity much beyond the borders of the prison-state. But I would like to extend his ideas to international relations, to suggest that the discipline now faces similar developments. Obviously, in an anarchical society there is no central watchtower to normalize relations, no panopticon to define and anticipate delinquency. Historically, the great powers

have reached relatively high levels of normalization by forging concerts of power, reciprocal codes of conduct, a body of international law. But this tenuous identity as a society was dependent upon a common diplomatic culture, as well as a collective estrangement from the "Anti-Christ Turk," the "colonial native," the "Soviet Threat," and the most recent pariah, the "international terrorist." In contemporary international relations, the diminution of the Soviet threat under Gorbachev and the renunciation of terrorism by PLO leader Arafat have removed critical points of collective alienation, and the efferent forces of states seeking resources and security grow stronger as America's ability to assert a hegemonic position declines. What power (some might prefer "regime" or "institution") can maintain stability and re-normalize relations in this (post)modern state of affairs, with multiplying state and non-state actors contesting the sovereign powers and truths behind "Western domination" (Hedley Bull's "Third World Revolt"), at the same time that the foundations of that domination are undergoing internal fragmentation and diversification?

That power is here and now, in the shadows and in the "deep black." It has no trouble seeing us, but we have had great difficulties seeing it. It is the normalizing, disciplinary, technostrategic power of surveillance. This modern panopticism takes many forms, but it is the communications intelligence (COMINT), electronic intelligence (ELINT), radar intelligence (RADINT), telemetry intelligence (TELINT), and photointelligence (PHOTOINT)—all operating under the 22,300 mile-high roof of technical intelligence (TECHINT)[21]—that constitute a new regime of power in international relations. Human intelligence (HUMINT) has played and continues to play an important role in normalizing relations through vigilance, but it lacks the ubiquity, resolution, and pantoscopic power of the technical intelligence system, as well as its apparent capability to provide value-free detailed information about the object of surveillance: "the picture does not lie."[22] Indeed, much of its power lies in this aura of representational truth that surrounds the image, in spite of the interpretational debates—from the alarmist interpretation of Soviet civil defense bunkers by former head of Air Force Intelligence, Major General Keegan, in the early 1970s, to the supposed discovery of Soviet MIG airfields and "Cuban" baseball fields in Nicaragua in the early 1980s—that have marked the history of photoreconnaissance. Admiral Stansfield Turner, more than any other director of the Central Intelligence Agency, promoted this view of technical intelligence: "What espionage people have not accepted is that human espionage has become a complement to technical systems. Espionage either reaches out into voids where technical systems cannot probe or double-checks the results of technical collection. In short, human intelligence today is employed to do what technical systems cannot do" (quoted in Burrows, 1986: v).

My purpose is not to rant against the "machine in the garden," as Leo Marx put it; neither is it to offer a paean to our new techno-gods. It is rather to point out a neglected problem of the surveillance regime, and to consider why it has been neglected. There is the obvious problem of secrecy and compartmentalized knowledge that surrounds the systems, and the attendant issue of accountability that automatically politicizes any inquiry. Technical intelligence systems are considered so sensitive that a new security classification was devised: SCI, for Sensitive Compartmented Information.[23] Perhaps, then, one reason why the politics of space surveillance has been understudied by the field of international relations is because there simply is no testable, scientific method to determine how it is controlled, used and budgeted. These remain matters for historical investigation, intertextual interpretation, and open-ended speculation—not the usual methods and concerns of behaviorists or neorealists, but prime material for a poststructuralist inquiry.

The central problem of the surveillance regime is that it normalizes relations by continuing *both* war and peace by other, technical means. The same satellite that monitors and helps us verify whether the Soviets are conforming to the INF treaty simultaneously maps the way for low-level, terrain-following cruise missiles. TENCAP (Tactical Exploitation of National Capabilities), using the latest generation of KH-12 and Milstar satellites, will provide field commanders with the real-time command, control, communications, and intelligence (C^3I) necessary to fight the war of the future—and perhaps to deter it, as immediate, local, conventional deterrence becomes a high priority with the prospect of a nuclear-free Europe. Indeed, something of a paradox seems to be at work: the greater the transparency and the faster the response time of the new satellites (like the Lacrosse and Magnum) that provide C^3I, the greater the opportunity for deterrence to "work." This paradox would seem to be demonstrated by one case—if it is to be believed—that Carter canceled a highly secret plan to attack Iran with five thousand assault troops the autumn after the failed hostage rescue because U.S. satellites detected large Soviet troop movements (twenty-two full divisions) heading toward Iran. This move was in turn made possible by the fact that the Soviets had gained access to U.S. satellite-relayed messages because the traitor John Walker had sold them the encryption key (see Barron, 1987: 24–25).

One policy implication of the new surveillance regime is that the superpowers have created a cybernetic system that displays the classic symptoms of advanced paranoia: hyper-vigilance, intense distrust, rigid and judgmental thought processes, and projection of one's own repressed beliefs and hostile impulses onto another. The very nature of the surveillance/cybernetic system contributes to this condition: we see and hear the other, but imperfectly and partially—*below* our rising expectations. This can induce paranoid behavior, that is, reasoning correctly from incorrect premises, as happened with the participants in a recent laboratory experiment at Stanford. Subjects unknowingly were subjected (through hypnosis) to a partial hearing loss; when placed in social situations they assumed that people were whispering about them and soon displayed symptoms of paranoia (Herbert, 1989: 62–63).

Forces internal to the national security state's surveillance system also reinforce paranoid behavior. Classic examples are the "bomber gaps" and "missile gaps" of the fifties and sixties, when Eisenhower and the CIA played superego to a warring military id that (ab)used the new U-2 photoreconnaissance to find bombers and missiles in every barn and silo of the Soviet Union.[24] Overclassification and overcompartmentalization of information in the national security state can lead to a form of overdetermined decision-making, with policy outcomes based on a surfeit of "deep," discrete sources that resist corrective feedback.

But what kind of feedback can possibly cure the modern cyber-paranoic? Perhaps our best hope and the best elevation for understanding the other at the highest reaches remains the much-maligned "summit." To be sure, there are many historical examples and counter-examples, but a recent case comes to mind: President Reagan approached his first summit with his Soviet counterpart with visions of the "Evil Empire," and came down from his third one saying (in Russian): "Trust, but verify."

Speed: the final frontier

In 1909 Filippo Marinetti gave notice in his famous *Futurist Manifesto* of an avantgarde movement for the modern industrial state: "The Futurist writer will make use *of free verse*, an orchestration of images and sounds in motion to express our contemporary life, intensified by the speeds made possible by steam and electricity, on land, on the seas, and in the air" (see Lista, 1986: 12–14).

To break out of the inertia of the prison-state as well as the prisonhouse of language, the Futurists exalted in paintings of the masses in perpetual motion, in race cars, airplanes, and city streets, and in poetry and manifestos of the emancipation of words from syntax, punctuation, the requirements of reason itself. Paintings and writings bore titles like *Dynamic Expansion + Speed* and *Technical Manifesto of Futurism*. The technology and "polyphony" of the urban space was their church and litany. The Futurists soon fell victim to their project of marrying an ideology of the avant-garde with art-in-action, which in Italy in the 1920s meant falling in with Mussolini's Fascist movement. But they burned brightly in that period, and they powerfully illuminated a new force in modern industrialized societies: speed.

Paul Virilio has almost single-handedly brought the issue of speed back into political and social theory. Trained as an architect, Virilio has curated museum exhibitions, studied military strategy, and written several remarkable books on topics ranging from the deterritorialization of international politics to the relationship of war to cinematic practices. It is not possible to summarize Virilio's work in this article. However, given the obvious importance of speed in international relations—from the rapid increase in weapon delivery speed and concomitant decrease in human response time, to the appearance of real-time representation and surveillance of the enemy—it does seem strange that Virilio's work has gone largely unnoticed in the discipline of international relations.[25]

In a word, Virilio's project is to politicize speed. The politics and power of wealth, war, and media have been studied, but not their political relationship to speed. In our own sub-field of international political economy we have taken steps to understand the relation of national wealth to violence, empire, and military power. But we have not given serious consideration to the political effects of excessive or insufficient speed in our systems of weapons, communications, and decision-making. Virilio is concerned about the issue because he believes a revolution has taken place in the regulation of speed. He outlined this argument in an interview with Sylvere Lotringer:

> Up until the nineteenth century, society was founded on the brake. Means of furthering speed were very scant. You had ships, but sailing ships evolved very little between Antiquity and Napoleon's time. The only machine to use speed with any sophistication was the optical telegraph, then the electric telegraph. In general, up until the nineteenth century there was no production of speed. They could produce brakes by means of ramparts, the law, rules, interdictions, etc ... Then, suddenly, there's the great revolution that others have called the Industrial Revolution or the Transportation Revolution. I call it a *dromocratic* revolution because what was invented was ... a means of fabricating speed with the steam engine, then the combustion engine. And so they can pass from the age of brakes to the age of the accelerator. In other words, power will be invested in acceleration itself. (1983: 44–45)

Virilio is preoccupied with the violence of speed, and running through his various works is the common theme that speed is the essence of war. It is speed that transforms the hand into a dangerous fist, or as Napoleon applied the concept to military strategy, "Force is what separates mass from power" (Virilio, 1983:31). But speed coupled with other technological changes has altered the battlefield: "Space is no longer in geography—it's in electronics. Unity is in the terminals. It's in the instantaneous time of command posts, multi-national headquarters, control towers, etc ... There is a movement from geo- to chrono-politics: the distribution of territory becomes the distribution of time. The distribution of territory is outmoded, minimal" (Virilio, 1983: 115). A radical claim, one that Virilio believes to be supported by the equally radical transformation of our visual representation of war. In *Guerre et Cinéma* (War and Cinema), Virilio gives a detailed history of the logistics of military perception and the use of cinematic techniques in warfare. As hand-to-hand combat gave way to long-range conflict, the enemy receded from sight. An urgent need developed to accurately see and verify the destruction of the enemy at a distance. The necessity of collapsing distance, of closing the geographical space between enemies, led to the joint development of modern techniques for war filming and killing.[26] In modern warfare, as the aim of battle shifts from territorial, economic, and material gains to immaterial, perceptual fields, the war of spectacle begins to replace the spectacle of war.[27]

Virilio's analysis of the increasing strategic significance of *battle-sight* over the more traditional battle-*site* can be verified in articles from a variety of defense journals.[28] But what lies between the texts is particulary illuminating. For instance, an advertisement in *Defense Review* for General Electric's "COMPU-SCENE V" extolls the "visionic edge": "In combat, the eyes have it: you watch the environment; you stay in contact with the threat; you aim the weapon; you search for cover. The more you see, the more you win. You see without being seen; you see first; you have tactical vision" (November 1989: p 38). General Electric can provide this military advantage because it "builds the best visionics simulation and training systems in the world." It would seem that as the "real" arms race begins to slow down, a "simulation race" is winding up: "GE continues to set the pace with COMPU-SCENE V, the most powerful member yet of the COMPU-SCENE family of computer image generators. COMPU-SCENE V delivers true photo realism, it comes with a mission generation capability that translates raw photography into real-world databases and it simulates the full range of visionic devices—a major step toward full mission rehearsal capability."

To read Virilio and then to read the technostrategic discourse provides an important message for students of war and peace: as the image becomes more credible than the fact, as time displaces space as the more significant strategic "field," and as the usefulness of our ultimate power, nuclear weapons, is increasingly called into question, the war of perception and representation deserves more of our attention and resources than the seemingly endless collection and correlation of data on war that goes on in the field of international relations. One does not need to look any further than the latest generation of weapons and strategy—Star Wars, the Stealth Bomber, the Lacrosse satellite, Discriminate Deterrence—to find ample proof that the empires of simulation, surveillance, and speed are growing in significance every day.

The beating of the bounds

I have no conclusions to offer, only a review of questions inspired if not answered by Virilio, Foucault, and Baudrillard. The grand question is, How have the new technologies of speed, surveillance, and simulation and their emerging discursive practices transformed the nature of international relations? Surrounding it are some more speculative queries. Does the rapidity and totality of nuclear and cinematic war point away from spatial, shooting wars and towards temporal, perceptual wars? Is the transparency offered by the panoptic surveillance machine leading toward a new regime of normalization? Will international conflict eventually be consigned to the cyberspace of increasingly sophisticated simulations? How can we gauge politically and judge ethically the power of simulation, surveillance, and speed to deconstruct (and reconstruct) not just the traditional boundaries of international relations but also the inadequately mapped boundaries between self and other, inside and outside, war and peace?

Might we someday see at these international borders a ritual like the one I witnessed on Ascension Day at the Marks and Spencer store in Oxford? The parsons at St. Michael's Church arrived with a crowd in tow to conduct the Beating of the Bounds, a ritual which dates back to the medieval practice of gathering to walk the boundaries of the parish and to mark them with the beating of sticks. I am sure that at one time—probably for a very long time—it was a deadly serious ritual, formally an act of gratitude to Christ but simultaneously a supplication to much older gods who kept the borders safe and the fields fertile. But on that spring day in Oxford the ritual had been opened up to interpretation, transgression, even parody, as most of the children and many of the adults joined in, pounding on the floor and shouting out "Mark! Mark!" in a way that was much more carnivalesque than pious.

Would that it be so, on the boundaries between the NATO and Warsaw forces, between Irish Catholics and Protestants, between Khomeini and Rushdie. Could it not be so, in a territory in which we have more say, the contested space of international relations theory? This is not to pretend that the boundaries do not "really" exist, or that they can be synthesized away. Rather, it is to see and study them as mythic markers for differences that we need but need not war over.

Author's note

This paper was first delivered at the London B/ISA Meeting in March 1989. I would like to thank Ruth Abbey, Kiaran Honderich, M. J. Peterson, Nick Rengger, John Santos, Gerard Toal, Michael Klare, and the Editors of *ISQ* for their help and criticism. For those commentators at the B/ISA panel who at the time found my conclusion too utopian, I apologize if it now—after Berliners have danced on the Wall—sounds too dated.

Notes

1 For critical enlightenment, as well as for casualty insurance, it is worth repeating Kant's opening remarks to his essay *Perpetual Peace*: " 'To Perpetual Peace' whether this satirical inscription on a certain Dutch shopkeeper's sign, on which a graveyard was painted, holds for *men* in general, or especially for heads of state who can never get enough of war, or perhaps only for philosophers who dream that sweet dream, is not for us to decide. However, the author of this essay does set out one condition: the practical politician tends to look down with great smugness on the political theorist, regarding him as an academic whose empty ideas cannot endanger the nation, since the nation must proceed on principles derived from experience; consequently, the theorist is allowed to fire his entire volley, without the worldly-wise statesman becoming the least bit concerned. Now if he is to be consistent—and this is the condition I set out—the practical politician must not claim, in the event of a dispute with a theorist, to detect some danger to the nation in those views that the political theorist expresses openly and without ulterior motive. By this *clausula salvatoria*, the author of this essay will regard himself to be expressly protected in the best way possible from all malicious interpretation" (1983: 341).

2 In one of his last interviews Foucault presented a persuasive argument for taking up a dialogical approach over against a polemical one: "Questions and answers depend on a game—a game that is at once pleasant and difficult—in which each of the two partners takes pains to use only the rights given him by the other and by the accepted form of the dialogue. The polemicist, on the other hand, proceeds encased in privileges that he possesses in advance and will never agree to question. On principle, he possesses rights authorizing him to wage war and making that struggle a just undertaking; the person he confronts is not a partner in the search for the truth, but an adversary, an enemy who is wrong, who is harmful and whose very existence constitutes a threat. For him, then, the game does not consist of recognizing this person as a subject having the right to speak, but of abolishing him, as the interlocutor, from any possible dialogue; and his final objective will be, not to come as close as possible to a difficult truth, but to bring about the triumph of the just cause he has been manifestly upholding from the beginning" (1984: 381–82). However, as I have argued elsewhere, this is not to support the kind

of mushy, uncritical eclecticism that is found in much of the "contending approaches" school (see Der Derian, 1988).

3 See Roland Barthes (1986: 11–12): "Hence, there exists today a new perspective of reflection—common, I insist, to literature and to linguistics, to the creator and the critic, whose tasks, hitherto absolutely self-contained, are beginning to communicate, perhaps even to converge, at least on the level of the writer, whose action can increasingly be defined as a critique of language … This new conjunction of literature and linguistics, which I have just mentioned, might provisionally be called, for lack of a better name, *semio-criticism*, since it implies that writing is a system of signs." And Foucault, "On the Genealogy of Ethics: An Overview of Work in Progress," (1984: 343): "I am not looking for an alternative; you can't find the solution of a problem in the solution of another problem raised at another moment by other people. You see, what I want to do is not a history of solutions, and that's the reason why I don't accept the word *alternative*. I would like to do the genealogy of problems, of *problematiques*."

4 On the displacement of "geopolitics" by "chronopolitics," see Virilio (1986).

5 In *The Twilight of the Idols*, Nietzsche exposes the origins of this tyranny of reason which first appears as but soon fences out dissident knowledge: "If one needs to make a tyrant of *reason*, as Socrates did, then there must exist no little danger of something else playing the tyrant. Rationality was at that time divined as a *savior;* neither Socrates nor his "invalids" were free to be rational or not, as they wished—it was *de riguer*, it was their *last* expedient. The fanaticism with which the whole of Greek thought throws itself at rationality betrays a state of emergency: one was in peril, one had only *one* choice: either to perish or be *absurdly rational*." (1968: 33).

6 The larger project, which attempts to answer questions raised in the final chapter on "Techno-diplomacy" in *On Diplomacy* with a reading of national security cultures, includes a critical inquiry into the late Hedley Bull's papers on diplomatic culture, interviews with specialists in terrorism and modeling at the RAND Corporation, discussions with lieutenant colonels from the War colleges, an intertextual analysis of over 520 issues (two years' worth) of the Defense Department's *Current News*, the absorption of over fifty espionage novels, and the deciphering of formerly classified CIA documents and NSC PROF notes on the Iran hostage crisis and the Iran-Contra affair that had been shredded or erased, rewoven like rugs or recovered from computer disks, and collected by the National Security Archive in Washington, D.C. For earlier samplings, see Der Derian, 1986, 1989a, 1989b. The project will be published as *Antidiplomacy: Speed, Spies, and Terror in International Relations* (Basil Blackwell, 1991).

7 See Kracauer, 1987 and 1963.

8 In a more recent work, Debord (1988) persuasively—and somewhat despairingly—argues that the society of the spectacle retains its representational power today.

9 For related analyses of the representational shift that marks modernity and postmodernity see also Baudrillard (1983b), Benjamin (1969), McLuhan (1964), and Kittler (1987).

10 An added impetus to leave reality behind can be found in the hyperrational test that much of international relations theory has set up for itself—the model's congruence with reality. See Keohane, 1989. As well, the clean, abstracted techniques of the game theoretic, or the structures of the more positivistic neorealists, have a certain technical appeal that the interpretive archives of genealogy and intertextualism do not. For eloquent yet varied defenses of genealogy and intertextualism in international relations theory, see the exchange between Richard Ashley and William Connolly in the epilogue to *International/Intertextual Relations*, pp. 259–342.

11 For other examples of military simulations, see Thomas Allen's fine book on the subject, *War Games: The Secret World of the Creators, Players, and Policy Makers Rehearsing World War III Today* (1987).

12 See Ward (1985) for a compilation of essays in honor of Harold Guetzkow, which provide a lengthy if uneven account of simulation in the discipline of international relations. See also Howard, 1987.

13 I was, in fact, counseled against conflating the terms by a top modeler at Rand, Paul Davis, who provided me with some valuable insights into the state of the art of simulations (interview, Rand Corporation, 18 February 1988). See also his monograph with Bankes and Kahan, 1986.

14 Two excellent criticisms of the internal assumptions of gaming can be found in a review of the literature by Ashley, 1983, and in Hurwitz, 1989.

15 A fuller account, based on teaching the prisoner's dilemma to—as well as learning it from—inmates at Gardner and Lancaster State Prisons in Massachusetts, interviews with lieutenant colonels from the U.S. Army War College in Carlisle, Pennsylvania, and Freedom of Information Act (FOIA) materials, can be found in Der Derian (1990).

16 See *The New York Times*, 20 August 1988, pp. 1 and 5: "The 53-page 'Investigative Report' appeared to confirm earlier news accounts that human error resulting from combat stress was among the main causes of the tragedy. 'Stress, task fixation, and unconscious distortion of data may have played a major role in this incident,' it said."

17 See *The New York Times*, 3 August 1988, pp. A1 and A6: "A Pentagon officer who previously served in an Aegis ship said crew train constantly with tapes that simulate every conceivable battle situation. But he said, 'the excitement factor is missing in such drills, because regardless of the realism of the simulation, it is just that, a simulation of the real thing."

18 The address, given to the City Club of Chicago, was the same one at which Quayle articulated his preference for offensive weapons systems: "Bobby Knight [the Indiana University basketball coach] told me this: 'there is nothing that a good defense cannot beat a better offense [sic].' In other words a good offense wins." See *The New York Times*, 9 September 1988, p. 1.

19 See "Sickness in the Cockpit Simulator," in *The New York Times*, 20 February 1989, pp. D1 and D5: "Identifying causes and cures for simulator sickness is difficult, Dr. Kennedy said, because the malady is both polygenic and polysymptomatic; that is, it has many causes and produces many different symptoms in different individuals. But most experts agree that the root of the problem is "cue conflict," which occurs when the body's senses receive information in conflict with each other or with the mind's expectations based on experience."

20 For three very different, very rich accounts of surveillance see Foucault (1977), Virilio (1984a), and Burrows (1986).

21 One may go beyond the favored geosynchronous parking spots to include the U.S. Vela spacecraft which watches for the double flash of a thermonuclear explosion from sixty thousand miles out. See Burrows (1986: 19–20).

22 For a study of the power of "traditional" espionage, see J. Der Derian (1989a).

23 Not that this classification prevented Christopher Boyce, employed in TRW's satellite program, and William Kampiles, a CIA watch officer, from stealing and selling to the Soviets detailed, comprehensive information about the Rhyolite and KH-11 satellite systems.

24 Burrows gives a good account of the inter-service rivalry and its effect on photo interpretation during this period. He quotes a former CIA officer who said that "To the Air Force, every flyspeck on film was a missile" (1986: 82–112).

25 The Anglo-American-centricity of international relations and the lack of translations might partially explain the neglect, but I would like to pre-empt any criticism of his difficult style by noting that his translated texts, *Pure War* and *Speed and Politics* are much more aphoristic and impressionistic than his much larger body of untranslated work.

26 See *Guerre et Cinéma*, "Si la première guerre mondiale est donc bien le premier conflit médiatisé de l'Histoire, c'est parce que les armes à tir rapide supplantent la multitude des armes individuelles. C'est la fin du corps à corps systematique, de l'affrontement physique, au profit du carnage à distance où l'adversaire est invisible ou presque, *á l'exception des lueurs de tir* qui signalent sa présence. D'où cette impérieuse nécessité de la visee optique, du grossissement telescopique, l'importance du *film de guerre* et de la restitution photographique du champ de bataille, mais aussi et surtout, la découverte du rôle militaire dominant de l'aviation d'observation dans la conduite des opérations" (1984a: 123). Translation: "If the First World War can be seen as the first mediated conflict in history, it is because rapid-firing guns largely replaced the plethora of individual weapons. Hand-to-hand fighting and physical confrontation were superseded by long-range butchery, in which the enemy was more or less invisible save for the flash and glow of his own guns. This explains the urgent need that developed for ever more accurate sighting, ever greater magnification, for *'filming the war'* and photographically reconstructing the battlefield; above all it explains the newly dominant role of aerial observation in operational training." (*War and Cinema*, Verso, London and New York, 1989, p. 69–70).

27 See *Guerre et Cinéma*, "Des premières armes spatiales de la seconde guerre mondiale à l'eclair d'Hiroshima, *l'arme de théâtre* a remplace le *théâtre d'opération* et, bien que démodé, ce terme d'arme de théâtre employe par les militaires est révélateur d'une situation: *l'historie des batailles c'est d'abord celle de la métamorphose de leurs champs de perception.* Autrement dit, la guerre consiste moins à remporter des victoires "matérielles" (territoriales, économiques …) qu'a s'approprier "l'immatérialité" des champs de perception et c'est dans la mesure où les modernes belligérants étaient decidé á envahir la totalité de ces champs que s'imposa l'idée que le véritable *film de guerre* ne devait pas forcement montrer la guerre ou une quelconque bataille, puisqu'a partir du moment où le cinéma etait apte à créer la surprise (technique, psychologique…) il entrait de facto dans la catégorie des armes" (1984a: 10). "From the first missiles of World War Two to the lightening flash of Hiroshima, the *'theatre weapon'* has replaced the *'theatre of operations'*. Indeed the military term 'theatre weapon', though itself outmoded, underlines the fact that *'the history of battle is primarily the history of radically changing fields of perception'*. In other words, war consists not so much in scoring territorial, economic or other material victories as in appropriating the *'immateriality'* of perceptual fields. As belligerents set out to invade those fields in their totality, it became apparent that the true war film did not necessarily have to depict war or any actual battle. For once the cinema was able to create surprise (technological, psychological, etc.), it effectively came under the category of weapons." *War and Cinema*, Verso, London and New York, 1989, p. 7–8.

28 See, for example, the special simulation issue of *National Defense* (November 1989), *Armed Forces Journal International* (November 1989); and *Marine Corps Gazette* (December, 1989).

References

ALLEN, T. (1987) *War Games: The Secret World of Creators, Players, and Policy Makers Rehearsing World War III Today.* New York: McGraw-Hill.

Armed Forces Journal International (1989) November, pp. 88–92.

ASHLEY, R. K. (1983) The Eye of Power: The Politics of World Modeling. *International Organization* 37(3): 495–535.

BARRON, J. (1987) *Breaking the Ring.* Boston: Houghton-Mifflin.

BARTHES, R. (1986) "To Write: An Intransitive Verb?" In *The Rustle of Language*, translated by R. Howard, pp. 11–12. New York: Hill and Wang.

BAUDRILLARD, J. (1983a) *Simulations.* New York: Simiotext(e).

BAUDRILLARD, J. (1983b) *Les Stratégies Fatales.* Paris: Bernard Grasset.

BENJAMIN, W. (1969) "The Work of Art in the Age of Mechanical Reproduction." In *Illuminations*, translated by H. Zohn, edited by H. Arendt. New York: Schocken Books.

BLANCHOT, M. (1986) *The Writing of the Disaster*, translated by A. Smock. Lincoln and London.

BURROWS, W. (1986) *Deep Black: Space Espionage and National Security.* New York: Random House.

CLAUSEWITZ, C. (1976) *On War*, translated and edited by M. Howard and P. Paret. Princeton:Princeton University Press.

Current News (1987) "Friday Review of Defense Literature." 7 August, p. 6.

DAVIS, P., S. BANKES, AND J. KAHAN (1986) "A New Methodology for Modeling National Command Level Decisionmaking in War Games and Simulations." Santa Monica, CA: RAND Corporation.

DEBORD, G. (1983) *Society of the Spectacle.* Detroit: Black and Red.

DEBORD, G. (1988) *Commentaires sur la Societé du Spectacle.* Paris: Editions Gerard Lebovici.

DER DERIAN, J. (1987) *On Diplomacy: A Genealogy of Western Estrangement.* Oxford: Basil Blackwell.

DER DERIAN, J. (1988) Introducing Philosophical Traditions in International Relations. *Millennium* 17(2): 189–193.

DER DERIAN, J. (1989a) "Spy versus Spy: The Intertextual Power of International Intrigue." In *International/Intertextual Relations: Postmodern Readings of World Politics*, edited by J. Der Derian and M. J. Shapiro, pp. 163–87. Lexington, MA: Lexington Books.

DER DERIAN, J. (1989b) Reading the National Security Culture (II). *Social Text* 22 (Spring).

DER DERIAN, J. (1990) The Simulation Syndrome: From War Games to Game Wars. *Social Text* 24 (Summer).

DER DERIAN, J. (1991) *Anti-Diplomacy: Speed, Spies, and Terror in International Relations.* Oxford: Basil Blackwell.

FOUCAULT, M. (1972) *The Archeology of Knowledge.* London: Tavistock.

FOUCAULT, M. (1977) *Discipline and Punish: The Birth of the Prison*, translated by Alan Sheridan. New York: Pantheon.

FOUCAULT, M. (1984) *The Foucault Reader*, edited by P. Rabinow. New York: Pantheon.

HERBERT, W. (1989) "Paranoia: Fearful Delusions." In *New York Times Magazine.*

HOWARD, N. (1987) The Present and Future of Metagame Analysis. *European Journal of Operational Research* 32: 1–25.

HURWITZ, R. (1989) "Strategic and Social Fictions in the Prisoner's Dilemma." In *International/ Intertextual Relations: Postmodern Readings of World Politics*, edited by J. Der Derian and M. J. Shapiro, pp. 113–134. Lexington, MA: Lexington Books.

KANT, I. (1983) *Perpetual Peace.* Indianapolis: Hackett Publishing.

KEOHANE, R. O. (1988) International Institutions: Two Approaches. *International Studies Quarterly* 32: 379–96.

KEOHANE, R. O. (1989) "Neoliberal Institutionalism: A Perspective on World Politics." In *International Institutions and State Power: 'Essays in International Relations Theory.* Boulder, CO: Westview.

KITTLER, F. (1987) Gramaphone, Film, Typewriter. *October 41*, Summer 1987.

KLEIN, B. S. (1989) "The Textual Strategies of Military Strategy: Or, Have You Read Any Good Defense Manuals Lately?" In *International /Intertextual Relations: Postmodern*

Readings of World Politics, edited by J. Der Derian and M. J. Shapiro, pp. 97–112. Lexington, MA: Lexington Books.

KRACAUER, F. (1963) *Das Ornament der Masse (The Mass Ornament)*. Frankfurt: Suhrkamp Verlag.

KRACAUER, F. (1987) The Cult of Distraction: On Berlin's Picture Palaces, translated by T. Y. Levin. *New German Critique* 40 (Winter).

LISTA, G. (1986) *Futurism*, translated by C. Clark. New York: Universe Books.

Marine Corp Gazette (1989) December, pp. 38–51.

McLUHAN, M. (1964) *Understanding Media*. New York: Signet.

National Defense (1989) November, pp. 19–65.

New York Times, 20 August 1988, pp. A1 and A5.

New York Times, 3 August 1988, pp. Al and A6.

New York Times, 9 September 1988, p. Al.

New York Times, 20 February 1989, pp. D1 and D5.

NIETZSCHE, F. (1968) *The Twilight of the Idols*. New York: Penguin.

REDECKER, J. (1986) "Crisis in Al Jazira: A Strategic Foreign Policy Simulation." Occasional Paper No. 4, Center for the Study of Foreign Affairs.

VIRILIO, P. (1975) *Bunker Archéologie*. Paris: Centre de Creation Industrielle.

VIRILIO, P. (1977) *L'Insécurité du Territoire*. Paris: Galilee.

VIRILIO, P. (1978) *Defense populaire et Luttes écologiques*. Paris: Galilee.

VIRILIO, P. (1980) *Esthetique de la Disparition*. Paris: Balland.

VIRILIO, P. (1983) *Pure War*. New York: Semiotext(e).

VIRILIO, P. (1984a) *Guerre et Cinéma: Logistique de la Perception*. Paris: Editions de l'Etoile.

VIRILIO, P. (1984b) *L'espace critique*. Paris: Christian Bourgeois.

VIRILIO, P. (1984c) *L'horizon négatif*. Paris: Galilee.

VIRILIO, P. (1986) *Speed and Politics*. New York: Semiotext(e).

VIRILIO, P. (1988) *La machine de vision*. Paris: Editions Galilee.

VIRILIO, P. (1989) *War and Cinema: The Logistics of Perception*, London and New York: Verso.

WALKER, R. B. J. (1990) "History and Structure in the Theory of International Relations." In *World Politics: Power, Interdependence, and Interdependence*, edited by D. Hoaglund and M. Hawes. New York: Hartcourt, Brace, Jovanich.

WARD, M., ED. (1985) *Theories, Models, and Simulations in International Relations*. Boulder, CO: West view Press.

4 Narco-terrorism at home and abroad

Source: *Radical America* (December 1991), vol. 23, nos. 2–3, pp. 21–26.

I'd like to begin in a rather odd place and time, in the village of Gerasimovka in the Ural Mountains of the Soviet Union, where over fifty years ago, a 13-year-old boy named Pavlik Morozov denounced his kulak father to the local authorities for hiding a pig in his basement. This was at the height of Stalin's dekulakization program, in which at least three million died by starvation, and many more were deported to labor camps, because they resisted the expropriation of their produce and farm animals. But Pavlik became a folk hero and a statue was erected in his honor.

The drug war hysteria in the US has certainly not reached the level of political persecution that existed in Stalin's era. But we need to recognize that we have already begun to build our own statues and camps for the war against drugs. I teach in the Massachusetts prison program and I have witnessed the incredible proliferation and overcrowding of prisons that cannot begin to accommodate the villains and victims of the drug wars. I am waiting for our drug "czar," William Bennett, to announce in true bureaucratic jargon the beginning of our radical denarcoticization program in the US.

I don't think that I exaggerate the threat. The signs are everywhere. Headlines tell us of sons and daughters turning in their parents for drug use, and, while I've not read of any statues being erected in their honor, we can witness the electronic equivalent on television, with the fleeting enshrinement of those battling drugs on such programs as "Call 911," "Crime Stoppers," and "America Crime Watch." And who can forget President Bush holding up that bag of crack cocaine purchased in a park across the street from the White House – after the DEA lured, *lured*, a drug dealer there for this media opportunity.

We see it in the popular culture as well. Just recently there was a special episode of a teenager informing on his drug-using parents on "21 Jump Street," a Fox TV program in which Johnny Depp's good looks and agonizing soul-searching are supposed to make up for the fact that he's little more than a glorified snitch. So I think we're in the middle of an anti-drug hysteria, and like other historical witch trials we're in so deep that we don't even realize it. It does have its comical aspects – like when the US troops reached Noriega's private headquarters and found among other things, Nazi paraphernalia, pornography, and 50 pounds of cocaine in the freezer. The cocaine later turned out be tamales. Perhaps the pornography will later turn out to be home videos.

How did we get here? To answer this question we have to engage in a critical history of what has been called narcoterrorism. We must look into the supposed origins of the war on drugs and how this particular war came to take on such importance in our international affairs.

Who's the terrorist in narcoterrorism?

It is difficult to pin a date on the origins of narcoterrorism, which is conventionally understood as the violent blending of illicit drug trade and political intimidation. The word itself first crops up in the early-80s, when Peruvian officials began to popularize the term by linking the *Sendero Luminoso* insurgency to the narcotics trade. But the war against it is better marked, with Nancy and Ronald Reagan sitting on a sofa somewhere in the White House a few years back, giving the American public the first high-level, televised debriefing of the war on drugs. It is important to put this in historical context, a time when Gorbachev seemed intent on unilaterally calling off the Cold War, and Khaddafi preferred to sulk in his tent rather than execute his threat to bring terrorism home to the United States, and we see narcoterrorism moving up the ranks to become our most immediate and dire foreign threat.

The charges flew in this period. We had Colombian cartels using drug profits to seduce left-wing guerrillas. The Syrians were growing opiates in the Bekaa Valley to fund Palestinian militias. And we were told that the Nicaraguan Sandinistas, as well as the Cubans, were providing transshipment for cocaine and using the profits to back Salvadoran rebels.

Our popular culture was selling a similar narrative – but the good guys and bad guys were often reversed. Before the mainstream media – or even the alternative press – were taking a critical attitude toward the Drug War, popular shows and films like "Miami Vice," "Lethal Weapon," and "Above the Law" were taking the first steps, dredging up the drug-running days of the CIA-proprietary, Air America in Southeast Asia, and moving their counter-insurgency operations to Latin America. They made the critical link between those drug-running days in Vietnam, Cambodia and Laos to drug-running and its political consequences in Latin America.

It became clear early on that Ron and Nancy's simple campaign of "Just Say No" was not going to defeat this new foreign enemy. That's the external context of the Drug War. Now let's turn to the internal context of the war against drugs.

First, you have the rise of internal gang warfare in major American cities, to such a level that counter-insurgency programs are adapted for urban warfare. We see a volatile combination emerging: internal terrorism in US cities, led by Jamaican and Colombian gangs and the expansionist LA gangs, Crips and Bloods, fighting for drug-trade turf, linked up with the international terrorism of the Mexican narcos who killed the DEA agent and the Medellin "Extraditables" who assassinated Colombian judges and other officials. All of these events were magnified by media overrepresentation, topped by the *video verite* of "Cops" and "America's Most Wanted" and the docudrama of the killing of the DEA agent in Mexico.

In quick fashion, our national security and the American way of life were put in danger. Narcoterrorism took on the qualities of a synergistic threat. For instance, Mayor Koch of New York advocated an air attack on Medellin. Daryl Gates, the chief of the Los Angeles Police, who at this point had become infamous for his anti-drug sweeps of the city with helicopters, armored vehicles, and thousands of police officers, outdid Koch by calling for an outright invasion of Colombia. I was living in LA at the time, at the edge of the barrio, and it sounded like a battle zone. The Drug Enforcement Agency became the first law enforcement agency to issue all of its members with submachine guns. Military AWACS began to patrol the Caribbean. The State Department was supplied with over 150 fixed-wing aircraft and Huey helicopters. The Customs Service and Coast Guard set up a Command, Control, Communications and Intelligence (C3I) Center in Miami and lined the Mexican border with radar-equipped blimps. The Green Berets set off to train paramilitary forces in Latin America for the war against narcoterrorism.

It was only a matter of time before stealth technology was introduced. I'm not referring to the stealth fighter-bomber's first mission in Panama, when it missed its target by a couple hundred feet, but to a front page article from the *Arizona Republic*, which reported that "National Guardsmen in Texas could be fighting the war on drugs dressed as cactuses, sneaking up on smugglers under the cover of night and prickly needles, according to a proposal submitted to the Defense Department."

"Stupid facts"

How did narcoterrorism come to claim precedence over all other forms of terrorism? One history – the official history – is made up of what President Reagan once referred to as "stupid facts," by which he meant, of course, stubborn facts. And there are some stubborn facts. I don't want to downplay the fact that US users spend between 100 and 150 billion dollars a year on narcotics, creating a demand that (according to the State Department's 1986 Internal Narcotics Strategic Contra Strategy Report) over 56 countries are ready to service in the capacity of growers, manufacturers, traffickers, or money launderers. And we should not allow that data to obscure the most important fact, that illegal drugs ruin and kill people.

But we have heard all this so often that they have become not stupid, but stupefying facts. They incur an inertia of helplessness, a mass mood that accepts the official view that only the experts, the police, the forces of law and order can handle the drug problem. But the problem clearly exceeds the capabilities of the best trained TNT (Tactical Narcotics Team) units which sweep a neighborhood clean of dealers one week, only to lose it the next, or the Drug Enforcement Agency which was recently forced out of Medellin, Colombia. The problem is that we have so demonized the drug problem that we have lost sight of its all too human form.

To compensate, I think we have to take into account some alternative facts and histories. Tobacco, an addictive drug, kills over 300,000 people a year;

alcohol 100,000 (including those by drunk drivers), while the use of all illegal drugs combined – cocaine, heroin, marijuana, angel dust, LSD, etc. – accounted for less than 4000 deaths in 1987. And, according to the 1989 figures, the use of illegal drugs in the United States is declining.

Yet the war on drugs continues to escalate. At times, US strategic interests have intersected with the interests of the drug trade. Some would claim that the US became entangled in this drug web. Others – and I would put myself in this camp – believe that we helped spin that web. The web-spinning theorist claims that we not only inherited the Vietnam war from the French, but also the opium trade which the French intelligence service, SDECE, had used to finance and win support of Hmong tribesmen against the Viet Minh. Even earlier, from 1948 on, the CIA had supposedly used drug smuggling routes and trade in the Golden Triangle to disguise intelligence operations against the Chinese Communists. And it is claimed that between 1966 and 1969, some of the players who later showed up in the Iran-Contra affair first perfected the guns-drug-secret warfare matrix in Laos; Thomas Clines, also CIA, worked with then Lieut. Colonel Secord to run cover air-supply missions.

The Iran-Contra hearings also revealed other drug connections, with the DEA involved in the hostage ransom attempt in Lebanon, and the CIA using of the Santa Elena airstrip in Costa Rica for the transshipment of illegal drugs and weapons. So I think that at the very least we can say that the US government has colluded with narcotics trafficking when it served US strategic interests.

Drugs as monopoly capitalism

But why is narcoterrorism now considered such a threat to US interests? Over the last thirty years, what is now called narcoterrorism was mainly perceived as a minor strategic threat and even a sometime ally in the battle against the much larger danger of communism. My own suspicion is that narcoterrorism is now being taken seriously – if not hysterically – because it has now taken on characteristics of monopoly rather than primitive capitalism, with a commensurate increase in political power. For instance, in Colombia, which is the source of 80% of the cocaine that reaches the US, right wing paramilitary squads, Marxist guerilla groups, and two major drug cartels have used drug profits to build up power bases that seriously challenge the sovereignty of the Colombian government. We have heard much of how the narcos have killed over 200 judges and court employees since 1981, and, most recently, assassinated the leading candidate for president. But what has been often ignored is the extent to which they supply a welfare system that the state cannot afford. Everything from health services and soccer fields to schools have been supplied by the narcos. And many peasants who have barely managed to survive on subsistence farming are provided not only with a cash crop and a guaranteed price for it, but just as importantly, a transportation system to get that crop to market. This is a very important reason for the support many give to the cartels. The narcos do not – could not – rule by terror alone. As war is for most states, terrorism is for the narcos – the last resort of a burgeoning agribusiness empire.

Providing a relatively lucrative living to everyone from the subsistence farmer to the ghetto dealer is the most important source of their power.

So the much ballyhooed solution of beating narcoterrorism by antiterrorism is certain to fail, as are schemes to make interdiction and eradication the top priority. The same plan was used with marijuana, which simply resulted in an increase in domestic production in Oregon and California as well as in the potency of the marijuana supply. There are already signs that the Colombian drug cartels, feeling the heat, are moving operations into the Brazilian jungles.

And even if we could develop the equivalent of a Narcotics Defense Initiative, some kind of impenetrable shield against organic drugs, designer and synthetic drugs could quickly fill the void. So I don't think that narcoterrorism will be stopped until the supply and demand of illegal narcotics are stopped, which means that the US must provide treatment and education, substitute businesses and jobs in the American cities, and crop alternatives to coca as well as the infrastructure of credit and roads in the Latin American countries.

However, I have to say that for political and economic reasons, I don't think this is going to happen in the near future. The worst-case scenario would be that incarceration – which is, let's face it, the preferred drug treatment program in the US – is exported as foreign policy. What this means is that the legal principle of *posse comitatus*, against the military making arrests as well as taking in policing duties, will be further eroded as actions are taken, through sanctions, surveillance, and even perhaps blockades, to imprison "criminal" nation-states.

To conclude, I'd like to return to that small village in the Ural Mountains. I'm happy to say that a few months ago the inhabitants of Gerasimovka tore down that statue of Pavlik in protest. I guess it was their own private step toward the democratization and restructuring of Soviet society. Yet here in America, as the Cold War ended we only plunged deeper into the Drug War, with media icons and prison gulags built everyday in its honor. We seem to have lost one enemy only to immediately construct another. Perhaps we can still learn something from those villagers. If we don't want our denarcoticization program to turn into a full-fledged political *pogrom*, if we don't want to face the prospect of tearing down similar statues in the future, we'd better start deconstructing right now, and everyday, the official stories behind the new Drug War.

5 The terrorist discourse

Signs, states, and systems of global political violence

Source: *World Security: Trends and Challenges at Century's End*, ed. M. Klare and D. Thomas, St. Martin's Press (1991), pp. 237–265.

> Why is it, that anything on this Earth we do not understand, we are pushed onto our knees to worship or to damn?
>
> The The, *"The Violence of Truth"*

From the 1978 news photograph of the kidnapped Italian Prime Minister Aldo Moro sitting under the banner of the *Brigate Rosse*, to the 1989 video murder of Lieutenant Colonel William Higgins by the Organization of the Oppressed on Earth in Lebanon, terrorism has attracted much public attention, a great deal of media commentary, and very little critical theory. After the 1980s, a decade marked by a rising number of incidents, the proliferation of terrorist studies, and the escalation of rhetoric by US Presidents, terrorism remains as resistant to comprehension as it is to remediation.[1]

This is not for the lack of intellectual effort. To explain the terrorist predicament, a welter of articles, academic books, professional reports, and special news programs have been produced. The predominant focus of the expert field has been on the psychological and organizational side of terrorism – its often fanatical motivations, unpredictable nature, and twisted techniques – resulting in models that range from complex and insightful to the crude and *identikit*.[2] Another group, popular in both journalistic and literary circles, has sought out – presumably for the purpose of retaliation and extirpation – the invisible hand that supplies and controls terrorism. Especially vocal are the counter-terrorist conspiracists, who see behind every Carlos, Agca, Abu Nidal (or the latest terrorist exemplar), the Soviet Union, Libya, Iran (or some other pariah state), acting as the central command of international terrorism.[3] Found somewhere between these camps are the liberal commentators, who study the particular features of democracies – an aversion to the use of naked force, an unrestrained media, hand-tying checks and balances – that make them appealing and vulnerable targets for terrorism. Generally more astute about the various religious, social, and economic causes of terrorism, the liberal theorists vacillate between remedies like better law enforcement and selective use of anti-terrorist forces.[4]

The matter of method

For all the academic, professional, and journalistic efforts of the 1980s, we seem far from a general theory of terrorism and further yet from any credible or generally acceptable plan for eradicating terrorism in the near future. To be sure, the "terrorist specialists" are not the only nor the most culpable party. Our ability to think and make judgments about terrorism has suffered from a corrosive mix of official opportunism, media hype, and public hysteria. The essential link between detached analysis and policy-making has become as attenuated as a fuse wire, ready to blow at the mere *threat* of a terrorist attack.

It is fairly easy – that is, politically expedient – to single out particular individuals as responsible for this state of affairs. Current candidates would include the political leader preoccupied with the "wimp-factor," the media magnate with an eye on profit-margins, or the think-tank courtier eagerly working the space between. But such an assessment of blame is to mimic the very cardboard construction of terrorist identities that presently pre-empts any serious attempt to comprehend terrorism.

It is more difficult – and certainly less popular – to assess the intellectual and structural obstacles blocking an inquiry into terrorism. The first obstacle is *epistemological:* even the most conscientious and independent student of terrorism faces a narrowly bounded discipline of thought. During the 1980s, terrorist studies became a fortress-haven at the edge of the social sciences, a positivist's armory of definitions, typologies, and databases to be wielded as much against the methodological critic as the actual terrorist who might call into question the sovereign reason and borders of the nation-state. The second obstacle is *ideological:* to gain official entry into the terrorist debate one must check critical weapons at the door, and join in the chorus of condemnation – or risk suspicion of having sympathy for the terrorist devil. What this means is that following a rash of terrorist incidents – at the moments of highest tension when sober thinking is most needed – responses other than instant excoriation and threats of retaliation are seen as "soft," or worse, collaborationist. As others have noted, this is very reminiscent of the regimentation of critical thinking by threat-mongering that marked Cold War I in the 1940s and 1950s and the most morbid moments of Cold War II in the early 1980s. Let Oliver North remind us once again: "It is very important for the American people to understand that this is a dangerous world, that we live at risk and this nation is at risk in a dangerous world."[5]

However, as Gorbachev worked hard to improve relations with the United States, and as the Soviet bloc began to disintegrate, it proved increasingly difficult to find, let alone maintain the credibility of an alien, uniform, foe. In the future, there will indeed be external dangers, but it is US *national identity*, not the United States as a nation, that it is truly at risk. Here lies the third, *ontological*, reason for the intractability of terrorism: it has been subsumed by the traditional gambit of defining and unifying a national identity through the alienation of others. In spite of the odds that we are more likely to die from a lightning strike, an automobile accident, or even a bee sting, many have come to accept the ubiquity of the terrorist threat as well as take on the identity of the victim.

Yet, even in polls taken immediately after a terrorist strike, the majority of Americans are reluctant to endorse military retaliation.[6] Common sense probably plays a conservative role: if polled, most Americans would probably not (for similar reasons) endorse surgical air-strikes on automobile plants or bee colonies to lessen the chances of an unlikely death. But I suspect something beyond common sense is at work. Reflecting the diverse and highly individualistic forces behind terrorism, we are not – nor can we be – of one mind, of one identity, or of one course of action when it comes time to think and act collectively *against* the terrorist threat. What the polls probably reflected is that after Vietnam (and before another Lebanon debacle), many preferred the *non*-identity of a silent but safe majority when it comes to taking on an enemy that is fearsome but faceless, anywhere and nowhere.

This is not to claim that one must sympathize with terrorism in order to understand it, although this chapter does attempt a better understanding of the terrorist *in situ*. Nor is it to pretend that a total comprehension of terrorism is possible, remedial, or even preferable, although this chapter does try to reconstruct our knowledge and to critique current practices of terrorism and anti-terrorism. Rather, it is to argue at the outset that any productive reading of terrorism requires a difficult, even contorted feat, of stepping outside of the one-dimensional identities that terrorism and the national security culture have implanted in both sides of the conflict.[7]

For some, this kind of intellectual activity might be considered subversive. Indeed, former Secretary of State George Shultz in a major policy address on terrorism stated that the US cannot effectively respond to terrorism unless Americans are of one mind on the subject: "Our nation cannot summon the will to act without firm public understanding and support." Without such a consensus we risk becoming, in Shultz's words, "the Hamlet of nations, worrying endlessly over whether and how to respond."[8] I believe, however, that it is time to take up a position of detachment towards terrorism that Hedley Bull approvingly referred to as "political nihilism."[9] After all, "when times are out of joint," as they were for Hamlet and as they appeared to be for the USA as the 1980s took a radical turn, we might find in Hamlet – who through his passionate yet intellectual introspection discovered just how rotten the declining state could be – a better guide than, say, Henry V – who, "because he did not know how to govern his own kingdom, determined to make war upon his neighbors."[10] We might also discover that there are more things in heaven and earth than are dreamt of in the official terrorist discourse, perhaps even the uncomfortable truth that there is some of the terrorist in us, and some of us in the terrorist. My response, then, to Shultz is more diplomatic than politic: the new *antidiplomatic* estrangement of international relations *requires* that we endlessly mediate the terrorist act and the response to it with a deeper and broader knowledge of *all* practices of global political violence. Otherwise, the will to act becomes inseparable from the will to know, and terrorism becomes indistinguishable from counter-terrorism.

Moreover, an alternative approach is needed because the problem of terrorism is implicated by a profound predicament that now confronts advanced societies.

Call it late capitalism, post-modernism, post-warring, or, as I prefer, neo-medievalism, it is a disturbing, anxiety-inducing condition in which traditional modes of knowledge and formations of identity no longer seem up to the task of representing, let alone managing international relations. Nation-states never enjoyed a true monopoly on the use of force, but now more than in any other post-Westphalian time – and certainly at an accelerated pace – the legitimacy of that monopoly has come under serious challenges from social, economic, technical, and military changes. Interdependent economies, global ecological concerns, penetration by surveillance and media technologies, the three-dimensionality and nuclearization of warfare – they have all been recognized as growing antidiplomatic forces undermining the sovereign privileges and obligations of the territorial state.[11]

Less noticed and understood is the emergence of a *terrorist discourse*, by which I refer to a global semiotic activity where violent powers and insurgent meanings clash.[12] With a nuclear stalemate curtailing superpower, and a global information economy boosting sign-power, it is increasingly in the discursive realm of terrorism that the "crises" of political legitimacy, national identity, and practical knowledge are being played out. Simultaneously brutalizing, repugnant, and fascinating, the terrorist repertoire – kidnapping, hijackings, and assassination – cannot alone account for its rise to the singular status of international crisis. In terrorist discourse a less visible battle is being fought – most desperately between the vanguards of aspiring powers and the rearguards of great powers – to reinscribe the boundaries of legitimacy in international relations.

In short, four important yet neglected theoretical points are being made here. In the study of terrorism, method matters: but very little critical consciousness of just how much it matters has been demonstrated in the field. Second, method *is* matter given the symbolic practices of terrorism, the limitations of physical anti-terrorism, and the simulacral projection of terrorism by the media, the representations of terrorism have taken on a powerful materiality. Third, because of changing configurations of power that rival traditional claims of international legitimacy, new critical methods are called for. Fourth, method alone cannot substitute for an ontological step that anyone seriously seeking truths about terrorism must take: questioning how our own identity is implicated and constituted by the terrorist discourse must precede any study of terrorism.

These critical considerations inform the analysis of modern forms of terrorism that follows. Taking into account the sheer volume of the terrorist archive, I can make no claims for comprehensiveness. My strategy is deconstructive *and* reconstructive: to provide a method which might displace, critique, and historicize received accounts of terrorism and, simultaneously, to present an alternative primer for reading terrorism in its multiple, de-territorialized forms.[13] What I wish to avoid is the subtextual ploy found in much of the terrorism literature where the theoretical organization of an inchoate body of thought pretends to reconcile the differences and contradictions of terrorism, thus "taming" rather than interpreting a heavily conflicted field.[14] At best, I hope to leave the reader with a critical method and the minimal amount of historical knowledge necessary to distinguish the politically dispossessed from the violently possessed, and to imagine possible forms of coexistence with the former, while galvanizing collective action against the latter.

Rites of passage

First, we must make the diversion promised in the preceding chapter. Entry onto the grounds of the terrorist discourse requires an initiating ritual of purification – otherwise known as definition. It is a difficult ritual, given that much of the semantic confusion as well as the urge for terminological purity is enmeshed in the discursive operations of terrorism and anti-terrorism. How are we to distinguish the terrorist from the bandit, criminal, or freedom fighter? What sets terrorism off from other forms of violent conflict? Why is one state's violence considered terrorist, while another's is anti-terrorist?

On the violence spectrum, terrorism is clearly somewhere between a rumble and a war. Or is it? In 1985, Secretary of Defense Weinberger called the TWA 847 hijacking and hostage-taking "a war and it is the beginning of war."[15] What could appear to be a logical trap – if terrorism is war, why isn't war terrorism? – or at the very least a chronological distortion – does terrorism precede its beginnings? – could also be interpreted to be a calculated definitional maneuver to invoke the strategies of war for a phenomenon that *by* definition resists such strategies. By first making terrorism discursively if not logically identical with war, Weinberger attaches justification for a military response, and then seeks to add credibility by declaring "it is the beginning of war." If the taking of the hostages becomes identical to war, then it also is the "beginning of war," because the US can and will use military force in retaliation for a form of conflict that, in fact, defies "traditional" beginnings, in the sense of hostilities with an extended duration or an official declaration between belligerents. Faced by the spasmodic immediacy of terrorism, Weinberger – who much preferred the *threat* of retaliation to the real thing – equates the terrorist discourse with war in the desire to install a compensatory, *deterrent* strategy.[16]

Other sources of confusion intrude. War clearly has its terrorist element: Dresden, Hiroshima, My Lai, Afghanistan all testify to the ability of states in an age of total war to sanction the killing and maiming of large numbers of civilians. Conversely, many terrorist groups employ the nomenclature of war (The Red *Army* Faction, the *Armed Forces* of National Liberation, the Red *Brigades*, the Provisional Irish Republican *Army*, the Holy *War*), *communiqués* full of military jargon, and many of the tactics of war, like tactical surprise, diversionary attacks, and psychological operations.

But ultimately, I believe, the definitional distinction between war and terrorism holds, which is why it should it be studied as an antidiplomatic discourse rather than a paramilitary form. War is a form of organized violence conducted by states, with commonly accepted (if not always observed) rules against bombing, assassination, armed assaults, kidnapping, hostage-taking, and hijacking of civilians – the type of actions that make up 95 percent of what is most often described as "terrorism."[17]

Terrorism, moreover, relies on unpredictable, randomized violence to achieve its various objectives.[18] However, the nature or type of violence utilized by terrorists does not provide sufficient criteria to define terrorism. Outgunned, outmanned, and outlawed by states, terrorists rely more on the intangible power of menacing symbols than on techniques of physical violence to achieve their goals. So, typologies and definitions of terrorism perform much like the airport security systems that seek to prevent terrorism: finely calibrated, they alert the reader to dangers that can prove to be so much loose change. Crudely set, they might miss entirely the non-ferrous, free-floating, *immaterial* threats that make up much of the terrorist arsenal; but regardless of the setting, they are supposed to work as much through deterrence as through detection.

This chapter eschews the intellectual equivalent of an anti-terrorist security system. It does not seek to define or detect, to stereotype or deter "the" terrorist. It takes an alternative route of plotting the many philosophical, historical, and cultural differences that have made the multiple forms of terrorism so difficult to understand and so resistant to remedy. To this end, I have interpreted terrorism as a strategy of intimidation and violence which can be delimited into eight formations: mytho-terrorism, anarcho-terrorism, socio-terrorism, ethno-terrorism, narco-terrorism, state terrorism, anti-terrorism, and pure terrorism. These formations should be read as an *array:* like soldiers on parade, this intellectual marshalling does not pretend to reproduce or capture the horror, uncertainty, and savagery of terrorism – it just temporarily represents and gives some order to it for the purpose of a critical review.

Mytho-terrorism

The first (if not primal) form is mytho-terrorism. At the root of much terrorism lies fear, desire, and violence – all the makings of myth. There is the reciprocal fear that comes from a relationship in which the less powerful simultaneously need and feel alienated from the more powerful. There is the desire for national, class, or simply *more* power to make a different world than the one inherited. And there is the violence that erupts when the desires of the alienated confront each other in mimesis and can no longer be negotiated, displaced, or ritualized away.[19]

Mythology and terrorism fuse when imagined solutions to intractable problems are pursued through new or unconventional rituals of violence. Mytho-terrorism has similar characteristics to other forms of ritual violence, like wars or general strikes, that bind together the deprived, the weak, the resentful, the repressed, or just the temporarily disadvantaged in a violent encounter with more powerful others.[20] The difference however – and this is the difference that both gives mytho-terrorism its power and anticipates its failure – is that its targets are identified by others as innocent victims, not guilty surrogates. What is tactically effective against the more powerful is strategically disastrous because terrorism's mythical justifications are sufficient to arouse the fears and anti-terrorism of the authorities, but not to assure the support of the mythical "people" in whose name the terrorist strikes. Executed in the name of an imagined group-identity, looking backward to a prior Golden Age, or anticipating a future utopia, mytho-terrorism can undermine an order through violence but is unable on its own to generate the necessary ritual substitutes for violence (in contrast, for instance, to the Eucharist, diplomacy, or jurisprudence).

The most potent forces behind mytho-terrorism are usually eschatological and millenarianistic: that is, they join redemption, social change, and cathartic violence in the pursuit of a new era. The eschatological millenarianism of the Crusades, the *jihad*, the Anabaptist insurrections of the sixteenth century, and indeed, the more radical forms of Catholic liberation theology and Islamic fundamentalism of today have inspired or sanctioned mytho-terrorism. The attempt to construct the Kingdom of Heaven on Earth has been marked by assassinations, violent uprisings, and all kinds of martyrdom. Understandably, many historians have turned once again to the Middle East to study possible transhistorical links between myth and terrorism.[21]

Even a superficial scan clearly shows that no one nationalist religion or religious nationalism has had a monopoly on mytho-terrorism. From the random killings of the messianic Zealots in their first-century struggle against the Romans, to the assassin *fidayeen* seeking to purify Islam in the twelfth and thirteenth centuries; from the terrorist attacks of the mid-twentieth century, of the Jewish Irgun blowing up British occupiers, to more recent cases of Christian Phalangists massacring Palestinians, and Islamic Hizballah car-bombing American and French soldiers; all have appealed to myth and resorted to violence to attain their other-worldly aims. Indeed, in the US's own back yard, such groups as the Order, the Covenant, and the Sword and the Arms of the Lord (CSA) have targeted American judges and FBI Arms for assassination in their apocalyptic pursuit of a second Christian millennium.

In mytho-terrorism as well as the other types of terrorism that follow, there is no clear-cut boundary of motivation or targets. Obviously, social, ethnic, ideological and other factors weigh heavily on any consideration of why people turn to terrorism. A short history of the Provisional Irish Republican Army would be a case in point. But it is important to recognize the power of the mythological element that binds and motivates a variety of terrorist groups with multiple grievances – and how this might handicap a purely reasonable inquiry or reaction. In the modern states-system, the pale of power is marked by mytho-terrorism, the boundary where legitimate, rational use of violence to attain goals comes up against the illegitimate, irrational use of violence. On this borderline, the intelligibility of terrorism is more likely to be discerned by a mythical reading than a rational analysis.

Anarcho-terrorism

A statement reprinted in the *New York Times* underscores the spreading threat posed by yet another form of terrorism:

> It was soon recognized at the Rome conference that very little could be done in the matter by diplomatic means. I, therefore, took the earliest opportunity

in the course of the conference of proposing that the sixteen chief officers of police of different nations who were present or their representatives should be formed into a special committee secretly to consider with closed doors and without minutes or written reports what steps could most advantageously be taken.[22]

These uncomfortably familiar remarks were made by Sir Vincent Howard, Great Britain's representative at the Rome Anti-Anarchist Conference – convened in 1906. The assassination of Tsar Alexander II by the *Narodnaya Volia* (the People's Will) in 1881, the Haymarket Square killings in 1886, an assassination attempt on H. C. Frick of Carnegie Steel by a Russian anarchist in 1892, the murder of the President of France by an Italian anarchist in 1894, the King of Italy assassinated in 1900, President McKinley shot by a follower of Emma Goldman in 1901, the assassination of the Empress Elizabeth of Austria: this is just a sampling of the rise of a new kind of international political violence, the amalgamation of anarchism and terrorism, or *anarcho-terrorism.*

Captured by the rapidly growing mass dailies, the anarchist archetype of the nineteenth-century terrorist – eyes borderline mad, revolver in one hand, bomb in the other – lingers long after its ideological origins have been forgotten, its technology antiquated. Certainly any elision of anarchism and terrorism risks simplifying the subject of a major political debate among some very heavy thinkers of nineteenth-century radicalism – including Proudhon, Bakunin, Marx, and Kropotkin – and furthering the modern slide into the false equation of anarchism = communism = terrorism. But at least a cursory knowledge of the originary forces behind anti-state political violence is needed if we are to understand much of the history of Euro-terrorism, for the anarchist message was to resonate in the discourse of, among others, the German Red Army Faction, the Italian Red Brigades, and the French Direct Action. Moreover, the anti-anarchist reaction at the beginning of the twentieth century certainly found its echo in the anti-terrorism summit conferences of the 1980s.

The common element of anarchism is violence against the state. The politics of reform is not an option, for its instruments of debate and persuasion are too weak when confronted by the cloaked violence of the state. Words are corruptible and ambiguous: violent deeds are pure and to the point. While vengeance, hate, and despair might secretly reside in the anarchist's heart and motivate his or her actions, there is an open and often overlooked archive of the destructionist intent of anarchism.[23] Most notorious is Sergey Nechaev's 1869 *Catechism of the Revolutionist.* In 21 points he constructs the identity of the anarcho-revolutionary: "a doomed man ... an implacable enemy of this world ... he knows only one science, the science of destruction."[24] Anarchist manifestos proliferated in this period, but it is in the series of increasingly vehementh debates between Nechaev and Bakunin against Marx and Engels that we can locate the heroic, individualist terrorist ethic that was rejected by socialists yet persists in the anarcho-terrorism of the modern Euro-terrorist groups like the small but deadly French Direct Action and Belgian Communist Combatant Cells.[25]

Socio-terrorism

Terrorism acquired its modern meaning in the French Revolution, when Robespierre, St. Just, and other Jacobins advocated the use of systematic social violence "to make right and reason respected" – and to get rid of some factional enemies in the process.[26] Originally a word with some positive social connotations, the heavy use of the guillotine and the internationalization of the French Revolution radically transformed the term. By 1795 "terrorist" had entered the lexicon as a clearly pejorative term when Edmund Burke referred to the "thousands of those hellhounds called terrorists."[27] Ever since, the word has been part of a sociopolitical game – a kind of "pin-the-term-on-the-class" – to condemn some forms of social violence and legitimize others.

The debate over who were the "real" socio-terrorists, those who endorse and conduct class warfare, erupted again in France in 1871. It is an important debate because it had a profound influence on future socialist and Marxist–Leninist positions on terrorism. After workers of the Paris Commune were charged by the British press with terrorist "incendiarism," Marx countered with cases of when the "British troops wantonly set fire to the Capitol at Washington and to the summer palace of the Chinese emperor," and "the vandalism of Haussmann, razing historic Paris to make place for the Paris of the sightseer."[28] But Marx's major concern was not explicating the class character of pyromania or urban planning. He was attempting to rebut the accusation that a revolutionary party in power was inherently terrorist, as was suggested by the Communards' execution of 64 hostages, including clergy and the Archbishop of Paris. Marx's reply bears quotation, not only because it is a seminal statement for future socialist positions on terrorism, but also because it makes short shrift of the out-of-context, *Reader's Digest*-ation of Marx that went on in the 1980s to prove that Communism equals Terrorism.

Marx first historically establishes that revolutionary socialists and colonial subjects have never been protected by the rules of war:

> The bourgeoisie and its army, in June 1848, re-established a custom which had long disappeared from the practice of war – the shooting of their defenceless prisoners. This brutal custom has since been more or less strictly adhered to by the suppressors of all popular commotions in Europe and India, thus proving that it constitutes a real "progress of civilization"!

In the disputed case of the Communards, Marx claims they were responding in kind to others, like the Prussians and the French statesman Thiers, who initiated the taking of hostages. Moreover, the Communard's efforts to negotiate a hostage-exchange were rebuffed, which Marx believed to have exposed "the unscrupulous ferocity of bourgeois governments":

> The real murderer of Archbishop Darboy is Thiers. The commune again and again had offered to exchange the archbishop, and ever so many priests in

the bargain, against the single Blanqui, then in the hands of Thiers. Thiers obstinately refused. He knew that with Blanqui he would give to the Commune a head while the archbishop would serve his purpose best in the shape of a corpse."[29]

Future theorists of socialism would draw on Marx's analysis to both condemn terrorism and to justify the extreme occasions when the use of terror against terror is necessary. At the height of the Russian civil war, Leon Trotsky, as head of the Red Army, wrote:

> The revolution "logically" does not demand terrorism, just as "logically" it does not demand an armed insurrection. What a profound commonplace! But the revolution does require of the revolutionary class that it should attain its end by all methods at its disposal – if necessary, by an armed rising; if required, by terrorism.[30]

Trotsky's defense of terrorism comes across as a *realpolitik* mix of Marx, Clausewitz, and Bismarck. Terrorism in itself is "helpless" as a political instrument unless adopted as a temporary measure against a reactionary class. "Intimidation," says Trotsky, "is a powerful weapon of policy, both internationally and internally;" and "War, like revolution, is founded upon intimidation."[31] The niceties of morality do not obtain in such extreme moments; or as he coldly puts it, "We were never concerned with the Kantian-priestly and vegetarian-Quaker prattle about the 'sacredness of human life.'" However, Trotsky is not one to make a virtue out of a necessity. The expedient use of terrorism must not obscure the higher aims of Marxism: "To make the individual sacred we must destroy the social order which crucifies him … and this problem can be solved only by blood and iron."[32]

Lenin was just as straightforward in his attitude towards terrorism. Early in the fight against Czarism, Lenin sought to distance the social democratic movement from the *Narodnaya Volia* as well as other populists and anarchists who were advocating or practicing terrorism and assassination against Czarist officials (often successfully, with the 1881 assassination of Czar Alexander II the most notable). Writing for the party paper *Iskra* in 1901, Lenin criticized the growing wave of terrorism:

> In principle we have never rejected, and cannot reject, terror. Terror is one of the forms of military action that may be perfectly suitable and even essential at a definite juncture in the battle, given a definite state of the troops and the existence of definite conditions. But the important point is that terror, at the present time, is by no means suggested as an operation for the army in the field, an operation closely connected with and integrated into the entire system of struggle, but as an independent form of occasional attack unrelated to any army … Far be it from us to deny the significance of heroic individual blows, but it is our duty to sound a vigorous warning against becoming infatuated

with terror, against taking it to be the chief and basic means of struggle, as so many people strongly incline to do at the present.[33]

But once in power and besieged by war and famine, Lenin finds terrorism defensible. In August 1918, he writes a "Letter to American Workers" for *Pravda:*

> How humane and righteous the bourgeoisie are! Their servants accuse us of resorting to terror … The British bourgeoisie have forgotten their 1649, the French bourgeoisie their 1793. Terror was just and legitimate when the bourgeoisie resorted to it for their own benefit against feudalism. Terror became monstrous and criminal when the workers and poor peasants dare to use it against the Bourgeoisie![34]

A few years later, Lenin was attacking the actions of the Social Revolutionary Party as anarchist and terrorist.[35] And Trotsky, exiled by a man who would make wide and brutal use of both internal and international terrorism, soon found himself in the position of defending his earlier use of terrorism against Stalin's.[36]

What does this prove? Only a minimal amount of the writings and history of socialism is required to dismiss the accusation that Marxism is identical to terrorism. A slightly more sophisticated if specious charge is that Marxism promotes the kind of relativism that condones terrorism. A more accurate, and I believe realistic, assessment would be that Marx, Lenin, and Trotsky endorsed a historicist perspective to make difficult and complex judgments on the effectiveness and justifiability of terrorism. It is another question, begged by Stalin's unchecked use of terrorism, whether they got it right. But this analysis of terrorism on a historical and social level can, I believe, contribute a better understanding of the motivations and actions of modern counterparts like the Farabundo Marti National Liberation Front (FMLN) in El Salvador, the New People's Army (NPA) in the Philippines, and the Sendero Luminoso in Peru who exploit (and are exploited by) the ambiguous boundary between social revolutionary and terrorist politics.

Ethno-terrorism

The pursuit of honor and justice, wealth and territory have been recurrent and seemingly eternal causes of violence in the history of the states-system. But from the dynastic rights of the "prince" to the popular rights of the nation there has been an evolution in the legitimacy of violence. The multiple, sometimes conflicting, even extra-terrestrial loyalties of medieval feudatories, and the "jealousies" and often capricious alliances of the royal houses made for unpredictable, unaccountable, or what today we would refer to as "irrational" political violence. It might be historically dubious – as well as morally specious – to consider it a sign of progress that when push comes to legal shove in the contemporary international system, a peoples' war is more likely now to determine the outcome than, say, individual trial by combat. But the tandem rise of the principles of national self-determination and nonintervention with the rights of war has brought a degree of *formally* democratic benefits to the international order.

Ironically, they have also abetted the rise of *ethno-terrorism:* the violent efforts of a national, communal, or ethnic group to acquire the status of a state. There are many nations or groups acting in the name of a nation, still pursuing the legitimacy and protection of statehood, like the Kurds or the Palestinians. There are nation-states which have lost – or have failed to fully acquire – the rights of self-determination because of enduring conditions of suzerainty that the great powers have installed at one time or another, as has been the case at different times in Central America and Eastern Europe. And the history (and still unfinished process) of de-colonization in which social and ethnic forms of terrorism merge into a violent prelude for state formation has been well documented.[37] Indeed, some radical analysts, like Franz Fanon writing of the Northern African case in *The Wretched of the Earth*, consider terrorism to be an essential element of de-colonization, both to liberate the physical territory and to free the colonized subject from years of psychic repression.[38]

The next explosion of ethno-terrorism, however, is more likely to be on the peripheries of the former Soviet Union than in the Western or developing regions of the world. Lost in the anti-terrorist din of the 1980s is the fact that it has been over five years since a major terrorist group has emerged in North America or Europe (the Combatant Communist Cells, or the CCC in Belgium). In the meantime, the potential for ethnoterrorism in the disintegration of the Soviet bloc had been willfully neglected by those on the right who persistently viewed the Soviet Union as an unchanging totalitarian monolith, as well as by those on the left who considered the United States to be the only imperial power of significance in the post-war system. The ingredients for a violent combustion are plentiful: 104 discrete nationalities in 15 republics, 20 autonomous republics, and 18 national districts have been radically reconfigured after the collapse of the Soviet Union; and at the fringes of power, mass movements in Latvia, Lithuania, Estonia, Moldova, Georgia, Armenia, Azerbaijan, Ukraine and other regions where expectations for autonomy and democracy have come up against great economic hardship. The prospect for outbreaks of ethno-terrorism in this area – whether by impatient minority groups (particularly in the Islamic republics) or newly subordinated majorities (like Russians and Gagauzians in Moldova) – has yet to be seriously studied.

It must be acknowledged that these positive developments – the breaking up of a monolithic Marxist–Leninist system (which had created conditions of totalitarian terrorism), the repudiation of the Brezhnev Doctrine (which had provided *ex post facto* justification for Soviet intervention into Czechoslovakia), the open rejection of the secret protocols of the 1939 Nazi-Soviet pact (which had led to the annexation of the Baltic Republics) – have a darker side. Alongside – and sometimes within – the display of progressive nationalism in the Baltic, Georgian, Azerbaijani, and Armenian Republics there lies an atavistic chauvinism. For instance, at the same time that Estonians declared their virtual sovereignty, they disenfranchised a sizeable portion of their Russian population, prompting widespread strikes and increased tensions. Christian Armenians and Muslim Azerbaijanis killed each other over their claims to the Autonomous Region of Nagorno-Karabakh, resulting in martial law. And in the Republic of Georgia, Soviet troops used shovels and toxic gas against nationalist protestors who were taking seriously Gorbachev's slogans of perestroika and glasnost. Elsewhere, in Rumania, Yugoslavia, Bulgaria, Uzbekistan and the Ukraine, the volatile ingredients for ethno-terrorism – territorial disputes (between Rumania and Hungary), economic disparities (in Yugoslavia between political, religious, and ethnic groups), cultural differences (between Slav and Turk in Bulgaria) – have also begun to surface after many years of repression.

Full of historical disparities, the experiences of the Jews, Basques, Irish, Sikhs, and others who waged long campaigns of ethno-terrorism against hegemonic powers nonetheless offer some insights for what might lie ahead for the former Soviet Union and its neighbors. Why some terrorist groups succeeded in their bids for statehood while others failed seems linked to their ability to mobilize and subsume social cross-sections of native populations against occupying or dominant powers that have lost the will and/or the way to rule. The mytho-terrorism of the Jewish Irgun, the anarcho-terrorism of the Serbian Black Hand, or the socio-terrorism of the Irish Republican Army alone were not sufficient to achieve their respective goals. It is ethno-terrorism, once legitimized as a stage in the transformation of nations into states, that has the best historical record among terrorist movements in achieving its goals.

However, this very ability to mount and sustain a long-term campaign of political violence makes ethno-terrorism a favored target of external manipulation, as well as a potential trigger for *systemic*, inter-state violence. Throughout history, ethno-terrorist groups have acted – sometimes as the vanguard, at other times as proxies – for *trans*national rivalries that have ended in global conflicts, such as the friction generated by pan-slavic and pan-germanic terrorism in the Balkans before the First World War, and the racial supremacist violence that fueled Italian, Japanese, and German fascism before the Second World War. Parallels could be drawn with the hydra offshoots of pan-Shiism like the Revolutionary Justice Organization, Organization of the Oppressed on Earth, and other groups under the umbrella of Hizballah that have proven their ability to light fuses that stretch far beyond the Middle East.

Narco-terrorism

It is difficult to pin a date on the origins of *narco-terrorism*, the violent blending of illicit drug trade and political intimidation. In the early eighties, blending Peruvian officials began to popularize the term by linking the Sendero Luminoso (Shining Path) insurgency to the narcotics trade; soon after the military arm of the Medellin drug cartel was similarly labeled. The war *against* narco-terrorism is better marked, with Nancy and Ronald Reagan in 1986 sitting on a sofa somewhere in the White House, giving the American public the first high-level, televised debriefing of the "war on drugs." At a time when Gorbachev seemed intent on unilaterally calling off the Cold War, and Khaddafi preferred to sulk in his tent rather than execute his threat to bring terrorism home to the United States, narco-terrorism moved up the ranks to become the most immediate and dire foreign threat to the US. The charges flew: Columbian cartels were using drug profits to suborn left-wing guerrillas, the Syrians were growing opiates in the Bekaa Valley to fund Palestinian militias, the Nicaraguan Sandinistas were providing transshipment for cocaine and using the money to back El Salvadoran rebels, and General Noriega of Panama was brokering protection deals between Castro and the Medellin cartel. US popular culture was selling a similar narrative, although the good guys and bad guys were often reversed: *Miami Vice, Lethal Weapon* and *Above the Law* took the first step in this reversal by dredging up the drug-running forays of the CIA-proprietary Air America in Southeast Asia, and reinstating their clandestine operations to Latin America.[39]

The discursive tactic of "just say no" quickly proved inadequate in the war against the new public enemy number one. A volatile combination emerged: internal terrorism in US cities, led by Jamaicans, Columbians, and the expansionist gangs of Los Angeles, the Crips and the Bloods; international terrorism, by the Mexican *narcos* who killed DEA (Drug Enforcement Agency) agents and the Medellin "Extraditables" who assassinated Columbian judges and other officials; and media over-representation, topped by the video *vérité/simulé* of *Cops* and *America's Most Wanted*. US national security *and* the American way of life now being at risk, narco-terrorism took on the qualities of a synergistic threat. In response, then Mayor Koch of New York advocated an air attack on Medellin, and Daryl Gates – the chief of the Los Angeles Police who had become infamous for his anti-drug sweeps of the city with helicopters and armored vehicles – outdid Koch by calling for an outright invasion of Columbia. Military AWACS began to patrol the Caribbean; the State Department was supplied with over 150 fixed wing aircraft and Huey helicopters for use in Columbia, Bolivia, and Peru; the Customs Service and Coast Guard set up a Command, Control, Communications and Intelligence Center (C^3I) in Miami, and lined the Mexican border with radar-equipped blimps; and the Green Berets set off to train paramilitary forces in Latin America for the war against narco-terrorism. It was only a matter of time before Stealth technology was introduced, as a front page article from the *Arizona Republic* reported that "National Guardsmen in Texas could be fighting the war on drugs dressed as cactuses, sneaking up on smugglers under the cover of night and prickly needles, according to a proposal submitted to the Defense Department."[40]

How did narco-terrorism come to claim precedence over all other forms of terrorism? One history, the official history, is made up of what President Reagan once referred to as "stupid facts," by which he meant of course the stubborn facts that US users spend between 100 and 150 billion dollars a year on narcotics, creating a demand that – according to the State Department's 1989 *International Narcotics Strategic Control Strategy Report* – over 56 countries are ready to service in the capacity of growers, manufacturers, traffickers, or money launderers.[41] Again, we should not allow the data to obscure the most important fact, that illegal drugs ruin and kill people. But we have heard all this so often that they have become not stupid but stupefying facts: they incur an inertia of helplessness, a mass mood that accepts the official view that only the experts, the police, the forces of law and order can handle the drug problem. But the problem clearly exceeds the capabilities of the best trained "TNT" (Tactical Narcotics Team) units which sweep a neighborhood clean of dealers one week, only to lose it the next, or the DEA, which was recently forced out of Medellin, Columbia. The problem is that the cultural economy of the day has so valorized the logistics, demonized the agents, and devalued the victims of the drug problem that we have lost sight of its all too human face.

To compensate, some alternative facts and histories are needed. Tobacco, an addictive drug, kills over 300,000 people a year, alcohol kills 100,000 (including those killed by drunk drivers), while the use of all illegal drugs combined – cocaine, heroin, marijuana, angel dust, LSD, etc. – accounted for less than 4,000 deaths in 1987.[42] From the latest available figures (1989), the use of illegal drugs in the United States is declining. Yet the war on drugs continues to escalate. This can be explained, I believe, only in the larger context of past examples of when US strategic interests intersected with the interests of the drug trade. Some would claim that the US became entangled in the drug web; others that we helped spin it.[43] The web-spinning theorists claim that we not only inherited the Vietnam war from the French, but also the opium trade which the French intelligence service, SDECE, had used to finance and win the support of Hmong tribesmen from the Vietnamese highlands in the struggle against the Vietminh guerillas. Even earlier, from 1948 on, the CIA had supposedly used drug smuggling routes and trade in the Golden Triangle to disguise intelligence and paramilitary operations against the Chinese Communists. It is also claimed that some of the players who later showed up in the Iran–Contra affair first perfected the guns–drugs–secret–warfare matrix in Laos in the 1960s, when Theodore Shackley was station chief of the CIA in Ventianne, General John Singlaub was chief of the SOG (Studies and Operations Group) which carried out secret raids into Laos, and Thomas Clines, also of the CIA, worked with (then) Lt Colonel Secord to run covert air-supply missions. The Iran–Contra hearings also revealed other drug connections, with the DEA involved in the hostage ransom attempt in Lebanon, and the CIA use of the Santa Elena airstrip in Costa Rica for the transshipment of illegal drugs and weapons.[44] There is a substantial body of evidence that leads one to conclude that agencies of the US government have at various times colluded with narcotics trafficking. At the very least, since about 1960 narco-terrorism has been mainly perceived as a minor strategic threat and as a sometime ally in the battle against (what was seen then as) the much larger danger of communism.[45]

My own suspicion is that narco-terrorism was finally taken seriously – if not hysterically – because it had taken on characteristics of a major transnational conglomerate rather than primitive capitalism, with a commensurate increase in political power.[46] In Columbia, the source of 80 percent of the cocaine that reaches the United States, right-wing paramilitary squads, Marxist guerrilla groups, and two major drug cartels have used drug profits to build up power bases that seriously challenged the sovereignty of the Columbian government. We have heard much of how the *narcotraficantes* have killed over 300 judges and court employees since 1981, and more recently, assassinated several candidates for president. Less often reported is the number of jobs, homes, health services, soccer fields, earthquake relief, and schools supplied by the *narcos* – amenities that the state cannot provide.[47] For many peasants they provide a cash crop, and more importantly, a transportation system that can get the "produce" to its far-flung markets. The *narcos* do not – could not – rule by terror alone: their notorious option of "Plata O Plomo" (lead or silver) captures this dual strategy. As war is for most states, terrorism is for the *narcos* the *ultima ratio* of their burgeoning agribusiness empire. Providing a relatively lucrative living for everyone from the subsistence farmer to the ghetto dealer – along with bribes for the underpaid police or military officer – is as important a source of power as the threat or use of terrorism. That many of the amnestied Columbian "druglords" have been able to set themselves up in well-appointed "prison-haciendas" attests to this power.

Hence, the much ballyhooed solution of beating narco-terrorism by anti-terrorism is certain to fail, as are schemes to make interdiction and eradication the top priority.[48] The same plan was used with marijuana, which simply resulted in an increase in domestic production as well as in the potency of the marijuana supply. There are already signs that the other Columbian drug cartels, like the Cali combine, are feeling the heat, and moving operations into Brazil, Bolivia and Ecuador. And even if we could someday develop the equivalent of a Narcotics Defense Initiative to shield the United States from foreign-produced narcotics, designer and synthetic drugs could quickly fill the void.[49] Narco-terrorism will not be stopped until the supply *and* demand of illegal narcotics are stopped, which means that the US must provide treatment and education, substitute businesses and jobs in the American cities, and crop alternatives to coca as well as an infrastructure of credit and roads in the Latin American countries. For political and economic reasons, that is unlikely to happen in the near future. The worst-case scenario, then, would be for incarceration, the preferred drug treatment program in the US, to be exported as foreign policy. The legal principle of *posse comitatus* against the military making arrests as well as taking on policing duties will be further eroded as actions are taken, through sanctions, surveillance, and even perhaps blockades, to imprison "criminal" nation-states.

State terrorism

If one were to parachute back into the early 1980s, attend a White House briefing, sit through a State Department news conference, or read Robert Gates's testimony (but not his critics') in the *New York Times*, one could walk away with the impression that terrorism was a violent activity orchestrated, supplied, and executed by a semi-permanent coterie of pariah states, among them Libya, North Korea, Iran, Syria, and the Soviet Union. In this period, "terrorism," over-used and lacking rhetorical sufficiency, had begun to show all the signs of semantic bleaching. Conservative spokespersons like Jeane Kirkpatrick, mainstream word-smiths like Claire Sterling, and White House spin-masters reissued and circulated a new term: *state terrorism*, by which they meant – among many other things – "premeditated, politically motivated violence perpetrated against noncombatant targets by clandestine state agents."[50]

What got lost in this ideological/semantical shuffle was a long history of state rule by terror: in modern times, Hitlerite Germany, Stalinist Russia, Suharto's Indonesia, Argentina's "Dirty War," Idi Amin's Uganda, Pol Pot's Khmer Rouge ... the list goes on. And today, South Korea, South Africa, and the People's Republic of China stand out as examples of how states – communist or capitalist in their economy but politically dictatorial – regularly resort to violent intimidation and political murder to maintain and further their power. Enhanced by a security, police, or military apparatus, internal state violence – or what we might generally call *endo-terrorism* – has achieved a much higher body count than any other form of terrorism. But Kirkpatrick and Antiterrorism, Inc., have a different form of terrorism in mind: state *exo-terrorism*. Defined as state-supported kidnapping, hostage-taking, or murder by proxy terrorists, state exo-terrorism is for the most part seen as a Middle Eastern continuation of war by condemnatory means: the motivations and actions of the terrorist groups that bombed the "Labelle" discotheque in Berlin, seized the cruise ship *Achille Lauro* and killed Leon Klinghoffer, hijacked TWA Flight 847, and killed Navy diver Robert Stethem, and kidnapped and killed Marine Lieutenant Colonel Higgins are defined and countered through their links to Libya's Khaddafi, Syrian intelligence, Iranian fundamentalist leaders, or with Moscow in the background. Secretary of State Shultz put it bluntly in a policy address: "States that support and sponsor terrorist actions have managed in recent years to co-opt and manipulate the terrorist phenomenon in pursuit of their own strategic goals."[51]

But if we stick to the strict definition of state exo-terrorism, would we not also need to include US sponsorship of the Contras, the delivery of missiles to the mujahideen, the 1985 mid-air "hijacking" by F-14s of the Egyptian airliner carrying the *Achille Lauro* terrorists, the 1986 "assassination" attempt on Khaddafi by US F-111s, and the 1987 "kidnapping" of suspected terrorist Fawaz Younis in international waters off Cyprus?[52] Is it only a matter of scale that separates legitimate state violence from illegitimate state terrorism? The official position is that US violence is defensive, retaliatory, and – hopefully – deterring. But can a mere prefix – the *anti* before "our" terrorism – support the distinction?

Anti-terrorism

The construction and maintenance of an unambiguous boundary between terrorism and anti-terrorism has become a preeminent function of the modern state. In the 1985 policy address, an indefinite "we" are told by Secretary of State Shultz that the distinction is self-evident, once "we settle on "our" definition of terrorism:

> We cannot afford to let an Orwellian corruption of language obscure our understanding of terrorism. We know the difference between terrorists and

freedom fighters, and as we look around the world, we have no trouble telling one from the other.[53]

If the definition of terrorism is the primary semantic battlefield in the struggle for international legitimacy, the delimitation of terrorism from anti-terrorism has became its bloodiest strategic site.[54] The official side of this struggle is embodied in the proliferation of anti-terrorist forces. Just about all of the major as well as many of the smaller powers have developed such elite anti-terrorist units: the Israeli *Sayaret Matkal*, the German *Grenzschutzgruppe* 9 (Border Protection Group 9) or GSG9, and the British Special Air Service or SAS, are among the more successful ones – if we are to judge by the movies made of their hostage rescues in Entebbe, Mogadishu, and London.[55] So far, however, Hollywood has shown little interest in the exploits of the US anti-terrorist unit, Delta Force, which gained the wrong kind of publicity in Operation Eagle Claw, the 1980 rescue attempt in Iran that ended in a calamity of malfunctioning helicopters, colliding aircraft, eight dead – and no one rescued.[56]

But a closer, colder scrutiny of the terrorist/anti-terrorist distinction reveals an ambiguity that both sides of the divide have sought to eliminate. This has been most tragically borne out in the killing ruins of Beirut, where all the violent players – state, anti-state, and non-state – seem to pause from their endless cycles of violence only long enough to argue who struck the first blow when, and thus to determine who is the *real* terrorist and the *real* anti-terrorist. Israel, Syria, Iran, and their Lebanese understudies reach back to originating myths (of "Judea and Samara," a "Greater Syria," or the *"dar al-Islam"* of the *jihad*) to justify their own actions – a "surgical" air strike, an indiscriminate shelling, a refugee camp massacre, a car-bombing, or a kidnapping – as an anti-terrorist action taken against terrorist foes.

At a less abstract, much more personal level, the distinction between retaliation and revenge, deterrent and destructive violence, combatant and noncombatant becomes almost meaningless. When asked by a visiting Arab-American delegation to release their hostages because they were innocent, the Hizballah captors of US citizens Joseph Cicippio and Terry Anderson replied that their family members killed by sixteen-inch shells from the US battleship *New Jersey* in 1984 and American bombs dropped from American planes piloted by Israelis had been just as innocent.[57] When terrorism persists, when its acts of violence intensify, accelerate, and accumulate, the word games behind it become superannuated. People *forget* the originary reasons, and blood feuds and revenge cycles take over. In "civilized" countries, it often becomes the task of intelligence agencies to carry out the "necessary" retributions that the public would not or could not sanctify. Cases like the Israelis' secret assassination campaign against PLO agents (that mistakenly killed an innocent Palestinian in Norway), former CIA director William Casey's support for the car-bombing of Sheikh Fadlallah (the bomb missed him but killed 80 others), a Lebanese leader of Shiism implicated in the bombing of the Marine barracks and the kidnapping and murder of CIA station chief William Buckley, or the KGB's retaliatory kidnapping and mutilation of a relative of Hizballah terrorists (resulting in the release of three Soviet envoys) are only the exposed skirmishes of what is probably a much deeper and wider intelligence war.[58] In *"de-civilized"* countries, like Lebanon, Columbia, and El Salvador, where feudal terror resurfaced and spread, anti-terrorist forces did not solve the terrorist "problem": they became just one among many warring militias and guerrilla groups.

Pure terrorism

Very little attention has been paid to the relationship between the nuclear balance of terror and modern terrorism. A few experts in the field have envisaged an ultimate bonding of the two, where a handful of terrorists steal or make their own nuclear device – or chemical weapon, biological contagion, or computer virus – to hold millions at a time hostage. But it is another kind of terrorist fusion – not this think-tank, worst-case scenario of what could be called "hyper-terrorism" – that warrants serious consideration.

First, we need to consider a possible paradox: has the nuclear stalemate, by bringing into an already violent family of nations a guarantee of limited peace – or more precisely, a state of non-war based on massive retaliation – served as the step-father to conventional terrorism? Historical parallels with another epoch point toward a possible answer. The classic foundations of colonization – a new mobility of power, technological superiority, and the cultivation of a pervasive fear of retribution – reappeared as attributes of the superpower system of nuclear terror. And like earlier apologists of colonization, those who have made a dogma of nuclear deterrence celebrate the stasis of a nuclear "peace" while denying any responsibility for the displacement of persistent rivalries and conflicts into new forms of violence.[59] Social critic Paul Virilio has tenaciously pursued this trend toward, in his words, *pure war*, declaring that "The art of deterrence, prohibiting political war, favors the upsurge, not of conflicts, but of *acts of war without war*."[60] In the global pure war that ensued, terrorism has emerged as its most virulent expression, triggering in turn an antibody reaction, anti-terrorism, that has proven, I believe, to be more devastating than the original "infection."

Socio-terrorists and anarcho-terrorists may of course claim, as did the Red Brigades in Italy and the Tupamaros in Uruguay, that this is the very purpose of terrorism – to reveal the repressive face of the state. However, this moral imperative of terrorism, treated as a truth that can only be proven by deed, is exposed as nothing more than a blood-soaked truism when the state provoked reveals its violent core once again – and nothing changes. To be sure, at world-historical moments like the French, Russian or Chinese revolutions, when governments lose the ability and the will to rule (usually in the aftermath of a major war) and some other group, class, or people is mobilized and ready to take power, then terrorism can indeed take on an important and usually spectacular role in transforming societies. But it should be clear from the weight of the cases outlined above that the heroics of terrorism, acting as a substitute for a mass movement, have only served to fortify the worst aspects of the modern state: its propensity for surveillance and secrecy, vigilantism and surrogate violence.[61] To push the family analogy one step further: fostered by the displacement of superpower violence, and orphaned by the masses in whose name they act, the modern terrorist in some ways resembles the repressed child who grows up into a serial killer, unable to distinguish the guilty parent from the innocent bystander. Conversely – sometimes perversely – we constitute and preserve our own "normalcy" by the terrorist's deviance.

This is not to belittle the moral turpitude of the terrorist – or the oppressive, alienating conditions that can give rise to terrorism. It is, rather, to highlight how pervasive and potentially universal terrorism – in all its guises – really is. As I stated at the outset, the fact that terrorism kills people should not be buried under a pile of words. But, contrary to prevailing moral *and* materialist views, the meaning and power of terrorism will not be found – to put it morbidly – under a pile of its victims. A new form of *pure terrorism*, as immaterial and diffuse as Virilio's pure war, has emerged as an international political crisis in which the violent intimidation and manipulation of a global media audience creates a pervasive state of insecurity and fear. This means that the critical production and distribution of the terrorist threat is not *territorial*, as is the case in conventional war, but *temporal:* its power is increasingly derived from the instantaneous representation and diffusion of violence by a global communication network. But before anyone assigns villainy to the disseminators of terrorist violence – as did former British Prime Minister Margaret Thatcher when she repeatedly called the media the "oxygen of terrorism" – they should recognize the *receptive* and *interpretive* power of a mass audience for whom (and often in whose name) terrorist rituals of violence are committed.[62]

Take again the bracketing terrorist acts of the 1980s: the murders of Aldo Moro and Colonel Higgins. Of the Red Brigade kidnapping of Moro, Claire Sterling wrote that "For speed, mobility, reconnaissance, logistics, staying power, and refinements in psychological warfare, it was a matchless performance."[63] True, but in stating the obvious she misses the more important point. "The real terror network" does not go through Moscow or Libya or Iran, but through a non-place, a cyberspace that reproduces and contextualizes the terrorist act for the global audience. In a manner, Sterling mimics the terrorist, attributing a surplus of power to the "heroic" individual as the author of violence, when it is the interventionist power of governments, the representational practices of the media, and the conformist interpretations of the audience that reconstitute and magnify the force of terrorism. The day after the Red Brigades released the photograph of Moro holding the 20 April issue of *La Repubblica* in his hands, it appeared on the front pages of over 45 major newspapers around the world.[64] I am sure that the video of Colonel Higgins hanging from a noose "captured" an even wider audience. The journey from the original terrorist deed to its propagandized destiny remains, I believe, the most important and under-studied area of terrorism.[65]

The future: post-modern or neo-medieval?

In the Middle Ages, power was fragmented along overlapping lines of religious, class, and national loyalties; a tenuous order was regularly shaken and reconfigured by kidnappings, hostage-takings, and assassinations; and, aside from rare and brief rebellions, a peasant majority was terrorized into a fatalistic subservience. In the 1980s, we read of Latin American drug "lords" and their retinues, equipped with small arms, anti-tank weapons, and air forces, challenging the sovereignty of states; of Shiite plots, hatched in Iran, to attack Israeli and American targets; and of warring fiefdoms in Lebanon, one side calling on Christian nations to help break a five-month old sea blockade, the other side vowing to fight "the new crusade" and to kill hostages should any Western power intervene.[66] The end of the Cold War merely added to the violence, with the demise of a Soviet endo-colonization producing new forms of endo-terrorism in Armenia, Georgia, Rumania, and, worst of all, in Yugoslavia.

Is modern terrorism now a containable "crisis," or is it a telling sign of a major shift "back to the future," from a world order based on the eminent domain of nation states to a segmented and sectarian system of warring economic, religious, political powers? Is the continuing terrorization of global politics, especially in the Middle East, a harbinger of a re-territorialization, as was the religious and civil terror that presaged the Thirty Years War of the seventeenth century? Or, more likely, a post-modern simulacrum of the Middle Ages, to be played out in C^3I omni-deterrence centers, covered by ABC News simulations with Peter Jennings, and – if necessary – fought out with secret or mercenary armies? In short, not the global village of interdependency die-hards, but something between Disneyland and Beirut as the model for the new global castle of antidiplomacy?

These speculations run against the grain of peace-mongering that marked the end of the 1980s. Perhaps there *are* reasons to be more optimistic, to discern emerging alternatives to national identities built upon violent antipathies. As a sign of the fractured state of the world order, hope for global solutions – sometimes in the guise of a new nostalgia – has gained ground. Full of promise were the globalist adherents of *nove myslenie* ("new thinking") that advised Gorbachev, the democratic parties in East/Central Europe, and the transnational social movements with various shades of Green in their politics.[67] More peculiar and still popular have been the New Age schemes, that range from the *est*-ian exhortations to think our way beyond war, to the apocalyptic musings of Ronald Reagan, that took on a science fiction character at one of his last question and answer sessions when he spoke longingly for the arrival of a *truly* alien threat to bring the world together in a final fight for good against evil.[68]

Contrary to the globalists, I believe that there are – and there will remain – irreconcilable differences and *many* evils at large in the world. Hence my hopes are on a smaller scale and come with a longer time span. For alternative models to terrorism for national liberation, social change, and other forms of self-determination, I look to the remarkable beginnings (yet incomplete accomplishments) of the Palestinian *intifada*, the journey of the Baltic national movements from underground to parliamentary status, the self-liberation of Central and Eastern Europe, and the fledgling democratization of formerly repressive regimes in Latin America. In these cases terrorism was confronted in all its forms and rejected in favor of a (relatively) non-violent resistance. They have done more to devalue the currency of terrorism than all of the official dealers in the anti-terrorist discourse. They also provide, I might add, an important lesson for everyone who profits by the terrorist discourse, a lesson once taught by history's most famous practitioner of nonviolence who upon discovering that his house of prayer had become a den of thieves left the chief priests alone – but threw out all the moneychangers.

But we are left with a much more secular concern: What to do? I have no global solution for the problem – and I would hope that the diverse and complex array of terrorism that I have presented in this chapter serves as a sufficient repudiation of national policy-makers *and* global salvationists who think that there is one. We can no more remedy the problem of terrorism than we can wipe out difference in the world; and were that possible, it would lead not toward a better world but a *final* solution. Alternatively, I offer in this chapter a much more modest yet potentially radical prospect, that through the deconstruction of the terrorist discourse we make possible a new constructive power to mediate antidiplomatic violence.

Notes

1 We have already noted how terrorism was on the top of the agenda at the first National Security Council meeting of the Reagan administration, and a primary target of Bush's. For a breakdown and explanation of terrorist incidents from 1980 to 1988, see *Patterns of Global Terrorism: 1988* (Department of State Publication, March, 1989), pp. 1–11 and 85.

2 Probably the best of a very large lot is *Inside Terrorist Organizations*, edited by David Rapoport (New York: Columbia University Press, 1988). The Rand Corporation churns out an enormous amount of material on the subject, including the very helpful if intimidating (with over 3,500 entries from 1968 to the present) *Chronology of International Terrorism*. In the Rand collection, I found articles by Brian Jenkins on the multiple strategies of terrorism, Jeffrey Simon on the perception of terrorist threats, and Bruce Hoffman on extreme right-wing terrorism the most useful. For those who need a quarterly fix of terrorist discourse, there is *Terrorism: An International Journal*, edited by Yonah Alexander.

3 See Claire Sterling, *The Terror Network: The Secret War of International Terrorism* (New York: Holt, Rinehart, and Winston, 1981); Christopher Dobson and Ronald Payne, *Terror! The West Fights Back* (London: Macmillan, 1982); Benjamin Netanyahu, *Terrorism: How the West Can Win* (New York: Farrar, Straus, Giroux, 1986); Yossi Melman, *The Master Terrorist: The True Story of Abu-Nidal* (New York: Avon Books, 1986): and *Fighting Back: Winning the War Against Terrorism*, edited by Neil C. Livingstone and Terrel E. Arnold (Lexington, MA: Lexington Books, 1986).

4 Paul Wilkinson's *Terrorism and the Liberal State* (London: Macmillan, 1977), Walter Laqueur's *Terrorism* (Boston: Little, Brown and Company, 1977), and *Terrorism, Legitimacy, and Power: The Consequences of Political Violence*, edited by Martha Crenshaw (Middletown, CT: Wesleyan University Press, 1983), are good examples of this genre. *Terrorism and International Order*, by Lawrence Freedman and other British international relations generalists (London: Royal Institute of International Affairs, 1986), offers a more philosophical and historical analysis. Official US policy in the eighties has vacillated between the conspiracy and liberal camps, but the most astute synthesis is Secretary of State Shultz's "Terrorism and the Modern World," an October 1984 address at the Park Avenue Synagogue in New York (Bureau of Public Affairs,

Current Policy No. 629). For a critical examination of the liberal attitudes toward terrorism, see Richard Rubenstein's *Alchemists of Revolution: Terrorism in the Modern World* (New York: Basic Publishers, 1987); and for a refreshingly anarchistic view, see Noam Chomsky's *Pirates and Emperors: International Terrorism in the Real World* (New York: Claremont, 1986). Finally, I believe three works stand out from the crowd, effectively using literary theory and cultural analysis to say something new about terrorism: Robin Wagner-Pacifici's *The Moro Morality Play: Terrorism as Social Drama* (Chicago: University of Chicago Press, 1986); Khachig Tololyan's "Cultural Narrative and the Motivation of the Terrorist," in *Inside Terrorist Organizations*, pp. 217–33; and *Terrorism and Modern Drama*, edited by John Orr and Dragon Klaic (Edinburgh: Edinburgh University Press, 1990).

5   *Taking the Stand: The Testimony of Lieutenant Colonel Oliver North* (New York: Pocket Books, 1987), pp. 26–7.

6   After Colonel Higgins's captors released the video of his hanging, 58 percent of those polled were for negotiations, 39 percent against; 40 percent supported a commando rescue attempt even if lives might be lost, while 50 percent were opposed; and 33 percent advocated the bombing of terrorist hideouts in Lebanon even if innocent people were killed, while 60 percent were against it. See *Time*, 14 August 1989, p. 15.

7   This is something I attempted to show in chapter 4 of *World Security: Trends and Challenges at Century's End*, edited by M. Klare and D. Thomas (New York, St. Martin's Press, 1991).

8   Shultz, "Terrorism and the Modern World," pp. 5–6.

9   Hedley Bull, "International Relations as an Academic Pursuit," *Australian Outlook* (26, no. 3, December 1972), pp. 264–5. While I clearly believe current world politics fully warrant Bull's *classical* stance of "political nihilism," I believe it can be positively supplemented by "post-classical" or "post-modern" approaches. Against charges that post-modernist and post-structuralist approaches are nihilist (like classical realism?), I have found the best theoretical defense to be William Connolly's account of a "projectional interpretation" that:

> draws part of its sustenance from an always-already-operative attachment to life as a protean set of possibilities exceeding the terms of any identity into which it is set … It then strives to thaw perspectives which tend to stay frozen within a particular way of life, to offer alternative accounts of threats to difference created by the dogmatism of established identities, and to advance different accounts of danger and possibilities crowded out by established regimes of thought.

(From "The Irony of Interpretation," *Politics and Irony*, edited by John Seery and Daniel Conway, St Martin's Press, 1992).

10   William Hazlitt, quoted in *The Complete Works of Shakespeare* (London: Collins, 1981), p. 277.

11   The expansion and acceleration of interdependence was recently highlighted in an event that warranted only a few inches in the *New York Times* (7 January 1990, p. 15), when world financial markets dipped on the news (later proven false) that Gorbachev had cancelled some upcoming meetings with foreign leaders to deal with domestic problems. For theoretical analysis of radical changes in international relations, see Paul Virilio, *Défense populaire et luttes ecologiques* (Paris: Editions Galilée, 1978); R. B. J. Walker, *One World, Many Worlds: Struggles for a Just World Peace* (Boulder, CO, 1988); and chapters 6 and 7 below.

12   "Semiotics" in this context refers to systems of sign usage – including words, visual images codes, or any signifying practices ("languages") – that convey relations of power and constitute meaning.

13   For those still unfamiliar (or just familiar enough to be contemptuous) with "deconstruction," it can be described as a skeptical (or in some hands, subversive)

reading of "texts" – any verbal or nonverbal sign-systems – that elicits the paradoxes, indeterminacy, and contradictions of any language-generated reality.

14 With an additional dash of hyperbole, French social critic Jean Baudrillard levels a similar charge: "Hence the stupidity and the obscenity of all that is reported about the terrorists: everywhere the wish to palm off meaning on them, to exterminate them with meaning which is more effective than the bullets of specialized commandoes..." See "Our Theater of Cruelty," *In the Shadow of the Silent Majorities and other essays* (New York: Semiotext(e), 1983), p. 117.

15 *New York Times*, 25 June, 1985, p. 1. More recently and in (unusually) clearer prose, former Secretary of State Alexander Haig echoed Weinberger in an editorial article: "We cannot allow a hostage crisis to paralyze the Government to the neglect of everything else ... But it is crucial to realize that we are in a war – a twilight war, to be sure, a war of unusual tactics – but one that requires continuing, strenuous efforts, not just a spasmodic reaction to the headlines." (*New York Times*, 15 August 1989, p. 21).

16 Weinberger's belief that the US should not use military force unless fully supported by the American people and Congress and only as a "last resort" became a matter of public record after his 18 November 1984 speech to the National Press Club. This view would seem to preclude preemptive or retaliatory anti-terrorist operations, and, indeed, Weinberger was opposed to the sending of the Marines to Lebanon *and* the hijacking by F-14 Tomcats of the Egyptian plane carrying the *Achille Lauro* terrorists. In his major statement on terrorism Secretary of State Shultz was much less equivocal on the equation of war with terrorism and the need for military retaliation: "We now recognize that terrorism is being used by our adversaries as a modern tool of warfare. It is no aberration. We can expect more terrorism directed at our strategic interests around the world in the years ahead. To combat it, we must be willing to use military force." See Jane Mayer and Doyle McManus, *Landslide: The Unmaking of the President, 1984–1988* (Boston: Houghton Mifflin, 1988), pp. 52–4, 140–2; and Shultz, "Terrorism and the Modern World," p. 5.

17 Brian Jenkins, *International Terrorism: The Other World War* (Santa Monica, CA: Rand, 1985), p. 12.

18 Although it is obvious that I am referring to *international* war and *international* terrorism, I have avoided the word because it is a misnomer: war and terrorism fought on individual, tribal, class and other terrain can have multi-level effects. Probably *global* is a better modifier for the phenomena under discussion, but I do not want arbitrarily to delimit the area to be investigated.

19 For a persuasive account of the roots of violence in "mimetic desire," and the historical attempt to control violence in substitutive rituals of sacrifice, see René Girard, *Violence and the Sacred* (Baltimore, MD: Johns Hopkins University Press, 1977).

20 For instance, see Georges Sorel's study of how the myth of violent collective action in the form of a general strike can act as a revolutionary force, in his *Reflections on Violence*, trans. T. E. Hulme and J. Roth (New York: Collier, 1961).

21 See N. Cohn, *The Pursuit of the Millennium* (London: Paladin, 1970); David Rapoport, "Fear and Trembling: Terrorism in Three Religious Traditions," *American Political Science Review*, 38, 3 (September, 1984), pp. 658–77.

22 *New York Times*, 17 June 1906. The setting up of a modern counterpart was also noted by the *New York Times* (9 December 1988), p. 14.

Anti-terror unit to talk strategy

... The assembly, commonly known as the "Trevi" group after their signing of the European Convention for the Prevention of Terrorism, will primarily deal with problems that have arisen concerning the extradition of terrorists.

23 Although Richard Rubenstein presumes in the label of "anarcho-communism" what needs to be historically demonstrated, his opening chapter to *Alchemists of Revolution*, "The Bogeyman, the Hero, and the Guy Next Door," is the best study to date of the complex psychological, political, and historical factors behind terrorism.

24 Sergey Nechaev, "Catechism of the Revolutionist," in *The Terrorism Reader*, edited by W. Laqueur and Y. Alexander (New York: Penguin, 1987), pp. 68–72.

25 See Laqueur, *Terrorism Reader*, pp. 47–9 and pp. 395–7, for useful bibliographical notes.

26 Saint-Just, *Fragments sur les institutions republicaines*, edited by A. Soboul (Turin: Einaudi, 1952), p. 49, quoted by F. E. and F. P. Manuel, *Utopian Thought in the Western World* (Oxford: Blackwell, 1974), p. 567.

27 W. Laqueur, *Terrorism* (London: Weidenfeld and Nicolson, 1978), p. 17.

28 Karl Marx, *Political Writings Volume III*, "The Civil War in France" (New York: Vintage, 1974), pp. 228–31.

29 Ibid., p. 230.

30 Leon Trotsky, "Terrorism and Communism," *The Basic Writings of Trotsky*, edited by Irving Howe (New York: Vintage Books, 1965), pp. 142–53.

31 Ibid., p. 146.

32 Ibid., p. 151.

33 V. I. Lenin, "Where to Begin?", in *Selected Works* (Moscow: Progress Publishers, 1968), pp. 38–9.

34 Ibid., p. 459.

35 See also Lenin's 1920 essay, "Left-Wing Communism – An Infantile Disorder," in which he attacks the "Socialist-Revolutionary Party" since it "considered itself particularly 'revolutionary', or 'Left' because of its recognition of individual terrorism, assassination – something that we Marxists emphatically rejected." *Selected Works*, p. 521.

36 See Leon Trotsky, *Their Morals and Ours* (New York: Pathfinder Press, 1969), where he uses the exigencies of the civil war to defend the Decree of 1919 – which called for taking hostages of relatives of commanders suborned from the Czar's Army – against "the institution of family hostages [by which] Stalin compels those Soviet diplomats to return from abroad" (p. 37–9).

37 See, for example, Eric Wolf, *Peasant Wars of the Twentieth Century* (New York: Harper and Row, 1969).

38 Franz Fanon, *The Wretched of the Earth* (Harmondsworth, UK: Penguin, 1967).

39 Judging from the pre-history of the key players, like Shackley, Clines, and Secord, re-exposed in the Iran–Contra affair, it would seem that fiction rang truer than fact, or at least Eliot Abram's version of it.

40 *Arizona Republic, 7* April 1989, p. 1. Less humorous and more threatening to civil liberties is the single-mindedness of US Democrats and Republicans on the threat of narco-terrorism. Senators Joseph Biden (Democrat, Delaware), and William Cohen (Republican, Maine) have co-sponsored a bill to establish a "Counter-Narcotics Technology Assessment Center" (CONTAC). Its task would be to "to coordinate research into high-technology anti-drug-trafficking techniques, including surveillance, advanced computers, artificial intelligence, and chemical and biological detection systems." See William Uncapher, "Trouble in Cyberspace: Civil Liberties at Peril in the Information Age," the *Humanist* (September/October 1991), pp. 10–11.

41 See *The International Narcotics Control Strategy Report* (Department of State Publication, March 1989). It is interesting to note that the United States is not included in the "Country and Regional Summaries" (pp. 19–24), nor in the list of "Worldwide Production Totals" (p. 15), in spite of the fact that the United States' annual rate of marijuana production rose during the 1980s to rival Columbia and Mexico as a major supplier. Since Section 481(h)(2)(A) of the Anti-Drug Abuse Acts of 1986 and 1988 requires that the President certify whether major drug producing and drug transit

countries have "cooperated fully" with the United States "to enforce to the maximum extent possible the elimination of illicit cultivation," the question arises whether the US should cut off aid to itself, or at least the marijuana-producing states within the US.

42 See *International Narcotics Control Strategy Report;* and Michael Massing, "Dealing with the Drug Horror," *New York Review of Books*, 30 March 1989, pp. 22–6. The *New York Times* does, however, report a rise in police officers killed in drug-related incidents to 14, out of a total of 78 for 1988 ("A Record 14 Officers Killed in '88 in Drug Incidents," 3 September 1989, p. 22). See also Michael Massing, "Noriega in Miami," *The Nation* (2 December 1991), pp. 697–704.

43 A sampling of this school would include Alfred McCoy's classic study, *The Politics of Heroin in Southeast Asia* (New York: Harper and Row, 1972); Peter Maas, *Manhunt: The Incredible Pursuit of a CIA Agent Turned Terrorist* (New York: Random House, 1986); Edward S. Herman, *The Real Terror Network; Terrorism in Fact and Propaganda* (Boston: Southend Press, 1982); and Jonathon Kwitney's *Crimes of Patriots* (New York: Norton, 1987).

44 See *Report of the Congressional Committees Investigating the Iran–Contra Affair* (Random House, 1988), pp. 130–1 and pp. 318–21.

45 Both narco-terrorism and the war against it can also be the occasion for insurgency and counter-insurgency on the sly: Juan E. Mendez, executive director of Americas Watch, has recently reported on the collusion between the Columbian military and the drug cartels in attacks on members and sympathizers of the leftist group *Union Patriotica* and guerilla movements (*New York Times*, 31 August 1989). In Peru, it would appear that the Maoist group *Sendero Luminoso* (Shining Path) has set up protection "rackets" with coca growers and tactical alliances with narco-traffickers. See also Eduardo Gamarra, "Militarizing Narcotics War may Threaten Latin Democracies," *Orlando Sentinel* (26 May 1991), p. G-1; Laura Brooks, "US Military Extends Drug War into Central America," *Christian Science Monitor* (25 June 1991), p. 1; and Charles Gepp, "US, Peru Sign New Anti-Drug Pact," (16 May 1991), p. 28.

46 President Bush confirmed this suspicion six months later in a speech, in which he stated that the cocaine cartels "are taking on the pretensions of a geopolitical force" and so "they must be dealt with as such by our military." Address by George Bush at the Commonwealth Club of San Francisco, 7 February 1990 (White House Office text). The most sophisticated argument for a non-military solution to the drug problem comes from Ethan Nadelmann, "US Drug Policy a Bad Export," *Foreign Policy* (Spring 1988), pp. 83–108.

47 See Michael Massing, "Dealing with the Drug Horror."

48 The State Department's Bureau of International Narcotics Matters spends about $100 million a year, of which only $3.6 million goes to crop-substitution and development assistance, while $45 million goes to eradicating crops, and $35 million on law enforcement and interdiction. See Massing, "Dealing with the Drug Horror."

49 One folly could well beget another: on 18 May 1989, the *Washington Times* reported that "House Democrats said yesterday that they will try next week to take money from President Bush's Strategic Defense Initiative research to pay for full funding of the war on illegal drugs." (p. 2). See also "In Drug War DoD Forces Had to Learn to Walk, but Now are Running," Jack Dorsey, *Sea Power* (January 1991), p. 76.

50 *Patterns of Global Terrorism: 1988*), p. v.

51 Shultz, "Terrorism and the Modern World," Current Policy No. 629, p. 2. President Reagan added some hyperbolic flourishes to say much the same thing at an address to the American Bar Association in July, 1985:

> So, there we have it: Iran, Libya, North Korea, Cuba, Nicaragua – continents away, tens of thousands of miles apart, but the same goals and objectives. I submit to you that the growth in terrorism in recent years results from the increasing

involvement of these states in terrorism in every region of the world ... [A]nd we're especially not going to tolerate these attacks from outlaw states run by the strangest collection of misfits, looney tunes, and squalid criminals since the advent of the Third Reich.

(Quoted from "The New Network of Terrorist States," Bureau of Public Affairs, Current Policy No. 721, pp. 2–3).

52 See, in particular, the section of the CIA's Nicaragua manual, *Psychological Operations in Guerilla Warfare* (republished by Random House in 1985), on "Implicit and Explicit Terror," which instructs the Contras to "Kidnap all officials or agents of the Sandinista government and replace them" (pp. 52–5).

53 Shultz, "Terrorism and the Modern World," p. 3.

54 Although "anti-terrorism" and "counter-terrorism" are often used interchangeably in both the official and academic terrorist discourses, I prefer to use only the term "anti-terrorism" to describe violent operations against terrorism. *Counter*-terrorism (the preferred term of the US State Department) implies, 1 believe, a competing structure (in the manner that Gramsci refers to a "counter-hegemony" or Foucault to a "counter-justice") that could, or intends to take the place of terrorism, although the stated policy is to deter and if possible *negate* terrorism rather than replace it with something else. For the official US policy of counter-terrorism – based on no concessions, and retaliation, legal prosecution, and law enforcement assistance – see the introduction *to Patterns of Global Terrorism*, pp. iii–iv. For a theoretical discussion of the anti/counter distinction, see A. Gramsci, *Selections from Prison Notebooks*, trans. and edited by Q. Hoare and G. N. Smith (London: Lawrence and Wishart, 1971), pp. 206–76; and M. Foucault, "On Popular Justice: A Discussion with Maoists," in *Power/Knowledge*, edited by C. Gordon (New York: 1980), pp. 33–5.

55 Although the roles of anti-terrorist and counter-insurgency forces, as well as the rationales of low-intensity conflict and covert action often overlap, I will focus only on anti-terrorism since the other topics are well-covered elsewhere. For a reasonably sober-minded assessment of the various military units involved, see James Adams, *Secret Armies* (New York: Bantam Books, units involved, 1989); and for a more analytical account of the doctrine of low-intensity conflict, see Michael Klare and Peter Kornbluh (eds), *Low-Intensity Warfare* (New York: Pantheon, 1988).

56 Nor do you hear much in the anti-terrorist lore of the Egyptian attempt to rescue a hijacked airliner in Malta that resulted in 57 of the 98 passengers and crew dead. Anti-terrorism, like its evil *doppelgänger*, relies heavily on the myth of invincibility; hence, much is made of its vaunted capabilities, and very little of its shortcomings – except through the blatant failures or occasional press leak.

57 "The Captors' Reasons," *New York Times*, 27 August 1989.

58 See Bob Woodward, *Veil: The Secret Wars of the CIA 1981–1987* (New York: Simon and Shuster, 1987), pp. 396–8, 416.

59 This begs the question of whether Western leaders have been too quick to dismiss as opportunist the claims of Southern leaders who have discerned a legitimating affinity between anti-colonial struggles and some modern forms of terrorism. A critical reading of the biennial UN General Assembly debates on international terrorism during the 1970s and 1980s could possibly shed some light on this question.

60 Paul Virilio, *Pure War* (New York: Semiotext(e), 1983), p. 27. See also Virilio's *Defense populaire et luttes ecologiques*, where he describes nuclear deterrence as being at the same time the catastrophic process of "une colonisation totale" (pp. 35–6).

61 "One cannot use violence against what is already violence, one can only reinforce it, take it to extremes – in other worlds, to the State's maximum power." Virilio, *Pure War*, p. 51.

62 We can find a sociological, historical and political equivalent to this diabolical conformity, to this evil demon of conformity, in the modern behaviour of the masses who are also very good at complying with the models offered to them, who are very good at reflecting the objectives imposed on them, thereby absorbing and annihilating them. There is in this conformity a force of seduction in the literal sense of the word, a force of diversion, distortion, capture and ironic fascination. There is a kind of fatal strategy of conformity. See Jean Baudrillard, *The Evil Demon of Images* (Sydney: Power Institute, 1987).

63 Sterling, *The Terror Network*, p. 80.

64 Actually Moro's hands are not visible, which at the time raised some doubts of the authenticity of the photograph. The artist Sarah Charlesworth has captured this terrorist cybernet in her presentation of 45 photographic facsimiles of newspapers that carried the image of the hostage Moro. Part of a much larger series, *Modern History* (1977–79), the collection was at New York's International Center of Photography in the summer of 1989. In the exhibition she goes beyond the obvious, Sterlingesque point that the Red Brigades made effective use of the media. Charlesworth's blanking out of all written text save the bannerheads of the newspapers reveals the power of context in terrorist discourse. For example, the Roman newspaper that originally received the photograph, *Il Messaggero*, filled two-thirds of the front page with it, with no other news pictures to distract the reader, while *l'Unita*, the newspaper of the Italian Communist Party, ran a much smaller one with two other photos of the forces of law and order, the *carabinieri*, busy at the scene. The London *Times* ran a small, tightly cropped photo of Moro, dwarfed by what *seems* to be a large photo of the Queen holding her new grandson, until one moves down the gallery wall, past the *Irish Times*, the New *York Times*, and the *Baltimore Sun* with multiple news photos as well, to the Toronto *Globe and Mail* which has the smiling monarch blown up three times the size of Moro. Stripped of the verbal signs, the newspapers reveal their ability to impart powerful meanings before the first caption or article is attached, through the image's cropping, placement, size and relation to other photographs. The viewer/reader is drawn into the process, to see how even the subtlest aspect of media coverage of terrorism becomes an indispensable part of the re-territorialization of global political conflict.

65 To be sure, there are many works on media coverage of terrorism. For example, see Alex Schmid and Janny de Graaf, *Violence as Communication: Insurgent Terrorism and the Western News Media* (Beverly Hills, CA: Sage, 1982); and *Terrorist Spectaculars: Should TV Coverage be Curbed?* (New York: Priority, 1986). But I believe Jean Baudrillard is the first to get inside the relationship of the global audience, the media, and terrorism, what he sees to be a circle of simulation that is not only ruptured from material referents but now engendering a political hyper-reality. See *A l'ombre des majorites silencieuses* (Paris: Cahiers d'Utopie, 1978), *Simulacre et Simulation* (Paris: Galilée, 1981), and *Les Strategies fatales* (Paris: Bernard Grasset, 1983); the edited translations in the Foreign Agent series (New York: Semiotext(e), 1983), *In the Shadow of the Silent Majorities* and *Simulations;* or *Jean Baudrillard: Selected Writings*, edited by Mark Poster (Stanford, CA: Stanford University Press, 1988).

66 See "Columbians Seize Drug Ring Suspect and 134 Aircraft" (p. 1); "Egypt Arrest 41; Sees Shiite Plot" (p. 6); and "France Says It Plans No Military Role in Lebanon" (p. 7) in *New York Times*, 22 August 1989.

67 It would appear that anti-terrorism is fast becoming (after disarmament) a primary site for cooperation with the Soviet Union. Confronting an increase in terrorist incidents (for instance, Aeroflot has suffered at least 11 hijackings since 1973, compared to the next highest airlines, TWA, Air France, and Kuwaiti, which have all been hijacked twice), the Soviet Union has set up a new hostage rescue unit and called for more intelligence-sharing on terrorism with Interpol and the CIA. There have also been high-level discussions on how jointly to combat terrorism: in January 1989, a group of 10 American

and 10 Soviet experts met in Moscow; in September 1989, Lt General Fjodor Sherbak, former deputy head of the KGB, and Maj. General Valentin Zvezdenkov, former head of KGB counter-terrorism, met at the Rand Corporation for closed-door talks with William Colby, former CIA Director, and Ray Cline, former CIA Deputy Director; and in 1990 Secretary of State James Baker and Soviet Foreign Minister Eduard Shevardnadze met to hold a second round of official talks on terrorism. See Glenn Schoen and J. Derleth, "KGB Fields New Hostage Rescue Unit," *Armed Forces Journal International* (October 1989), p. 22; and Robin Wright, "US and Soviets Seek Joint War on Terrorism," *Los Angeles Times*, p. 1.

68 The speech was to the National Strategy Forum in Chicago in May, 1988, and his response was to someone who asked what he thought was the most important unsolved problem in international relations. The last part of his reply was:

> But I've often wondered what if all of us in the world discovered that we were threatened by a power from outer space – from another planet. Wouldn't we all of a sudden find that we didn't have any differences between us at all – we were all human beings, citizens of the world – wouldn't we come together to fight that particular threat?

6 S/N: International theory, balkanisation and the new world order

Source: *Millennium Journal for International Studies* (Winter 1991), vol. 20, no. 3, pp. 485–506.

> Why do we tell stories? For amusement or distraction? For 'instruction,' as they said in the seventeenth century? Does a story reflect or express an ideology, in the Marxist sense of the word? Today all these justifications seem out of date to me. Every narrative thinks of itself as a kind of merchandise.
>
> Roland Barthes, *L' Express* interview, 31 May 1970

This essay is a story drawn from a travelogue that begins in July 1985 aboard the Baltic Peace and Freedom Cruise and ends in June 1990 at a Billy Bragg concert in Prague. It is both a travelogue in the conventional sense of a record of events that I kept as an observer and minor participant, and a study (in the root sense of *travel + logue*) of how words and images travel and take on a discursive power in international relations.[1] In the first part of this essay, a genealogy of one concept in particular, 'balkanisation', is undertaken to show how discursive practices delimit the conditions of possibility for a new Central and Eastern European order.[2] The second part is an experimental argument for the political and intellectual benefits of dissidence in international relations. The third is a speculative inquiry: it looks down the road from a moribund nowhere to somewhere new, from the degenerative utopia of the communist order to the possibility of a regenerative heterotopia emerging from the Eastern and Central European experience.[3] In short, this travelogue inscribes the political transformation of a region, the intellectual practices of a discipline and the prospects for a new world order.

There are many reasons not to take this journey. A foreigner (that is, a generalist without the right papers and worse, carrying French luggage) is not very welcome in the specialist's domain of Soviet and European politics. Yet I believe there are pressing reasons for the incursion. The foremost reason is the manner and method by which the remarkable and rapid transformations of the last five years have been politically charged and intellectually neutralised by a one-sided, parochial triumphalism in which vocal conservatives declare an end to history, confused liberals choke on its dust and the rest, the 'happy peoples' as Hegel called them in *The Phenomenology of Spirit*, are left with no history.[4] I have argued elsewhere that the primacy of space over time in international theory, of geopolitics over chronopolitics, has hampered our ability to keep up with, let alone presage, the impact of real time representations of rapid political change.[5] In this essay, I move from critique to an alternative method that might possibly allow us to weigh the impact of sudden diachronic moments of change against the synchronic structure of the international order. A second reason for a travelogue to assess a political order is the anthropological advantage afforded by an extraterritorial, alien status. This is not to pretend, by way of a sovereign method, that this will take one out of the power-knowledge loop and onto some detached position of objectivity. Rather, it can help to defamiliarise the orthodox, disciplined process of understanding the world *as it is* (the realist imperative) in opposition to *what it is not* (the utopian fallacy), a binary method of reasoning that invariably works to reinforce and to reconstitute the order of things.[6] Hence, this essay intends to devalue high structural analysis built upon noncontested concepts and parsimonious models by flooding the marketplace of international theory with imported, post-structural narrations. In international political economy, one might call this 'dumping'.

A third reason can be found in the nature of language itself. This essay is a self-reflexive study of 'S/N' in international politics. What does this mean? In telecommunications parlance, this refers simply to the signal-to-noise ratio that is produced by the technical reproduction of a sound or image. By now, we all have some sense of how noise and nonsense disseminate and accumulate in technologically advanced societies, especially when they approach or engage in warfare.[7] Given the heavily mediated yet heterogeneous nature of world politics, it is not surprising that international relations enjoys no diplomatic immunity against the high 'S/N' of late modernity. The only real surprise is the nonrecognition of that fact in international theory. A warning, then: this hybrid travelogue contains some videographic out-takes on eastern and central Europe that might be considered by some in the field to be too 'loud' for a scholarly journal.[8]

But there is (as least) one other important meaning for 'S/N'. This essay, in both its content and unconventional style, endorses the possibility of positive change through a critical pluralism. In a critical pluralism, language is not the tool of some external thought or purpose (say, a research program, a career or a revolution), but the very space in which the will to power and truth confronts the empire of circumstance; imagined dialogues take on powerful monologues of the past, and the play of difference challenges the permanent war of essential identities. Hence, the sign 'S/N' has a stereographic as well as videographic sense in this essay. The oblique bar acts as a linguistic sign of the most significant condition of otherness (and challenge to order) in international relations today: not simply the state versus the nation or sovereignty versus nationalism, but the difference (historical, cultural, ideological) between them that makes and unmakes both identities. It is this *alternation* (the 'other' nation that constitutes sovereign identities) that this essay reimagines.

The matter of the order of things

First there is the matter of order, or more precisely, the method by which we make the idea of order matter in international relations. An obvious preliminary point: order matters most when it is lost or in the process of being lost, especially during the break-up of empire. Traditionally, the speculative range at such moments in international theory reconstructs a broadband spectrum: at the one extreme lies tyranny, at the other anarchy, and via media, the optimal order of things. Hedley Bull, following this trialectic, opens his inquiry into order in world politics, *The Anarchical Society*, with Saint Augustine's view of the best possible order.[9] With one eye on the City of God and the other on Rome under barbarian attack, Augustine defined order broadly as 'a good disposition of discrepant parts each in its fittest place'. Not a definition that would pass muster with most political scientists, but one nonetheless that evokes the important dualism of a pattern of politics that is necessitated by dangerous exogenous alternatives and made possible by endogenous goals and values.[10]

At historical ruptures comparable to the fall of Rome (like the disintegration of Christendom and the arrival and eventual defeat of Napoleon), the issue of order arises time and again, causing thinkers to anxiously (or nostalgically) look backward for a reconstruction of the old order while others bravely (or recklessly) look forward to the building of a new order. For instance, one could plot the move from a medieval to a modern view of order with the divergent visions of Dante's *De Monarchia* and Machiavelli's *Prince*, the first calling for a return to a Christian, universalist monarchy, the second for states roughly concurrent with national, particularist interests.[11]

The modern debate has ranged somewhat further, on the merits and perils of multipolarity over against the stability afforded by hegemonic powers or alliances in a bipolar system.[12] And to be sure, there have been numerous predictions of the imminent end of a world order based on state sovereignty, whether because of technological innovations like the telegraph, radio or airplane, the coming resolution or revolution of class conflict, the global threat of exterminism or even the New Age promise of harmonic convergence. But now in our own field of international relations, at a time when radical transformation of superpower politics has taken place, the owl of Minerva seems to be grounded.

Not, then, simply a case of being shot down by the ideologues, or left in the jet-stream of events, but grounded by confusion over the question of what might constitute a better, if not the best and fittest, order. The disintegration and reformation of the Soviet bloc (and with it the power to define an order through an alien threat) led George Bush, President of the United States, to declare at National Press Club banquets as well as Veteran of Foreign Wars outings that the new enemy is 'uncertainty', 'unpredictability' and 'instability'.[13] Similarly, in the Soviet Union, events signaling an impending state of chaos have reached such a level that they go unreported in the news; not because of censorship, but because they are no longer thought to be newsworthy.[14]

Of course, some warning noises about the impact of imperial decline on international order have been heard, most notably from thinkers in the historical camp of political economy, like Robert Gilpin and Paul Kennedy, who have read the numbers and seen the symptoms from a bottom-up, materialist perspective.[15] But there is another form of order deserving scrutiny that operates at the level of cultural economy, by which I mean the flow and exchange of valorized signs and symbols. Michel Foucault charts this terrain with remarkable finesse in the Preface to *The Order of Things*, in which he offers his own 'trialectic' or order.[16] He first identifies an order's 'system of elements' as the classification of resemblances and differences which define and establish its most basic form. These act as the 'fundamental codes of a culture' which govern and through governance, constitute an order and make us feel at home in it:

> Order is, at one and the same time, that which is given in things as their inner law, the hidden network that determines the way they confront one another, and also that which has no existence except in the grid created by a glance, an examination, a language: and it is only in the blank spaces of this grid that order manifests itself in depth as though already there, waiting in silence for the moment of its expression.[17]

Foucault then locates the other constitutive boundary of an order, the reflexive pale where 'there are the scientific theories or the philosophical interpretations which explain why order exists in general, what universal laws it obeys, what principle can account for it, and why this particular order has been established and not some other'.[18] Between these two regions lies an extraterritorial expression of order, no less powerful in its ordering effects, that is more resistant to analysis. It is here that a culture, imperceptibly deviating from the empirical orders prescribed for it by its primary codes, instituting an initial separation from them, causes them to lose their original transparency, relinquishes its immediate and invisible powers and frees itself sufficiently to discover that these orders are perhaps not the only possible ones or the best ones. This culture then finds itself faced with the stark fact that there exist, below the level of its spontaneous orders, things that are in themselves capable of being ordered, that belong to a certain unspoken order; the fact, in short, that order exists.[19]

It is to this space between the codes of a culture and the dominant scientific and philosophical interpretations of the day that this essay travels. It retraces the path of a concept that moved from a natural position upholding a superpower order, to critical attitudes toward the order of things and, once historically transvalued, to a multiplicity of contested meanings that no single power or doctrine could possibly fix.[20]

The discourse of 'balkanisation'

Balkanisation is generally understood to be the break-up of larger political units into smaller, mutually hostile states which are exploited or manipulated by more powerful neighbours. It takes only a cursory knowledge of the history of international relations to find some fault with this definition. Indeed, such a definition could be used to describe the entire history of the states-system (from the disintegration of the Holy Roman Empire through the rise of nationalism to the process of decolonization) as one of 'balkanisation', in which existing structures broke up into smaller pieces.[21] Nor does it take an acute sensibility to sniff out the presence of a great power *telos* operating in the definition. That is, there exists a finite process of state formation leading to the most stable order.[22] Yet this usage of 'balkanisation' seems to have enjoyed the standing of common wisdom and thus avoided critical scrutiny. A genealogy of the term is called for in order to understand how one meaning became paramount over contending definitions; what kind of order was produced and served by balkanisation; and its legacy for post-Cold War politics.

The term itself has explicit geopolitical origins. The root of the word, 'balkan', means mountain in Turkish, and the history of the politics of the region reflects this geographical fact. Recurrent invasions passed through the valleys of the Danube and its tributaries while the surrounding mountains isolated the settler groups. What developed was a condition described by John McManners, in *The Near Eastern Question and the Balkans*, as 'inner fragmentation and outer accessibility'. Rather than forging unity, conquest multiplied the diversity of peoples in the region. A pattern emerged: after the various conquerors left, nationalist and tribal strife would erupt along the fault lines created by years of colonisation.

An exemplary case was the Russo-Turkish war of 1876. Abetted by a panslavist movement and a militant Orthodox Church, Russia exploited internal ethnic and religious differences, and then legitimised its intervention in Bulgaria with the Treaty of San Stefano. Great Britain, which had previously fought in the Crimean War not in support of Turkey but to thwart Russian expansion, grew alarmed by the regional shift in the balance of power towards Russia. Another Great Power congress was convened, and the Treaty of Berlin of 1878 attempted to redress alignments by redrafting the borders of the region. What was the result? Balkanisation in everything but name: Russia and Bulgaria disputed the Dobrya; Serbia and Bulgaria quarreled over the Pirot; Bulgaria and Greece sparred over Thrace; Greece and Albania fought over Eprius; Austria-Hungary annexed Bosnia-Herzegovina, and if there were more synonyms for fighting we could go on about the multiple conflicts that erupted among Bulgarian-speaking Greeks, Greek-speaking Slavs, Albanised Serbs, Turks and Albanians in Macedonia.[23] At the time, these persistent local rivalries with systemic reverberations went under the orientalist rubric of the 'Eastern Question'. After two Balkan wars, the question, Who would fill the power vacuum left by the decline of two empires, the Ottoman and the Austrian-Hungarian? had two eager respondents: Germany, in pursuit of *lebensraum*, pushed eastward (a carrying forward of the nineteenth century *drang nach osten*); while Russia, full of Slavic fratemalism and seeking warm water ports, pushed westward. Never resolved, the question was to be gorily debated in the First World War.

Although the phenomenon of balkanisation was very much in evidence in the late nineteenth century, it was only after the First World War that it gained official linguistic recognition. According to the Oxford English Dictionary, it first appeared in two magazines in the 1920s: the *19th Century Magazine* ('Great Britain has been accused by French observers of pursuing a policy aimed at the Balkanisation of the Baltic provinces.'); and *Public Opinion* ('In this unhappy

Balkanised world ... every state is at issue with its neighbors.') From its original use, balkanisation clearly had a negative connotation of hostility toward neighbours and a threat to the existing international order. And the early usage carries with it the sense of the failure of the post-war order, for what was the purpose of the peace following the First World War but to bring an end to the danger of balkanisation?

This issue is raised by Arnold Toynbee in *The Western Question in Greece and Turkey*, the only book that I have found to mention the political origins of the term, although it does so only in passing. Toynbee attributes its origins to German social democrats who used it to describe the deleterious effects that the 1918 Treaty of Brest-Litovsk between Germany and the Soviets would have on the Baltic provinces, soon to be independent states. With this clue in hand, I searched through the writings of pre-war German, Russian and Polish social democrats, Kautsky, Lenin, Trotsky, Luxemburg and Liebknecht among them. I was surprised to discover a meaning of balkanisation that never made it into the general discourse of international relations, nor, for that matter, into the Oxford English Dictionary.

In a report from January 1909 in the *Kievan Thought*, a correspondent wrote that the Balkans were 'Europe's Pandora's Box and that only a single state of all Balkan nationalities, built on a democratic, federative basis – on the pattern of Switzerland and the North American republic – can bring international peace to the Balkans and create conditions for a development of productive forces'. After two Balkan wars and on the eve of the First World War, the same correspondent provided the key elements of balkanisation in a 1914 article called 'The Balkan Question':

> The balance of power in the Balkans created by the Congress of Berlin in 1879 was full of contradictions. But up by artificial ethnographical boundaries, placed under the control of imported dynasties from German nurseries, bound hand and foot by the intrigues of the Great Powers, the people of the Balkans could not cease their efforts for further national freedom and unity.

This essay, along with others from the war years, would be published in the United States, in 1918, under the title *The War and the International*. In bold print the author set out the conditions for peace:

No reparations, the right of every nation to self-determination. The United State of Europe – without monarchies, without standing armies, without ruling feudal castes, without secret diplomany.[24]

Four years later the same correspondent, Leon Trotsky, became the first foreign minister of the Soviet state and led a delegation to those very 'balkanising' negotiations at Brest-Litovsk. Ten years later, he applied the concept of balkanisation to the Ruhr crisis:

> Victorious France is now maintaining her mastery only by Balkanising Europe. Great Britain is inciting and backing the French policy of dismembering

and exhausting Europe, all the time concealing her work behind Britain's traditional mask of hypocrisy ... Just as federation was long ago recognised as essential for the Balkan peninsula, so now the time has arrived for stating definitely and clearly that federation is essential for Balkanised Europe.[25]

From these quotes and their historical context, we can find the intertextual origins of balkanisation and the reason for its first political transvaluation. Balkanisation was forged as an important conceptual weapon in the Marxist lexicon to describe what was seen to be a form of endo-colonisation in Europe. The persistence of national rivalries was interpreted as a remnant of a feudal past now exacerbated by the uneven development of capital. During the war and for a short period afterwards, Trotsky and others in the Comintern leadership advocated a solution, which never amounted to much more than a slogan, for balkanisation: a united state of Europe which would be economically united, politically socialist and ethnically federated. In this same period, Lenin also was taking a liberal view on the nationalist question, likening the right of self-determination to the right of divorce – as rights that should be interpreted as necessary freedoms to maintain a family, not as a moral imperative to break it up. But Trotsky did not find permanent revolution at Brest-Litovsk. With ample assistance from the allied powers, he found a permanent state of 'neither war nor peace' that persisted, in one form or another of the Cold War, until 1989. Nor did he find a united state of Europe, unless one is willing to take a long (and revisionist) view toward the coming union of Europe in 1992. And Lenin's enlightened view of nationalism was quickly tested by the Poles' bid for self-determination in 1919 and found wanting when he advocated an invasion of Poland by the Red Army.

At this point, balkanisation began to travel: to describe the precarious position of the newly independent Baltic Republics, the resurgence of old grievances in the Danube and the state of the world in general. It still carried a negative description of chauvinism gone hostile and of meddlesome intervention by outside parties. But it traveled politically as well, gradually losing the remedial prescription of the social democrats. In other worlds, balkanisation lost its pink petticoats and donned the starched collar of the Wilsonian liberals.[26]

I do not intend to rehearse the history of the failure of these ideals to materialise in either the Communist International or the League of Nations. I wish, rather, to challenge the conventional wisdom that the Marxists and the Wilsonians were at epistemological loggerheads, divided by the formers' materialism and the latters' idealism. A study of their use of balkanisation (as well as its use of them) reveals a telling affinity. Both believed geo-economic factors, in particular the size of a state and the internationalisation of a single mode of production, to be the critical determinants of a state's viability and an international order's stability. Both shared a progressive view of history – that a growing economic interdependence would diminish nationalist rivalries and bring about a better, more just order. Both shared epistemologies based on a closed structure of binary oppositions: for the Marxists, balkanisation or federation, barbarism or socialism, nationalism or internationalism; for the Wilsonians, balkanisation or confederation, despotism or liberal constitutionalism, nationalism or cosmopolitanism. And, most importantly, both world-views proved unable to resolve the fundamental contradictions between the principle of self-determination and the requirements of international order.

To be sure, other cultural, geographical, historical and economic factors evade this simple dichotomisation of order versus justice. Sentiments as politically powerful as they are intellectually elusive (like France's desire for both revenge over the loss of Alsace and Lorraine and war reparations from Germany, or Germany's resentment over the loss of territory to the Poles) need to be taken into consideration. But from the reconstruction of a post-war order, the conditions for a future balkanisation were assured. A third of Poland's population spoke German; Poles, Russians, Germans and Magyars made up a third of Czechoslovakia's population; and over a million Maygars became part of Romania. And in the two successful cases of nation-state formation, Czechoslovakia and the Baltic Republics, conditions of balkanisation were established that led to the two great injustices that assured the outbreak of a Second World War: the seizure of the Sudetenland and the carving up of the Baltic region by Germany and the Soviet Union in the secret protocol of the Ribbentrop-Molotov Pact of 1939. It is then ironic that shortly after the attempted Nazi *putsch* in Austria, a learned observer of the Balkans, R.W. Seton-Watson, would write that balkanisation was 'a cheap phrase about central Europe current after the War'.[27] In fact, balkanisation clearly had legs.

Floating signifiers: aboard the Baltic Star

15 January [1985]. Received invitation to participate in the Baltic Peace and Freedom Cruise. Sounds like a ship of fools.

22 January. Sounded out friends about cruise and Stockholm conference on the Baltic future. Most of them confused: why a cruise through the 'Balkans'? K. and B. [two Soviet specialists] thought it sounded like an émigré provocation, advised against it. Fear of balkanisation.

1 February.
Dear Mari:
I accept your invitation. To say the least, it sounds intriguing, and I think it might just have the potential to break through the intellectual logjam created by academics who don't like to change maps and texts too often and by superpower politicians who like to keep their spheres of influence intact. So although I am somewhat skeptical of the outcome, I am eager to participate in an area of discussion which has been (not so benevolently) neglected. What happens when Baltic peoples assert their right to self-determination; when and under what circumstances might it happen; what will be its effect on the international system; how does the Baltic Question fit into the debate of order versus justice in superpower politics: these are a few of the questions I would like to bring up in my presentations.

25 March. Received program of cruise panel and Stockholm University conference. I think I made a mistake. Boat panel is with Vladimir Bukovsky (ex-*gulag*), Alex Stromas (Lithuanian émigré academic), a Polish Solidarity official and 'Swedish parliamentarian' (?). In Stockholm, with Imants Lesinskis, KGB defector from Latvia. Suspect a set-up: I've been billed as 'peace activist, former member of Oxford Mothers Against Nuclear War'.

MOSCOW, JULY 15 (TASS) TASS NEWS ANALYST VIKTOR PONOMARYOV IT HAS BEEN LEARNT FROM THE REPORTS OF FOR-EIGN NEWS AGENCIES REACHING HERE THAT CERTAIN CIRCLES OF THE NATO COUNTRIES HAVE STARTED A SERIES OF DANGEROUS PROVOCATIONS IN THE BALTIC SEA ZONE … ONE CAN CLEARLY SEE THE STYLE OF +LANGLEY EXPERTS+ IN THE SCENARIO OF PROVO-CATIONS. THE +JUDGES+, +WITNESSES+ AND THE +VICTIMS+ WILL RUBBERSTAMP THE +VERDICT+ WHICH HAS LONG BEEN ENDORSED IN THE QUIET OF THE CIA'S OFFICES, WILL THEN GO TO STOCKHOLM ACCOMPANIED BY A BUNCH OF OVERHEATED +FREE EMIGRE YOUTH+ WHERE A SPECIALLY CHARTED PIRATIC SHIP IS ALREADY WAITING FOR THEM … THE SHIP WILL CRUISE IN CLOSE PROXIMITY TO THE SOVIET UNION'S TERRITORIAL WATERS. IN PASSING ALONG THE SEA BORDER IT IS PLANNED TO SEND LARGE QUANTITIES OF ANTI-SOVIET PAPERS ONTO THE COAST OF THE SOVIET BALTIC REPUBLICS USING FOR THIS PURPOSE SPECIAL UNSINKABLE CONTAINERS AND AIR BALLOONS. HEAPS OF SUBVER-SIVE LEAFLETS ARE ALREADY BEING DELIVERED FROM THE CIA'S DEPOTS … THE STAND THAT WILL BE TAKEN WITH REGARD TO THESE PROVOCATIONS BY RESPONSIBLE POLITICIANS FROM THE EUROPEAN GOVERNMENTS, PRIMARILY THOSE OF DENMARK AND SWEDEN WHOSE TERRITORIES AND VESSELS MAY BE USED IN THE PLANNED EXTREMIST ACTIONS, WILL CLEARLY SHOW HOW SIN-CERE THEY ARE IN THEIR ASSURANCES TO THE EFFECT THAT THEY ARE EAGER TO ACTIVELY PROMOTE THE NORMALISATION OF THE INTERNATIONAL SITUATION, THE CONSOLIDATION OF GOOD NEIGH-BOURLY RELATIONS IN EUROPE AND IN THE BALTIC SEA ZONE.

25 July. Arrived in Stockholm and went to the headquarters of the cruise in the Old Town. A bomb scare clears the building. I accuse Mari of staging it for publicity; he seems to have missed the joke. As we walk out and reach the police line, there is a very loud bang. Some of the reporters fell to the ground (former war correspondents?). The Swedish police had decided to blow up a suspicious-looking briefcase that had been left in a doorway. Nobody claims it.

26 July. Boarding the boat delayed while dogs sniff every suitcase. Lots of singing mixed with accusation – anyone with cheap shoes and a camera is suspected of being a KGB agent. One of the accused turns out to be a cameraman for the BBC.

TASS hysterical news releases have done the trick: over 40 reps from the western media are coming along. However, seems to be no one from the US press, except guy from Radio Free Europe (the CIA provocateur?). The news people get the cabins with portholes.

27 July. Gave presentation today. Aside from invective and continuous spray of spittle from S. it went OK. Writer from *Toronto Life* liked the line 'better mass whimsy than mass destruction' and bought me a drink in the stem bar. While there, overheard the captain of the ship (always in the bar) say to a reporter that 'the Soviet Navy, on their way back from their biggest maneuvers in history, will grab my ship and take it to Riga. They will interrogate you for three days and me for two and then let us go'. The organisers couldn't get any other ship but this one: on his last voyage, the captain miscalculated a turn and hit an island.

Superpower Estrangement and the Baltic National Identity

When I first received your invitation to participate in the Baltic Peace and Freedom Cruise, I must admit to some reluctance ... My concern was that this cruise and the Baltic Futures Seminar would be marked by an emotional intensity at the default of a rational analysis of how the Baltic Question has been a monologue of the superpowers. In the end, I decided to participate in the hope that my empathy for your case might temper – and render more acceptable – some critical comments I have to make about Baltic nationalism.

I must also say that my doubts were not assuaged by the name of this conference. In the first Cold War and in the new one in which we find ourselves, both words have been appropriated for political and often disinformational purposes: the West has claimed freedom for their own, while the Soviets have staked out peace. My doubts, then, are about the pairing of these concepts: is it a marriage of convenience to legitimise one more one-sided attack on a superpower? If so, your call for human rights will ring as hollow as Reagan's and Gorbachev's, who see human rights' abuses everywhere in the other's sphere of influence, but are blind to them in their own. Or does this represent a genuine attempt at a dialogue, to reunite two concepts, two movements which superpower politics and parochial interests has torn apart in the first place? In the end, I decided that the strategy of the peace movement itself dictates participation, for there must be, at the very least, an initial trust of independent groups' intentions if we are to break the political deadlock caused by Cold War obsessions with capabilities.

The intention of this floating conference, as I understand it, is to investigate the possibility of opening between the two blocs a space in which Baltic cultures might freely develop in peace. When compared with the military might of NATO and the Warsaw Pact, the capabilities of this cruise do indeed seem paltry. Yet through your imaginative staging of this event, the spontaneous support gained at demonstrations, and a forthright relationship with the media, you have managed to magnify many-fold the raw power of committed Balts. Nonetheless, we should all be aware that the most immediate and tempting capability of this cruise is potentially a negative one: it is much easier, and much more dangerous, to provoke superpowers than to mediate between them. That said, we should not allow the superpowers a monopoly on defining what constitutes a provocation: otherwise, they will surely and without a struggle pre-empt the terrain and rights of independent groups such as your own.

[I] think it is a positive act for the Baltic future, and the first sign of a political or cultural organisation coming of age, to open the Baltic Question to outsiders, in particular to those from the peace movement who are sympathetic to the problem of human rights but are critical of strategies which entail purely national solutions. For very good reasons, peace activism in the United States has involved participation in the debates and struggles against human rights abuses in Central America, South Africa and other areas in and at the borders of the United States' sphere of interests. For a variety of reasons, the most obvious one being the political expediency (let's call it what it is – the hypocrisy of President Reagan's human rights policy), the peace movement has been less inclined to forge links with human and national rights movements emanating from the Soviet bloc. This has been less true in Europe and, as peace movements also come of age and come to grips with the complexity of global politics, I think it will be increasingly less true in the United States as well. Two examples would be the European Nuclear Disarmament group in Britain and the Campaign for Peace and Democracy/East and West, based in New York but beginning to find wide support across the United States. These groups are not shouting into the wind: they have formed links and given support to groups on the other side of the two bloc divide, to independent groups equally committed to human rights and peace rights. Examples include: Charter 77 in Czechoslovakia, one of the oldest; Swords into Ploughshares in East Germany; the Dialogue group in Hungary; the Moscow Trust Group; and, most recently, the formation of the Freedom and Peace Movement in Poland. There have been stirrings in the Baltic as well, with a petition for the establishment and extension of a Nordic Nuclear Free Zone to the Baltic region. At least eight of the organisers have ended up in prison camps or psychiatric hospitals; in fact, one of them shared a cell with the released Anatoly Shcharansky. What all these groups have in common is a history of challenging the Yalta state of affairs and state of mind, which puts bloc stability before civil liberties and national security before national self-determination.

I believe it would be a positive action on the part of the Baltic groups in the West to build bridges with these independent, non-aligned movements. But some might rightly say, 'let's be practical: what does the peace movement have to offer to the Balts besides a moral position superior to the superpowers?' We must acknowledge that not a single missile has been removed from the European theatre because of the peace movements. But we should also measure the success of peace movements and human rights groups by their ability to demystify the demonology of the Cold War and to open between the two superpowers a discursive space in which alternative strategies for defense and human rights might freely develop. They have been active in continuous compaigns to publicise and fight for human and peace rights activists in the eastern bloc. They surely can take some credit for the pressure European governments have put on the US government to begin arms talks with the Soviets. And more importantly for the Baltic cause, they are working to create the conditions for a detente from below, a relaxation of tensions which is necessary if there is to be any possibility of better conditions in the Baltic region.

[I] have left for last the question of nationalism, because it is the most contentious and potentially divisive issue for peace and human rights activists. Obviously, nationalism has been and can continue to be a positive, powerful force for liberating peoples from conditions of exo- and endo-colonisation. Just as apparent, I hope, is the case with which nationalism can deteriorate into an exclusivist chauvinism. The obvious, however, can sometimes make us oblivious to unpleasant considerations: given the geopolitical position of the Baltic states, a violent expression of self-determination could well be the last refrain before self-extermination. For those who view the Baltic future with a backward-looking nationalism, who remember a post-war state of flux which gave rise to free Baltic states, who envisage similar opportunities from crisis. I say look again, and then multiply the dangers by the megatonnage of destruction in the superpowers' arsenals.

I wish to make it clear that I am not questioning the Baltic right to self-determination. Rather, I am challenging the blind advocacy or pursuit of national rights which precludes a discussion of less dangerous paths to that end. The question, then, is not whether, but how, to rejuvenate and preserve a free Baltic national identity. By now, one historical lesson should have been learned by all Balts: balance of power politics will not do it. You have in the past, and perhaps you might again, win independence by playing one great power off another. But you did not, and will not, keep that independence because smaller powers, in particular those with any geo-strategic significance, are not players, but expandable pawns in the great powers' games. Once you seek redress in power politics, you leave the court of international law and human rights behind and enter the international free market of threat-exchange. There is little, if any, autonomy for small powers in this arena: your destiny is determined by secret protocols (like the Molotov-Ribbentrop Pact of 1939) or in tacit and not so tacit revisions to the Yalta agreements (like the Sonnenfeldt doctrine).

How then are the Baltic republics to make the transition from occupied, threatening (to both superpowers) non-entities, to liberated, non-threatening entities? It would be supremely arrogant for an outsider such as myself, and indeed presumptuous for Balts living outside of the Soviet Union, to give advice for those who would undoubtedly suffer for it. It is up to them to decide what strategy for peace and freedom is appropriate. But it will help their cause, I believe, to know that they have supporters in the West who are opting for a third way, for a dealigned, demilitarised, and most urgently, debrutalised Baltic region; who believe that finlandisation is a better prospect for Balts and the world than balkanisation; and *who are trying to forge links of human, not national interests, in international relations.*

I should leave it at that, but 'that' is not really adequate. I have attempted an analysis of the Baltic Question in the hope that the moment and movements of change might be advanced. But what can we do now? There is a weapon, one that I have witnessed at close quarters aboard the Baltic Star. I have seen it deflate puffed-up bureacrats, challenge the arrogance of security services and, at the same time, boost the morale of Balts. For lack of a better, more impressive academic sounding term, I will borrow from the Czech writer Kundera and simply call in the Baltic Joke, which I have, over the last few days enjoyably observed (and often been the butt of) as satire, buffoonery, caricature, wit and self-deprecation. Against the deadly serious, yet absurd, superpower strategy of mass destruction, what better way to fight despair and the Yalta powers than a dissident strategy of mass whimsy.

28 July. 'Soviet patrol boat threatens shipload of Baltic protesters', *Toronto Star*:

> ABOARD THE BALTIC STAR – A Soviet patrol boat last night sped on a collision course off the coast of Estonia for this small ship carrying 400 Baltic exiles – including 20 Canadians – veering away only at the last minute. At the same time, a Soviet fishing trawler cut across the Baltic Star's bow and stopped in its path – forcing the ship's captain to change course.

29 July. Left the bow, where a Swedish Liberal Party member was droning on, for the stem bar which was full of other exiles, older Balts; most of them seem to have become disaffected with the youthful, liberal views (and enthusiasms) of the cruise – their anti-communist views not receiving much of a hearing. They were all watching a black and white video, something with Nazis in it and lots of martial music. Suddenly realised it was a German propaganda film of Operation Barbarossa – the German invasion (liberation?) of Russia in 1941. They seemed to be enjoying it.

30 July. Lunch with Lesinskis at Stockholm University, KGB defector, before the panel, his two Swedish secret service handlers sitting on either side of me, looking very athletic and sharp in tailored suits, but with gym bags that clank on the seats. L. very talkative until I ask him about his fellow defector, Shevchenko. Later some confusion about the seating arrangements on stage. In the middle of the introductions one of the handlers comes from behind the side curtain to move a large vase from in front of me to in front of L. I suddenly feel very exposed.

9 August. 'Balts manage to *embarrass the Soviets', New Statesman*:

> A cruise and conference organised by Baltic refugees from Estonia, Latvia and Lithuania has been trying to get the 'Baltic Question' back on the political agenda.

[The] trip was dogged by practical and political difficulties. Both the ship – the Baltic Star – and the organising committee received bomb threats; the ship was shadowed all the way by Soviet, Finnish, and Swedish secret services, and diverted from its agreed course by a Soviet military pincer movement; and 400 Finnish Communist MPs unsuccessfully tried to prevent the ship from docking in Helsinki.

Following Baltic Star's arrival, the streets of Helsinki witnessed the largest political demonstration for decades – in support of the cruise. After the demonstration, cruise members went to the Soviet embassy but were forced away by police, who made one arrest and two detentions.

Toward the end of the voyage, participants unanimously agreed to a series of demands for the establishment of peace, human rights and freedom in the Baltic region. Those who took part describe the debates as 'non-dogmatic' and 'filled with real spontaneity'.

Accordingly to one recent visitor to the Baltic states, Balts themselves view the cruise as a positive action. In the words of a representative from the Swedish peace campaign, it seems that 'detente from below' might be taking its first but uneasy steps in the area.

Static wor(l)ds

Admittedly this essay itself, like many pirate videos, has a high 'S/N'. With any span of time in the retelling and editing of stories, distortion and dropouts are inevitable and, in this case, international. Only the totally sovereign power can pretend to transmit a message that gives no sign of its constitutive and often distortive medium. Yet the fictionally sovereign superpowers keep on trying, whether in the form of the socialist realistic projection of Soviet power, or the televisual simulation of America's greatness. Similarly so in international theory, where sovereign methods pursue total transparency in their representational practices and rationalist models chase after complete congruency with reality. The result: the intractable issues and irrational events of world politics never quite fit into a 'research programme'. Hence, this hybrid travelogue.

I have adapted the form of the travelogue as a textual experiment in perspectivism (in all its historical, political, cultural, technical forms) in the hope that it might convey the extraordinary level of media (in all of its representational forms) interference and influence in world politics that has, for the most part, resisted theoretical scrutiny in international theory.[28] It is not meant to serve as a prismatic corrective that will yield a more truthful vision of Central European politics. Nor should this travelogue be confused with its nineteenth century apotheosis: it does not move at the leisurely speed of trains and ships, speak imperially for the mute other of establish documentary authority through a photographic mirroring of reality. That moment of sovereign certitude has vanished. Or so it would seem, until one crosses genres into the discipline of international relations which is dominated by a seeming diversity of approaches (neorealism, rational and public choice theory, correlates of war analysis, game theory, neoliberal institutionalism), but nearly all of which continue to share the rationalist perspective of the nineteenth century that all that is reasonable is true.[29]

Has this travelogue taken 'balkanisation' someplace new? It has shown how the concept travelled almost invisibly from converging Marxist and idealist usages to define its binary opposite, the optimal order of things. Contrasting the historical materiality and ideological baggage of the concept of the abstract, philosophical, or in Foucault's words, 'unspoken' nature of 'order', one can better understand how balkanisation came to play such a discursively powerful role in our understanding of what constitutes the 'best and fittest' order.

Where might its next port of call be? Surely the demise of a bipolar order and the resurgence of endo-colonisation as a disordering force will once again see the revalorisation of 'balkanisation'. However, with the institutionalisation and formalisation of an European union, the concept should begin to shed its Eurocentric skin. Perhaps, then, 'balkanisation' is ready for a return to its Ottoman origins. Take for example President Bush's recent condemnation of the Iraqi invasion of Kuwait as a 'ruthless assault on the very essence of international order and civilized ideals'.[30] We know what he means by 'the very essence of international order' by its violation (that is, the dictatorial interference in the affairs of another state).

A critical history of how 'balkanisation' has travelled could yield a very different, much less essentialist definition of 'order' in the Middle East. Saddam Hussein followed a great power tradition of solidifying his sphere of interest by the annexation of a much smaller state that only exists because of an earlier colonial balkanisation. Yet his actions were met by a level of global solidarity and a hailstorm of rhetoric unmatched since Hitler blitzkrieged into Europe. To be sure, the swallowing up of an oil producing state is bound to be less digestible than, say, the invasion of Lebanon by Syria or the occupation of the West Bank by Israel.[31]

I believe the reaction to the Iraqi invasion confirms a conclusion that I have reached from my study of balkanisation: the international order is once again being defined by the idealist practices resembling those of the 1920s and 1930s. Or rather, *neo*-idealist.[32] This ground has been theoretically prepared by developments in the field of international relations since the 1970s. The promulgation of western values, the spread of liberal-democratic capitalism, the decline of the state and the role of force, a belief in progress towards a more unified global order, an emphasis on economic links, a concern for human rights and a sense of intellectual commitment toward these ends mark much of the interdependency and world order model project theory that came out of the 1970s. Oddly enough, now it and many of its second generational 'institutionalist' adherents go under the rubric of 'neo-realism'. I contend that their teleological vision of world order contains cultural historical and epistemological blindspots that I hope this travelogue has called into question. Balkanisation can lead to disorder, anarchy and a 'bad infinity' of political powers, but that threat must be continually weighed against the history of its discursive power to maintain and promote unjust orders.

The necessary appendix

Two signs of the acceleration of history have begun to proliferate in international relations. The first is the conditional footnote leading off many journal articles ('this is the definitive statement as of date X'). The second is the appendix intending to bridge all the unforeseen events that transpire between the submission and publication dates. This essay does not pretend to be an exception to the current rule of circumstance in world politics; it is just slightly less transparent about its inability to represent events that are, in fact, current. Since this paper was presented at an American Political Science meeting in 1990, there has been a war in the Persian Gulf, the independence of the Baltic Republic and the rise of secessionist movements and violence in the Balkans. I am thus compelled to say more on the question of international order – especially since President Bush has chosen to embrace the discourse as his *ur*-text for world politics.

Beginning with Gorbachev's reforms, something happened in international political discourse: as the sovereign bipolar powers and truths that determined the exchange value of key words began to slip, wild fluctuations in the marketplace of ideas began to surface. Dangerous, perhaps, but also liberating. Vaclav Havel, in his earlier role as wordsmith rather than powerbroker, wrote of the malleability of words-as-weapons in the political arena:

> No word ... comprises only the meaning assigned to it by an etymological dictionary. The meaning of every word also reflects the person who utters it, the situation in which it is uttered, and the reason for its utterance. The selfsame word can, at one moment, radiate great hopes; at another, it can emit lethal rays. The selfsame word can be true at one moment and false the next, at one moment illuminating, at another, deceptive. On one occasion it can open up glorious horizons; on another, it can lay down the tracks to an entire archipelago of concentration camps. The selfsame word can at one time be the cornerstone of peace, while at another, machine-gun fire resounds in its every syllable.[33]

We have already seen how keywords of the Cold War were used in this manner: '*peace*', '*freedom*', '*justice*' and '*human rights*' are but a few of the words that were appropriated by both sides for polemical and often disinformational purposes. While the United States identified itself with the word freedom, the Soviets did the same for peace; justice came in two incommensurable forms, economic (Soviet) and political (US). The condemnation of human rights violations were used as a continuation of the Cold War by other means; attacks were only made within the other superpower's sphere of influence. But then, as the superpowers were beset by both internal and external challenges, and their hegemonic hold over words continued to erode, one term became the primary battlefield of the diplomatic discourse. And since, as Havel claims, 'all important events in the real world – whether admirable or monstrous – are always spearheaded in the realm of words', we must pay heed to this new term.[34]

We (just who is left out by this inclusionary 'we' will be discussed below) are entering, constructing, or perhaps just wishfully invoking a 'new world order'. President Bush is often given credit for coining the term, and certainly his liturgical use of it has cleansed the term of its embarrassing roots in Hitler's *Die nueue Ordnung*, an altogether different kind of architecture for the world. First given a trial run by the President at a news conference in August 1990, 'the new world order' was inaugurated in a television speech to the American public in September and then formally inducted into the diplomatic lexicon at a February address to the Economic Club of New York. In both cases, it was used to describe an American-led, United Nations-backed system of collective security.

Surely Soviet diplomacy deserves, at the very least, equal credit. In a September 1987 *Pravda* article (its less than felicitous title of 'The Reality and Guarantees of a Secure World' perhaps explains its lack of media coverage in the West), Gorbachev presented all the ingredients for the new world order that President Bush would later popularise: a wider role for international law, a stronger United Nation's Security Council and new global institutions to deal with environmental, military and economic challenges. Moreover, Gorbachev used the term itself (or at least as Tass translated it) well before President Bush did, informing a gathering of the World Media Association in Moscow in April 1990 that, 'We are only at the beginning of the process of shaping a new world order'. In September 1990, Deputy Foreign Minister Vladimir Petrovsky, opening the General Assembly debate at the United Nations, declared that it was time to 'get down to creative work on shaping a new world order'.

However, before we can begin to assess the import of the 'new' world order, we must have some understanding of what happened to the 'old' one. We have seen how order is most important (more so than freedom, justice, or even peace) when it is in the process of breaking down or when it has already vanished, especially when empires fall apart. Reform in the Soviet Union, the Soviet withdrawal from Afghanistan, Chernobyl, freedom and democracy movements in East and Central Europe, removal of intermediate nuclear forces from Europe, the reunification of Germany, the relative decline of the American economic hegemony, even the growing hole in the ozone layer, were just a few of the important transformative events of the late 1980s that challenged the Cold War norms and ideological practices of superpower diplomacy. Significant as these changes are, it took more than these changes to alter the order upon which international politics rests.

Like all things new and revolutionary in the international system, it was to be a war that gave birth to a new world order. Neo-Hegelians like Francis Fukuyama, late of the State Department, would like us to believe that it was the era of the Cold War, marked by the demise of communism and the triumph of liberalism, that ushered in what was to be a peaceful, if boring, new world order. However, in August 1990, Saddam Hussein rudely reminded the world that there remained many unhappy people who were willing to exploit and struggle against the colonial legacy of the states-system. What we were to witness in the events leading up to the Gulf War was not a Hegelian 'end of history', but an 'irony of history'. The French social critic Jean Baudrillard anticipated the deadly irony that might result when the superpowers chose (or, given the politico-economic costs, had no choice but) to end the dialectic of superpower deterrence:

> Like the real, warfare will no longer have any place – except precisely if the nuclear powers are successful in de-escalation and manage to define new spaces for warfare. If military power, at the cost of de-escalating this marvelously practical madness to the second power, reestablishes a setting for warfare, a confined space that is in fact human, then weapons will regain their use value and their exchange value: it will again be possible to *exchange warfare.*[35]

When the Soviet Union decided to back the United Nations sanctions rather than Iraq, its erstwhile regional ally, and then to back down when President Bush rejected Gorbachev's peace proposal, an 'exchange of warfare' was guaranteed. This is not said to affix blame on either one party or another, to endorse a balance of power politics or to wax nostalgic over the loss of the nuclear balance of terror. It is simply said to identify a watershed moment for diplomacy. Bipolar power and truths gave way to a new universalism. Note: *uni*-versalism, not *multi*-versalism, for much as the 'invisible hand' of *laissez-faire* economics performed in nineteenth century British foreign policy, the universalist ideals of collective security, liberal economics and politics, and international law promote (the more critical might say 'cloak') the unipolar power of the United States. This is evidenced by the suzerainty that the US exercised over the coalition in military planning and warfighting in the Gulf, but also in its broader strategic aims, unchanged since 1945, of maintaining its position as the global military power.

In the 1990 Gulf War, words lost out not just to war, but to images. We were treated to videos of smart bombs unerringly hitting their targets, cruise missiles seemingly reading street signs as they made their way down the boulevards of Baghdad and a victorious ground war of one hundred hours that ended in fewer coalition casualties (no one was keeping track of the Iraqi dead) than in the exercises leading up to it. Of course, images can cut both ways: the video images of the lone Chinese student staring down a column of tanks in Tiananmen Square, the foot of an unknown Lithuanian sticking out from under the tread of a Soviet tank in Vilnius or a group of Los Angeles policemen beating a black motorist work against the power of those prone to use violence before dialogue. But in the Gulf War, the tightly controlled, aesthetically clean images presented an appealing portrait of military technology solving intractable diplomatic problems. This was a war whose victory was measured in the field of perceptions not political reality and played out in the method and metaphor of gaming, not the history and horror of warring. In short, when a war of spectacle manages to displace the spectacle of war, diplomacy risks becoming the last rather than the first option of the superpower.

As the 'new world order' fails to live up to its lofty ideals, nostalgia for old order, or worse, calls for a rebirth of an authoritarian 'new order' could result. As ethnic chauvinism, religious fundamentalism and economic turmoil grow (or less abstractly, as Azerbs and Armenians, Kurds and Iraqis, Serbs and Croats, Israelis and Palestinians reach for each others' throats), I am sure that in both Washington and Moscow there are diplomats who nod at the Islamic saying. 'Better 100 years of tyranny than one day of anarchy'. We will, I predict, be seeing much more of our friend, 'balkanisation'.

In the harsh terms of *Realpolitik*, the end of the Cold War simply means the end of the Soviet Union as a counter-balance to American hegemony. To believe that this is a guarantee of peace and stability requires a leap of faith or a dose of patriotism that is unsuited for the critical thinker. However, the one lesson that should have been learned from the events of 1989 is that international relations cannot be reduced to the will to power. Events might have been triggered by a relative decline in the superpowers, but in the end it was the will to *truth* that changed the map of Europe and the Soviet Union.

Therein lies the greatest challenge for diplomacy. Perhaps at one time, 'one God, one Pope, one Emperor' was necessary and sufficient for the world. But the fragmentation of the diplomatic culture, the diffusion of power along new political and national fault lines and the continued level of uneven economic development means that the selfsure monologues of the past are no longer feasible – even if they are dressed up in the universalist rhetoric of the new world order. Nor can we depend on or believe in some spiritual, dialectical or scientific processes to overcome or transcend the domestic and international divisions, ambiguities and uncertainties that mark current international politics. Rather, we must find a way to live with cultural difference. Indeed, our very existence depends upon it: not (necessarily) in some apocalyptic sense, but in our deep ontological need for otherness in the formation of sovereignty and construction order.

The insights of two artists might help us better understand this. The first is Billy Bragg, a Scottish singer who is difficult to categorise: saying that he performs solo with an electric guitar and sings militant songs does not really say enough. His June 1990 performance in Prague, during the week of the first democratic elections in Czechoslovakia since 1948, captured a moment and some disturbing truths about the consolidation of identity through the constitution of difference.[36] Unlike the widely covered Joan Biaz concert the night before at the immense Peoples Sports Palace (piously dull) or the Paul Simon concert two nights later in the packed Old Town Square (drearily sentimental), Havel was not there. Bragg performed in the Zimin stadium, a grand old name for an old hockey rink, in front of anarchists, punks, young army recruits still in uniforms, and yes, there were genuine hippies. The performance was brilliant as were the asides, and the crowd showed its appreciation by maintaining the kind of Mazurka-St. Vitus-Rokenrol frenzy throughout. But it was the first of three encores that shifted the mood. He brought a Czech up on stage for a word-by-word translation of the first song – the *Internationale*. After about ten minutes of this half, the audience began whistling (booing) and shouting things like, 'Communism is Nazism', A few bottles were thrown. Unfazed, he launched into the next song, 'dedicated to the ironic soul of the Czechs': 'Waiting for the Great Leap Forward'. And for the finale, Bragg was joined by Michael Stripe from R.E.M. and Natalie Merchant from the

10,000 Maniacs, to sing 'The One I Love'. In the space of three songs, Bragg forced his audience to confront the political difference that had constituted their identities, the ironic difference that allowed them to escape those fixed identities and the free identity cultivated from a care for difference. And most of the audience had a good time at the same time.

The second insight comes from the great Soviet linguist and literary theorist, Mikhail Bakhtin. Although writing about the work of Dostoevsky, he best plots the link between word and world orders, showing us how diplomacy (like language itself) must negotiate the meaning and values that constitute identity out of difference. He provides what I believe should be the first and last entry for a travelogue of the new world order:

> To be means to be for the other, and through him, for oneself. Man has no internal sovereign territory; he is all and always on the boundary; looking within himself, he looks *in the eyes of the other* or *through the eyes of the other* ... I cannot do without the other; I cannot become myself without the other; I must find myself in the other, finding the other in me.[37]

Notes

This essay is a revision of a paper originally given at the American Political Science Meeting in San Francisco, CA in September 1990. I would like to thank Jean Bethke Elshtain, Kiaran Honderich, and Adam Lerner for their criticisms and John Ruggie for his poetic response.

1 This essay attempts at a conceptual and historical level of what Edward Said skillfully achieves at a theoretical and literary level in his essay, 'Traveling Theory', *Raritan* (Winter 1982), pp. 41–67, sharing with it some of the way stations that Said sets out in an introductory paragraph:

> There is, however, a discernible and recurrent pattern to the movement itself, three or four stages common to the way any theory or idea travels. First, there is a point of origin, or what seems like one, a set of initial circumstance in which the idea came to birth or entered discourse; second, there is a distance traversed, a passage through the pressure of various contexts as the idea moves from an earlier point to another time and place where it will come into a new prominence; third, there is a set of conditions – call them conditions of acceptance, or as an inevitable part of acceptance, resistance – which then confronts the transplanted theory or idea, making possible its introduction or toleration, however alien it might appear to be; fourth, the now fully (or partly) accommodated (or incorporated) idea is to some extent transformed by its new uses, its new position in a new time and place.

2 It will take another story to explain the rise in discursive power of historical concepts like 'finlandisation', 'ottomanisation' and 'medievalisation', and the decline of political concepts like communism, imperialism, capitalism, etc.

3 *Utopias* afford consolation: although they have no real locality, there is nevertheless a fantastic, untroubled region in which they are able to unfold; they open up cities with vast avenues, superbly planted gardens, countries where life is easy, even though the road to them is chimerical. *Heterotopias* are disturbing, probably because they secretly

undermine language, because they make it impossible to name this and that, because they shatter or tangle common names, because they destroy 'syntax' in advance, and not only the syntax with which we construct sentences, but also that less apparent syntax which causes words and things (next to and also opposite one another) to 'hold together'.

See M. Foucault, *The Order of Things: An Archaeology of the Human Sciences* (New York: Vintage Books, 1973), p. xviii. For an anthropological appreciation of the power of a regenerative disorder, see J. Clifford, *The Predicament of Culture* (Cambridge, MA: Harvard University Press, 1988), p. 141.

4 There is another possibility, that the origins of the new 'endism' lie less in ideology or a philosophy of history than in a new sedentariness. In our perpetual desire to avoid the evidence that there is no first principle of truth, final meaning, redemptive end – only eternal recurrence – we mistake our own inertia amidst rapid change for arrival. In his essay 'The Last Vehicle', Paul Virilio argues that the speed of travel and information gives an additional priority of arrival over departure, of distance/speed over distance/time and likens the phenomenon to the Tokyo swimming 'pools' in which the swimmer in a greatly reduced space swims vigorously against a current and stays stationary. See P. Virilio, 'The Last Vehicle', in D. Kamper and C. Wulf (eds), *Looking Back on the End of the World* (New York: Semiotext(e), 1989), pp. 106–19. A more familiar example would be the step machines, now so popular that people wait for elevators in health clubs to wait in line to use the machines. And for an elaboration on the appeal of 'endism', see my 'Reply to Rosenau: Fathers (and sons), Mother Courage (and her children), and the End of the World (as we know it)', Roundtable on Superpower Scholars, 1990 International Studies Association Meeting, forthcoming in J. Rosenau (ed.), *International Relations Voices: Dialogues of a Discipline in Flux* (Boulder, CO: Westview Press).

5 See J. Der Derian, 'The (S)pace of International Relations: Simulation, Surveillance, and Speed', *International Studies Quarterly* (September, 1990), pp. 295–310; and J. Rosenau, ibid.

6 See E. Said, *Orientalism* (Harmondsworth: Penguin, 1985), who quotes Hugh of St. Victor: 'The man who finds his homeland sweet is still a tender beginner; he to whom every soil is as his native one is already strong; but he is perfect to whom the entire world is as a foreign land'. Richard Ashley and Rob Walker endorse a similar intellectual position of exile in the introduction to the *International Studies Quarterly* Special Issue, 'Speaking the Language of Exile: Dissidence in International Studies', (September 1990), pp. 259–68.

7 The reply of the poet Robert Graves to an interviewer's question, 'Why had he not been able to make people understand the nature of the First World War when home on leave?' makes the point simply and eloquently: 'You couldn't: you can't communicate noise. Noise never stopped for one moment – ever', *Listener*, 15 July 1971, p. 74, quoted by P. Fussell, *The Great War and Modern Memory* (New York: Open University Press, 1975), p. 170.

8 This does not mean there is a video-tape to accompany the essay. 'Videographic' is used to convey the technical characteristics (time-shifting, channel-switching, erasability of the archive, etc.) as well as the philosophical implications (the intuitive and simulacral power of movement, as external physical reality, and image, as internal psychic consciousness) of the latest and most pervasive form of representation. The term draws on Henri Bergson's notions of 'movement-image' and 'cinematographic' illusion, first presented in *Matter and Memory* (1896) and *Creative Evolution* (1907) and reinterpreted by Gilles Deleuze in *Cinema I: The Movement Image* (Minneapolis, MN: University of Minnesota Press, 1986) and *Bergsonism* (New York: Zone Books, 1988). For an assortment of views on the philosophical impact of videography, see the special issue of *Block* (Autumn 1988) on 'The Work of Art in the Electronic Age'; Jean Baudrillard, *The Evil Demon of Images* (Sydney: Power Institute of Fine Arts, 1987); and Michael Shapiro, 'Strategic Discourse/Discursive Strategy: the Representation of "Security Policy" in the Video Age', *International Studies Quarterly* (September 1990), pp. 327–40.

9   See H. Bull, *The Anarchical Society: A Study of Order in World Politics* (New York: Columbia University Press, 1977), pp. 4–5. I believe Benedict Kingsbury first applied the idea of a 'trialectic' working in Bull's analysis in a presentation at the 1986 British International Studies Association paper.

10   For an a very persuasive account of the influence of Augustine on classical international theory, see Roger Ivan Epp, *Power Politics and the Civitas Terrena: The Augustinian Sources of Anglo-American Thought in International Relations* (Ph.D. Dissertation, Queen's University Belfast, June 1990).

11   For the first account of the modern world order, see A.H.L. Heeren, *Manual of the History of the Political System of Europe and its Colonies* (London: Bohn, 1873), p. x. This was written in response to what he perceived as the demise of that very order. In the Preface to the 1809 first edition, Heeren stated that, 'while the author was thus employed in elaborating the history of the European states system, he himself saw it overthrown in most essential parts … Its history was in fact written upon its ruins'.

12   See K. Deutsch and J. Singer, 'Multipolar Power Systems and International Stability', *World Politics* (Vol. 16, No. 3, 1964), pp. 390–406; K. Waltz, 'International Structure: National Force and the Balance of World Power', *Journal of International Affairs* (Vol. 21, No. 2, 1967), pp. 215–31; R. Keohane, 'The Theory of Hegemonic Stability and Changes in International Economic Regimes, 1967–1977,' in O. Holsti, et al. (eds.), *Changes in the International System* (Boulder, CO: Westview, 1980); and A. Watson, 'Systems of States', *Review of International Studies* (Vol. 16, 1990), pp. 99–109.

13   Saddam Hussein has temporarily given the US foreign policy a purpose and identity again, but the personalities and issues (despite the hyperbolic and historically specious identification of Hussein with Hitler and Kuwait with Czechoslovakia) lack the necessary grandeur to become a sustainable global threat.

14   See C. Bohlen, 'A Glasnost Nightmare: The News is all Bad', *New York Times*, 18 August 1990.

15   See P. Kennedy, *The Rise and Fall of the Great Powers* (New York: Random House, 1987); R. Gilpin, *War and Change in World Politics* (Cambridge: Cambridge University Press, 1981); and R. Gilpin, *The Political Economy of International Relations* (Princeton, NJ: Princeton University Press, 1987).

16   Foucault, *op. cit.,* in note 3, pp. xv–xxiv.

17   Ibid., p. xx.

18   Ibid.

19   Ibid.

20   This does smell of relativism, even nihilism. For those who consider relativism or nihilism a graver danger to the international society than totalitarian truths, I would recommend large doses of Kundera. Outside of Nietzsche, the best short statement on the subject comes from the French literary critic, Maurice Blanchot, 'The Limits of Nihilism', in D. Allison (ed.), *The New Nietzsche* (Boston, MA: MIT Press, 1985), p. 122:

> Here, then, is a first approach to Nihilism: it is not an individual experience or a philosophical doctrine, nor is it a fatal light cast over human nature, ctenally vowed to nothingness. Rather, Nihilism is an event achieved in history, and yet it is like a shedding off of history, a moulting period, when history changes its direction and is indicated by a negative trait: that values no longer have value by themselves. There is also a positive trait: for the first time the horizon is infinitely opened to knowledge – 'All is permitted'.

21   I realise the historical specificity of this claim as well, but if we measure the success of Italian (in the nineteenth century) and German unification (1848–1871), as well as

the current process of reunification against the failure of pan-Slavism, pan-Arabism, pan-Africanism, pan-shi'ism, etc., then I believe the claim is a valid one.

22 In an Oxford University lecture, Hedley Bull stated that the leading theorist of nationalism in the nineteenth century, Giuseppe Mazzini, also believed that there was a finite number of nations seeking liberation.

23 For an exhaustive account of the pre- and inter-war ethnic conflicts of Europe, see Elie Kedourie, *Nationalism* (London: Hutchinson, 1961), pp. 118–31.

24 L. Trotsky, *The War and the International* (Wellawatee: Wesley Press, 1971), p. 34.

25 L. Trotsky, *The First Five Years of the Communist International.*

26 There is some evidence to suggest that the appropriation was direct and nearly coterminous: one source claims that Woodrow Wilson had asked the publisher for the proofs of Trotsky's 1914 pamphlet in which he advocated self-determination, democratic principles and an end to secret diplomacy. See the preface to Trosky, *op.cit.,* in note 24.

27 R.W. Seton-Watson, 'The Danubian Problem', *International Affairs* (September–October 1934).

28 Roland Barthes puts it much better in the Preface to Sade, *Fourier, Loyola* (New York: Hill and Wang, 1976), p. 10:

> The social intervention of a text (not necessarily achieved at the time the text appears) is measured not by the popularity of its audience or by the fidelity of the socioeconomic reflection it contains or projects to a few eager sociologists, but rather by the violence that enables it to exceed the laws that a society, an ideology, a philosophy establishes for themselves in order to agree among themselves in a fine surge of historical intelligibility. This excess is called: writing.

29 For example, William Ivin's quote, 'The nineteenth century began by believing that what was reasonable was true, and it would end up by believing that what it was a photograph of was true'. See William M. Ivins, Jr., *Prints and Visual Communications* (1953), quoted by Andy Grundberg, 'Ask It No Questions: The Camera Can Lie', *New York Times*, 12 August 1990.

30 'We must not delude ourselves. Iraq's invasion was more than a military attack on tiny Kuwait; it was a ruthless assault on the very essence of international order and civilized ideals.' George Bush, Address to the Veterans of Foreign Wars, *New York Times,* 20 August 1990.

31 A comparison of the reaction to the 1923 crisis between France and Germany over the Ruhr, a vital coal producing region, might be edifying.

32 The use of this term and much of my analysis of it comes from an Oxford University lecture that Hedley Bull gave on the subject, much of it a dissection of the work of Joseph Nye and Robert Keohane, which he categorised as 'neo-idealist'.

33 V. Havel, 'Words on Words', *The New York Review of Books,* 18 January 1990.

34 Ibid.

35 J. Baudrillard, *Fatal Strategies,* in M. Poster (ed.), *Jean Baudrillard: Selected Writings* (Stanford, CA: Stanford University Press, 1988), p. 191.

36 I borrow the phrasing on identity/difference from William Connolly.

37 M. Bakhtin, *The Problems of Dostoevsky's Politics*, (trans.), C. Emerson (Minneaplos, MN: University of Minnesota Press, 1984) pp. 311–12.

7   Cyberwar, video games, and the Gulf War syndrome

Source: *Antidiplomacy: Spies, Terror, Speed and War* (Cambridge, MA and Oxford, UK, 1992), pp. 173–202. [JDD]

> Let us take a limited example, and compare the war machine and the State apparatus in the context of the theory of games.
>
> Gilles Deleuze and Felix Guattari, *Nomadology: The War Machine*

This is not a final chapter; it does not conclude. It happens to come at the end of a book and at the beginning of a "new world order," which is sufficient reason to apply the theoretical claim of this book – that new technostrategic, antidiplomatic forces in international relations require a poststructuralist approach – to the first, and surely not the last, late modern war.

Let me stress – in case the "excess of writing" is not emphatic enough – the word "approach": not "analysis," "system," "methodology," or "model," but an "approach," which recognizes the impossibility of pure congruence of thought and object, and yet draws the self into the event. Social scientific theory can act as a proxy in war, as did organization and systems theory in Vietnam, to distance the observer from the secondary reality of war, the killing of another human, in the name of studying the primary purpose, to vanquish the enemy. A poststructuralist approach closes the distance to death, asking first before any other question, how is my own identity implicated in a study of the killing of others? This is not to take up an a priori pacifist or belligerent position, but to understand fully the forces in a de-territorialized, hyper-mediated, late modern war already at work to *fix* that position before one has even begun to consider it. During the war, as the level of killing became inversely proportional to the level of knowing the Other, I tried to disturb that position. This chapter is the unfinished result.

Mind games

> Do we not feel the breath of empty space?
>
> F. Nietzsche, *The Gay Science*

BC – Before Cyberspace – our leaders read books during world crises. Much has been made of the fact that during the Cuban Missile Crisis John Kennedy was heavily influenced by Barbara Tuchman's *Guns of August*. In his memoirs of the event, Kennedy's brother Robert claims that the President's decision-making was tempered at critical moments by Tuchman's account of how Europe stumbled into the First World War.[1] In the midst of the Persian Gulf War I wondered what George Bush was reading: after watching George Bush, Saddam Hussein, and even a note-taking journalist watch CNN, I stopped wondering and watching, and started reading (mainly Oswald Spengler's *The Decline of the West*) and writing again.[2]

With this war, cyberspace came out of the research labs and into our living rooms. The written word lost out to the video of a bomb that did not need books to be smart; to cruise missiles that read the signs of Baghdad's streets better than most of us read the signs of the war; to a hyperreal Gulfspeak that "attrited" all critics who clung to the archaic notion that words meant what they said and said what they meant. The result is that the majority of Americans – not just the President – had neither the time nor the ability to read, write, or even reflect effectively about the war. For six weeks and one hundred hours we were drawn into the most powerful cyberspace yet created, a technically reproduced world-text that seemed to have no author or reader, just enthusiastic participants and passive viewers. This is not to reify or deify some new technological force in our society. But it is to recognize the possibility that we have become so estranged from the empty space left by the decline of American hegemony and the end of the Soviet threat that we eagerly found in cyberspace what we could no longer find in the new global disorder – comfort and security in a superior technostrategy.[3]

But do not misread me: this chapter is not a literacy campaign, a neo-Luddite attack on new technologies, or an exercise in cyber-bashing. I am merely offering a cautionary tale, of how the technical preparation, execution, and reproduction of the Gulf War created a new virtual – and consensual – reality: the first *cyberwar*, in the sense of a technologically generated, televisually linked, and strategically gamed form of violence that dominated the formulation as well as the representation of US policy in the Gulf. In name only, cyberspace had its origins in science fiction: its historical beginnings and technological innovations are clearly military (from the primitive link flight simulators of the 1940s to the ultra-modern S1MNET-D facilities in Fort Knox, Kentucky), and now its widest civilian application has been by the media, continuing the Gulf War by the most technical and immediate means. Yet clearly it is science fiction that alerted us to the dangers of cyberspace, and now popular culture that drives the message home.[4]

Indeed, popular journalism seems much more attuned to the phenomenon than academic critics. Consider, for instance, these two assessments of the Gulf War:

> The trouble is that order is a 19th century term that suggests Metternichian arrangements of large, heavy, somewhat static entities. History in the late 20th century seems to belong more to chaos theory and particle physics and fractals – it moves by bizarre accelerations and illogics, by deconstructions and bursts of light.[5]

and:

> It will not suffice to do extended textual readings of Pentagon briefings or
> Hussein's speeches. One must also know something about American culture,
> Iraqi history, etc. The whole deconstructive line of solipsism is obviously
> worthless or worse in this case. Are we talking about a discourse or are we
> talking about a war?[6]

When *Time* magazine (the first quote) begins to read like a critical theorist, and
a critical theorist (the second quote) begins to read like *Time*, one begins to suspect
that not only the Iraqi Republican Guard was out-flanked in the Six Weeks and
One Hundred Hours War. Like old generals the anti-war movement fought the
last war, while popular journalism and popular culture represented a new war
of speed, surveillance, and spectacle – a "pop" war ready-made for the video
arcade. As the critics of the war hunkered down for a long war and high US
body counts, the rest of America climbed aboard the accelerating, solipsistic,
deconstructive war machine. In effect, the "New" Left fought a disastrous war of
position, constructing ideologically sound bunkers of facts and history while the
"New" World Order fought a highly successful war of maneuver, enfilading the
horrors and ugly truths of war with high-speed visuals and a high-tech aesthetics
of destruction.[7]

The modernist school of criticism ignored the new phenomenon of cyberwar
and carried on with the important task of building an edifice of facts unobfuscated
by false consciousness and disinformation, à la Chomsky ("Just take a look at
the logic of the situation as it is evolving in the Gulf").[8] But efforts to construct
a critical *and* universal counter-memory were handily isolated as anti-American
and dismissed as Utopian. Just as a foreign implant is set upon by antibodies,
the "radical" lessons of the Vietnam war and the Cold War not only suffered
pathological rejection but became the perverse justification for a hot, curative war
("By God, we've kicked the Vietnam Syndrome once and for all," said George
Bush the morning after).

An alternative, late-modern tactic against total war was to war on totality itself,
to delegitimize *all* sovereign truths based on class, nationalist, or internationalist
metanarratives, à la Lyotard ("we have paid a high enough price for the nostalgia
of the whole and the one").[9] Let me once again put my cards on the table: this is the
strategy of this chapter, as it was for the presentations that I made at teach-ins and
conferences on the war. Contrary to the claims of some of the New Left, I found
neither quietism nor conservatism but activism and imaginative criticism coming
from deconstructionist, feminist, literary and cultural critics with a bad (po-mo)
attitude who organized and participated in anti-war events. To be sure, the attitude
comes with a highly advertised side-effect: there is no absolute guarantee that
a new pragmatic basis for justice and truth – rather than an infinite regress of
language-games and textual free-play – will result from political encounters. But
better strategically to play with apt critiques of the powerful new forces unleashed
by cyberwar than to hold positions with antiquated tactics and nostalgic unities.

As was proven by the accelerated pace of this war, to overcome someday is already a day too late.

All critics of the war, however, were caught (with apologies to the Rolling Stones) between Iraq and a hard place, between the history of a civilization and its sanctioned destruction, between the new Hitler in the bunker and Bush at the helm of the New World Order. From the start patriotic reflexes, journalistic practices, and presidential politics worked to sublate this difference into synthetic moral ends: naked aggression must be stopped, a nation-state's sovereignty restored, and a new regional peace constructed. Translated: We must war for peace. Vindication came in the aftermath: roughly 100,000 Iraqi military dead minus precisely 266 US dead equals victory. What was left for the critic? Only the less decidable *after-image*, the still unfinished product of the war between matter and perception that would determine the dominant memory of this conflict.[10]

Here we might learn a lesson from the military: let the target determine the strategy. The most powerful objectives of a post-war, anti-war movement must be the instant after-image, the war that was technically reproduced on the screen between the events and on. This site of perceptions was immediately targeted by the state and the war machine to provide what the economy no longer can: the foundation for a resurgent American hegemony. What was it that made the image so irresistible, and the after-image so resistant to criticism? Conversely – and inevitably – what new foundations will be produced by resistance to it?

I believe that these questions of position and maneuver, of theoretical bunkers and critical de-bunking, require a mix of modern and late-modern armaments. This chapter is a cross-border operation, violating the territorial principle of non-intervention that delimits both the theory and the system of international relations. Hence my use of still photographs of moving images, the crude black and white alienation from a living color war, and the play of agonistic video games, to reveal what scientific procedures of causality cannot: how an immaterial conflict was given such serious substance through a war of simulations. In my targeting of the after-images of war I aim to transgress disciplinary boundaries and at the risk of regressing with multiple representations. But this is, I believe, the only means by which the critical theorist might approximate and expropriate the language, video, and war games of the strategists of a late-modern war.

Where better to begin and end than with the first and last *shot* of the Six Weeks and One Hundred Hours War: the night bombing of Baghdad and the night liberation of Kuwait City, reproduced by television cameras equipped with night-vision technology and transmitted in real-time by portable satellite link-ups. The grainy, ghostly green images of the beginning and the end of the war stick. They seem more real, more authentic than all the packaged images that were sandwiched in between. Call it the new *video vert:* a powerful combination of the latest technology, the lowest quality image, the highest representation of reality. It reproduced a twisted Manichean truth: light – a tracer bullet, a secondary explosion, a flaring match – is danger; darkness – by camouflage, stealth, the night – is safety. Correspondents quickly learned that in wartime it was better to dwell and deal in the latter. The motto "We own the night" (originating in the seventh

Infantry Division) became the slogan of the war and the reality of its coverage. When obfuscating military briefers and mandatory "security reviews" extended the ownership beyond the battlefield, the press and the public, already blind-sided in Grenada and neutered by the pool system in Panama, eagerly seized on the hi-tech prosthetics offered by the military. Words became filler between images produced by gun-cameras using night-vision or infrared that cut through the darkness to find and destroy targets lit up by lasers or radiating heat. Perhaps if a few journalists had known what all night-fighters know, that night-vision degrades depth perception, then the appeal of the videographic reproduction of the war might have been diminished. But from the beginning moving images took out fixed words, and photocentrism triumphed over logocentrism. The combination of surgical video strikes and information carpet bombing worked.

To be sure, for every public viewing of the war there was also a private perspective. I for one missed the collective moment of first images. Circling over Chicago's O'Hare airport when the bombs started to fall on Baghdad, I first heard of the war on the radio of a taxi. The first mediation came from the driver, who had not said a word during the trip until he turned around to give me change. In the thickest of Russian accents he said: "They told me it would be over in three weeks – I was in Afghanistan for three years."

The discordance of the first word with first images lasted right up to the last day of the war. Fast forward to the end of the Ground War, to the televised victory briefing by "the chief architect of the ground war," better known as the commander of allied forces in the Persian Gulf, General Norman Schwarzkopf. Working his charts full of red and blue markers, he presented the keystone to the building that Norm built.

> I think this is probably one of the most important parts of the entire briefing I could talk about. As you know, very early on, we took out the Iraqi Air force. We knew that he had very limited reconnaissance means. And therefore, when we took out his air force, for all intents and purposes, we took out his ability to see what we were doing down here in Saudi Arabia. Once we had taken out his eyes, we did what could best be described as the Hail Mary play in football.[11]

Stretching from the first days of the Six Weeks War to the last minutes of the One Hundred Hours War, these two simple statements by two disparate "mud soldiers" frame the architecture of cyberwar. The construction and destruction of the enemy other would be:

- measured in time not territory
- prosecuted in the field of perception not politics
- authenticated by technical reproduction not material referents
- played out in the method and metaphor of gaming, not the history and horror of warring.

In short, a cyberwar of chrono-strategic simulations for pax Americana II.

Video games

> It is precisely when it appears most truthful, most faithful and most in conformity to reality that the image is most diabolical ...
>
> Jean Baudrillard, *The Evil Demon of Images*

The simulated nature of the war was apparent at the outset, but took on a critical consciousness when ABC correspondent Cokie Roberts asked General Schwarzkopf, via satellite link-up, to comment on it:

Roberts: You see a building in a sight – it looks more like a video game than anything else. Is there any sort of danger that we don't have any sense of the horrors of war – that it's all a game?

Schwarzkopf: You didn't see me treating it like a game. And you didn't see me laughing and joking while it was going on. There are human lives being lost, and at this stage of the game [*sic*] this is not a time for frivolity on the part of anybody.

In the space of a single sound-bite Schwarzkopf reveals the inability of the military and the public to maintain the distinction between warring and gaming in the age of video. We were enchanted by the magic of applied technologies, seduced and then numbed by the arcane language of the military briefers, satisfied by the image of every bomb finding its predestined target. The wizards in desert khaki came out from behind the curtain only long enough to prove their claims on TV screens, to have us follow their fingers and the arcs of the bombs to the truth. At some moments – the most powerful moments – the link between sign and signifier went into Möbius-strip contortions, as when we saw what the nose-cone of a smart bomb saw as it rode a laser beam to its target, making its fundamental truth claim not in a flash of illumination but in the emptiness of a dark screen. William Tecumseh Sherman meets Jean-Paul Sartre in a sick syllogism: since war is hell and hell is others, bomb the others into nothingness.

Schwarzkopf's difficulty in separating war from its gaming is understandable. Back in October 1990 Schwarzkopf revealed in a *USA Today* interview that the US military was ready for war in the Gulf over a year before, because two years earlier they had learned that Iraq "had run computer simulations and war games for the invasion of Kuwait."[12] He did not mention – it is doubtful that he did not know – that the software for the invasion simulations was supplied by an American company. In the same interview Schwarzkopf stated that he programs "possible conflicts with Iraq on computers almost daily." Having been previously stationed in Florida as head of the US Central Command – at the time a "paper" army without troops, tanks, or aircraft of its own – he had already earned a reputation as an adept simulation jockey.

In fact, Schwarzkopf sponsored a highly significant computer-simulated command post exercise which was played in July 1990 under the code name of Exercise Internal Look '90.[13] According to a Central Command news release issued at the time, "command and control elements from all branches of the military will be responding to real-world scenarios similar to those they might be expected to confront within the Central Command AOR consisting of the Horn of Africa, the Middle East and Southwest Asia." When Kuwait was invaded by Iraq, the war game specialist who put Exercise Internal Look together, Lt General Yeosock, was moved from fighting "real-world scenarios" in Florida to taking command of all ground troops – except for the special forces under Schwarzkopf – in Saudi Arabia. The war gamers went to cyberwar.

War games

> How much better is this amiable miniature than the Real Thing! Here is a homeopathic remedy for the imaginative strategist. Here is the premeditation, the thrill, the strain of accumulating victory or disaster – and no smashed or sanguinary bodies, no shattered fine buildings, nor devastated countrysides, no petty cruelties, none of that awful universal boredom and embitterment, that tiresome delay or stoppage or embarrassment of every gracious, bold, sweet, and charming thing, that we who are old enough to remember a real modern war know to be the reality of belligerence.
>
> H. G. Wells, *Little Wars*

What Cokie Roberts and her journalist cohort had only begun to suspect, that the line between war and game was becoming irrevocably blurred, was common knowledge in the realm of popular culture – and down at the mall video arcade. Two films stand out as genre setters. The first is the late seventies, post-Watergate, pre-*Challenger* film *Capricorn One* based on the premise that the military and NASA would – and had the technological capability to – simulate a successful Mars landing after the "real" mission aborts. The second is the Reagan-era film *War Games*, a story of a young hacker who taps into an Air Force computer simulation and nearly triggers a nuclear war between the superpowers.

There are as well the ubiquitous video games. "Tank," one of the earliest and most popular, was a stripped-down version of an Army training simulation. Its graphics and sound effects now seem neolithic when compared to the simulations available for home computers. To name a few: from Navy simulations there is *Harpoon, Das Boot Submarine, Wolf Pack*, and *Silent Service II;* from the Air Force, *Secret Weapons of the Luftwaffe, Nighthawk*, F–117A *Stealth Fighter, A–10 Tank Killer*, and *F–15 Strike Eagle.* Judging from a sampling of "non-military" (narrowly defined) games, the future appears to be neo-medieval, inter-galactic, and eco-sensitive in nature. A keyboard jockey can choose among: *Warlord, Crusades of the Dark Savant, Dusk of the Gods, The Two Towers, Hyperspeed, Rules of Engagement, Armada 2525*, and *Xenocide;* and for those seeking eco-simulations, *Populous, Civilization, SimCity, SimEarth*, and *Global Dilemma.*

Of course, simulations – *the continuation of war by means of verisimilitude –* have a much longer and much wider history.[14] Prussia used *Kriegsspiel* ("war play") before their victories over the Austrians at Sadowa in 1866 and the French in 1870; Major William Livermore of the Army Corp of Engineers joined William McCarry Little and Rear Admiral Alfred Thayer Mahan at the Naval War College to set up the United States' first modern system of war gaming in 1889; and Japan made effective use of war games to achieve an unexpected victory over the Russians in 1904. Moreover, there is something of a law of uneven development at work in the field of war gaming. For instance, the Afghanistan resistance combined highly flexible sand box and toy soldier war games with hi-tech weaponry like the Stinger to defeat their far superior enemy, the Soviets – who, one could argue, were fighting the wrong war game. In this same period the US military research labs began to develop simulations for smart ground and air weapons-systems that operated without pilots or drivers, taking us further along the slide into sci-fi war gaming and robotic war-fighting.

Logos wars

> What entered Megavac 6-v as a mere *logos* would emerge for the TV lenses and mikes to capture in the guise of a pronouncement, one which nobody in his right mind – especially if encapsulated subsurface for fifteen years – would doubt.
>
> P. K. Dick, *The Penultimate Truth*

The most powerful dialogue of the TV cyberwar – if measured by the allocation of image resources – was the war of logos. It speaks for itself, but a genealogy helps us to understand how the media construct their own simulation cyberspace. Just around the time that Schwarzkopf wrapped up Operation Internal Look, the networks began to prepare their own war simulations. Most of them booked time at National Video on 42nd Street in New York City, a cutting edge video graphics lab known for its production of MTV logos.

NBC, cash-poor, went for the see-cubed-eye look, no fancy graphics, of the image of the news set as command and control HQ of *America at War.* CBS and ABC revealed the limits of simulated imagination when they replayed *Time-Newsweek's* simultaneous cover story of Bruce Springsteen: both came up with *Showdown in the Gulf.* ABC had the distinguishing underlay of a radar screen, but soon jettisoned the High Noon theme for a simpler logo, *The Gulf War.*

But it was ABC's *Primetime Live* and CNN's *Headline News* that would be the front runners if there were an Emmy award in the special category of War Graphics. *Primetime* went for the Cruise Missile simulation. In successive frames the missile goes through some remarkable ground-hugging, terrain-following maneuvers, and just as it looms large – as the viewer realizes who the target is – *The Gulf War* logo and Diane Sawyer fade in. CNN, riding a high ratings wave, took the most innovative approach. It used as an underlay the military video of the week, and as the smart-bomb or missile homed in on the logo, *War in the Gulf*, block-lettered in fascistoid orange and black, rotated in over the destroyed target. Scary enough to hope that hologram TV never arrives.

To be sure, a more significant logomachy was in evidence at the less graphic, more subtextual level of semantics. Before the first shot was fired, language was enlisted in the war effort. Until we had sufficient troops in place "to deter and defend," the hostages in Iraq were cautiously referred to as "detainees." In late fall, after 250,000 more troops had arrived, George Bush shifted linguistic gears and called for the "unconditional surrender" of Saddam Hussein. When reminded shortly afterwards that this demand exceeded the requirements of the UN resolutions, he replied "that's just semantics." By February, with the air war going well and ground exercises for invasion taking place daily, General Colin Powell stripped US strategy toward Iraq of any nuance or ambiguity: "First we're going to cut it off, and then we're going to kill it."

But enough has been said about the systematic corruption of language by military practices. It quickly became a commonplace that truth was the first casualty of war.[15] But this was a slogan in need of a theory, of how truth is *produced* in the continuation of war by other, simulated means.

Theory games

In short, by opposition to the philosophico-juridical discourse which addresses the problem of sovereignty and law, this discourse which deciphers the permanence of war in our society is essentially a discourse where the truth functions as a weapon for a partisan victory, a discourse sombrely critical and at the same time intensely mythical.

Michel Foucault, *Résumé de Cours* (Collège de France, 1975–76)

Writing for the *Frankfurter Zeitung* in 1926, marveling at the immense popularity of the newly constructed picture palaces in Berlin, Siegfried Kracauer chronicled the emergence of a "cult of distraction." It is in these new "optical fairylands," he wrote, that "distraction – which is meaningful only as improvisation, as reflection of the uncontrolled anarchy of the world – is festooned with drapes and forced back into a unity that no longer exists."[16] In Kracauer's view the picture palaces served as a kind of Hegelian asylum from Weimar disorder, ornate spaces where the alienated Berliner could seek reunification through a new, totally imaginary, cinematic (yet organic) *Zeitgeist*.

Taking his first measure of film production, Walter Benjamin wrote in his 1936 essay, "The Work of Art in the Age of Mechanical Reproduction," of the corresponding loss of authenticity, aura, and uniqueness in art. Benjamin believed mechanically reproduced art, especially film, to be especially useful to if not generative of Fascism, for the rendering of politics into aesthetics had the advantage of mobilizing the masses for war without endangering traditional property relations. He quotes the Futurist Marinetti to chilling effect:

War is beautiful because it establishes man's dominion over the subjugated machinery by means of gas masks, terrifying megaphones, flame throwers, and small tanks. War is beautiful because it initiates the dreamt-of metalization of the human body ... War is beautiful because it creates new architecture, like that of the big tanks, the geometrical formation flights, the smoke spirals from burning villages, and many others ... Poets and artists of Futurism! ... remember these principles of an aesthetics of war so that your struggle for a new literature and a new graphic art ... may be illumined by them![17]

Surveying the rise of a consumer society, anticipating the failure of conventional, radical, *spatial* politics in 1968, Guy Debord, editor of the journal *Internationale Situationniste*, opened his book *Society of the Spectacle* with a provocative claim: "In societies where modern conditions of production prevail, all of life presents itself as an immense accumulation of *spectacles.* Everything that was directly lived has moved away into a representation." At the root of this new form of representation was the specialization of power, with spectacle coming to speak for all other forms of power, becoming in effect "the diplomatic representation of hierarchic society to itself, where all other expression is banned."[18]

After analyzing the political economy of the sign and visiting Disneyland, Jean Baudrillard, the French master of edifying hyperbole, notified the inhabitants of advanced mediacracies that they were no longer distracted by the technical reproduction of reality, or alienated and repressed by their overconsumption of its spectacular representation. Unable to recover the "original" and seduced by the simulation, they had lost the ability to distinguish between the model and the real: "Abstraction today is no longer that of the map, the double, the mirror or the concept. Simulation is no longer that of a territory, a referential being or a substance. It is the generation by models of a real without origin or reality: a hyperreal."[19]

Paul Virilio's project to politicize the violence of speed, reviewed in chapter 6, illuminates the events of the Gulf War. Indeed, his account of the linking of the logistics of military perception and surveillance to the use of video in warfare anticipates many of the representational practices of the first "real" cyberwar. The last years of the Vietnam War foreshadowed the hi-tech display that bedazzled the public and befuddled the critics. Recounting a Vietnam pilot's story of how he was sent back repeatedly to bomb the same target, just to please the photo interpreters, Virilio remarks: "People used to die for a coat of arms, an image on a pennant or flag; now they died to improve the sharpness of a film. War has finally become the third dimension of cinema."[20] In the Gulf War, the necessity of speed and capabilities of new technologies made video "the third dimension of war." This was confirmed by Colonel Tom Diamond, commander of Combat Photography in the Gulf:

> In the field, any time and anywhere in the world, we could take a photo, point a portable satellite cellular phone system, and send images as fast as we could take them, so that the time between when the event occurred and when we could get it to the national command authority was reduced to forty seconds transmission time. Now we were helping decision-making. We can make a difference in a battle.[21]

The consequence, foreseen by Virilio, is that in modern warfare, as the aim of battle shifts from territorial, economic, and material gains to immaterial, perceptual fields, the spectacle of war is displaced by the war of spectacle.

This is not to claim that in the Gulf War the truth was collaterally damaged as some incidental victim of a necessary violence. The truth – in the Nietzschean sense of "illusions whose illusionary nature has been forgotten"[22] – was constructed out of and authorized by spectacular, videographic, cyberspatial simulations of war.

Game wars

> I hate to say it, but once we got rolling it was like a training exercise with live people running around. Our training exercises are a lot harder.
>
>   Captain Kelvin Davis (after American troops captured Kuwait City)[23]

We were primed for this war. Simulations had infiltrated into every area of our lives, in the form of news (re)creations, video games, flight simulators, police interrogations, crime reenactments, and, of course, media war games. Six days into the invasion of Kuwait Tom Brokaw on *NBC News* staged a war game with former US officials standing in for Hussein and Bush. It ended with "Hussein" threatening to "send home body bags every day" and Brokaw warning us that "before too long we may have the real thing." In October 1990 Ted Koppel on ABC *Nightline* weighed in with his "Ides of November" war game. This war game differed from previous ones presented by Koppel (two on terrorism and one on nuclear war): there was not a pasha from Kissinger Associates in sight, and the talking-heads barely had equal time with the video simulations. Constructed and narrated by the authors of the book *A Quick and Dirty Guide to War* and the wargame *Arabian Nightmare*, the program featured stock clips of war exercises, computer simulations of bombing runs, many maps, and a day-by-day pull-down menu of escalating events. The post-game commentary (known in the ranks as a "hot wash-up") was conducted by two military analysts armed with pointers, James Blackwell and Harry Summers, Jr. They ended with a split decision – and a final cautionary note that "no plan survives contact with the enemy."

By the first ultimatum in January, the representational boundary between the simulation and the "real thing" was as attenuated as a fuse wire. War continued by means of simulation in its media representation as well as through its military preparation. Before the ground war the US conducted a series of highly publicized war exercises, the largest being an amphibious Marine landing called "Imminent Thunder." In fact, no landing crafts were used because the seas were running too high. Nonetheless, the simulation "worked." When the allied troops reached Kuwait City they found in a school house used by the Iraqi military as a headquarters a room-sized model of the city. On a sand tableau there were, to scale, wooden ships, buildings, roads, barbed wire – and all the Iraqi guns pointing toward the sea attack that never came.

For those still retaining some control over their television sets during the war, there were illuminating intertexts to be seen on non-news channels. My local movie channel ran a Eastwood–Norris–Bronson–Stallone series to coincide with the real thing. But it was in switching over to the *Fox* station that I discovered the hoariness of the simulation theme when an episode on war games appeared on *Star Trek* – not on *The Next Generation* with its virtual reality holodeck, but on the toggle-switch and blinking-lights original. Called the "Ultimate Computer," the episode pits Kirk against the "M5 Multitronic Unit" in a war game. After the crew is removed from the ship, Kirk is told by the creator of the computer "to sit back and let the machine do the work." As machine proves more adept than man, Kirk goes through several existential crises; that is, until the machine mistakes the game for war and destroys another ship by unfriendly fire. Angered and impassioned, Kirk stops soliloquizing and regains control of the ship by convincing the computer that by killing humans it has violated its primary purpose of protecting them.

It took Captain Kirk to pull the plug on the national security doublespeak of the Gulf War: we kill to live. Ironically, it was Peter Arnett reporting not from Baghdad but from Ben Tre, Vietnam, who had recorded an earlier instance of that naked mechanical truth: "it became necessary to destroy the town to save it."

Science fiction offers other insights that journalism and lagging social science cannot provide. In the movie *Aliens*, when the Colonial Marines are being buffeted as they enter the atmosphere of the planet where the unknown awaits them, Ripley (Sigourney Weaver) asks the obviously anxious Lieutenant how many combat drops this is for him. He replies "Thirty-eight," pauses, and then adds "- Simulated." He quickly proves incapable of responding to situations that do not follow his simulation training. Both Kirk and Ripley should have been on the bridge of the USS *Vincennes* on 3 July 1988 when its radar operator and the tactical information coordinator mistook – after nine months' simulation training with computer tapes – an Iranian Airbus for an attacking Iranian F-14 and shot it down.

Even more useful is the intertext of strategic power and popular culture provided by Tom Clancy. Clancy's first bestseller, the *Red October*, has a hyperbolic blurb from former President Reagan. His second novel, *Red Storm Rising*, a thinly fictionalized mosaic of NATO war games, was authoritatively cited by Vice President Quayle in a foreign policy speech to prove that the US needs an anti-satellite capability. In his third, *Patriot Games*, Clancy magnifies the threat of terrorism to prove that state counter-terrorism works, a view endorsed by Secretary of Defense Weinberger in a laudatory review of the book for the *Wall Street Journal* – which was then reprinted in the Pentagon's *Current News* for the edification of the 7,000-odd Defense and State Department officials who make up its readership. His fourth novel, *The Cardinal of the Kremlin*, in which Clancy plots the plight of a mole in the Kremlin, affirms the need to reconstruct the impermeable borders of the sovereign state with Star Wars. His fifth novel, *Clear and Present Danger*, opens with a quote from Pascal, "Law, without force, is impotent," and closes with the unrepressed message that the US will be impotent if it does not use – prudently of course – its technological edge in night-vision, GBU-15 laser-guided bombs, and satellite surveillance against drug cartels.

Taken together, Clancy's novels anticipate the strategic simulations that filled our screens during the Gulf War. Jammed with technical detail and seductive ordinance, devoid of recognizable human characters, and obliquely linked to historical events, they act, from the Cold War to the Drug War, as free-floating intertexts for saving the reality principle of the national security state: namely, that the sovereign state's boundaries, like those between fiction and fact, simulation and reality, can once again be made impermeable to any threat posed by this year's model of evil.

There is of course a fundamental and ultimate difference between war and its game: people die in wars. But this distinction also suffered erosion in the Gulf War. If we subtract the number of Coalition soldiers (the Iraqi dead never "figured") killed or injured by "friendly fire" and accidents, there were more casualties in the war exercises leading up to "G-Day" (the beginning of the ground war) than during the war itself.

End game

> This is a war universe. War all the time. That is its nature. There may be other universes based on all sorts of other principles, but ours seems to be based on war and games. All games are basically hostile. Winners and losers. We see them all around us: the winners and the losers. The losers can oftentimes become winners, and the winners can very easily become losers.
>
> William S. Burroughs, *The War Universe*

Was this a just war, or just a game? For the winners, both: for the losers, neither. To suggest as I have done in this video-essay that it could be both or neither simultaneously is to challenge the US effort to construct out of this war a new world order based on one truth, one winner, one loser. To offer as I do nothing in its place but a Nietzschean "breath of empty space" is to risk those familiar charges of relativism, or worse, nihilism. But this cyberwar is the *result* of the US effort to fill and to delimit the new void left by the end of the Cold War, the end of the old order, the "end of history." While the architecture of the new world order may be built of simulations, its hegemonic effect will be all too real for those nation-states that have little to gain from it.

Of course, the post-war historical possibilities are not so clear-cut, a nihilistic case of either all or nothing being permitted. But "the end of the Cold War" – that is, the end of the Soviet Union as a counterbalance to American hegemony – *has* re-opened a space – as illustrated above by Baudrillard's quote – for *both* war and peace."[24]

But Baudrillard does not get it quite right. If anything has been proven by this war, it is that simulations now rule not only in the war without warring of nuclear deterrence, but also in the post-war warring of the present.[25] It was never in question that the US would win the military conflict. But it did not win a "war," in the conventional sense of destroying a reciprocating enemy. What "war," then, did the US win? A cyberwar of simulations. First the pre-war simulation, Operation Internal Look 90, which defeated the Made in America Iraqi simulation for the invasion of Kuwait. Second, the war game of AirLand Battle which defeated an Iraqi army that resembled the game's intended enemy, the Warsaw Pact, in hyperreality only. Third, the war of spectacle, which defeated the spectacle of war on the battlefield of videographic reproduction. And fourth, the post-war after-simulation of Vietnam, which defeated an earlier defeat by assimilating Vietnam's history and lessons into the victory of the Gulf War.

Have we, "by God," kicked the Vietnam Syndrome in Iraq? I am sure that as long as there is a great global gap in power and wealth there will be tenacious under-dogs with a taste for grey flannel – and more swift kicks to follow. But the score is being kept. Almost 25 years ago at the Bertrand Russell War Crimes Tribunal in Stockholm, Jean-Paul Sartre rendered a verdict that bears remembering:

> It [the US] is guilty, by plotting, misrepresenting, lying and self-deceiving, of becoming more deeply committed every instant, despite the lessons of this unique and intolerable experience, to a course which is leading it to the point of no return. It is guilty, self-confessedly, of knowingly carrying on this *cautionary* war to make genocide a challenge and a threat to peoples everywhere. We have seen that one of the features of total war was a constant growth in the number and speed of means of transport; since 1914, war can no longer remain localized, it must spread through the world. Today the process is becoming intensified; the links of the *One World*, this universe upon which the United States wishes to impose its hegemony, are ever closer.[26]

Perhaps it is time to diagnose a "Gulf War Syndrome," the pathological need to construct and destroy a lesser enemy to restore and revive US hegemony in the "new world order." Iraq served its purpose well as the enemy other which redefined our own essential identities: but it was the other enemy, the new threat posed by the de-territorialization of the state and a disintegrating bipolar order that required the violent reconstitution of new monological truths.

The new disorder requires a commensurate de-territorialization of theory. We can no longer reconstitute a single site of meaning or reconstruct some neo-Kantian cosmopolitan community, that would require a moment of enlight-ened universal certainty that has long past. Nor can we depend on or believe in some spiritual, dialectical or scientific process to overcome or transcend the domestic and international divisions, ambiguities, and uncertainties that mark the antidiplomatic age of spies, terror, speed, and war. Rather, we must find a way to live with and recognize the very necessity of difference, the need to assert heterogeneity before we can even begin to understand our role in the lives of others. This is not yet another Utopian scheme to take us out of the "real" world, but a practical strategy to live with less anxiety, insecurity, and fear in what Mikhail Bakhtin described as "exotopy," and Michel Foucault as "heterotopia." These environments make possible broader realms of freedom where the heteroglossia of language bespeaks a heterodoxy in world politics, where radical otherness in international relations is assumed and asserted in dialogue, not repressed and expressed in violence.

The strategy from the first to this last chapter, to construct a counter-simulation to war and antidiplomacy, is in the end only one of many beginnings towards one of many heterotopias. Not an endgame, then, but a game with no end, no winners, no losers, no rules but one: play in peace.

Notes

1 See Robert F. Kennedy, *Thirteen Days: A Memoir of the Cuban Missile Crisis* (New York: W. W. Norton, 1971), pp. 40, 105.
2 The inspiration for the chapter comes mainly from the powerful (and admittedly, orientalist) opening to Spengler's chapter on "Problems of the Arabian Culture." See Oswald Spengler, *The Decline of the West* (New York: Viking, 1927), vol. II, chapter 7, pp. 186–9:

> In a rock-stratum are embedded crystals of a mineral. Clefts and cracks occur, water filters in, and the crystals are gradually washed out so that in due course only their hollow mould remains. Then come volcanic outbursts which explode the mountain; molten masses pour in, stiffen, and crystallize out in their turn. But these are not free to do so in their own special forms. They must fill up the spaces that they find available. Thus there arise distorted forms, crystals whose inner structure contradicts their external shape, stones of one kind presenting the appearance of stones of another kind. The mineralogists call this phenomenon Pseudomorphosis.
>
> By the term "historical pseudomorphosis" I propose to designate those cases in which an older alien Culture lies so massively over the land that a young Culture, born in this land, cannot get its breath and fails not only to achieve pure and specific expression-forms, but also to develop fully its own self-consciousness. All that wells up from the depths of the young soul is cast in the old moulds, young feelings stiffen in senile works, and instead of rearing itself up in its own creative power, it can only hate the distant power with a hate that grows to be monstrous.

3 This begs the onto-theological question that I raised in the Introduction (see p. 4).
4 The most comprehensive definition of cyberspace that I have heard comes from Michael Benedikt (professor of architecture at University of Texas at Austin), taken from the *Collected Abstracts from the First Conference on Cyberspace*:

> Cyberspace is a globally net-worked, computer-sustained, computer-accessed, and computer-generated, multi-dimensional, artificial, or "virtual" reality. In this world, onto which every computer screen is a window, actual geographical distance is irrelevant. Objects seen or heard are neither physical nor, necessarily, presentations of physical objects, but are rather – in form, character, and action – made up of data, of pure information. This information is derived in part from the operation of the natural, physical world, but is derived primarily from the immense traffic of symbolic information, images, sounds, and people, that constitute human enterprise in science, art, business, and culture.

See also Philip K. Dick, *The Simulacra* (New York: Ace Books, 1964) and *The Penultimate Truth* (London: Triad, 1984); and the book in which William Gibson coined the term "cyberspace," *The Neuromancer* (New York, Ace Books, 1984).

5 Lance Morrow, *Time*, 18 March 1991, p. 21.
6 Todd Gitlin, "Theory in Wartime: An Interview with Todd Gitlin," *Linguafranca*, February 1991, p. 26. Another position of radical critics that I witnessed at various teach-ins and in journals like *Z* and *Lies in Our Times* was to attribute the war to a plan by the US and Israel to lure Saddam Hussein into Kuwait and then spring the trap. This was such a perfect conspiracy that these same people were predicting as late as January US casualties in the several thousands, a protracted war, and mass resistance. When this scenario failed to develop they fell back on a conspiracy theory to explain why the war was so popular, so swift, and so total – and why their theoretical analysis was so far off.
7 See P. Virilio, *Bunker Archéologie* (Paris: Centre Georges Pompidou, 1975), p. 42, on the dangers of "bunker architecture": "Le bunker est devenu un mythe, à la fois présent et absent, présent comme objet de répulsion pour une architecture civile transparente et ouverte, absent dans la mesure où l'essential de la nouvelle forteress est ailleurs, sous nos pied, désormais invisible."
8 See N. Chomsky, *On Gulf Policy* (Westfield, New Jersey: Open Magazine Series, 1991), p. 1.
9 See J.-F. Lyotard, *The Postmodern Condition: A Report on Knowledge* (Minneapolis, MN: University of Minnesota Press, 1984), pp. 81–2.
10 See Henri Bergson, *Matter and Memory* (New York: Zone Books, 1988), and Walter Benjamin, "On Some Motifs in Baudelaire," in *Illuminations* (New York: Schocken, 1969).
11 *New York Times*, 28 February 1991, p. A8. I doubt whether we will ever see a "Norm knows football" advertisement (Bo can rest easy), for the only "Hail Mary" play of the war was Iraq's desperate long bomb SCUD attacks. Chris Hables Gray (from the University of California at Santa Cruz) later pointed out to me that the appropriate football analogy for the Allies' strategy was using the air game to set up the ground game, followed by a fake up the middle and power sweep around the left side. And most of the military officers that I interviewed referred to it as the "end-run" play.
12 *USA Today*, 8 October 1990, p. 8.
13 See J. Der Derian, "War Games May Prove Deadly," *Newsday*, 9 December 1990.
14 See T. Allen, *War Games: The Secret World of the Creators, Players, and Policy Makers Rehearsing World War III Today* (New York: McGraw Hill, 1987); and P. Perla, *The Art of WarGaming* (Annapolis, MD: Naval Institute Press, 1990).
15 Since journalists were as reluctant to credit the quote as they were keen to repeat it, it should be noted that Senator Hiram Johnson said in 1917 that "[T]he first casualty when war comes is truth." Of course, the corruption of language is not always intentional. For instance, General Colin Powell's reference to the US forces as "Desert Storm Troopers" during a victory – speech before a convention of Veterans of Foreign Wars went unreported, probably because it was considered to be an innocent slip.
16 See F. Kracauer, "Cult of Distraction: On Berlin's Picture Palaces," trans, by T. Y. Levin, in *New German Critique*, 40 (Winter, 1987), p. 95; and Kracauer's *Das Ornament der Masse* (Frankfurt a.M.: Suhrkamp Verlag, 1963), forthcoming as *The Mass Ornament*, translated and edited by T. Y. Levin (Cambridge, MA: Harvard University Press).
17 See W. Benjamin, "The Work of Art in the Age of Mechanical Reproduction," *Illuminations*, edited by H. Arendt (New York: Schocken, 1969), pp. 241–2.
18 See G. Debord, *Society of the Spectacle* (Detroit: Black and Red, 1983), no. 1, pp. 1 and 23. In a more recent work, Debord persuasively – and somewhat despairingly – argues that the society of the spectacle retains its representational power in current times: see *Commentaires sur la Société du Spectacle* (Paris: Editions Gerard Lebovici, 1988).
19 See J. Baudrillard, *Simulations* (New York: Semiotext(e), 1983), p. 2. The original French version, *Simulacres et Simulation* (Paris: Editions Galilée, 1981), has more on the simulacral nature of violence in cinema. See in particular his readings of *China Syndrome, Barry Lyndon, Chinatown*, and *Apocalypse Now*, pp. 69–91.

20 See *War and Cinema*, p. 85.

21 Tom Diamond, "Combat Camera," *Arts and Entertainment* documentary, 22 November 1991.

22 Paul de Man, *The Resistance to Theory* (Minneapolis, MN: University of Minnesota Press), p. 67.

23 *Newsweek*, 11 March 1991, p. 17.

24 See "Fatal Strategies," in *Jean Baudrillard: Selected Writings*, edited by M. Poster (Stanford, CA: Stanford University Press, 1988), p. 191, quoted in chapter 7:

> Like the real, warfare will no longer have any place – except precisely if the nuclear powers are successful in de-escalation and manage to define new spaces for warfare. If military power, at the cost of de-escalating this marvelously practical madness to the second power, reestablishes a setting for warfare, a confined space that is in fact human, then weapons will regain their use value and their exchange value: it will again be possible *to exchange warfare.*

Backing up Baudrillard's claim is a recent report that the Pentagon has produced, in secret, seven "illustrative" post-Cold-War "war scenarios," all of them potential regional conflicts except for the last, which envisions the rise of an "REGT" (Resurgent/Emergent Global Threat) by the year 2001. See Patrick Tyler, *New York Times*, 17 February 1992, p. A8.

8 ACT IV: Fathers (and sons), Mother Courage (and her children), and the dog, the cave, and the beef

Source: *Global Voices: Dialogues in International Relations*, ed. James N. Rosenau (Boulder, CO and Oxford, UK: Westview Press, 1993), pp. 83–96.

Prologue

Ever since the Sophists ran circles around Socrates, Plato and his followers have sought revenge by staging the triumph of reason over rhetoric. The practice persists: Nearly all students of political science cut their theory teeth on the Socratic dialogues, a practice that gives them a good start in the Western tradition of what the French literary critic Jacques Derrida referred to in *Of Grammatology* as *logocentrism*, the metaphysical conceit that the spoken word is closer to reality, always prior to and therefore more authentic than the written word.[1] But it is in a later work, *The Post Card: From Socrates to Freud and Beyond*, that, inspired by his discovery in Oxford's Bodleian Library of a postcard reproduction of a thirteenth-century illustration that shows Socrates at a table *writing* while Plato directs him from behind, Derrida addressed the distance between the writer, speaker, and reader. He reverses the modernist proclivity for the instructive dialogue in a deconstructive reading of what he calls "[P]lato's dream: To make Socrates write, and to make him write what he wants, his last command, *his will. To make* him write what he wants by letting him write what he wants."[2] In effect, Derrida sends the postcard back to the original writer, stamped address unknown, message untraceable, destiny forgotten.

Honored by Jim Rosenau's invitation to engage in a dialogue on the state of international relations theory—and weary of the polemics that only serve to sustain the exclusionary borders of that fictionally sovereign state—I weighed the epistemological costs of an *ersatz* dialogue against the didactic (not to mention, of course, careerist) opportunities of a response. Not all considerations were intellectual or professional. Would it be possible to respond in kind—and still be kind? Were the differences in approach too wide, the prehistory of the debate too nasty?

Let us first look at the most obvious difference, that between generations. Rosenau's dual intention in Act I—with a dialogue form as his vehicle—is to preempt criticisms that "superpower" social science cannot avoid a national bias by taking some critical first steps toward the formation of a more global yet less hegemonic social science. Here Rosenau certainly deserves credit for rejecting the easier form of polemical solo in favor of a more difficult—and much more entertaining—pas de deux between a "Senior American Scholar" and a "Junior U.S. or Foreign Scholar." (Should we assume from the difference in titles that Junior, state-bounded, will someday grow into Senior's continental status?) Rosenau might be surprised to learn in this regard that he shares common ground with the "mature" Foucault, who in one of his final interviews eloquently stated his preference for dialogue over against polemic:

> Questions and answers depend on a game—a game that is at once pleasant and difficult—in which each of the two partners takes pains to use only the rights given him by the other and by the accepted form of the dialogue. The polemicist, on the other hand, proceeds encased in privileges that he possesses in advance and will never agree to question. On principle, he possesses rights authorizing him to wage war and making that struggle a just undertaking; the person he confronts is not a partner in the search for the truth, but an adversary, an enemy who is wrong, who is harmful and whose very existence constitutes a threat. For him, then, the game does not consist of recognizing this person as a subject having the right to speak, but of abolishing him, as the interlocutor, from any possible dialogue; and his final objective will be, not to come as close as possible to a difficult truth, but to bring about the triumph of the just cause he has been manifestly upholding from the beginning.[3]

In intention, at least, Rosenau presents us with a conversation rather than a contest. In execution, however, the exchange between SAR and JUSOFS is a dialogue only in a formal sense, containing all kinds of double-talk and monological reasoning. Neither of Rosenau's characters wins or loses in the conventional sense; nor do they, however, seem to gain or contribute new insights in the exchange. Instead of negotiating their differences, they scuttle sideways, like two crabs relying on first claw and then shell to protect their sovereign territories. They leave the cafeteria with their one-dimensional identities intact, each seeing in the other either a condescending old duffer or an impudent young Turk.

Fine criticisms, but as the elder spokesperson (no ageism or sexism here) would probably say, put up or shut up, which is, of course, yet another arbitrary delimitation of intellectual options—but one nonetheless with a pragmatic, injunctive power. Still, to reply in kind with a "dialogue"—or to rebut with an unkind polemic—would probably only serve to rigidify the extant borders of both IR and world politics. How, then, to open up Rosenau's formative dialogue to a supplementary reading without making deceptive moves to transcend or negate it? The best option, I believe, is to apply the insights of Mikhail Bakhtin's intertextual theory of *dialogism*, which shows how all understanding, like language itself, is a responsive act that depends upon prior discourses as well as anticipating future ones.[4] Since it is through the communicative acts of negotiating meaning and values with others that the self is constituted, identity *requires* difference: "[T]he psyche," says Bakhtin, "enjoys extraterritorial status."[5]

Yet, in world politics, the self clearly "enjoys" territorial and sovereign protection. This can partially be explained by the heightened sense of insecurity and long history of estrangement that have created "deep identities" and a rationalist faith in the state to keep the contingencies of life at bay. These artesian sources of monological, sovereign reasoning in IR, which bubble up just when global dangers threaten to overcome the abilities of the nation-state to control them, induce a self-fulfilling dread and denial of an extraterritorial identity.[6]

In this context, consider first Bakhtin's critique of monologism:

> Ultimately, *monologism* denies that there exists outside of it another consciousness, with the same rights, and capable of responding on an equal footing, another and equal I (*thou*). The monologue is accomplished and deaf to the other's response; it does not await it and does not grant it any *decisive* force. Monologue makes do without the other; that is why to some extent it objectivizes all reality. Monologue pretends to be the *last word*.[7]

And then the last words of Bakhtin, written in 1974:

> There is no first or last discourse, and dialogical context knows no limits (it disappears into an unlimited past and in our unlimited future). Even *past* meanings, that is those that have arisen in the dialogue of past centuries, can never be stable (completed once and for all, finished), they will always change (renewing themselves) in the course of the dialogue's subsequent development, and yet to come. At every moment of the dialogue, there are immense and unlimited masses of forgotten meanings, but, in some subsequent moments, as the dialogue moves forward, they will return to memory and live in renewed form (in a new context). Nothing is absolutely dead: every meaning will celebrate its rebirth.[8]

I believe Bakhtin's distinction provides a particularly apt exposé of what passes for criticism and debate in both Rosenau's dialogue and in the field of IR in general. Many might find fault with Rosenau's dialogue for leaving out particular voices: that of the woman, the third world thinker, the long-wave enthusiast, ad nauseum. In contrast, I (and others who have been lumped together as poststructuralist thinkers) would target Rosenau's construction of opposites— war/peace, male/female, domestic/international, objective/subjective—to define the phenomena and delimit the possibilities of IR. This criticism would also call into question the teleological claims (sometimes explicit but more often implicit) that some spiritual, revolutionary, or scientific process is at work to transcend, overcome, or rationalize these harmful binary oppositions. The aim is to study the powers behind the construction and enforcement of such oppositions and to understand how it is the "space between" rather than the binary units themselves that matter most in IR.[9]

Language, then, is the model: Our efforts to fix the meaning of what something is by establishing what it is not is always already warped by the space between sender and receiver, sign and referent, *langue* (the social code) and *parole* (individual message), author and reader. The heteroglossia of language—the

constant renegotiation of meaning and values that goes on with each utterance—
bespeaks a heterodoxia in world politics where radical alterity should be assumed
and asserted rather than subsumed and repressed. These strategies shift if not
obliterate Rosenau's seemingly natural (that is, necessary) fact-value dichotomy
in which the anguished social scientist seeks to expunge subjective factors from
his objective analysis.

In short, the goal should not and cannot be a single identity or grand theory
for IR, be it in the formation of SAR's global social science or the end result
of JUSOFS' marxoid dialectic. The aim is to live with and recognize the very
necessity of heterogeneity for understanding ourselves and others. Paul de Man,
in his exposition of Bakhtin's principle of *exotopy*, made this point with a high
level of sophistication:

> On the other hand, dialogism also functions … as a principle of radical
> otherness. … [F]ar from aspiring to the telos of a synthesis or a resolution, as
> could be said to be the case in dialectical systems, the function of dialogism is
> to sustain and think through the radical exteriority or heterogeneity of one
> voice with regard to any other … The self-reflexive, autotelic or, if you
> wish, narcissistic structure of form, as a definitional description enclosed with
> specific borderlines, is hereby replaced by an *assertion* of the otherness of the
> other, preliminary to even the possibility of a *recognition* of his otherness.[10]

A dialogical reading of Rosenau raises several questions. Is it possible to imagine
and construct such a dialogue between SAR and JUSOFS in which their identities
are not predetermined or fixed by national, class, or chronological origins external
to the dialogue but constantly interacting and shifting in the interlocutionary space
between the self and the other? Informed by this psychic interdependency, would
such characters be less willing, perhaps even unable, to declare the other persona
non grata in this extraterritorial land? In this move from a metalinguistic concept to
an interdiscursive relationship, does dialogism exceed its function as a metaphor
or formal model and point the way toward a re-formation of IR? Ultimately, the
answer probably depends most on just how jealous each is of the right to the
last word.

What follows is my effort to construct a hybrid dialogue that takes into account
these concerns. Yes, it is overly self-conscious and predictably self-serving; but, as
compensation and consolation, it is always aware—and celebratory—of the always
absent other that evades the enclosure acts of this and other dialogues in IR.

Scene 1 – Fathers (and sons): the formation of orthodoxy in IR

(*A dialogue heard from behind the curtain.*)

"A Nihilist," his father said slowly. "As far as I can judge, that must be a word
derived form the Latin *nihil*—*nothing*, the term must therefore signify a man
who … will admit nothing?"

"Better still, a man who will respect nothing," Paul Petrovich interjected, and then resumed his buttering.

"Who looks at everything critically," Arcady remarked.

"And what is the difference?" his uncle inquired.

"There is a difference. A Nihilist is a man who admits no established authorities, who takes no principles for granted, however much they may be respected."

"Well then? Is that a good thing?" his uncle interrupted.

"That depends on the circumstances, Uncle. It's good in some cases and very bad in others."

(*On stage:*)

FATHERS: So let's get right to the crux of it: You want to send me to the dustbin of history, to disenchant my power over you, to *kill* me.

(AND SONS): You're just like those old generals Marx, Weber, and Freud, always ready to fight the last theory war. This is not about you and me: This is about a late modern condition where ambiguity and contingency, speed and surveillance, spectacle and simulation rule. The worry over theoretical heroes and heroic theories is touching but not very timely.[11]

FATHERS: But then what do we have to talk about?

(AND SONS): Not much.

(*Take two:*)

FATHERS: Let's start again. How do you explain the new interest in theory in IR?

(AND SONS): The easy answer? It's simply a generational anxiety triggered not by the end of history but by its acceleration. What once appeared transparent and predictable has taken on a strange new veneer, simultaneously superficial and opaque. As history conspires to reduce the international relations theorist to the intellectual status of armchair pundit, *decline denial* sets in. You can see it in the schizophrenic split of the traditionalist camp of IR in the United States, with the cynical neo-Machiavellians on one side, feeding on new perceptions of persecution while clinging to the reasonable belief that history will repeat. This of course allows them to recycle ideas and lecture notes one more time before retirement. On the other side, we find the hubristic neo-Hegelians, pumped up with a chauvinist pride that grows before the fall, who have unilaterally declared an end to history, leading some in their ranks to gloat while others wax nostalgic.

FATHERS: And where do you find yourself?

(AND SONS): Trying to think anew about new problems, in spite of and in opposition to the disciplinary conformity that stifles such efforts.

But that conformity seems to be breaking up. I believe that the current proliferation of approaches that we are witnessing matches not just the depth and breadth of new problems but also the loss in a consensus on the best means to measure and map the new spaces of world politics.

FATHERS: But hasn't every generation of scholars viewed their era, their predicament, their theories as the most dangerous, the most turbulent, the most radical?

(AND SONS): I agree—and dissent. To paraphrase R.E.M. …

FATHERS: What?

(AND SONS): My point precisely. Michael Stipe of R.E.M. sings that it is the end of the world—*as we know it.* What this means is that before we can know and, in the act of knowing, reconstruct a "new" world, we face the perpetual task of deconstructing "old" epistemologies: Otherwise, "endism" begets yet another cycle of mythical "originism." This move is fully evidenced in your writings as well as in the recent spate of preferred readings on the decline of U.S. and USSR hegemony. What began as an intellectual attempt to understand the rise and fall of great powers quickly deteriorated into the elevation and denigration of particular scholars and their political sponsors: in other words, a metonymic event, or intellectual simulacrum of decline denial. It all started off as a collegial, indeed, Ivy League event, with Gilpin from Princeton kicking off to Kennedy from Yale who was first tackled by Nye from Harvard. Then play was stopped when Fukuyama from State walked off the field with the ball, declaring an end to the game (and going free-agent to pick up a new million-dollar book contract).

FATHERS: So you see no progress, no hope for a general theory of IR, no better worlds?

(AND SONS): Not now, not when grand theory goes schizo. When the preferred readings of declining hegemonic powers split, distort, and weaken, we *should* expect some pretty bizarre symptoms in the field of IR. But over and against the background noise of dissent, a powerful message can still be heard. It echoes Hegel (but without the irony) when he states in *The Phenomenology of Spirit* that "Happy peoples have no history." Crudely templated to our own experience, this means now that we have won the Cold War (the only meaningful war), it is time—as it was immediately following the two other great conflicts of the twentieth century—for us to settle into a new political as well as epistemological isolationism. But I would argue from the above evidence that the victory celebrations have deafened the most superpowerful scholars to a host of new and urgent messages. In effect, they have unilaterally left the proverbial forest with the falling trees, where the majority of peoples of the world are unhappily making history and yet trying to make sense of all the noise.[12]

FATHERS: (*with increasing exasperation*): But where do *you* stand?

(AND SONS): I suppose somewhere in this constructed space of a false quiet. One can detect the traces of dissonance—generational, cultural, sexual—that run silent, run deep, and never quite break the surface tension of your theory, or for that matter, IR discourse in general. Perhaps they are little noticed or under-debated because they threaten to break the bounds of civil dialogue and further divide the field between those who hear noise and those who hear music, between those who say the party is over and those who say let's party, between those who see tradition as a safe harbor and those who see it as an anchor.

Scene 2 – Mother courage (and her children): re-forming IR?

FATHERS: (*cross-dressed as MOTHER COURAGE*): I think it's about time that we heard some female voices in IR—as long as they don't sound too shrill, or god forbid, too French.[13]

(AND SONS): (*keeping a wary eye out for [HER CHILDREN]*): I'm not sure that it matters what you think. An insurgent matrix of generational and gendered difference has already created pressure from below and outside the discipline. So why rehearse lines that have been better executed by others?[14]

(HER CHILDREN): (*arriving*): Like the threads, Mom. Care to check my papers before I enter this dialogue?

FATHERS: (*dressed-down*): Always trying to provoke me, aren't you?

(HER CHILDREN): Well, I could force my way in, but that's more your style.

FATHERS: A cheap shot.

(HER CHILDREN): Is it? Have you ever looked up "force" in Webster's? The first definition is "to make a person (or animal) do something by force; compel." The second is, simply, "to rape (a woman)." You've got to love those parentheses.

FATHERS: So what's your belabored point?

(HER CHILDREN): Very simple: In international relations, force equals rape. You have nations violated, interfered with in a violent manner. The recurring "rape" of Poland, or the "rape" of Czechoslovakia, are powerful, transhistorical analogues. In international relations (and dictionaries), women (like animals) suffer a parenthetical rape: It happens at the edges of war and colonial conquest and appears only at the fringes of a few classical narratives.[15]

(AND SONS): So boys are bad and girls are good?

(HER CHILDREN): Nice try, but as long as we're the dominant voice in this act, reductio ad absurdum won't cut it. I'm not saying that *all* violence is phallocentric, or that feminist IR should confine itself to such a thesis. I'm just trying to open up for discussion what some in the field consider to be an inappropriate motivation for scholarly research: righteous anger. And here I refer not only to violence against women but the role of phallocentric force against men as well. If you believe that the civilizing march of progress has rendered this an archaic and inappropriate topic for IR, then I suggest you take a look at a video I brought along.

(*The videotape from a prime-time news program opens with a long overhead shot of a Hungarian in freshly de-Stalinized Romania being brutally beaten. A small group of men disperse after the beating, except for one man who lingers and aims a final kick at the supine Hungarians testicles. The dead man doesn't move: Satisfied, the live one moves on. It is a loop video.*)

MOTHER COURAGE: All fine and good, but your anger is just the mirror image of male violence. Where will that get you?

(HER CHILDREN):   Why should I listen to you? Your so-called courage is nothing more than a willingness to accept defeat on the big issues while gaining the petty victories that allow you to survive the Theory Wars. Your cynicism, your numbing of outrage, and your reduction of expectations—you are nothing but a realist *poseur.*

MOTHER COURAGE: "You listen because you know I'm right. Your rage has calmed down already. It was a short one and you'd need a long one. But where would you find it?"[16]

(HER CHILDREN):   There's plenty of injustice to go around.

MOTHER COURAGE: You think that a global anger will re-form a global condition? Take it from an old camp follower: It's better to feed the Theory Wars than to be its sacrificial fodder.

FATHERS (AND SONS):   Speaking of food, where's the beef?

Scene 3 – The dog (and the beef)

(SON) (*approaches the front of the cave*): Who are you?

DOG: Where's the beef?

(SON):   What beef?

DOG: (*barks but does not bite*): Grrrr.

(SON):   There's more on the menu of life than beef. Have you tried tofu?

DOG: Grrrrr.

(SON):   Okay, Okay. What kind of beef? Chuck, flank, filet mignon?

DOG: Beef is beef.

(SON):   Yes and no. In some cultures beef is used as a ritual sacrifice to the gods. And believe it or not, some people use it to signify something of substance, like, say, a research program.

Suddenly a little old lady, Walter Mondale, and Ronald Reagan appear. She begins to hit Mondale over the head with an umbrella for taking her beef patty. Reagan, having no beef, is grinning widely. The DOG goes for the leg of the (SON), who grabs the burger from Mondale and gives it to the DOG. The DOG lets go of the (SON)'s leg and disappears into the cave. The (SON) is left alone in front of the cave. A strange creature approaches.

(SON): Where's the beef?

Epilogue

I would like to end by returning to the theme that set the stage of Rosenau's dialogue: the impact of rapid change on IR. Rosenau deserves much credit: Confronting a strange new world, SAR does not leave the forest for the manicured suburbs of IR. He witnesses the rapidity of change and interprets the turbulence of international relations as intellectual imperatives for opening up the discipline to questions of cultural difference, generational identity, and critical approaches. But I think SAR might be making a possibly fatal error: He seems to be running to catch up to events that are in fact bearing down on him at very high speed.

Let me explain this point with a few outtakes from the remarkable events in Eastern and Central Europe. First, there is the speech by President Vaclav Havel of Czechoslovakia to the joint session of the Congress in February 1990, widely (but not very deeply) covered in the media. His opening remarks highlighted the acceleration of history: "The human face of the world is changing so rapidly that none of the familiar political speedometers are adequate. We playwrights, who have to cram a whole human life or an entire historical era into a two-hour play, can scarcely understand this rapidity ourselves."[17] Curiously, the *New York Times* excerpted the above remarks in the following day's paper but expurgated Havel's completion of the thought: "And if it gives us trouble think of the trouble it must give to political scientists who spend their whole life studying the realm of the probable and have even less experience with the realm of the improbable than the playwrights."[18]

The easy criticism, one that does not break the rationalist (or alliterative) constraints of Rosenau's entitlement, is that superpower scholars are too *slow:* They/we have lost the alacrity and celerity to keep up with events. This observation echoes Carr's concern that historians are failing to evolve in synchronicity with structural changes in world politics. But left out of the equation is an important new force in IR: the acceleration of mass by information.

A second outtake: the circle of Peter Jennings quoting playwright (not yet President) Vaclav Havel who was quoting the scholar-journalist Timothy Garton Ash: "In Poland it took ten years, in Hungary ten months, in East Germany ten weeks; perhaps in Czechoslovakia it will take ten days."[19]

Events in the Soviet Union, Eastern Europe, and Central Europe give eloquent testimony to the pace, improvisation, and intertextuality of change. But the lesson I have drawn from these events clearly exceeds Carr's or Rosenau's prescriptions for understanding rapid change. The real-time representation and transmission of global change are such that running to keep up with events is no longer sufficient. International relations is passing, I believe, from what could be called a classical *Heraclitian dilemma* to a postmodern *Doppler conundrum*. In effect, there is a new game of chicken being played out in IR between the onrushing event and the sometimes recoiling, sometimes advancing observer, who becomes unsure of the source and direction of change: Is it varying according to its relative velocity to the observer? Is it being warped by the mediation of transmission? Is it, in short, objectively knowable, before it is upon or beyond us? Global change is now witnessed as closely and as similarly as the passing of a train is first experienced, and we seem to be simultaneously repelled from and attracted to the waxing and warping of a new power that might just leap the rails.

Paul Virilio, whose work has gone largely unnoticed in IR, has given serious consideration to the political effects of excessive or insufficient speed in our systems of weapons, communications, and decision-making.[20] Virilio believes a revolution has taken place in the regulation of speed: "Space is no longer in geography—it's in electronics. Unity is in the terminals. It's in the instantaneous time of command posts, multi-national headquarters, control towers, etc. ... There is a movement from geo- to chrono-politics: the distribution of territory becomes the distribution of time. The distribution of territory is outmoded, minimal."[21] But where does this leave the superpower scholar? Out of breath or full of bluster? Extraterritorial and patriotic? Bewildered yet cynical? Passive or active?

A third outtake: better to bank on a dated metanarrative than risk a new adventure in story-telling: "But Mr. Norris said when it comes to ideas for screenplays, he's staying away from the fast-moving events in Eastern Europe."[22]

Or, finally, a fourth outtake: from Adam Michnik, a powerful rebuttal and lesson from the Solidarity leader who found the events in Eastern Europe extraordinary and exceptionalist: "A striking characteristic of the totalitarian system is its peculiar coupling of human demoralization and mass depoliticizing. Consequently, battling this system requires a conscious appeal to morality and an inevitable involvement in politics. This is how the singular anti-political political movement emerged in Central and Eastern Europe."[23]

My last words to Rosenau? It is in the very *de-scription* of IR that we might write an antidiplomatic diplomatic dialogue for its future.

Notes

1 See, in particular, Jacques Derrida, *Of Grammatology* (Baltimore, MD: Johns Hopkins University Press, 1977).

2 Jacques Derrida, *The Post Card: From Socrates to Freud and Beyond* (Chicago: Chicago University Press, 1987), p. 52.

3 See "Polemics, Politics, and Problemizations," in P. Rabinow, ed., *The Foucault Reader* (New York: Pantheon Books, 1984), pp. 381–382.

4 For a fuller understanding of how identity is not internally but dialogically constructed in a verbal community, see Mikhail Bakhtin, *The Dialogic Imagination: Four Essays by M. M. Bakhtin*, ed. Michael Holquist (Austin: University of Texas Press, 1981);

Tzvetan Todorov, *Mikhail Bakhtin: The Dialogical Principle* (Minneapolis: University of Minnesota Press, 1984); and Paul de Man, "Dialogue and Dialogism," in *The Resistance to Theory* (Minneapolis: University of Minnesota Press, 1986).

5 Mikhail Bakhtin, *Marxism and the Philosophy of Language* (New York: Seminar Press, 1973), p. 39.

6 See William Connolly, *Identity/Difference: Democratic Negotiation of Political Paradox* (Ithaca and London: Cornell University Press, 1991), for an incisive study of the impact of the "globalization of contingency" on public identities.

7 Mikhail Bakhtin, *Problems of Dostoevsky's Poetics*, trans. Caryl Emerson (Minneapolis: University of Minnesota Press, 1984), p. 318.

8 Mikhail Bakhtin, "Concerning Methodology in the Human Sciences," quoted by Todorov in *Dialogical Principle*, p. 110.

9 This has been an ongoing project, crudely begun in "Hedley Bull and the Idea of a Diplomatic Culture," a paper presented at the annual meeting of the British International Studies Association, 1986; outlined in an introductory essay, "The Boundaries of Knowledge and Power in International Relations," in James Der Derian and Michael Shapiro, eds., *International/Intertextual Relations: Postmodern Readings of World Politics* (Lexington, MA: Lexington Press, 1989), pp. 3–10; and completed in my book, *Antidiplomacy: Spies, Terror, Speed, and War in International Relations* (Oxford: Basil Blackwell, 1992). The dialogical approach has also been adroitly applied to IR by Richard Ashley in his essay, "Living on Border Lines: Man, Poststructuralism, and War," in Der Derian and Shapiro, eds., *International/Intertextual Relations*, pp. 259–322. And R. B. J. Walker has convincingly taken apart the "inside/outside" dichotomy upon which much of IR rests in *Inside/Outside: International Politics as Political Theory* (Cambridge: Cambridge University Press, 1993).

10 De Man, "Dialogue and Dialogism," p. 109.

11 On the appeal of "heroic theory" and "sovereign voices" in IR, see Richard Ashley, "Untying the Sovereign State: A Double Reading of the Anarchy Problematique," *Millennium Journal of International Studies* 17, no. 2 (Summer 1988): 227–262; and Richard Ashley, "Living on Border Lines: Man, Poststructuralism, and War," in James Der Derian and Michael Shapiro, eds., *International/Intertextual Relations: Postmodern Readings of World Politics* (Lexington, MA: Lexington Press, 1989), pp. 259–321.

12 Nancy Huston makes this point in another context, of the exclusion of women from the making of war and war narrative. See "Tales of War and Tears of Women," *Women Studies International Forum* 5, no. 3/4 (1982): 271.

13 For example, Robert Keohane's view that the "postmodern project is a dead-end in the study of international relations—and that it would be disastrous for feminist international relations theory to pursue this path." See "International Relations Theory: Contributions of a Feminist Standpoint," *Millennium* (Summer 1989): 249.

14 On the debate between "French" and "American" varieties of feminism, see, for example, Toril Moi, "Feminism, Postmodernism, and Style: Recent Feminist Criticism in the United States," *Cultural Critique* (Spring 1988): 3–22. On the introduction of feminist theory into IR, see *Millennium* (Winter 1988), a special issue on women in international relations; V. Spike Peterson and Jane Jaquette, conference report, "Clarification and Contestation: Woman, the State and War: What Difference Does Gender Make?" Occasional Paper, Center for International Studies, University of Southern California, Los Angeles, 1989; and Christine Sylvester, "Reconstituting a Gender Eclipsed Dialogue" (Act II of this volume).

15 The remarkable exception is Tzvetan Todorov's *The Conquest of America*, trans. R. Howard (New York: Harper and Row, 1984).

16 From the "real" Mother Courage, just before she sings "The Song of the Great Capitulation." See Bertolt Brecht, *Mother Courage and Her Children*, trans. Eric Bentley (New York: Grove Press, 1963), p. 67.

17 *New York Times*, February 22, 1990.

18 *Congressional Record*, February 22, 1990. Perhaps this helps us to better understand why Havel met with Frank Zappa in Prague before he met with political scientists at Georgetown University.

19 Timothy Garton Ash, "The Revolution of the Magic Lantern," *New York Review of Books*, January 18, 1990, p. 42.

20 See P. Virilio, *Bunker Archeologie* (Paris: Centre de Creation Industrielle, 1975); *L'Insecurite du Territoire* (Paris: Galilee, 1977); *Vitesseet Politique* (Paris: Galilee, 1978) *Speed and Politics: An Essay on Dromology*, trans. M. Polizzotti (New York: Semiotext[e], 1986); *Defense Populaire et Luttes Ecologiques* (Paris: Galilee, 1978); *Esthetique de la Disparition* (Paris: Balland, 1980); *Pure War* (New York: Semiotext[e], 1983); *Guerre et Cinema: Logistique de la Perception* (Paris: Editions de l'Etoile, 1984); *L'espace Critique* (Paris: Christian Bourgeois, 1984); *L'horizon Negatif (Paris:* Galilee, 1984); and *La Machine de Vision* (Paris: Editions Galilee, 1988).

21 P. Virilio, *Pure War*, p. 115.

22 *New York Times*, March 30, 1990.

23 Adam Michnik, "Notes on the Revolution," *New York Times Magazine*, March 11, 1990, p. 44.

9　The value of security

Hobbes, Marx, Nietzsche, and Baudrillard

Source: *The Political Subject of Violence*, ed. G.M. Dillon and David Campbell, Manchester University Press (1993), pp. 94–113.

> Now, what is going to happen to us without
> the Barbarians? They were, those people, after all,
> a kind of solution.
>
> C. P. Cavafy, "Waiting for the Barbarians," in
> *C. P. Cavafy: Selected Poems*, tr. E. Keely and P. Sherrard,
> © 1975 Princeton University Press. Reprinted by permission.

Decentering security

The rapidity of change in the international system, as well as the inability of international theory to make sense of that change, raises this question: Of what value is security? More specifically, just how secure is this preeminent concept of international relations? This evaluation of security invokes interpretive strategies to ask epistemological, ontological, and political questions – questions that all too often are ignored, subordinated, or displaced by the technically biased, narrowly framed question of *what* it takes to achieve security. The goal, then, of this inquiry is to make philosophically problematic that which has been practically axiomatic in international relations. The first step is to ask whether the paramount value of security lies in its abnegation of the insecurity of all values.

No other concept in international relations packs the metaphysical punch, nor commands the disciplinary power of "security." In its name, peoples have alienated their fears, rights and powers to gods, emperors, and most recently, sovereign states, all to protect themselves from the vicissitudes of nature – as well as from other gods, emperors, and sovereign states. In its name, weapons of mass destruction have been developed which have transfigured national interest into a security dilemma based on a suicide pact. And, less often noted in international relations, in its name billions have been made and millions killed while scientific knowledge has been furthered and intellectual dissent muted.

We have inherited an *ontotheology* of security, that is, an *a priori* argument that proves the existence and necessity of only one form of security because there currently happens to be a widespread, metaphysical belief in it. Indeed, within the concept of security lurks the entire history of western metaphysics, which was best described by Derrida "as a series of substitutions of center for center" in a perpetual search for the "transcendental signified."[1] From God to Rational Man, from Empire to Republic, from King to the People – and on occasion in the reverse direction as well, for history is never so linear, never so neat as we would write it – the security of the center has been the shifting site from which the forces of authority, order, and identity philosophically defined and physically kept at bay anarchy, chaos, and difference.

Yet the center, as modern poets and postmodern critics tell us, no longer holds. The demise of a bipolar system, the diffusion of power into new political, national, and economic constellations, the decline of civil society and the rise of the shopping mall, the acceleration of *everything* – transportation, capital and information flows, change itself–have induced a new anxiety. As George Bush repeatedly said – that is, until the 1992 Presidential election went into full swing – "The enemy is unpredictability. The enemy is instability."[2]

One immediate response, the unthinking reaction, is to master this anxiety and to resecure the center by remapping the peripheral threats. In this vein, the Pentagon prepares seven military scenarios for future conflict, ranging from *latino* small-fry to an IdentiKit super-enemy that goes by the generic acronym of REGT ("Reemergent Global Threat"). In the heartlands of America, Toyota sledge-hammering returns as a popular know-nothing distraction. And within the Washington beltway, rogue powers such as North Korea, Iraq, and Libya take on the status of pariah-state and potential video bomb-site for a permanently electioneering elite.

There are also prodromal efforts to shore up the center of the International Relations discipline. In a newly instituted series in the *International Studies Quarterly*, the state of security studies is surveyed so as to refortify its borders.[3] After acknowledging that "the boundaries of intellectual disciplines are permeable," the author proceeds not only to raise the drawbridge but also to caulk every chink in the moat.[4] Recent attempts to broaden the concept of "security" to include such issues as global environmental dangers, disease, and economic and natural disasters endanger the field by threatening "to destroy its intellectual coherence and make it more difficult to devise solutions to any of these important problems."[5] The field is surveyed in the most narrow and parochial way: out of 200-plus works cited, esteemed Third World scholars of strategic studies receive no mention, British and French scholars receive short shrift, and Soviet writers do not make it into the Pantheon at all.

The author of the essay, Stephen Walt, has written one of the better books on alliance systems;[6] here he seems intent on constructing a new alliance within the discipline against "foreign" others, with the "postmodernist" as arch-alien. The tactic is familiar: like many of the neoconservatives who have launched the recent attacks on "political correctness," the "liberals" of international relations make it a habit to base their criticisms on secondary accounts of a category of thinking rather than on a primary engagement with the specific (and often differing) views of the thinkers themselves.[7] In this case, Walt cites IR scholar Robert Keohane on the hazards of "reflectivism," to warn off anyone who by inclination or error might wander into the foreign camp: "As Robert Keohane has noted, until these writers 'have delineated ... a research program and shown ... that it can illuminate important issues in world politics, they will remain on the margins of the field.' "[8] By the end of the essay, one is left with the suspicion that the rapid changes in world politics have triggered a "security crisis" in security studies that requires extensive theoretical damage control.

What if we leave the desire for mastery to the insecure and instead imagine a new dialogue of security, not in the pursuit of a utopian end but in recognition of the world as it is, *other than us*? What might such a dialogue sound like? Any attempt at an answer requires a genealogy: to understand the discursive power of the concept, to remember its forgotten meanings, to assess its economy of use in the present, to reinterpret – and possibly construct through the reinterpretation – a late modern security comfortable with a plurality of centers, multiple meanings, and fluid identities.

The steps I take here in this direction are tentative and preliminary. I first undertake a brief history of the concept itself. Second, I present the "originary" form of security that has so dominated our conception of international relations, the Hobbesian episteme of realism. Third, I consider the impact of two major challenges to the Hobbesian episteme, that of Marx and Nietzsche. And finally, I suggest that Baudrillard provides the best, if most nullifying, analysis of security in late modernity. In short, I retell the story of realism as an historic encounter of fear and danger with power and order that produced four realist forms of security: epistemic, social, interpretive, and hyperreal. To preempt a predictable criticism, I wish to make it clear that I am not in search of an "alternative security." An easy defense is to invoke Heidegger, who declared that "questioning is the piety of thought."[9] Foucault, however, gives the more powerful reason for a genealogy of security:

> I am not looking for an alternative; you can't find the solution of a problem in the solution of another problem raised at another moment by other people. You see, what I want to do is not the history of solutions, and that's the reason why I don't accept the word *alternative*. My point is not that everything is bad, but that everything is dangerous, then we always have something to do.[10]

The hope is that in the interpretation of the most pressing dangers of late modernity we might be able to construct a form of security based on the appreciation and articulation rather than the normalization or extirpation of difference.

A genealogy of the concept

In traditional realist representations of world politics as the struggle for power among states, the will to security is born out of a primal fear, a natural estrangement and a condition of anarchy which diplomacy, international law and the balance of power seek, yet ultimately fail, to mediate.[11] By considering some historical meanings of security that exceed this prevailing view, I wish to suggest "new" possibilities and intelligibilities for security. Admittedly, this brief genealogy is thin on analysis and thick on description. But my intention is to provoke discussion, and to suggest that there is more than a speculative basis for the acceptance of a concept of security that is less coherent and dogmatic, and more open to the historical complexity and contingent nature of international relations.

In its earlier use, "security" traveled down a double-track and, then, somewhere at the turn of the nineteenth century, one track went underground. Conventionally understood, security refers to a condition of being protected, free from danger, safety. This meaning prevailed in the great power diplomacy of the modern states-system. In 1704, the *Act of Security* was passed by the Scottish Parliament, which forbade the ascension of Queen Anne's successor to the throne of Scotland unless the independence of the Scottish kingdom was "secured."[12] In 1781, Gibbon conveyed a specifically geopolitical meaning when he wrote in *The Decline and Fall of the Roman Empire* that "the emperor and his court enjoyed … the security of the marshes and fortifications of Ravenna."[13] Coeval, however, with the evolution of security as a preferred condition of safety was a different connotation, of security as a condition of false or misplaced confidence in one's position. In *Macbeth*, Shakespeare wrote that "Security is Mortals cheefest Enemie."[14] In a 1774 letter, Edmund Burke impugned "The supineness, neglect, and blind security of my friend, in that, and every thing that concerns him."[15] And, as late as 1858, the *Saturday Review* reported that "Every government knew exactly when there was reason for alarm, and when there was excuse for security."[16]

Clearly, the unproblematical essence that is often attached to the term today does not stand up to even a cursory investigation. From its origins, security has had contested meanings, indeed, even contradictory ones. Certainly, the tension of definition is inherent in the elusiveness of the phenomenon it seeks to describe, as well as in the efforts of various users to fix and attach meanings for their own ends. Yet there is something else operating at the discursive level: I believe there is a talismanic *sign* to security that seeks to provide what the *property* of security cannot. The clue is in the numerous citations from sermons found in the *Oxford English Dictionary*. They all use security to convey the second sense, that is, a careless, hubristic, even damnable overconfidence. The excerpts range in dates from the sixteenth to the nineteenth century: "They … were drowned in sinneful security" (1575); "This is a Reflection which … should strike Terror and Amazement into the securest Sinner" (1729); one, claiming that "It is an imaginary immortality which encloses him in sevenfold security, even while he stands upon its very last edge" (1876).[17]

Mediating between these two senses of security lies a third. In the face of a danger, a debt, or an obligation of some kind, one seeks a security, in the form of a pledge, a bond, a surety. From the 1828 *Webster*: "Violent and dangerous men are obliged to give security for their good behavior, or for keeping the peace."[18] In Markby's *Elementary Law* (1874), the word is given a precise financial meaning: "I shall also use the word security to express any transaction between the debtor and creditor by which the performance of such a service (one capable of being represented in money) is secured."[19] A security could also be "represented" in person. Shakespeare again, from *Henry IV*: "He said, sir, you should procure him better Assurance, the Bardole: he wold not take his Bond and yours, he lik'd not the Security."[20]

Hobbes and epistemic realism

> Nor is it enough for the security, which men desire should last all the time of their life, that they be governed, and directed by one judgement, for a limited time; as in one Battle, or one War. For though they obtain a Victory by their unanimous endeavour against a foreign enemy; yet afterwards when either they have no common enemy, or he that by one part is held for an enemy, is by another part held for a friend, they must needs by the difference of their interests dissolve, and fall again into a War amongst themselves.
>
> –Thomas Hobbes, *Leviathan*

For his representation of security, Hobbes preferred the axiomatic style of Euclid and the historical reasoning of Thucydides to the poetic excess of Shakespeare. Both Hobbes and Shakespeare contributed interpretations that exceeded and outlived their contemporary political contexts and historical emulations.[21] However (and unfortunately), since Hobbes rather than Shakespeare enjoys a paradigmatic status in international relations, a short overview of his foundational ideas on realism and security is needed.

In chapter 10 of the *Leviathan*, Hobbes opens with the proposition that "The Power of a Man ... is his present means, to obtain some future apparent Good."[22] Harmless enough, it would seem, until this power is put into relation with other men seeking future goods. Conflict inevitably follows, "because the power of one man resisteth and hindereth the effects of the power of another: power simply is no more, but the excess of the power of one above that of another."[23] A man's power comes to rest on his *eminence*, the margin of power that he is able to exercise over others. The classic formulation follows in chapter 11: "So that in the first place, I put a general inclination of all mankind, a perpetual and restless desire of power after power, that ceaseth onely in Death."[24]

The implications for interpersonal and interstate relations are obvious. Without a common power to constrain this perpetual struggle there can be no common law: "And Convenants, without the Sword, are but Words, and of no strength to secure a man at all."[25] In the state of nature there exists a fundamental imbalance between man's needs and his capacity to satisfy them – with the most basic need being security from a violent and sudden death. To avoid injury from one another and from foreign invasion, men "confer all their power and strength upon one Man, or upon one Assembly of men, that man reduce all their Wills, by plurality of voices, into one Will."[26] The constitution of the Leviathan, the sovereign state, provides for a domestic peace, but at a price. Hobbes's solution for civil war displaces the disposition for a "warre of every man against every man" to the international arena.[27] Out of fear, for gain, or in the pursuit of glory, states will go to war because they can. Like men in the precontractual state of nature, they seek the margin of power that will secure their right of self-preservation – and run up against states acting out of similar needs and desires.

In these passages we can discern the ontotheological foundations of an epistemic realism, in the sense of an ethico-political imperative embedded in the nature of things.[28] The sovereign state and territoriality become the necessary effects of anarchy, contingency, disorder that are assumed to exist *independent* of and *prior* to any rational or linguistic conception of them. In epistemic realism, the search for security through sovereignty is not a political choice but the necessary reaction to an anarchical condition: Order is man-made and good; chaos is natural and evil. Out of self-interest, men must pursue this good and constrain the evil of excessive will through an alienation of individual powers to a superior, indeed supreme, collective power. In short, the security of epistemic realism is ontological, theological and teleological: that is, metaphysical. We shall see, from Marx's and Nietzsche's critiques, the extent to which Hobbesian security and epistemic realism rely on social constructions posing as apodictic truths for their power effects. There is not and never was a "state of nature" or a purely "self-interested man"; there is, however, clearly an abiding fear of violent and premature death that compels men to seek the security found in solidarity. The irony, perhaps even tragedy, is that by constituting the first science of security, Hobbes made a singular contribution to the eventual subversion of the metaphysical foundations of solidarity.

Marx and social realism

> Of course, the measure of the power that I gain for my object over yours needs your recognition in order to become a real power. But our mutual recognition of the mutual power of our objects is a battle in which he conquers who has the more energy, strength, insight and dexterity. If I have enough physical strength I plunder you directly. If the kingdom of physical strength no longer holds sway then we seek to deceive each other, the more dextrous beats the less.
>
> –Karl Marx, Notes on James Mill's *Elements of Political Economy*

Marx took probably the most devastating – and certainly the most politically influential – shot at the metaphysics of Hobbesian security. I will avoid the obvious gesture of recounting how Marx put Hegel – and with him the state – back on material footing, and instead focus on Marx's early polemic against the universalist guise of the state, "On the Jewish Question."[29]

In the essay, Marx traces the split between civil society and the state to the spread of secularized traditions of Judaism and Christianity. In an essentialist if not racialist manner, Marx locates the earliest "spirit of capitalism" in the Judaic practices of usury and the "chimerical nationality of the Jew ... of the trader and above all the financier."[30] He attributes to it a powerfully corrosive effect that sunders Christianity's universalist spirit into the "spirit of *civil society*, of the sphere of egoism, of the *bellum omnium contra omes*." The "war of all against all" is not the residue of an imagined state of nature, but the universalization of the "capitalist spirit" of Judaism "under the reign of Christianity," which "dissolves the human world into a world of atomistic, mutually hostile individuals." Like Hobbes, Marx is a realist in that he acknowledges a universal struggle for power; and he is clearly indebted to Hobbes for his nominalist demythologization of power.

But Marx goes one step further, identifying the source of the Leviathan's power not in a free association of alienated power, but in "the separation of man from man ... the practical application of the right of liberty is the right of private property." The desire for security, then, does not emerge from some external state of nature: "rather, security is the guarantee of the egoism of civil society." It is not a Hobbesian fear or self-interest that gives rise to security; it is money, as "the alienated essence of man's labour and life, this alien essence dominates him as he worships it." This elevation of the egoistic partiality to a metaphysical universality conceals the real divisions created by alienated labor. Not the Leviathan but Mammon binds together society: "The god of the Jews has been secularized and has become the god of the world." The state takes on this universalist identity, becoming the "mediator to which man transfers all his unholiness and all his *human freedom*."

In Marx, alienation gives rise to a struggle for power which necessitates the security of a state, whereas, in Hobbes, alienation is a consequence of the struggle for power. Moreover, in Marx the power struggle is not a permanent condition: it is historically and class specific, and once the contradiction between a social production of wealth and the private exercise of power comes to its dialectical resolution, the state would become obsolescent – and with it the security dilemma. For Hobbes, the struggle for power is permanent and universal; hence the state is unlikely to wither away. Moreover, it is improbable that a supra-state Leviathan could be constructed: "In states and commonwealths not dependent on one another, every commonwealth has an absolute liberty to do what it shall judge most conducive to their benefits."[31] Marx sees this extra-territorial liberty to be as chimerical as Hobbes's domestic version. Just as the power of partial economic interests dominates the whole of civil society through the abstract universality of the state, Marx considered interstate politics to be the "serf" of a "universal" financial power hiding a narrow class interest.[32]

Nietzsche and interpretive realism

> In the last analysis, "love of the neighbor" is always something secondary, partly conventional and arbitrary – illusory in relation to *fear of the neighbor*. After the structure of society is fixed on the whole and seems secure against external dangers, it is this fear of the neighbor that again creates new perspectives of moral valuation.
>
> –Friedrich Nietzsche, *Beyond Good and Evil*

Nietzsche transvalues both Hobbes's and Marx's interpretations of security through a genealogy of modes of being. His method is not to uncover some deep meaning or value for security, but to destabilize the intolerable fictional identities of the past which have been created out of fear, and to affirm the creative differences which might yield new values for the future.[33] Originating in the paradoxical relationship of a contingent life and a certain death, the history of security reads for Nietzsche as an abnegation, a resentment and, finally, a transcendence of this paradox. In brief, the history is one of individuals seeking an impossible security from the most radical "other" of life, the terror of death which, once generalized and nationalized, triggers a futile cycle of collective identities seeking security from alien others–who are seeking similarly impossible guarantees. It is a story of differences taking on the otherness of death, and identities calcifying into a fearful sameness. Since Nietzsche has suffered the greatest neglect in international theory, his reinterpretation of security will receive a more extensive treatment here.

One must begin with Nietzsche's idea of the will to power, which he clearly believed to be prior to and generative of all considerations of security. In *Beyond Good and Evil*, he emphatically establishes the primacy of the will to power: "Physiologists should think before putting down the instinct of self-preservation as the cardinal instinct of an organic being. A living thing seeks above all to *discharge* its strength – life itself is will to power; self-preservation is only one of the most frequent results."[34]

The will to power, then, should not be confused with a Hobbesian perpetual *desire* for power. It can, in its negative form, produce a reactive and resentful longing for *only* power, leading, in Nietzsche's view, to a triumph of nihilism. But Nietzsche refers to a *positive* will to power, an active and effective force of becoming, from which values and meanings – including self-preservation – are produced which affirm life. Conventions of security act to suppress rather than confront the fears endemic to life, for "... life itself is *essentially* appropriation, injury, overpowering of what is alien and weaker; suppression, hardness, imposition of one's own forms, incorporation and at least, at its mildest, exploitation – but why should one always use those words in which slanderous intent has been imprinted for ages."[35] Elsewhere Nietzsche establishes the pervasiveness of agonism in life: "life is a consequence of war, society itself a means to war."[36] But the denial of this permanent condition, the effort to disguise it with a consensual rationality or to hide from it with a fictional sovereignty, are all effects of this suppression of fear.

The desire for security is manifested as a collective resentment of difference– that which is not us, not certain, not predictable. Complicit with a negative will to power is the fear-driven desire for protection from the unknown. Unlike the positive will to power, which produces an aesthetic affirmation of difference, the search for truth produces a truncated life which conforms to the rationally knowable, to the causally sustainable. In *The Gay Science*, Nietzsche asks of the reader: "Look, isn't our need for knowledge precisely this need for the familiar, the will to uncover everything strange, unusual, and questionable, something that no longer disturbs us? Is it not the *instinct of fear* that bids us to know? And is the jubilation of those who obtain knowledge not the jubilation over the restoration of a sense of security?"[37]

The fear of the unknown and the desire for certainty combine to produce a domesticated life, in which causality and rationality become the highest sign of a sovereign self, the surest protection against contingent forces. The fear of fate assures a belief that everything reasonable is true, and everything true, reasonable. In short, the security imperative produces, and is sustained by, the strategies of knowledge which seek to explain it. Nietzsche elucidates the nature of this generative relationship in *The Twilight of the Idols*:

> The causal instinct is thus conditional upon, and excited by, the feeling of fear. The "why?" shall, if at all possible, not give the cause for its own sake so much as for a *particular kind of cause*–a cause that is comforting, liberating and relieving. ... That which is new and strange and has not been experienced before, is excluded as a cause. Thus one not only searches for some kind of explanation, to serve as a cause, but for a particularly selected and preferred kind of explanation–that which most quickly and frequently abolished the feeling of the strange, new and hitherto unexperienced: the most *habitual* explanations.[38]

A safe life requires safe truths. The strange and the alien remain unexamined, the unknown becomes identified as evil, and evil provokes hostility–recycling the desire for security. The "influence of timidity," as Nietzsche puts it, creates a people who are willing to subordinate affirmative values to the "necessities" of security: "they fear change, transitoriness: this expresses a straitened soul, full of mistrust and evil experiences."[39]

The unknowable which cannot be contained by force or explained by reason is relegated to the off-world. "Trust," the "good," and other common values come to rely upon an "artificial strength": "the feeling of *security* such as the Christian possesses; he feels strong in being able to trust, to be patient and composed: he owes this artificial strength to the illusion of being protected by a god."[40] For Nietzsche, of course, only a false sense of security can come from false gods: "Morality and religion belong altogether to the *psychology of error*: in every single case, cause and effect are confused; or truth is confused with the effects of *believing* something to be true; or a state of consciousness is confused with its causes."[41]

Nietzsche's interpretation of the origins of religion can shed some light on this paradoxical origin and transvaluation of security. In *The Genealogy of Morals*, Nietzsche sees religion arising from a sense of fear and indebtedness to one's ancestors:

> The conviction reigns that it is only through the sacrifices and accomplishments of the ancestors that the tribe *exists*–and that one has to *pay them back* with sacrifices and accomplishments: one thus recognizes a *debt* that constantly grows greater, since these forebears never cease, in their continued existence as powerful spirits, to accord the tribe new advantages and new strength.[42]

Sacrifices, honors, obedience are given but it is never enough, for the ancestors of the *most powerful* tribes are bound eventually to grow to monstrous dimensions through the imagination of growing fear and to recede into the darkness of the divinely uncanny and unimaginable: in the end the ancestor must necessarily be transfigured into a *god*.[43]

As the ancestor's debt becomes embedded in institutions, the community takes on the role of creditor. Nietzsche mocks this originary, Hobbesian moment: to rely upon an "artificial strength": "the feeling one lives in a community, one enjoys the advantages of communality (oh what advantages! we sometimes underrate them today), one dwells protected, cared for, in peace and trustfulness, without fear of certain injuries and hostile acts to which the man *outside*, the "man without peace," is exposed ... since one has bound and pledged oneself to the community precisely with a view to injury and hostile acts.[44]

The establishment of the community is dependent upon, indeed it feeds upon, this fear of being left outside. As the castle wall is replaced by written treaty, however, and distant gods by temporal sovereigns, the martial skills and spiritual virtues of the noble warrior are slowly debased and dissimulated. The subject of the individual will to power becomes the object of a collective resentment. The result? The fear of the external other is transvalued into the "love of the neighbor" quoted in the opening of this section, and the perpetuation of community is assured through the internalization and legitimation of a fear that lost its original source long ago.

This powerful nexus of fear, of external and internal otherness, generates the values which uphold the security imperative. Indeed, Nietzsche locates the genealogy of even individual rights, such as freedom, in the calculus of maintaining security:

> My rights are that part of my power which others not merely conceded me, but which they wish me to preserve. How do these others arrive at that? First: through their prudence and fear and caution: whether in that they expect something similar from us in return (protection of their rights); or in that they consider that a struggle with us would be perilous or to no purpose; or in that they see in any diminution of our force a disadvantage to themselves, since we would then be unsuited to forming an alliance with them in opposition to a hostile third power. *Then*: by donation and cession.[45]

The point of Nietzsche's critical genealogy is to show that the perilous conditions that created the security imperative – and the western metaphysics that perpetuate it – have diminished if not disappeared; yet, the fear of life persists: "Our century denies this perilousness, and does so with a good conscience: and yet it continues to drag along with it the old habits of Christian security, Christian enjoyment, recreation and evaluation."[46] Nietzsche's worry is that the collective reaction against older, more primal fears has created an even worse danger: the tyranny of the herd, the lowering of man, the apathy of the last man which controls through conformity and rules through passivity. The security of the sovereign, rational self and state comes at the cost of ambiguity, uncertainty, paradox – all that makes a free life worthwhile. Nietzsche's lament for this lost life is captured at the end of *Daybreak* in a series of rhetorical questions:

> Of future virtues – How comes it that the more comprehensible the world has grown the more solemnities of every kind have decreased? Is it that fear was so much the basic element of that reverence which overcame us in the presence of everything unknown and mysterious and taught us to fall down before the incomprehensible and plead for mercy? And has the world not lost some of its charm for us because we have grown less fearful? With the diminution of our fearfulness has our own dignity and solemnity, our own *fearsomeness*, not also diminished?[47]

It is of course in Nietzsche's lament, in his deepest pessimism for the last man, that one finds the celebration of the overman as both symptom and harbinger of a more free-spirited yet fearsome age. Dismissive of utopian engineering, Nietzsche never suggests how he would restructure society; he looks forward only so far as to sight the emergence of "new philosophers" (such as himself?) who would restore a reverence for fear and reevaluate the security imperative. Nietzsche does, however, go back to a pre-Christian, pre-Socratic era to find the exemplars for a new kind of security. In *The Genealogy of Morals*, he holds up Pericles as an example, for lauding the Athenians for their "*rhathymia*" – a term that incorporates the notion of "indifference to and contempt for security."[48]

It is perhaps too much to expect Nietzsche's message to resonate in late modern times, to expect, at the very time when conditions seem most uncertain and unpredictable, that people would treat fear as a stimulus for improvement rather than cause for retrenchment. Yet Nietzsche would clearly see these as opportune times, when fear could be willfully asserted as a force for the affirmation of difference, rather than canalized into a cautious identity constructed from the calculation of risks and benefits.

Baudrillard and hyperrealism

> Like the real, warfare will no longer have any place – except precisely if the nuclear powers are successful in de-escalation and manage to define new spaces for warfare. If military power, at the cost of de-escalating this marvelously practical madness to the second power, reestablishes a setting for warfare, a confined space that is in fact human, then weapons will regain their use value and their exchange value: it will again be possible to *exchange warfare*.
>
> –Jean Baudrillard, *Fatal Strategies*

Fine allegories, Baudrillard would say of Marx and Nietzsche. Nietzsche's efforts to represent the deeper impulses behind the will to security, as well as

Marx's effort to chart the origins of the struggle for power, to pierce the veil of false consciousness that has postponed revolution, to scientifically represent the world-to-be, are just examples of a representational mirroring, a doubling of late-modernity's cartography of the world-as-it-is. "For it is with the same Imperialism," says Baudrillard, "that present-day simulators try to make the real, all the real coincide with their simulation models."[49]

Baudrillard goes beyond Nietzsche in his interpretation of the death of god and the inability of rational man or the proletariat to fill the resulting value-void with stable distinctions between the real and the apparent, idea and referent, good and evil. In the hyperbolic, often nihilistic, vision of Baudrillard, the task of modernity is no longer to demystify or disenchant illusion – as Nietzsche realized, "*with the real world we have also abolished the apparent*"[50] – but to save the reality principle, which in this case means, above all else, the sovereign state acting in an anarchical order to maintain and if possible expand its security and power in the face of penetrating, de-centering forces, like the ICBM, global capital, military (and now civilian) surveillance satellites, the international or domestic terrorist, the telecommunications web, environmental movements and transnational human rights conventions, to name a few of the more obvious forces. In his now familiar words: "It is no longer a question of a false representation of reality (ideology), but of concealing the fact that the real is no longer real."[51]

The idea that reality is blurring, or has already disappeared into its representational form, has a long lineage. It can be traced from Siegfried Kracauer's chronicling of the emergence of a "cult of distraction" in the Weimar Republic,[52] to Walter Benjamin's incisive warning of the loss of authenticity, aura, and uniqueness in the technical reproduction of reality,[53] to Guy Debord's claim that, in modern conditions, spectacles accumulate and representations proliferate[54] and, finally, to Jean Baudrillard's own notification that the simulated now precedes and engenders a hyperreality where origins are forgotten and historical references lost.[55] In his post-Marxist work, Baudrillard describes how the class struggle and the commodity form dissolved into a universal play of signs, simulacra, and the inertia of mass culture – and the revolution went missing along with the rest of reality. We are at end-times: but where Marx saw a relentless, dialectical linearity in capitalism leading to social revolution, Baudrillard sees only a passive population depending on the virtuality of technology to save a defunct reality principle.

War serves as the *ultima ratio* of all four thinkers. The Gulf War, and the postwar attempt to set up a "new world order," provides rich material for Baudrillard's thesis that security has now entered the realm of hyperreality. Back in 1983, when Baudrillard wrote of the renewed possibility of an "exchange of warfare," he had already spotted the dark side to a possible end of the ultimate simulation of the Cold War, nuclear deterrence. And if ever a war was "engendered and preceded by simulation," it was the Gulf War. We were primed for this war. Simulations had infiltrated every area of our lives, in the form of news (re)creations, video games, flight simulators, police interrogations, crime reenactments and, of course, media war games.[56] From the initial deployment of troops to the daily order of battle, from the highest reaches of policymaking to the lowest levels of field tactics and supply, a series of simulations made the killing more efficient, more unreal, more acceptable.[57] Computer-simulated by private contractors, flight-tested at the Nellis Air Force Base, field-exercised at Fort Irwin in the Mojave Desert, and re-played and fine-tuned everyday in the Persian Gulf, real-time war games took on a life of their own as the real war took the lives of more than 100,000 Iraqis.

But there is also evidence that simulations played a critical role in the decision to go to war. In an interview, General Norman Schwarzkopf revealed that, two years before the war, U.S. intelligence discovered, in his words, that Iraq "had run computer simulations and war games for the invasion of Kuwait."[58] In my own research, I learned that Iraq had previously purchased a wargame from the Washington military-consulting firm BDM International to use in its war against Iran; and almost as an aside, it was reported in September 1990, on *ABC Nightline*, that the software for the Kuwait invasion simulation was also purchased from a U.S. firm.[59] Moreover, Schwarzkopf stated that he programmed "possible conflicts with Iraq on computers almost daily." Having previously served in Tampa, Florida as head of the U.S. Central Command – at the time a "paper" army without troops, tanks, or aircraft of its own – his affinity for simulations was and is unsurprising.

In fact, Schwarzkopf sponsored a highly significant computer-simulated command-post exercise that was played, in late July 1990, under the code-name of "Exercise Internal Look, '90." According to a Central Command news release issued at the time, "command and control elements from all branches of the military will be responding to real-world scenarios similar to those they might be expected to confront within the Central Command AOR consisting of the Horn of Africa, the Middle East and Southwest Asia." The war game specialist who put Exercise Internal Look together, Lt. General Yeosock, moved from fighting "real-world scenarios" in Florida to command of all ground troops – except for the special forces under Schwarzkopf – in Saudi Arabia.

Perhaps it is too absurd to believe that the Gulf War was the product of one U.S. wargame designed to fight another wargame bought by Iraq from an American company. Perhaps not. My purpose is not to conduct an internal critique of the simulation industry, nor to claim some privileged grounds for ascertaining the causes of the war.[60] Rather, my intent is to ask whether, in the construction of a realm of meaning that had minimal contact with historically specific events or actors, simulations demonstrated the power to construct the reality they purport to represent–and international security suffered for it. The question is whether simulations can create a new world order where actors act, things happen, and the consequences have no origins except the artificial cyberspace of the simulations themselves.[61]

Indeed, over the last decade there has been a profusion of signs that a *simulation syndrome* has taken hold in international politics. According to Oleg Gordievsky, former KGB station chief in London, the Soviet leadership became convinced in November 1983 that a NATO command-post simulation called

"Able Archer '83" was, in fact, the first step toward a nuclear surprise attack.[62] Relations were already tense after the September shootdown of KAL 007 – a flight that the Soviets considered part of an intelligence-gathering mission – and since the Warsaw Pact had its own wargame, which used a training exercise as cover for a surprise attack, the Soviets assumed the West to have one as well. No NATO nuclear forces went on actual alert, yet the KGB reported the opposite to Moscow. On November 8 or 9, flash messages were sent to all Soviet embassies in Europe, warning them of NATO preparations for a nuclear first strike. Things calmed down when the Able Archer exercise ended without the feared nuclear strike, but Gordievsky still maintains that only the Cuban missile crisis brought the world closer to the brink of nuclear war.

On a smaller, more conventional scale, the mistaking of war for its simulation was repeated in July 1988, when the radar operator and the tactical information coordinator of the *U.S.S. Vincennes* misidentified an Iranian Airbus as an attacking Iranian F-14, even though the ship's highly sophisticated Aegis radar system registered an unknown airplane flying level at 12,000 feet. The nine months of simulation training with computer tapes that preceded the encounter proved more real than the reality of the moment. In effect, the Airbus disappeared before the surface-to-air missile struck, transmuted from an airplane with 290 civilians into an electronic representation on a radar screen and, then, into a simulated target.

The Gulf War is the preeminent, but probably not the last, case of a simulation syndrome manifesting itself in the discourse of national security. Baudrillard was right, in the sense that simulations would rule not only in the war without warring of nuclear deterrence, but also in the postwar warring of the present.[63] It was never in question that the coalition forces would win the military conflict. But they did not win a "war," in the conventional sense of a destroying a reciprocating enemy. What "war," then, did the U.S. win? A cyberwar of simulations. First, the prewar simulation, Operation Internal Look '90, which defeated the "Made in America" Iraqi simulation for the invasion of Kuwait. Second, the war game of AirLand Battle, which defeated an Iraqi army that resembled the game's intended enemy, the Warsaw Pact, in hyperreality only. Third, the war of spectacle, which defeated the spectacle of war on the battlefield of videographic reproduction. And fourth, the postwar after-simulation of Vietnam, which defeated an earlier defeat by assimilating Vietnam's history and lessons into the victory of the Gulf War.

Perhaps Baudrillard's *and* Marx's worst scenarios have come true: the post-Cold War security state now has the technology of simulation as well as the ideological advantage of unipolarity to regenerate, at relatively low cost to itself, an ailing national economy and identity through foreign adventures. We should expect, then, endo- as well as exo-colonial wars, trade wars and simulated wars to figure in the new world order. Iraq served its purpose well as the enemy "other" that helped to redefine the Western identity: but it was the *other* enemy, the more pervasive and elusive threat posed by the de-territorialization of the state and the disintegration of a bipolar order that has left us with a "Gulf War Syndrome," in which the construction and destruction of the enemy other is measured in time, not territory; prosecuted in the field of perception, not politics; authenticated by technical reproduction, not material referents; and played out in the method and metaphor of gaming, not the history and horror of warring.

Not a conclusion but a provocation

People in the newly sovereign republics of the former Soviet Union report greater fear and insecurity than they felt before they became independent. ... Indeed, the data show that the greatest perceived threats are closest to home, with most of those asked more fearful of their neighbors than anyone else, reflecting the lingering unease among ethnic groups living side by side in the former republics.

–"Many in the Former Soviet Lands Say They Feel Even More Insecure Now," Bruce Weber, *New York Times*, April 23, 1992.

If security is to have any significance for the future, it must find a home in the new disorder through a commensurate deterritorialization of theory. We can no longer reconstitute a single Hobbesian site of meaning or reconstruct some Marxist or even neo-Kantian cosmopolitan community; that would require a moment of enlightened universal certainty that crumbled long before the Berlin Wall fell. Nor can we depend on or believe in some spiritual, dialectical or scientific process to overcome or transcend the domestic and international divisions, ambiguities, and uncertainties that mark the age of speed, surveillance and simulation.

This is why I believe the philosophical depth of Nietzsche has more to offer than the hyperbolic flash of Baudrillard. Can we not interpret our own foreign policy in the light of Nietzsche's critique of security? As was the case with the origins of an ontotheological security, did not our debt to the Founding Fathers grow "to monstrous dimensions" with our "sacrifices" – many noble, some not – in two World Wars? Did not our collective identity, once isolationist, neutralist and patriotic, become transfigured into a new god, that was born and fearful of a nuclear, internationalist, interventionist power? The evidence is in the reconceptualization: as distance, oceans and borders became less of a protective barrier to alien identities, and a new international economy required penetration into other worlds, *national interest* became too weak a semantic guide. We found a stronger one in *national security*, as embodied and institutionalized in the National Security Act of 1947, as protected by the McCarran-Walter Act of 1952, and as reconstructed by the first, and subsequent National Security Council meetings of the second cold war.

Nietzsche speaks a credible truth to increasingly incredible regimes. He points toward a way in which we might live with and recognize the very necessity of difference. He recognizes the need to assert heterogeneity against the homogenizing and often brutalizing forces of progress. And he eschews all utopian schemes to take us out of the "real" world for a practical strategy to celebrate, rather than exacerbate, the anxiety, insecurity and fear of a new world order where radical otherness is ubiquitous and indomitable.

Notes

1 J. Derrida, "Structure, Sign, and Play in the Discourse of the Human Science," A. Bass, trans., *Writing and Difference* (London: Routledge and Kegan Paul, 1978), p. 279.
2 The same mantra has since been repeated by President Clinton.
3 Stephen M. Walt, 'The Renaissance of Security Studies', *International Studies Quarterly* 35, no. 2 (June 1991): 211–239.
4 Walt, "Renaissance," p. 212.
5 Ibid., p. 213.
6 Stephen Walt, *The Origins of Alliances* (Ithaca: Cornell University Press, 1987).
7 The political theorist William Connolly has also noted this tendency among international relations theorists, and refers to it as the "strategy of condemnation through refraction." See William E. Connolly, *Identity/Difference–Democratic Negotiations of Political Paradox* (Ithaca: Cornell University Press, 1991), pp. 49–63.
8 Walt, "Renaissance," p. 223.
9 M. Heidegger, "The Question concerning Technology" (David Krell, ed.), *Martin Heidegger: Basic Writings* (New York: Harper & Row, 1977), p. 317.
10 M. Foucault, "On the genealogy of ethics," interview by P. Rabinow and H. Dreyfus, *The Foucault Reader* (New York: Pantheon, 1984), p. 343.
11 See J. Der Derian, chapter 4 on "Mytho-diplomacy," pp. 47–68 and chapter 7 on "Anti-diplomacy," pp. 134–67, in *On Diplomacy–A Geneology of Western Estrangement* (Oxford: Basil Blackwell, 1987).
12 See *Oxford English Dictionary*, vol. 9, p. 370.
13 Edward Gibbon, *The Decline and Fall of the Roman Empire* (1781), xxxi, III, p. 229, quoted in *OED*, vol. 9, p. 370.
14 William Shakespeare, *Macbeth* (1605), III, v. 32, quoted in *OED*, vol. 9, p. 370.
15 E. Burke, *Letter to Marq. Rockingh.*, quoted in *OED*, vol. 9, p. 370.
16 *Saturday Review* (17 July 1858), p. 51, quoted in *OED*, vol. 9, p. 370.
17 *OED*, vol. 9, p. 370.
18 Ibid.
19 Ibid.
20 Ibid.
21 See S. Greenblatt, *Shakespearean Negotiations: The Circulation of Social Energy in Renaissance England* (Berkeley: University of California Press, 1990).
22 Thomas Hobbes (C. B. Macpherson, ed.), *Leviathan* (Harmonsworth: Penguin, 1968).
23 Thomas Hobbes (F. Tonnies, ed.), *Elements of Law* (Cambridge: Cambridge University Press, 1928), p. 26.
24 Hobbes, *Leviathan*.
25 Ibid., p. 223.
26 Ibid., p. 227.
27 Ibid., p. 188.
28 For a theoretical exposition of the ontotheological character of "epistemic realism," see Connolly, *Identity\Difference*, pp. 70–71; and William Connolly, "Democracy and Territoriality," *Millennium* (Winter 1991): 474 and 483n. See also David Campbell, *Writing Security: United States Foreign Policy and the Politics of Identity* (Minneapolis: University of Minnesota Press, 1992).
29 A fuller account of this essay can be found in Der Derian, *On Diplomacy*, pp. 138–141.
30 K. Marx, "On the Jewish Question" (L. Easton & K. Guddat, eds.), *Writings of the Young Marx on Philosophy and Society* (New York: Anchor Books, 1967), pp. 216–248.
31 Hobbes, *Leviathan*, p. 64.

32 Marx, "On the Jewish Question," p. 245.

33 This echoes an interpretation first presented by Gilles Deleuze in *Nietzsche and Philosophy* (Minneapolis: University of Minnesota Press, 1983), which inspires much of my analysis of Nietzsche on fear and security.

34 F. Nietzsche, *Beyond Good and Evil*, no. 13.

35 *Beyond Good and Evil*, no. 259.

36 *Will to Power*, no. 53. In an equally significant passage, which links social valuation and biology, Nietzsche warns against interpreting particular legal institutions as anything more than temporary, life-restricting constructs. That is, to the extent that the legal order is "thought of as sovereign and universal, not as a means in the struggle between power complexes, but as a means of *preventing* all struggle in general" it must be seen as hostile to life. (*On the Genealogy of Morals*, II, no. 11)

37 F. Nietzsche, *The Gay Science*, no. 355.

38 Nietzsche, *Twilight of the Idols*, no. 5.

39 Nietzsche, *Will to Power*, no. 576. On the flip side of this influence of timidity, as man has over time overcome particular fears, the now rational, causal object or instance now gives pleasure precisely because it used to inspire fear. Therefore Nietzsche contends that the "feeling for nature" is possible now due to our previous invocation of mystical meaning and intention. See also *Daybreak*, no. 142.

40 *Will to Power*, no. 917.

41 *Twilight of the Idols*, "The Four Great Errors," no. 6.

42 F. Nietzsche (W. Kaufmann, ed. and trans.), *On the Genealogy of Morals* (New York: Random House, 1967), pp. 88–89. See also Der Derian, *On Diplomacy*, pp. 53–56, for a fuller account of how the reciprocity of this relationship between the living and the dead is projected as a mytho-diplomatic mediation between alien peoples.

43 Ibid.

44 *Genealogy of Morals*, II, no. 9.

45 *Daybreak*, no. 112. Bret Brown pointed out to me the connection that Nancy Love makes between Nietzsche and Marx on the relationship of rights to security in *Marx, Nietzsche, and Modernity* (New York: Columbia University Press, 1986): "Marx says, '*security* is the supreme social concept of civil society, the concept of *police*, the concept that the whole of society is there only to guarantee each of its members the conservation of his person, his rights and his property.' Nietzsche says, 'How much or how little is dangerous to the community, dangerous to equality … now constitutes the moral perspective.' They agree that freedom is oppression and equality is inequality, so security is insecurity. Again from different perspectives, they argue that liberal democracy secures an alienated existence." (p. 157).

46 *Daybreak* no. 57.

47 Ibid., no. 551.

48 *Genealogy of Morals*, I, 11.

49 J. Baudrillard, *Simulations* (New York: Semiotext(e), 1983), p. 2.

50 See F. Nietzsche, *Twilight of the Idols*, pp. 40–41; and Der Derian, "Techno-diplomacy," Chapter 9, of *On Diplomacy*, pp. 199–200.

51 Baudrillard, *Simulations*, p. 48.

52 See F. Kracauer, "Cult of Distraction: On Berlin's Picture Palaces," (T. Y. Levin, trans.), *New German Critique*, 40 (Winter 1987): 95; and S. Kracauer, *Das Ornament der Masse* (Frankfurt a.M.: Suhrkamp Verlag, 1963); S. Kracauer (T. Y. Levin, trans. and ed.), *The Mass Ornament* (Cambridge: Harvard University Press, 1995).

53 See Walter Benjamin (H. Arendt, ed.), "The Work of Art in the Age of Mechanical Reproduction," *Illuminations* (New York: Schocken, 1969), pp. 241–42.

54 See Guy Debord, *Society of the Spectacle* (Detroit: Black and Red, 1983), no. 1, 45, pp. 1 and 23. In a more recent work, Debord persuasively – and somewhat despairingly – argues that the society of the spectacle retains its representational power in current

times: see *Commentaires sur la Société du Spectacle* (Paris: Editions Gerard Lebovici, 1988).

55 Baudrillard, *Simulations*, p. 2.

56 Whether it took the form of representing criminality on "America's Most Wanted," where alleged crimes are re-enacted for the public benefit, or docu-dramatizing espionage on ABC primetime news, with a stand-in for the alleged spy Felix Bloch handing over a briefcase to a KGB stand-in, a genre of truthful simulations had already been established. There are as well the many commercially available war simulations. To name a few: from Navy simulations there is *Harpoon, Das Boot Submarine, Wolf Pack,* and *Silent Service II*; from the Air Force, *Secret Weapons of the Luftwaffe, F-19 Stealth Fighter, A-10 Tank Killer,* and *F-15 Strike Eagle*; and for those seeking more serious global simulations, *Populous, Balance of Power, SimCity,* and *Global Dilemma.* On the heels of the Gulf War, wargames like *Arabian Nightmare* (in which the player has the option to kill American reporters like Ted Koppel) and the *Butcher of Baghdad* were added to the list.

57 Simulations in this context could be broadly defined here as *the continuation of war by means of verisimilitude*, which range from analytical games that use broad descriptions and a minimum of mathematical abstraction to make generalizations about the behavior of actors, to computerized models that use algorithms and high resolution graphics to analyze and represent the amount of technical detail considered necessary to predict events and the behavior of actors.

58 See J. Albright, "Army mastermind stays ahead of the 'game,'" *Atlanta Constitution*, October 25, 1990, p. 1.

59 See T. Allen, *War Games* (New York: McGraw Hill, 1987), p. 4; and "ABC Nightline" transcript, September 26, 1990, p. 3.

60 Two excellent criticisms of the internal assumptions of gaming can be found in a review of the literature by R. Ashley, "The eye of power: the politics of world modeling," *International Organization* 37, no. 3 (Summer 1983); and R. Hurwitz, "Strategic and Social Fictions in the Prisoner's Dilemma," pp. 113–34, in: Michael Shapiro and James Der Derian, eds., *International/Intertextual Relations: Postmodern Readings of World Politics* (Lexington: Lexington Books, 1989).

61 This is not to suggest that the 500, 000+ troops in Kuwait were not real; rather, to point out that their being there might well have been a consequence of a "reality" constructed out of the imagined scenarios created within the computer war games.

62 C. Andrews and O. Gordievsky, *KGB: The Inside Story* (New York: HarperCollins, 1991), pp. 583–605; and conversation with Gordievsky, 7–9 November 1991, Toronto, Canada.

63 The art of deterrence, prohibiting political war, favors the upsurge, not of conflicts, but of "*acts of war without war.*" Paul Virilio and Sylvere Lotringer (Mark Polizotti, trans.), *Pure War* (New York: Semiotext(e), 1983), p. 27. See also Timothy Luke, "What's Wrong with Deterrence? A Semiotic Interpretation of National Security Policy," pp. 207–230, in: Shapiro and Der Derian, *International/Intertextual Relations.*

10 The CIA, Hollywood, and sovereign conspiracies

Source: *Queen's Quarterly* (Summer 1993), vol. 100, no. 2, pp. 329–347.

From Humphrey Bogart to Harrison Ford, Hollywood's most popular screen heroes have employed various means to thwart devious adversaries, and their efforts almost invariably culminate in the venerable sock-on-the-jaw. But the sovereign borders that once enabled these heroes to identify their foes have been blurring for some time. And although high-tech ordnance has allowed cinema's lone crusaders to pack more of a punch, James Der Derian wonders whether the punch alone has become the genre's raison d'être.

Since conspiracies are of such dangerous consequences alike to princes and to private persons, I cannot well omit to discuss their nature, for it is plain that many more princes have lost their lives and their states in this way than by open war, because it is given to but few to make open war on a prince, whereas anyone can conspire against him.

Niccolo Machiavelli, "On Conspiracies," *The Discourses*

In 1933 George Bernard Shaw paid a visit to America, at the time an unusual country whose secretary of state held to the novel notion that "gentlemen do not read each other's mail." Shaw's only formal speaking engagement was at the New York Metropolitan Opera House, where he presented a lecture to the American Academy of Political science. The talk, "The Political Madhouse in America and Nearer Home," was full of droll remarks about the "follies and futilities" of the "Hundred-percent American." Although a preface to the published version cushioned Shaw's satirical jabs ("the truth is that the Hpc American is a harmless and well-meaning child compared to the Hpc Englishman, Frenchman, German Nazi, or Japanese") he nonetheless sounded a warning against the spread of a made-in-America, world-class danger. Shaw's greatest fear, it would seem, was that America's worst character flaw would be globally projected through its mastery of a new technology:

> But I do reproach you for a special American propaganda of Anarchism which is having most serious effects throughout the world. Formerly you were not able to affect public morals and public feeling much on the other side of the Atlantic. But now you have an instrument called the cinematograph and a centre called Hollywood, which has brought public and private morals under your influence everywhere.
>
> (Shaw 5, 20)

The nature and extent of this "Anarchism" was surely exaggerated by Shaw to make a quasi-humorous point, but Shaw returned to the subject with a didactic seriousness:

> No: the doctrine with which Hollywood is corrupting the world is the doctrine of anarchism. Hollywood keeps before its child audiences a string of glorified young heroes, everyone of whom is an unhesitating and violent Anarchist. His one answer to everything that annoys him or disparages his country or his parents or his young lady or his personal code of manly conduct, is to give the offender a "sock" in the jaw.

And for good measure, he went on to punctuate his criticisms by citing an anonymous, native source:

> An eminent American, whom I will not name, has sent me a letter which I received yesterday morning. It says "Do not judge the United States by its two plague spots: Hollywood and New York." I was not surprised. Hollywood is the most immoral place in the world.

What if we were, 60 years later, to judge America by Hollywood, not for the sake of argument but as an overdue genealogy of morals conveyed by the most powerful of the global media? That is, what if we take Shaw seriously, not as a moralist *per se* but as a soothsayer who read the early symptoms right and got the cure wrong? I am suggesting that we accept Shaw's view of Hollywood as a screen upon which America's values are projected – and then rendered dangerous as a *plot* – in order to judge the representational power of one of Hollywood's most successful genres, the spy film. More specifically, let us interpret the spy film as symptomatic of highly contingent, late modern times, when borders are increasingly porous, dangers ubiquitous, politics ambiguous; when the fear and suspicion spreads that there must be someone, the *anarchist* or *terrorist*, behind the proliferation of danger; that there must be a panoptic system, *espionage*, to uncover and to keep track of it; that there must be, if necessary, a violent strategy, *counter-terrorism*, to fight it; and finally, that there must be some way, *conspiracy theory*, to make sense of it. And when all these forces fail to achieve their plotted ends, as they surely and dramatically must, there must be a heroic, rugged individual, Shaw's "Anarchist," who will rise to the occasion and give "the offender a 'sock' on the jaw."

If danger and high anxiety produce the categorical imperative, the moral "must" behind the spy genre, it is the desire to secure a sovereign self-identity that sustains the conspiratorial narrative, and raises it to the power of theology. "Ye shall know the truth, And the truth shall make you free," reads the inscription on the entry to the CIA. Cinema and espionage share, mediate, and magnify the constitutive power of the sovereign gaze: knowing the truth implies, indeed necessitates, seeing the other as alien, different, threatening. Otherwise, and all the same, there would be no big budgets for Hollywood or Langley. Obviously it is not only the intimate relationship of power to knowledge, and identity to difference, that draws us to the spy film. The spy and the *cinéaste* are twinned – as is their *eros* and *thanatos* – by their radical relationship to the otherness of death: extreme and defiant, at once above and beyond life and therefore the law – they can act with the freedom (to seduce) and the license (to kill) that everyman lost a long time ago.

There is the temptation, when confronted by the elusiveness of the spy genre, to mimic the plot technique of the conspiratorial text, to expend energies in a search for the key or cipher that will unlock the protective enigmas of sovereign power. But if we have learned anything from an early master of the genre, Alfred Hitchcock, it is the ultimate futility of such a quest: like the nonexistent secret clause of the naval treaty in *The Foreign Correspondent* or the non-person "George Kaplan" in *North by Northwest*, it is the absence at the centre, the vanishing point, what Hitchcock referred to as the "nothing at all" or "McGuffin," that propels all action and consumes the resources of the protagonist.[1] The cipher hides, by its very absence, the nothingness at the core of all sovereign conspiracies, making all the mysteries, suspenses, and chases, which serve to cloak that emptiness, signs without a referent, symptoms without a cause.

For anyone who thinks that this role of pure semblance in film has no counterpart in "real" life, I suggest a close reading of the recent Senate hearings to confirm director-designate of the CIA James Woolsey, a latter-day St. George who picks up the sword of metaphor to meet the radical metamorphosis of danger:

> Yes, we have slain a large dragon. But we live now in a jungle filled with a bewildering variety of poisonous snakes. And in many ways the dragon was easier to keep track of.
> (CIA transcript, "Senate Intelligence Committee hearings on the nomination of James Woolsey to be director of central intelligence" 2)

To suggest that the Holy Grail of espionage is a Hitchcockian "McGuffin" is not, as some might read it, a call for theological adventurism or intellectual nihilism; rather it is to treat the signs, simulations, and symptoms of espionage, that is, spy films, seriously – *because that is all we really have to go by*. Symptomatic of the strange, indeed, mythical times in which we live, the spy film has become a more credible guide than the incredible reality it supposedly represents.

To understand this, then, one must resort to a symptomology, or as it was once called in medicine, and is now called in literary theory, a *semiology*, in the sense of a study of the cinematic signs of espionage as symptoms of a general disorder whose cure (*pharmakon*), sovereignty, is also its poison.[2]

I believe the doctor of reality, Nietzsche, offers the best diagnosis of Shaw and the contemporary analysts and pundits who wish to protect the moral health and sovereign borders of America, not just from external threats, but from the perceived threat of that "other" media, the fictional one not constrained by (just the) facts (ma'am). In *The Twilight of the Idols*, Nietzsche endorses the power of semiology to expose the interdependent relationship between the morality business and the politics of sovereign representations:

> To this extent moral judgment is never to be taken literally: as such it never contains anything but nonsense. But as *semeiotics* it remains of incalculable value: it reveals, to the informed man at least, the most precious realities of cultures and inner worlds which did not know enough to "understand" themselves. Morality is merely "sign" language, merely symptomatology; one must already know *what* it is about to derive profit from it.
>
> (Nietzsche 55)

A half-century after Shaw, as the circulation of moral values from Hollywood goes global, there is a growing margin of profit to be had from a study of the "sign language" of spy films. Indeed, Shaw found his Cassandra-echo in a recent *New York Times* editorial by its former managing editor, A.M. Rosenthal. Sent out to pasture a few years ago, Rosenthal takes care to fill his regular column, "On My Mind," with literally unreadable ruminations and politically objectionable droppings. Since Rosenthal's sinecure, I have religiously avoided the upper-right corner of the Op-Ed page, but the title of his March 30 piece, "America the Terrorist," proved too irresistible. It begins with great promise:

> From Presidents on down, officials of the United States engage in murder, treason, bombing and torture – all on the soil of the country. ... Military and intelligence agencies send executives into the streets to shoot Americans and foreigners or blow them up in their hotels. ... Politicians can get away with faking their own assassinations to get elected and with other scams, like drug control.

Borderline ravings, yes, but clearly an improvement over his earlier *oeuvre*. With the Oscars a day away I should have foreseen the moral punchline which followed: "The crimes mentioned above were detailed in four movies I have seen. Millions around the world also saw them, or will." Rosenthal, always somewhat behind the curve, singles out *JFK*, *Lethal Weapon* and, surprisingly, *Bob Roberts*, for their critical depiction of the American government and the CIA in particular. He saves the most opprobrium and space for a more recent film, *Point of No Return*. Starring Bridget Fonda, the film is an American remake of Luc Bresson's

La femme Nikita, a stunning contribution to the popular French film genre, Late Cynicism. Rosenthal describes it as "a beauty, a collector's item of Satanization that should play big in Teheran." After detailing the various crimes against humanity committed by Fonda under the auspices of an American intelligence agency – "presumably the CIA" – Rosenthal poses the power-packed rhetorical question that must have sent a hundred agents (Hollywood, not intelligence) reaching for their cellular phones:

> I wonder – did the producers themselves give a thought to the idea of showing American officials capable of bombing terrorism against American civilians in an American city? Would they still make that scene after the bombing of the World Trade Center? How does this hit you: The CIA did it?

The shades of Shaw begin to take on definition when Rosenthal resorts to an anonymous foil to make a pathetic point:

> But it's fiction – what's the harm? A movie maker I particularly admire said that when I brought up Hollywood's killer-image of government... But granted that most of the films are taken as fiction – at least by Americans – they still amount to deliberate defamation of the American governmental system and they still make me sick.

Rosenthal's texts have always been prone to auto-deconstruction, that is, inadvertently speaking the truth out of the side of mouth that does not have the foot in it. But it is rare that documentation would so swiftly follow to prove that the truth of the matter is even stranger – and potentially more damning – than Rosenthal's limited political imagination. On the same day of the *New York Times'* editorial, the *Village Voice* came out with a seven-page article by Robert Friedman, "The CIA and the Sheikh," which traced in detail the links between CIA funding of anti-Soviet Afghanistan Islamic fundamentalists, who, having defeated their immediate enemy, were now turning their considerable training and weaponry against the "Great Satan," America.[3] So, "The CIA did it"?

For an answer to that one, best stay tuned for the made-for-TV movie(s), "The Sheikh Omar Abdel Rahman Story." In the meantime, that between-time (with apologies to Gramsci) when reruns are in their last cycle and pilots for the new season have not yet been aired, it is more profitable to sift through some of the other morbid political, moral, and epistemological symptoms mooted by Shaw and Rosenthal. Although it is easy to lampoon their moral priggishness, they appreciate the economy of meaning that circulates between imaginative and political discourses of sovereignty, from the emblematic figures of the cowboy to gangster to spy to statesman – and back again. And they take seriously, if only to condemn it, the primary "sign language" of the genre, conspiracy theory. But they have trouble understanding the appeal of conspiratorial reasoning, how it has become a more attractive alternative to conventional logic as "true" stories become stranger than their fictional representations.

If we leave behind our rational garb and take a plunge into this river of real-time representation of espionage and terror – and give it a Hollywood "Anarchist" treatment – all kinds of serendipitous insights might follow. In brief, the message of the signs as I read them is that we can measure the attenuation of sovereign discourses by the lack of measure in the response to any new threat or challenge to them. To be sure, it is a tragedy that six people were killed in the bomb blast, and there is good reason to keep track of potential threats to our safety. But how are we to gauge the level of response to those deaths and putative global dangers against the "normal" homicides and crimes that visit New York City and the world every day?

While it is still fresh, reconsider the immediate aftermath and after-images of the World Trade Center incident. On the first day, Governor Mario Cuomo set the stage: 'The damage looks like a bomb; it smells like a bomb; it's probably a bomb." He went on to declare that "normalcy" cannot return "to this safest and greatest city and state and nation in the world until the culprits are caught" (*Economist* 25 March 6–12). Considering that this statement came at the end of a week in which six residents of the Bronx were lined up and shot through the back of the head, and a seventh, in a related incident, was assassinated outside a Bronx courthouse, one must ask, what constitutes "normalcy"? The answer: abnormal events such as this one.

Put another way, the *Ur*-text of sovereignty, the myth of the sovereign state, is woven from a web of words, tropes, and concepts with sticky meanings which entrap the critically unwary. Constant discursive repairs must be made to this web of meaning, for it is under daily assault by a range of external and internal forces, material and immaterial challenges. The list is long and by now familiar: accelerating economic flows, viral epidemics, acid rain and acid-wash jeans, ICBMs and BCCIS, Sony, Krupps, and Time-Warner, TRW, IBM, and CNN. But these challenges effect only low-order maintenance repairs to sovereignty, like selective tariff-borders and tactical ideological operations. These sovereignty effects simultaneously provide the illusion of protection and immure the citizen from the costs that might attend such protection. It takes a brick falling through the web, a rented Rider van full of K-Mart explosives, to reveal the highly tenuous and highly ambiguous nature of sovereignty – and to call forth the radical otherness of the conspiracy text. Whether it is the CIA or the mujahedeen – or both – the conspiracy text underwrites the "abnormality" of an unprotected territory and unpredictable death.

The moral outcry that surrounded the film *JFK* a good illustration of this. As demonstrated by a variety of polls taken over the last three decades, lone gunman theories and monocausal explanations early on proved inadequate to explain the death of the president. Falling apart on their own illogics, the official stories were quickly displaced by conspiratorial reasoning. Much more interesting – and telling – than the technical debate over the distortion of the facts in the film *JFK* was the underlying epistemological assumption that there could only be one "truth" – authorized by the Warren Commission – and only one way to represent it – through the objectivity of the juridical process and, in a pinch, journalism (preferably print).

Director Oliver Stone *was* criticized for his deviations from the official story, but the real moral assault was aimed at his refusal to accept the epistemic privileging of the single representation of truth. His refusal was not so much manifested in the substance of the film, but in what Derrida identifies as the author's will to power in the text, his *style*. Stone chose a style of authenticity identified early on by Walter Benjamin as most appropriate for an age of cinematic reproduction: "the work must raise to the very highest level the art of quoting without quotation marks. Its theory is intimately linked to that of montage" (Benjamin 3). The rapid montage editing-in of "real" talking and exploding heads with hyperreal actors and simulated re-enactments – standard fare on tabloid TV and ubiquitous at supermarket check-outs – was considered sacrilegious when dealing with the death of such a mythical figure as John Kennedy.

The highest expression in the film of this montage construction of truth comes during the restaurant meeting of Jim Garrison with his prosecution team, when the assassination plot is woven together through a syntactic series of rapid flashbacks featuring the darkroom construction of a key photograph of Oswald, his dramatic capture in the movie theatre, and the subsequent interrogation where he claims to have been a patsy. The dinner scene is shot in real-time, full technicolour; the darkroom scenes as a re-creation in shadows of black, white, and infra-red; and the interrogation in grainy news-reel. In an act of cinematic mimicry, the photographed head of Oswald is eventually paired by a cut-and-paste job with the body of an anonymous figure, creating the damning *Life* magazine photograph of Oswald with a copy of the *Militant* newspaper and *the* rifle. In real-time, Garrison's assistant narrates her hypothesis that the photograph must be a fake because the sun's shadow on the nose of Oswald – actually a photograph of Gary Oldman (and a body double?) – does not correspond with the shadow cast by the body.

In this remarkable series of buzz-cuts across real-time and cinematic space, between representation and simulation, even the slackest viewer cannot escape the point driven home by Stone's trademark sledge-hammer style: the authority of the truth is constructed through the technical reproduction of reality – and it is through an over-representation of reality that Stone deconstructs any claims for the authenticity of an "original" version of the truth. Stone's crime was not to distort reality but to mimic its media reproduction with such dizzying detail and technical prowess that he creates a simulation of the assassination that, in the fitting hyperbole of Jean Baudrillard, precedes and engenders the reality that it purports to represent. So, "The CIA did it"?

As the technologies of representation proliferate and infiltrate into all walks of life, this problem of over-represented truths compounds. In a giddy moment of the presidential campaign, Bill Clinton captured this new *Zeitgeist* (and raised suspicions in some camps that he did inhale):

This is an expressive land that produced CNN and MTV. We were all born for the information age. This is a jazzy nation, thank goodness, for my sake, that created be-bop and hip-hop and all those other things. We are wired for real time.

(Karen de Witt *New York Times* 28 February 1993)

The acceleration of communication coupled with the seeming ubiquity of contingency has produced a global interconnectivity that lends itself to the grand (and oddly reassuring) narratives of conspiracy. Again, Walter Benjamin puts it best: "In times of terror, when everyone is something of a conspirator, everybody will be in a situation where he has to play detective."[4]

The cultural critic Frederic Jameson believes that this new global mapping of the world has generated a "geopolitical aesthetic," a technological, artistic form of perception that best envisions the antagonistic forces of an integrative capitalism and an atomistic international politics. He cites an early expression of it in the spy film *Three Days of the Condor* (Pollack, 1975). More specifically, he centres on the opening credits, flashed in computer fonts while printers, scanners, and disk drives whirr and clatter in the back ground. Espionage is reduced to the commodification of information, excepting of course the film's Shavian "Anarchist," Robert Redford, the iconoclastic researcher for the CIA who reads books and stumbles upon a conspiracy within the CIA bent on securing world oil supplies by whatever means necessary. Redford explains who he is – and who he is not – to Faye Dunaway, his (initially) unwilling accomplice:

> I am not a spy. I just read books. We read everything that is published in the world. We feed the plots into the computer, and check it against CIA actual operations and plans. We read adventure and novels and journals … who would invent a job like that?

But I think Jameson misses the signalling of a conterminous if not displacing force field behind the conspiratorial attraction. Not quite at the hyper-speed of *JFK*, the plot is constituted by factors of time: the speed of the computers, the flow of information, the critical time in which Redford is absent from his building, the shuttle-traffic between Washington and New York, the creation of a telephone cyberspace that out-paces the CIA's tracking devices. Indeed, the dreadfully arty sex scene with Dunaway is generated by Redford's desire to "just have it all stop." Even the title change from book to film is significant: from *Six Days of the Condor* (Grady 1974) to three. Taken together, we can detect an early manifestation of a chronopolitical aesthetic, where the pace of information and capital flows becomes as important a factor as the place of static borders and geopolitics.[5]

The third aesthetic of the conspiratorial text could be more broadly described as technopolitical. The exemplary case that blurs and blends the realms of fiction and fact into a powerful intertext of international intrigue remains the Tom Clancy "techno-thriller." Clancy's first bestseller, *Hunt for the Red October*, modeled on the unsuccessful run of a Soviet frigate for the Swedish coast, sported an appreciative blurb from President Reagan. His second novel, *Red Storm Rising*, a thinly fictionalized mosaic of NATO war games, was authoritatively cited by

Vice President Quayle in a foreign policy speech to prove that the US needed an anti-satellite capability. In his third, *Patriot Games*, Clancy magnified the threat of terrorism to prove that state counter-terrorism works, a view endorsed by Secretary of Defense Weinberger in a laudatory review of the book for the *Wall Street Journal* – which was then reprinted in the Pentagon's *Current News* for the edification of the 7,000-odd Defense and State Department officials who make up its readership. The author's fourth novel, *The Cardinal of the Kremlin*, in which Clancy plots the plight of a mole in the Kremlin, affirmed the need to reconstruct the impermeable borders of the sovereign state with Star Wars. His fifth novel, *Clear and Present Danger*, opens with a quote from Pascal, "Law, without force, is impotent," and closes with the unrepressed message that the US will be impotent if it does not use – prudently of course – its technological edge in night-vision, GBU-15 laser-guided bombs, and satellite surveillance against drug cartels. His most recent novel, *The Sum of All Fears* is too long, too hubristic, too *conspiratorial* to reduce to a pat synopsis.

Taken together, Clancy's novels anticipate the strategic simulations that filled our screens during the Gulf War. Jammed with technical detail and seductive ordnance, devoid of recognizable human characters – except, once again, the outsider on the inside, Jack Ryan – and obliquely linked to historical events, they act as free-floating signifiers for saving the reality principle of the national security state: namely, that the sovereign state's boundaries, like those between fiction and fact, simulation and reality, can once again be made impermeable to any threat posed by this year's model of evil.

To this effect, the three aesthetics take on a syncretic power in the film version of *Patriot Games*. The first film ever (publicly) to have an assist by the CIA, it elevates the terrorist threat to the magnitude necessary to justify the full utility of the surveillance machine. Verisimilitude is established early in the film, right after the attack on the "Royals" by a splinter group of IRA terrorists. Three critical scenes are geopolitically and chronopolitically linked, without a cut, through use of a "live" report by CNN, which shrinks into a television set watched by the terrorists as they change the licence plates of their get-away cars; the terrorists are seeking an instant intelligence report – as is CIA director James Earl Jones, who watches the same CNN report in Langley; his dyspeptic reaction reflects on the screen as it shifts locales in a pull-back shot that opens up into the hospital room where Jack Ryan's wife nervously watches as she hovers over her "Anarchist" husband, recovering from wounds suffered in his rash attack on the terrorists. Everyone is wired to real-time, interconnected by the cyberspatiality of CNN.

The global reach of these aesthetics is driven home in the brief moment when moral qualms come up against technological capability – and fall short. After Ryan has made full use of his intuition, intellectual drive, and a couple of Keyhole satellites to identify the desert training camp of the Irish terrorists, he is brought up to a strange, darkened room full of high-clearance officials watching television screens. At first confused, he begins to understand what he is witnessing: the real-time results of his research, an assault by the British counter-terrorist unit, the SAS, on the terrorist camp. For the first time his face registers some kind of moral doubt, even repugnance, when an infra-red image of a body darkens as it dies, and a coffee-sipping suit watching the action from a safe tele-distance cooly remarks, "*That* is definitely a kill."

There is another side to this, mentioned earlier, the appealing side of the conspiratorial aesthetic, which produces and is sustained by the tension between fear and desire. The world system might, on the face of it, be speeding out of control, yet we cling to the metaphysical faith and find perverse pleasure in the cinematic confirmation that somewhere under the table, in the highest corporate or governmental office, someone is pulling the strings – or at the very least, is willing with the best technology, fastest speed, and longest reach to intervene secretly, if sinisterly, when necessary. It then makes sense to find in coeval events, synchronicities, even odd accidents, the intellectual evidence and psychological comfort of the hidden hand. In other words, the fictional sovereignty of the self and the state melds and materializes as a truth at such moments of high conspiracy and eventful contiguity. Everything, everyone can stop, connect, and find a place to be in the cinematic representation of this scheme of things.[6]

Marshall McLuhan and C. Wright Mills almost got it right: as refugees from uneven levels of modernity seek sanctuary in the global castle, as meaning is molecularized by a pervasive media, as reason leaps from the window of vulnerability, as morality plays nightly on prime time, the Hollywood medium with its vast resources has become the ultimate message parlour of *both* the power élite and its critics. The message it is sending today is not so different from the one foreordained by Shaw. Over the years Hollywood has expanded its resources, extended its reach, and the role of the "Anarchist" has maintained its dramatic appeal. Now the hero gets a technological assist – like *Aliens*' Ripley during her epic battle against the mother-bitch alien, or *Patriot Games*' Ryan as he relies on satellite reconnaissance.

But with the Soviet empire gone and the American one showing all the signs of over-reach, should we not expect a representational shift, if only for the absence of a powerful enemy, a source of oppressive authority? In other words, as international anarchy looms larger, should not the appeal of the "Anarchist" diminish? Or perhaps the centrality of the figure reflects a deeper instinct in America, a salubrious one at that, best captured by biker Brando's famous reply in *The Wild One* when asked what he was rebelling against: "Whaddyagot?" In other words, rebellion for rebellion's sake?

Like the genre itself, this essay has been long on imaginative speculations – and comes up short on plausible answers. At best, and at the margins, a study of the cinematic signs of espionage outlines the emptiness at the centre which is sovereignty, the collapsing black hole of state power and morality to which conspiracy theory is drawn. They tell us, through a symptomatic reading, that the search for a cipher to the espionage text is misguided, leading not to a key of understanding but to the "McGuffin," the nonexistent yet powerful pretext which informs "natural" cinematic and security states of fear and suspense. Once deprived of a solid centre or a worthy enemy, espionage takes on the shabby look of a protection racket, where a variety of racketeers operating inside and outside the penetrated borders of sovereignty create the mayhem and disorder that require their special services.[7]

My final reply to Shaw and Rosenthal must, then, rely on and reflect the forces of chance, contiguity, and contingency which espionage and the conspiracies of sovereignty seek to rule. In 1975, two French thinkers were focusing their considerable intellectual energies on the representational power of sovereignty. Paul Virilio, architect and social critic, was curating an exhibition on "*Bunker Archéologie*" at the *Musée des Arts Décoratifs*, a photo-installation which presented the Maginot Line as the last serious attempt to provide a territorial defence of sovereignty. In an accompanying essay, "*La Forteresse*," he envisioned the de-territorialization of sovereignty giving rise to a new identity of self-defence, the "double-agent":

> *La transparence, l'ubiquité, la connaissance totale et instantanée, voilà ce qu'il faut pour survivre. ... L'espionnage devient un phénomène de masse. ... Les professionnels de l'espionnage sont litteralément doublés, d'une part par la prolifération des systèmes d'informations, et de l'autre par le développement considérable de la délation dans les masses, les amateurs. Les agents spéciaux n'ont plus le monople du déviolement, de la trahison; c'est le perfectionnement des organes technologiques de perception et de détection qui les remplacent un peu partout dans de nombreuses missions.*
>
> (Virilio 29–30)

And in 1975, as Professor of History of Systems of Thought at the *Collège de France,* Michel Foucault presented a *résumé de cours* for the year's lecture topic, "*Il faut defendre la société.*" Like Virilio, he warned of the perverse effects that were to be expected from the attenuation of traditional forms of sovereignty. He opened with the declaration, "*Pour mener l'analyse concrete des rapports de pouvoir, il faut abandonner le modèle juridique de la souveraineté,*" and ended with a critical call to philosophical arms, for a counter-intelligence and a counter-mythology to state power:

> *En somme, par opposition au discours philosophico-juridique qui s'ordonne au problème de la souveraineté et de la loi, ce discours qui déchiffre la permanence de la guerre dans la société, est un discours essentiellement historico-politique, un discours où la vérité fonctionne comme arme pour une victoire partisane, un discours sombrement critique et en même temps intensément mythique.*
>
> (Foucault)

If this all sounds too incredible, conspiratorial, allegorical, or just too French, remember that when a dragon dies, a variety of snakes spring forth from its belly. What this is about, after all, is the ultimate absurdity: the reason of states.

Notes

1 See *Everything You Always Wanted to Know about Lacan (But Were Afraid to Ask Hitchcock)*, ed. Slavoj Zizek (London: Verso, 1992).

2 'The god of writing is thus also a god of medicine. Of "medicine": both a science and an occult drug. Of the remedy and the poison. The god of writing is the god of the *pharmakon.'* See Jacques Derrida, "Plato's Pharmacy," in *Dissemination*, from *A Derrida Reader: Between the Blinds*, ed. Peggy Kamuf (New York: Columbia University Press, 1991) 123.

3 The connective tissue is sometimes thin, but Friedman presents the case that Sheikh Omar Abdel Rahman, the leader of the El Salaam Mosque in Jersey City who has been linked to El Sayyid Nosair (supposed assassin of Rabbi Meir Kahane) and Mohammed Salameh (alleged bomber of the World Trade Center), enjoyed at one time or another US government protection. The evidence largely rests on the CIA's backing of the sheikh and his mujahedeen supporters in Afghanistan and Pakistan during their efforts to topple the Afghan government left behind by the Soviets when they departed in February 1989. But Friedman places great weight (perhaps too much so for an array of bureaucracies that have been known in the past to commit the odd bungle) on the fact that the sheikh was able to gain a tourist visa to the US, and later a green card, in spite of the fact he was on the State Department's terrorist watch-list. One week later the *New York Times* also began to investigate the possible links of the US government to the World Trade Center bombing. See Robert I. Friedman, "The CIA and the Sheikh," *Village Voice*, 30 March 1993, 20–1; and Alison Mitchell, "After Bombing, New Interest in Brooklyn Holy War Recruiters," *New York Times*, 11 April 1993, 23.

4 Walter Benjamin, *Charles Baudelaire: A Lyric Poet in the Era of High Capitalism*, trans. Harry Zohn (London: Verso, 1983), 40. My analysis here has benefited from a dialogue with four thinkers: for a fresh and penetrating perspective on Benjamin's outline for a transgressive form of knowledge, see Jeneen Hobby, "On Raising Consciousness in Walter Benjamin" (Ph.D. dissertation, 1993); for a critical, Lacanian, interpretation of espionage, see Carol Pech, "Deciphering the Gaze: A Different Look at Espionage" (unpublished essay); for a full appreciation of the political effects of the "globalization of contingency," see William E. Connolly, "Identity and Difference in Global Politics," *International/Intertextual Relations: Postmodern Readings of World Politic*, (New York: MacMillan, 1989), 323–42; and for the details, Bret Brown.

5 For more on the representation of chronopolitics in espionage literature, see Der Derian, "The Intertextual Power of International Intrigue," *Antidiplomacy: Spies, Terror, Speed, and War*, (Oxford: Basil Blackwell, 1992), 40–70. And for those who appreciate Hegel's (robotic) owl of Minerva flying at twilight in *Blade Runner*, I offer as an aside the significant absence of being-in-the-world of the one employee who does not show up for work on the day of the hit in *Three Days of the Condor:* "R. Heidegger."

6 This is more easily put than explained. It might be better to question a few of the contiguities of "real" real-time representations that, with little imaginary work, seem more *irreal* than their fictional representations. What, say, of the moment when Clair George, former head of Operations and most-senior CIA official to be charged in the Iran-contra affair, gave testimony at his trial while Oliver North appeared that night on the NBC sit-com, "Wings," playing his parody as himself, promoting his book, *Under Fire*? What of Jack Ryan's attempt to save the "Royals" in *Patriot Games* at the very moment they were self-destructing in their "real" tabloid life, with the aid of what appear to be MI6 intercepts and leaks of royal telephone sex? Was the World Trade Center bombed because the "perps" knew, as anyone would who has seen *Three Days of the Condor*, that it housed the New York City headquarters of the CIA? Or in one of the stranger moments of cinematic and intelligence forces working together to keep the dark forces at bay, what are we to make of the recent Freedom of Information Act revelations of the 25-year alliance between Walt Disney and Edgar Hoover – during which Disney spied on

"Communistic agitation" in the film industry and made some script changes in episodes of the *Mickey Mouse Club* show for the FBI, and in exchange was made a "full Special Agent in Charge," which meant, according to a memo from Hoover, "affording you a means of absolute identity throughout your lifetime" (see Herbert Mitgang, "Disney Link to the FBI and Hoover is Disclosed," *New York Times*, 6 May 1993, C17). To paraphrase the president, have we been cross-wired by real time?

7 I recently experienced a slightly more benign form of this protection racket while taking a taxi with some friends late at night in Chicago. The driver, after telling us that he was taking a short-cut through the most dangerous area of the city, declared that he would give anybody 50 bucks to walk the neighbourhood. When I called his bluff he retracted the offer, which clearly was intended to make all of the occupants of the cab feel safer, and award him a higher tip for it. My argument is that the state similarly produces sovereignty effects by the manufacture or magnification of threats.

Works Cited

Benjamin, Walter N. "Theoretics of Knowledge, Theory of Progress," *The Arcades Project*, *The Philosophical Quarterly*, Fall-Winter 1983–84, 3.

Connolly, William E. "Identity and Difference in Global Politics," *International/Intertextual Relations: Postmodern Readings of World Politics*. New York: MacMillan, 1989.

Der Derian, James. "The Intertextual Power of International Intrigue," *Antidiplomacy: Spies, Terror, Speed, and War*. Oxford: Basil Blackwell, 1992.

Derrida, Jacques. "Plato's Pharmacy," in *Dissemination*, from *A Derrida Reader: Between the Blinds*. ed. Peggy Kamuf. New York: Columbia University Press, 1991.

de Witt, Karen. "Washington Has an Oval Office That's Decidedly Not Square," *New York Times*, 28 February 1993.

Economist, 6–12 March 1993, 25.

Foucault, Michel. *Resumes des Cours: 1970–1982*. Paris: Julliard, 1989.

Friedman, Robert I. "The CIA and the Sheikh," *Village Voice*, 30 March 1993, 20–1.

Jameson, Frederic. *The Geopolitical Aesthetic: Cinema and Space in the World System*. Bloomington: Indiana University Press, 1992.

Mitchell, Alison. "After Bombing, New Interest in Brooklyn Holy War Recruiters," *New York Times*, 11 April, 1993, 23.

Mitgang, Herbert. "Disney Link to the FBI and Hoover is Disclosed," *New York Times*, 6 May 1993, C17.

Nietzsche, Friedrich. *Twilight of the Idols*. trans. R.J. Hollingdale. Middlesex, UK; Penguin, 1968.

Pech, Carol. "Deciphering the Gaze: A Different Look at Espionage" (unpublished essay).

Shaw, George Bernard. *The Political Madness in America and Nearer Home*. London: Constable, 1933.

Virilio, Paul. "La Forteresse," in *Bunker Archeologie*. Paris: Centre Georges Pomidou-CCI, 1975.

Zizek, Slavoj, ed. *Everything You Always Wanted to Know about Lacan (But Were Afraid to Ask Hitchcock)*. London: Verso, 1992.

11 Great men, monumental history, and not-so-grand theory

A meta-review of Henry Kissinger's *Diplomacy*

Source: Forum review article, *Mershon International Studies Review* (April 1995), vol. 39, no. 1, pp. 173–180.

Editor's Note: In the first issue of the Mershon International Studies Review the Forum section featured a debate concerning the recently published book by Alexander L. George, Bridging the Gap: Theory and Practice in Foreign Policy (1993). The primary thesis of the book, that both scholars and practitioners of foreign policy benefit from better communication and collaboration, went unchallenged. In this chapter, James Der Derian, who authored On Diplomacy (1987) and Antidiplomacy (1992), offers a critique of this assumption through a meta-review of the recent book by analyst-turned-politician Henry Kissinger: Diplomacy (1994a).

Diplomacy is a history of the attempt by statesmen to bring order to international politics through a balancing of war and diplomacy, national interest and morality, domestic values and international necessities. For Kissinger, lessons derived from the balance of power politics of classical figures like Richelieu, Metternich, and Bismarck must be applied to current times if the "new world order" is ever to become more than a slogan of aspiration. This is especially true for the United States, where the recurrent tension between Theodore Roosevelt's realism and Woodrow Wilson's idealism must be skillfully and diplomatically balanced if the U.S. is not to slip back into the twin dangers of isolationism and exceptionalism.

Certainly it would be worth examining how the author became individualized in a culture like ours, what status he has been given, at what moment studies of authenticity and attribution began, in what kind of system of valorization the author was involved, at what point we began to recount the lives of authors rather than of heroes, and how this fundamental category of "the-man-and-his work criticism" began.

(Michel Foucault, 1984: 101)

How can one begin to review the book of the peerless statesman who won the Nobel Peace Prize—and approved the wiretapping of his then executive assistant, now National Security Adviser, Anthony Lake? Who opened the door to China— and recommended the secret bombing of Cambodia? Who has now written a book of such immodest scope and size that it graces the summer cover of *Esquire*—as modest cover for supermodel Christie Brinkley on the beach?

Of course, the book is not the man (and Kissinger not Nixon). But Henry Kissinger, the fifty-sixth Secretary of State and former professor at Harvard University, long ago lost control over what little remained of his author-function, to a host, or, as he has been prone to see it, to a parasitic body of envious academics, resentful bureaucrats, sound-bite pundits, not to mention, popular culture mavens. Kissinger is just too controversial, too multifaceted, too *big* for one review. Hence, this *Forum* is a review of reviews, or meta-review, of his latest work, *Diplomacy*. It is, then, not so much a review of Kissinger's text, as it is a review of what lies (sometimes in both senses of the word) between the lines: its discursive, ideological, and functional effect on a variety of writers/critics who convey the multiple, conflictive, and sometimes intersecting interests of the government, the university, and the media. The list of reviewers is long as well as impressive, and I have chosen from it what I believe to be a reasonable cross-sampling. The reviews of historians Gordon Craig, Ernest May, and Simon Schama are included as much for their learned reputations as for the toniness of their publishers—the literary iron triangle of *The New York Review of Books, The New York Times Book Review*, and the *New Yorker* respectively. Charles Powell, a foreign affairs adviser (albeit for Prime Minister Thatcher) provides more of a practitioner's perspective in the *National Review.* Journalists Walter Issacson, Anthony Lewis, and Russell Watson represent the more popular media—*Time, The New York Times*, and *Newsweek.* And two International Relations theorists, Hedley Bull and Fred Halliday, and former adviser to President Nixon, H. R. Haldeman, drop in to fill out the portrait of Henry Kissinger as scholar and practitioner of diplomacy. Through a dialogue of these reviews I do not seek, as the literary critic Roland Barthes (1986: 52) put it, "to establish what the author meant," but "what the reader understands;" and in this special case, that means how different understandings of American foreign policy are produced.

First, however, all reviewers of Kissinger seem compelled, either out of respect for the author or out of fear of a perfunctory full-page retort, to engage in the *de rigueur* ritual of revealing their own interests. Walter Issacson is a good exemplar. In his review of *Diplomacy* for *Time* (April 11, 1992), Issacson admits coming "to this book as an interested party," but then takes care to establish his middle-of-the-road credentials by noting the mixed reactions of critics to his own biography of Kissinger, "which many of his detractors, and some of his putative friends, said pulled too many punches, and which his fervent defenders (himself among them) decried as too harsh" (Issacson, 1992: 82). This strategy of detachment is attractive yet deceptive. It might arbitrarily yield a *via media*, but it is no guarantee of objectivity. The same, of course, holds for a meta-review. But to the extent that a meta-review speaks in a plurality of other voices—or more precisely, writes among a number of other texts—it might just offer a wider approach toward that highly contested terrain, the "truth" of the matter.

Nonetheless, since it is impossible to avoid the task of selecting one review over another (why, for instance, Walter Issacson and not Lyndon LaRouche?), as well as interpreting one as more plausible than another (one man's slander is another's truth-claim), a ritual disclaimer appears to be a necessary form of casualty insurance for the always hazardous passage from reader to critic. So I wish to inform all readers that fate and proximity have caused me to rub shoulders with two former aides to Kissinger who saw fit to sue him for illegal wiretaps placed on their telephones during the Cambodian invasion. I admit to a passing friendship with one of them, Tony Lake (and his dog, Tucker, too); and as an exploited adjunct professor at Columbia University, I shared an office with Mort Halperin (but avoided the telephone). I have also written a book on the same topic of diplomacy, only slightly less pretentiously titled than Kissinger's (*On Diplomacy: A Genealogy of Western Estrangement*), which does not show up in his index. Going further back, I once organized a sit-in at my high school during the invasion of Cambodia. When there was greater clarity to my moral universe, I thought "War Criminal" a more appropriate middle-name than "Alfred." And I was always somewhat dumbfounded why so many glamorous women showed up at Kissinger's side at celebrity events.

Thus, ritually cleansed through confession of guilty associations, intellectual rancor, political prejudice, and personal envy, I-become-one can objectively meta-review *Diplomacy*.

"Great men"

As most reviewers note in their lead paragraphs—after remarking on either the brilliance or the flaws of the book—*Diplomacy* is not really about diplomacy. It is mainly a history of a number of famous dead statesmen (the Great Helmsman and the Iron Lady briefly break the white male ranks) whose ghosts live on in the very much alive if under-employed Kissinger. "Henry Kissinger's *Diplomacy*," says Ernest May in *The New York Times Book Review*, "is a book of maxims disguised as a history of statecraft" (p. 3). Some see this as a positive attribute: "Despite its title, the book is not actually about diplomacy, an activity practiced by indisputably superior beings, but ultimately on a par with Japanese flower-arranging and Scrabble," writes Charles Powell (p. 63) in the *National Review*. Others are agnostic on the question. In *Newsweek*, Russell Watson states, "His new book, *Diplomacy*, is less a history of the statesman's craft than a celebration of great men who practiced it single-mindedly, from Cardinal Richelieu to President Reagan" (p. 42). And a long time observer of diplomatic practice, Gordon Craig, writes in *The New York Review of Books*, that "Henry Kissinger's *Diplomacy* is highly selective in what it includes. Despite its title and the fact that it is dedicated to 'the men and women of the Foreign Service of the United States of America,' it says almost nothing about them or about diplomacy proper, its origins and the development of its procedures, or the great ambassadors of the eighteenth and nineteenth centuries and their accomplishments" (p. 8). But Craig charitably finds the omission "understandable," given the quickening superannuation of traditional diplomacy by summit conferences and—perhaps Kissinger's most significant institutional contribution to the trade—shuttle diplomacy.

Ernst May's review pushes the point furthest and finds fault to the degree that *"Diplomacy* ... is 'great man history'" (p. 3). The book favors historical figures like Richelieu, Metternich, and Bismarck who preferred the principle of power over the power of principle in their analysis and conduct of foreign affairs. Others, like Gladstone who placed more faith in Christian values than balance of power, or Napolean III who relied too much on popular opinion, are held up as bad examples for contemporary statesmen. But the book also suffers from other historical misdemeanors. Not only does it favor the personality and testimony of a few great men (who happen to bear no little resemblance to Kissinger himself), but it does so at the neglect of forces and trends which cannot be reduced to the actions of individuals. This might be due to Kissinger's failure "to acknowledge a canon," and May gives as an example (incorrectly, it turns out)—the lack of a single reference to Sir Harold Nicolson's similarly titled 1939 classic. Finally, and perhaps most pointedly, given Kissinger's professorial beginnings, May claims that *Diplomacy* "makes the types of mistakes for which students fail to get pass degrees in history." "To cite just three examples," says May (usually a sure sign in a review that just *x* number of examples were actually spotted): European diplomats did not need a primer from Woodrow Wilson on the idea of self-determination; the use of a quote from Lloyd George, on his intent to "squeeze Germany until the pips squeak," was "wrong and unjust" (p. 24); and the knowledge of German generals about Hitler's plans for world domination was misrepresented by Kissinger's skewed interpretation of the 1937 Hossbach memorandum.

May's final verdict? Some classic maxims for diplomacy derived from a highly selective group of great men—but at the sacrifice of good history.

Wasting no time or ink, Kissinger responded three weeks later with a full-page riposte in the "Letters" section of *The New York Times Review of Books* (Kissinger, 1994b)—which led, in turn, to a letter from May. One could attempt to adjudicate the truth-claims of each. But even where one of them might have gotten it factually wrong (Nicolson *was* footnoted, and there were only a few top generals at the meeting made famous by the Hossbach Memorandum), the criticisms still ring true. (Kissinger, under the originality imperative, does seem disinclined to acknowledge intellectual debts; and May does come off as overly pedantic about the number of generals.) One can attempt to decipher some deeper meaning from the exchange, as suggested by Kissinger's assertion that May's review is full of "personal invective" and "personal aspersions" (1994b: 31). Indeed, in the spring of 1970, May, along with thirteen colleagues from Harvard, came to have lunch with Kissinger at the White House, during which they registered their opposition to the Cambodia incursion. From Kissinger's book as well as his earlier memoirs, in which Kissinger viewed this belated opposition to a war begun by the Eastern Establishment to be one more sign of their abdication of responsibility, it can be safely adduced that there is as much a personal as a professional history at work here.

I believe, however, that it is more fruitful to leave the fact-checking to the copy-editors, and psychologizing to the armchair therapists, and take instead a closer look at the author-function revealed by this exchange. First identified by Michel Foucault in his seminal essay, "What is an Author?" (Foucault, 1984), the primary function of the modern author is, as represented by modern critics and in contradiction to traditional views, to *reduce* meaning: "The author is the principle of thrift in the proliferation of meaning" (Foucault, 1984: 118). Instead of an open text inspired by a genial writer, the author is presented as a site of exclusion, where meaning ceases to circulate. Foucault writes:

> In fact, if we are accustomed to presenting the author as a genius, as a perpetual surging of invention, it is because, in reality, we make him function in exactly the opposite fashion. One can say that the author is an ideological product, since we represent him as the opposite of his historically real function ... The author is therefore the ideological figure by which one marks the manner in which we fear the proliferation of meaning.
>
> (1984: 119)

Is this not what we witness as well in the Kissinger-May exchange, and in modern criticism in general: one more attempt to regulate and fix meaning, not as a reflection but in opposition to the highly ambiguous, widely contingent nature of international politics? What if we reopen the gates, not to prove the authenticity, originality, or accuracy of Kissinger's work, but to ask, as does Foucault, how the text is being used, for what purposes it is appropriated, where does it circulate unimpeded, and what subjects are reconstituted by its discursive economy? We might then be better able to judge the man by the history that he writes.

Monumental history

Speaking from his preferred territory of deep background, Kissinger once remarked to a reporter that "As a professor, I tended to think of history as run by impersonal forces. But when you see it in practice, you see the difference personalities make" (Issacson, 1992: 13). This belief is amply confirmed by his political as well as literary work, and *Diplomacy* is no exception. However, even a historian like Gordon Craig, who has ably demonstrated his own sympathies for the role of individuals in diplomacy in his co-edited work, *The Diplomats* (Craig and Loewenheim, 1994), finds that Kissinger tends to fix his focus too narrowly on heroic figures whose histories just too neatly add up to a Kissingerian exemplar of diplomacy. After praising Kissinger's effort to redress the balance between justice and order through a cautionary tale of statecraft at its *realpolitik* best and legal-moralist worst, Craig finishes the review with the dry yet cutting comment that Kissinger "does not say that a prerequisite of success would be a negotiator as inventive and as tireless as he was himself, but we are perhaps justified in believing that this is assumed" (p. 14).

Another historian, Simon Schama, takes up in a *New Yorker* review where Craig left off. He too testifies to the virtues of a book in which "the tragedies of the Old World are summoned to sober the dangerous innocence of the New" (p. 93). He finds the account of Great Power diplomacy of the nineteenth and early twentieth centuries, "studded with epigrams and lapidary utterances on the practice of power." But as the narrative approaches the reign of "Nixinger," when the ego and insecurity of both men reached a synergistic high, the "book seems to harden into a brittle defensiveness" (p. 93). Schama clearly has a weak spot for Kissinger's use of an "unrepentantly old-fashioned" form of diplomatic history and concurs with him that "American ahistoricism is the cause of our most damaging acts of moral hubris." But he too thinks that Kissinger, at telling moments, gets his history wrong, and blessed with more space than May, he carefully outlines not just what but *why* he gets it wrong. Most damning is his meticulous counter-history of the protagonist of *Diplomacy*, Cardinal Richelieu. Schama argues that Richelieu's Christianity was hardly the fig-leaf for *raison d'etat* that Kissinger makes it out to be. Kissinger fails to take into account the possibility that Richelieu's alliances with foreign Protestants were made so that they could be free to quash his main domestic foe, the Protestant Huguenots. It is a telling example of how Kissinger can be brilliant in his focus on the great game outside and between states, yet is purblind to domestic causes, especially ones with despotic outcomes that can undermine the work of the most adept statesmen. Unlike many of the other reviews, the shadow of Watergate looms large in Schama's interpretation of the work.

Yet all of these valid criticisms seem to scratch the surface of a deeper, more worrying aspect of Kissinger's particular form of historicism. Nietzsche, I think, provides some insights into the Germanic soul that lurks within Kissinger's outward appreciation of America's exceptionalism. In his short work, *The Use and Abuse of History*, Nietzsche writes of a "monumental history" that "lives by false analogy; it entices the brave to rashness, and the enthusiastic to fanaticism by its tempting comparison." "Imagine," asks Nietzsche, "this history in the hands—and the head—of a gifted egoist or an inspired scoundrel; kingdoms would be overthrown, princes murdered, war and revolution let loose, and the number of 'effects in themselves'—in other words, effects without sufficient cause—increased" (Nietzsche, 1957: 16).

I will refrain from pursuing any false analogies to Cambodia, Allende, Angola (Fred Halliday's review is one of the rare ones that does not). I do, however, agree with Nietzsche (as I imagine Kissinger might) that "History is necessary above all to the man of action and power who fights a great fight and needs examples, teachers and comfort he cannot find them among his contemporaries" (Nietzsche, 1957: 12). This is a lesson brought home when one compares Kissinger's *Diplomacy* to the ahistorical, hyper-rationalist, poorly written work that makes up much of contemporary writing on foreign policy in the universities. The history might be overly monumental and the men too great to be true, but the prose is crisp, the insights sharply rendered, and there is a sense of irony to match the recurrent tragedy that defines so much of international politics. However, put bluntly, Kissinger's history suffers for the lack of a higher purpose. To be sure, he professes a desire to redress the balance between morality and power in U.S. foreign policy. But it is buried under what Nietzsche calls "an excess of history," by which "life becomes maimed and degenerate, and is followed by the degeneration of history as well" (Nietzsche, 1957: 12). Nietzsche understands the likes of Kissinger all too well:

> Monumental history is the cloak under which their hatred of present power and greatness masquerades as an extreme admiration of the past. The real meaning of this way of viewing history is disguised as its opposite; whether they wish it or no, they are acting as though their motto were: "let the dead bury the—living."
>
> (1957: 17)

As dramatically demonstrated by a less likely critique of Kissinger's diplomacy as well as *Diplomacy*, the dead *can* bury the living—particularly when the dirt comes packaged in the seemingly inexhaustible medium of CD-ROM. *The Haldeman Diaries: Inside the White House* (The Complete Multimedia Edition) proves all too well what Kissinger espouses in *Diplomacy*. International politics is driven by personalities, but not by their great or even their middling qualities. The *Diaries* is a study in the banality of power, how the petty and often malicious effects of insecure personalities are played out, one might even say displaced, on the stage of national security. And Kissinger is no exception. The entries on Kissinger are numerous, but Anthony Lewis (1994) and others have focused on one particular entry, December 21, 1970, when Kissinger (Henry) and Nixon (P) discuss the withdrawal of American troops in the context of upcoming presidential elections. At first cut, the conversation reeks of crass, if not criminal, opportunism:

> Henry was in for a while, and the P discussed a possible trip for next year. He's thinking about going to Vietnam in April, or whenever we decide to make the basic end of the war announcement. His idea would be to tour around the country, build up Thieu, and so forth, and then make the announcement right afterwards. Henry argues against a commitment that early to withdraw all combat troops because he feels that if we pull them out by the end of '71, trouble can start mounting in '72 that we won't be able to deal with, and which we'll have to answer for at the elections. He prefers, instead, a commitment to have them all out by the end of '72, so that we won't have to deliver finally until after the elections and, therefore, can keep our flanks protected. This would certainly seem to make more sense, and the P seemed to agree in general, but wants Henry to work up plans on it.
>
> (Haldeman, 1994)

No document speaks for itself, and Lewis makes contentious use of this one to assert that the peace reached with North Vietnam in 1972 could have been reached in 1969, were it not for domestic, that is, electoral politics. Kissinger was quick to reply, with another letter to the editor (Kissinger, 1994c). His defense is scattershot: he does not recollect the episode; there is no other paper evidence (Nixon's memoirs as well as Kissinger's own *Diplomacy* are cited as proof); Nixon was probably just blowing off steam about the upcoming election; and most importantly, there is no evidence that "the terms offered by Hanoi in 1972 existed since 1969." But Kissinger has one target in mind, the same as in *Diplomacy:* the kind of "indulgent moralism" displayed by Lewis and others which distracts from "the reality of serious moral dilemmas" in foreign affairs.

Yet, as further proof of the banality of power, what Lewis, Kissinger, and Haldeman fail to note—but the White House log book does not—is that this important meeting on December 21 was followed that very afternoon by Elvis Presley's first and only visit to the Oval Office.

The *Diaries* are full of less damning but, by sheer quantity and monotony, ultimately more convincing evidence that the primary theses of *Diplomacy* are highly suspect. The foreign policy of Kissinger and Nixon was not determined by the deep thoughts of prudent statesmen engaged in balance of power politics, but by intense bureaucratic warfare overlayed by personality conflicts, electoral machinations that would make Machiavelli weep, the deep insecurities of wide and shallow egos, and even one martini too many at the wrong moment in the decision-making cycle.

"Not-so-grand-theory"

Whatever the historical anomalies, no one can fault Kissinger for theoretical inconsistency. From his first book *A World Restored* (1957) to *Diplomacy*, he has maintained a theoretical defense of balance of power politics, and with it, a conservative preference for the maintenance of order over the promulgation of justice, since, in his world-view, they are fundamentally incompatible properties which all-too-often come at the expense of the other. At best, statesmen can balance them, as they would power itself. Hence, in his pantheon of the "Greats," the ideas of iron-and-blood men like Richelieu, Metternich, and Bismarck get top billing over pen-and-ink types like Grotius, Kant, and Vattel, who in contrast were arguing for the inherent compatibility and necessary interdependence of justice and order in world politics.

Kissinger's theory is grand to the extent that it seeks to produce from the manipulation of history some universal rules of behavior for statesmen—or, from a critical perspective, as C. Wright Mills (1959: 22) called it in his critique of grand theory, "a trans-historical strait-jacket." In *Diplomacy*, fear, deceit, and the lust for power are represented as historical givens, and balance of power in the service of objective national interests is the best institution to check these primal forces which seem to be deeply embedded in the nature of man. However, Kissinger's theory is not-so-grand in more ways than one. He wishes to assert the historical contingency of world politics and to challenge the academic belief that the interactions of individuals can be reduced to scientific coda. This is all fine and good, but he wants simultaneously to distill universal lessons and norms from those interactions. Moreover, this normative element of his theory is implicit in most of his historiography, and only emerges in the form of epigrams or maxims which often ring true in the immediacy of his narrative but are not subject to any counter-history or critical theory which might test their universal, transhistorical value—not to mention extant alternatives or other philosophical possibilities. In other words, he wants to eat his historical cake and have more than just speculative crumbs left on the plate. His history is driven by a policy imperative; again, not reprehensible in itself, but certainly not the makings of the best scholarship.

Finally there is the matter of style. Some might think this a minor matter, but I hold to Jacques Derrida's view that style is the author's will to power in text— and there is a considerable will at work in this particular text. In a review of the first volume of Kissinger's memoirs, *The White House Years*, Hedley Bull (1980: 484) remarked that "Kissinger's academic writings have sometimes seemed excessively, even comically Wagnerian." But Bull does not apply the criticism to the memoirs, for Kissinger has come to inhabit, indeed, to constitute the history he once wrote: "But in this book grand opera does not seem out of place: Kissinger himself is a real life *prima donna*, the policy-maker *manqué* has become the policy-maker, his grandiose prescriptions and portentous warnings do not seem contrived but clearly express the deepest of convictions: his conception of international politics has become part of the history of the United States and we are compelled to take it seriously" (Bull, 1980: 484–85).

But now, although not quite out on the street, Kissinger is out of the Ring (or at least the Beltway), and as if by compensation, he *over*-writes the greatness of past heroes. One thinks of Marx's famous revision of Hegel, that tragedy repeats itself as farce. But I think Nietzsche, Wagnerian apostle-turned-apostate, again provides a better diagnosis for Kissinger's desire to "maxim"-ize the recurrent, tragic lessons of history rather than find in philosophy the possibility for ways of being in the world that do not reside in fear, deceit, and insecurity. In both his added preface to *The Birth of Tragedy*, "Attempt at a Self-Criticism," and the later *Case of Wagner*, Nietzsche (1967: 183) sees the tragic pessimism of Wagner as a necessary sickness that must be overcome, that can be overcome by a philosophical "resistance" to its seductive world-weariness and "blackest obscurantism."

> What does a philosopher demand of himself first and last? To overcome his time in himself, to become "timeless." With what must he therefore engage in the hardest combat? With whatever marks him as the child for his time. Well then! I am, no less than Wagner, a child of this time; that is, a decadent: but I comprehended this, I resisted it. The philosopher in me resisted.
>
> (Nietzsche, 1967: 155)

Perhaps Kissinger identifies such a critical resistance too closely with the academic establishment that never seemed to forgive him for Vietnam (nor, admittedly, to acknowledge fully its own early support of the war). But his grave warnings of tragedy to come, should his advice not be heeded, and of the dangers of an optimism unchecked by the realities of history sound too much like the Wagnerian benediction that Nietzsche warns against for those traveling in troubled waters:

Bene navigai, cum naufragium feci (When I suffer shipwreck, I have navigated well).

References

BARTHES, ROLAND. (1986) *Writing Reading: The Rustle of Language.* Translated by Richard Howard. New York: Hill and Wang.

BULL, HEDLEY. (1980) Kissinger: The Primacy of Geopolitics. *International Affairs* 56(3).

CRAIG, GORDON. (1994) Looking for Order. *The New York Review of Books*, May 12, p. 8.

CRAIG, GORDON, AND FRANCIS LOEWENHEIM, eds. (1994) *The Diplomats, 1939–1979.* Princeton: Princeton University Press.

FOUCAULT, MICHEL. (1984) What is an Author? In *The Foucault Reader*, edited by Paul Rabinow. New York: Random House.

HALDEMAN, H. R. (1994) *The Haldeman Diaries: Inside the Nixon White House, The Complete Multimedia Edition.* Santa Monica: Sony Electronic Publishing.

HALLIDAY, FRED. (1994) Lying Abroad. *London Review of Books*, July 21, pp. 7–8.

ISSACSON, WALTER. (1992) *Kissinger: A Biography.* New York: Simon and Schuster.

KISSINGER, HENRY A. (1994a) *Diplomacy.* New York: Simon and Schuster.

KISSINGER, HENRY A. (1994b) Letter to the Editor. *The New York Times Book Review*, April 24, p. 31.

KISSINGER, HENRY A. (1994c) Letter to the Editor. *The New York Times*, June 3.

KISSINGER, HENRY A. (1957) *A World Restored: Metternich, Castlereagh, and the Problems of Peace, 1812–1822.* Boston: Houghton Mifflin.

LEWIS, ANTHONY. (1994) Guilt for Vietnam. *The New York Times*, May 30, p. 24.

MAY, ERNEST. (1994) The "Great Man" Theory of Foreign Policy. *The New York Times Book Review*, April 3, p. 3.

MILLS, C. WRIGHT. (1959) *The Sociological Imagination.* New York: Oxford University Press.

NIETZSCHE, FRIEDRICH. (1967) *The Birth of Tragedy and The Case of Wagner.* Translated by Walter Kaufmann. New York: Random House.

NIETZSCHE, FRIEDRICH. (1957) *The Use and Abuse of History.* New York: Macmillan.

POWELL, CHARLES. (1994) No Diplomat. *National Review*, June 13, p. 63.

SCHAMA, SIMON. (1994) The Games of Great Men. *The New Yorker*, pp. 92–97.

WATSON, GEORGE. (1994) Review of *Diplomacy.* In *The Friday Review of Defense Literature, Department of Defense Current News*, June 17, pp. 2–4.

WATSON, RUSSELL. (1994) An Element of Guile. *Newsweek*, April 11, p. 42.

12 Post-theory

The eternal return of ethics in international relations

Source: *New Thinking in International Relations Theory*, eds. Michael Doyle and John Ikenberry (New York: Westview Press, 1997), pp. 55–75.

Postmodernism: This word has no meaning. Use it as often as possible.
[—Modern-day Dictionary of Received Ideas]

This paper consists of little more than a list and a question, and nothing less than a provocation for International Relations (IR).

First, a list of all things post. Postmodernism, postmodernity, poststructuralism. Postphilosophy, *posthistoire*, post-Enlightenment, post-ideology. Postbehavioralism, postpositivism, postfeminism, post-analytical. Post-realism, post-idealism, postrationalism, post-Marxism, post–international relations. Post-Fordism, postindustrialism, postcapitalism, postdevelopment, postcolonialism. Post–Cold War, post-Yalta, postwar. Postmodern architecture, postmodern film, postmodern culture, postmodern science, postmodern sportswear. Postmodern parody, pastiche, and irony, Post-modernism *avant la lettre*. Post-postmodernism, Post-Toasties, pre(post)erous. Post-theory. Postscript.

Second, the question, one that precedes all others about the topic, the approach, and yes, sometimes the fad, of postmodernism in International Relations. This is the question that surrounds and keeps one distant from it, the question that goes unasked in polite company: Why bother?

My answer can only be partial, in both senses of the word. The topic is too wide, too diverse, and in many ways too *out-of-date* to be recounted in one chapter. I am, as well, too closely self-identified with postmodernism to claim a neutral, impartial position. Yet there has been in IR a disposition to take the path of least intellectual resistance in dealing with postmodernism—to dismiss it by polemic or ignore it through arrogance. I intend only to scan the general question of *what* postmodernism is and to focus instead on *why* one should be bothered by postmodernism as a global phenomenon and on why one might consider poststructuralism as an appropriate theoretical response.

Let me enumerate the reasons why one should bother with and be bothered by poststructuralism, make my theoretical case, and then leave for last an empirico-postmodernist proof. First, I believe poststructuralism is a valuable—indeed an invaluable—intellectual tool for understanding the ways of postmodernity, or as I prefer, late modernity. Second, poststructuralism offers an ethical way of being in highly contingent, highly relativist times. Third, and most important for the discipline of IR, poststructuralism provides a reflexive method for constantly challenging and testing the validity of the first two claims.[1] Other current approaches in IR might be able to meet one or even two of these claims, but they fail to fulfill all three of them.

The toolbox of poststructuralism

I do not intend to provide here a primer on poststructuralism (which I have done elsewhere).[2] I wish to make the case that late modern times require poststructuralist, *among other*, critical pluralist approaches. However, to make sure that we are leaving from the same starting gate, it might be useful to review some of the conceptual distinctions that I presented in two earlier books, *International/Intertextual Relations* and *Antidiplomacy*.

My opening list of all things post does not prove anything. However, it should suggest, even to the epistemologically challenged, that we are witnessing some kind of an epochal rupture with modernity that signals the emergence of a different, perhaps even new social condition. The use of "postmodern" to designate this shift predates Lyotard, Habermas, Derrida, Foucault, and other "Frankfurters" (critical theorists) and "French Fries" (poststructuralists): It can be traced at least back to Beefeaters (non-Marxist, pre–Mad Cow materialists), like the historian Arnold Toynbee who in 1954 referred to the emergence of a "postmodern" period in volume nine of his *Study of History*. I prefer to use the term "late modernity" rather than "postmodernity" to describe this shift, not out of some semantic purism, but first, to better distinguish a historical, social condition ("late modernity," "postmodernity") from a theoretical response ("pastmodernism," "poststructuralism"); second, to avoid the kind of historical periodization of a clean break that belies that the time-warp quality of late modernity, where past, present, and future seem to meld in real-time representations and simulations; and third, because "postmodernism" in general has begun to take on more meanings than it can sensibly carry, as suggested by the semihumorous quote that opens this chapter.

Some years ago I voiced some trepidation about the use of "postmodernism" in the preface to *On Diplomacy*[3] (which was only heightened when I later heard Devo's song "Post-post-modern Man"). But one lesson I learned upon my reentry into North American IR—which has always been more a taxonomy than a subject matter—is that without a label, a box, or a school, one does not exist. So I became a postmodernist, without meaning—or meaning to.

It is much easier, and less controversial, to say what I mean by the phenomenon of "late modernity/postmodernity." What I wrote in shorthand back in 1989 holds up, I believe, fairly well today:

> [I]ncreasingly postmodern world politics is very much in need of post-structural readings. The basis for the claim, and our written response to its implications, can be traced to an overdetermined (yet underdocumented)

"crisis" of modernity, where foundational unities (the autonomous subject, the sovereign state, grand theory) and synthetic oppositions (subject-object, self-other, inside-outside) are undergoing serious and sustained challenges. We are witnessing changes in our international, intertextual, inter*human* relations, in which objective reality is displaced by textuality (Dan Quayle cites Tom Clancy to defend anti-satellite weapons), modes of production are supplanted by modes of information (the assemblyline workplace shrinks, a computer and media-generated cyberspace expands), representation blurs into simulation (Hollywood, and Mr. Smith, goes to Washington), imperialism gives way to the Empire of Signs (the spectacle of Grenada, the fantasy of Star Wars serve to deny imperial decline). With these tectonic shifts, new epistemological fault lines develop: the legitimacy of tradition is undermined, the unifying belief in progress fragments, and conventional wisdom is reduced to one of many competing rituals of power used to shore up a shaky (international) society.[4]

I make my case for the diverse approaches that make up poststructuralism in my book *Antidiplomacy*.[5] My toolbox for the task draws from the works of Nietzsche, Bakhtin, Barthes, Bataille, Blanchot, Foucault, Deleuze, Derrida, Lyotard, Rorty, Kristeva, Said, Jameson, Lacan, Irigaray, Spivak, Baudrillard, Virilio, and other critical and postmodernist thinkers. I provide some of the protocols that inform poststructuralism and distinguish it from the traditional approaches of IR. My goal was then and is now to move the engagement with poststructuralism in IR from closed, defensive positions to an open, dialogical terrain. Not so long ago mental flak jackets were de rigueur if one so much as uttered the "P-word" among IR scholars. To be sure, the poststructuralists were not blameless in this regard, but the ghost of Vince Lombardi—the best defense is a good offensive(ness)—haunted IR long before po-mo came on the scene. I like to believe that the era of mindless dismissal by one side and reflexive defensiveness by the other is on the wane, as IR as well as the other social sciences appropriate the key concepts (if not the more radical implications) of postmodernism.[6]

That said, I am not about to produce an easy target in the form of a pat definition of an intellectual approach that is, by definition (*pace* Nietzsche, "only that which has no history can be defined") the product of inversion, a going beyond, a calling into question of essentialist structures, not least among them definitions. So, by way of post-Hegelian negation, I offer a consideration of what poststructuralism is not by what critics have claimed that it is. I will limit myself to four of the most reasonable criticisms.

First, poststructuralism is not, as critics have claimed, inherently antiempirical. It does in my own work and in others contain a "research program," but not one that assumes that the object of research is immaculately reproduced by the program. Poststructuralism differs from rationalist approaches in that it does not hold that international theorists mirror the reality of world politics through their intellectual analysis. Both use and are used by language: meaning endlessly differs and is deferred through the interpretive interaction of theorist and text.

Rationalists cling to the faith that there is an objective reality out there that is waiting for the right method to come along and in the name of scientific progress make use of, make sense of, give order to it. However, the realities of world politics increasingly are generated, mediated, even simulated by successive technical means of reproduction, further distancing them from some original and ultimately mythical meaning. From diplomatic notes to popular postcards, from engravings to photographs, from radio to television, from textbooks to the internet, reality has shifted into the domain of virtual technologies. It also signals the arrival if not yet the acceptance of a broader range of plural realisms for a newly multipolar, multicultural International Relations.

Second, critics assert that not only is there no ethics to poststructuralism, but also that it advocates a relativist, even nihilist position. The poststructuralist response is that relativism is an historical response to the metaphysical desire for the last word and highest truth that long predates the arrival of Foucault, Derrida, Rorty, et al. on the late modern scene. It has taken many forms, from the "vulgar" relativism of Raskolnikov (where "all is permitted") to the "refined" relativism of Isaiah Berlin ("to realize the relative validity of one's convictions and yet stand for them unflinchingly, is what distinguishes a civilized man from a barbarian").[7] It has been interpreted by Nietzsche as proof of eternal recurrence ("There is no pre-established harmony between the furtherance of truth and the well-being of mankind")[8] and promoted by John Stuart Mill as the stepchild of progress: "It is hardly possible to overrate the value, in the present low state of human improvement, of placing human beings in contact with persons dissimilar to themselves, and with modes of thought and action unlike those with which they are familiar. ... Such communication has always been, and is peculiarly in the present age, one of the primary sources of progress."[9]

A poststructuralist response is not, then for all its purported relativism, axiomaticailly apolitical or amoral: It is in fact an attempt to understand— *without* resort to external authorities or transcendental values—why one moral or political system attains a higher status and exercises more influence than another at a particular historical moment. If there is a practicoethical injunction to poststructuralism, it is to identify and to assess the dangers of systems of thought (like universal rationalism) and systems of politics (like Pax Americana) that deny the historical reality and pragmatic appeal of relativism. As political theorist William Connolly describes it, the current worry of academics about relativism is "untimely"; indeed, their acts of theoretical closure and nostalgia for lost certainties reveal an anxiety about the openness of late modernity:

> Nor is relativism the consummate danger in the late-modern world, where every culture intersects with most others in economies of interdependence, exchange, and competition. Relativism is an invention of academics who yearn for a type of unity that probably never existed, who worry about an alienation from established culture that seldom finds sufficient opportunity to get off the ground, and who insist that ethical discourse cannot proceed unless it locates its authority in a transcendental command.[10]

In contrast, the ethics of poststructuralism is located in and through the construction of subjectivity. It does not reside outside as a set of principles to guide individual behavior, but as a prior and necessary condition for identity formation.[11] Ethics begins with the recognition of the need for the other, of the need for the other's recognition. It proceeds, in other words, from an interdependency of caring and responsibility that cannot be separated from the pluralism and relativism of multiple identities. An ethical way of being emerges when we recognize the very *necessity* of heterogeneity for understanding ourselves and others.

Third, a poststructuralist approach does not seek to reduce IR to a linguistic practice; nor does it claim that there is *no* truth, *no* values, *no* reality. Rather, it aims to refute the claim that there is an external being, supreme epistemology, ultimate theory that can prove, adjudicate, verify an existence or truth independent of its representation. It is not, then, "all is permitted," but rather "all is questionable," in recognition that the most pernicious truths are the effects of unchallenged interpretations. A poststructuralist approach proceeds on this suspicion by investigating the interrelationship of power and representational practices that elevate one truth over another, that legitimate and subject one identity against another, that make, in short, one discourse matter more than the next.[12] Such an investigation requires a semio-critical approach, one that might dismantle and invert empirico-positivist categories by revealing their internal (conceptual and logical) contradictions and external (descriptive and interpretive) inadequacies.[13]

Let me second-guess one reaction to the last sentence—and perhaps even those before—and say, What? Which leads to the fourth criticism: Could this not all be said more simply? Just as we have begun to be familiar with Hegel's "mediation of mediation," Marx's "alienation of alienation," Sartre's "totalization of totality," along come Deleuze's "rhizomes," Foucault's "geneal- ogy," Baudrillard's "precession of simulacra," Derrida's *"differance"* with a difference. Do we really need this level of linguistic difficulty, this rhetorical excess, this pastiche posing to understand the world? For many the reply has been, no, no, and once again, no to po-mo.[14]

At the disciplinary level, this question and others like it reflect the continuing domination of a philosophical realism in IR—from its logical positivist to rational choice forms—which holds that the purest, most parsimonious statement most accurately, usefully, authentically expresses a thought or reflects an event. At the level of common sense, they suggest a natural preference for conceptual rigor and clarity. After all, even Wittgenstein in his most radical linguistic assault on foundationalist philosophy—a challenge that anticipates poststructuralism—states unequivocally that "everything that can be put into words can be put clearly."[15]

These questions could be dismissed as parochial concerns or philistine conceits. They could be interpreted as the residue of a particularist sign system posing as a universal discourse. Or, as in the reaction to relativism, they reflect a longing for simpler times expressed in simpler terms. At times the debate has an uncomfortably familiar ring to it, reminiscent of conversations overheard at a gallery when someone declares—usually while standing in front of a cubist, an abstract expressionist, or some other avant-garde work of art—"I could do that."

Of course, few can, and worse, many do not know why they cannot. Nevertheless these questions, if only for their repetition in IR, deserve a serious response.

One often-used justification is that new, sometimes difficult words must be coined for new phenomena. In his preface to an English translation of *Capital*, Engels felt compelled to apologize to his new audience: "There is, however, one difficulty we could not spare the reader: the use of certain terms in a sense different from what they have, not only in common life, but in ordinary Political Economy. But this was unavoidable. Every new aspect of a science involves a revolution in the technical terms of that science."[16]

But something else is going on. It is expressed more self-consciously by Hegel than Marx, when he stated that "the familiar, just because it is familiar, is not cognitively understood." [17] In *other* words (literally), we might be able to get closer to the constraints of meaning, to understand the *aporia*, or gap between rhetoric and rationality that invariably opens up when a critical language is applied to the various constructions of language. This "making strange" through language, then, is meant to disturb. Why its continental, rhetorical form should be more disturbing in IR than its positivist, modeled form is for the most part a matter of acceptable styles and disciplinary practices, although I suspect that a paradigmatic incommensurability might also be at work.[18]

The most effective (that is, most powerful) style in IR is (like power itself) the one that appears as most transparent and least visible. One post-structuralist might use style as a physics teacher uses iron filings, to *reveal* (and simultaneously to reinscribe) the rhetorical force fields that draw us to this statement, repel us from that one. Another might use it as a clown uses greasepaint, to *distort* (and simultaneously to parody) the "normal" face that cannot express the excess of meaning and the absurdities of life. For the poststructuralist, style is a sign, if not *the* sign, of the author's will in the text. It can be, as Derrida has artfully demonstrated, as light as a feather ("*stylo*,") or as dangerous as a dagger ("*stylet*").[19] But sometimes it takes an excess of poststructuralist style to understand how the neopositivist stylelessness of the North American journals *American Political Science Review, International Organization*, or *International Studies Quarterly* precedes inquiry, delimits debate, suppresses alternative modes of expression—and in the process preempts practical possibilities for change.[20]

Enmeshed in a similar debate in the 1960s about the "dangerous language" of the "new criticism," Roland Barthes launched an attack on the ideological assumptions implicit in the call for clarity. His response to his critics helps us to understand why traditional IR theory seems perennially predisposed to an epistemological status quo:

> When a word like dangerous is applied to ideas, language or art, it immediately signals a desire to return to the past. ... Discourse reflecting upon discourse is the object of a special vigilance on the part of institutions, which normally contain it within the limits of a strict code: in the literary State, criticism must be controlled as much as a police force is: to free the one would be quite as

"dangerous" as democratizing the other: it would be to threaten the power of power, the language of language.[21]

This important interrelationship of language, ethics, and identity, so long neglected in traditional IR, finds its seminal expression in the writings of the linguist and literary theorist Mikhail Bakhtin.

How our efforts to fix the meaning of what something is by establishing what it is not is always already warped by the space between the sender and receiver, sign and referent, *langue* (the social code) and *parole* (individual message), author and reader. The heteroglossia of language—the constant renegotiation of meaning and values that goes on with each utterance—bespeaks a heterodoxia in world politics, where radical alterity should be assumed and asserted rather than subsumed and repressed.[22] This shifts if not obliterates the positivist fact-value dichotomy in which the anguished social scientist seeks to expunge subjective factors from objective analysis.

In this context, consider first Bakhtin's critique of monologism:

Ultimately, *monologism* denies that there exists outside of it another con- sciousness, with the same rights, and capable of responding on an equal footing, another and equal *I (thou)*. The monologue is accomplished and deaf to the other's response; it does not await it and does not grant it any *decisive* force. Monologue makes do without the other; that is why to some extent it objectivizes all reality. Monologue pretends to be the *last word*.[23]

And then, from the last writings of Bakhtin in 1974:

There is no first or last discourse, and dialogical context knows no limits (it disappears into an unlimited past and in our unlimited future). Even *past* meanings, that is, those that have arisen in the dialogue of past centuries, can never be stable (completed once and for all, finished), they will always change (renewing themselves) in the course of the dialogue's subsequent development, and yet to come. At every moment of the dialogue, there are immense and unlimited masses of forgotten meanings, but, in some subsequent moments, as the dialogue moves forward, they will return to memory and live in renewed form (in a new context). Nothing is absolutely dead: every meaning will celebrate its rebirth.[24]

This is a distillation of Mikhail Bakhtin's intertextual theory of *dialogism*, which shows how all understanding, like language itself, is a responsive act that depends upon prior as well as anticipates future discourses.[25] Since it is through the communicative acts of negotiating meaning and values with others that the self is constituted, identity *requires* difference: "The psyche," says Bakhtin, "enjoys extraterritorial status."[26]

Yet in world politics the self clearly "enjoys" territorial and sovereign protection. This can partially be explained by the heightened sense of insecurity and long history of estrangement that have created "deep identities" and a rationalist faith in the state to keep the contingencies of life at bay. These artesian sources of monological, sovereign reasoning in IR, which bubble up just when global dangers threaten to overcome the abilities of the nation-state to control them, induce a self-fulfilling dread and denial of an extraterritorial identity.[27]

A dialogical reading of traditional approaches in IR might raise several questions. Is it possible to imagine and construct a new dialogue in IR, one in which identities are not predetermined or fixed by national, class, or chronological origins external to the dialogue but rather are constantly interacting and shifting in the interlocutionary space between the self and the other? Informed by this psychic interdependency, would they be less willing, perhaps even unable, to declare the other persona non grata in this extraterritorial land? In this move from a metalinguistic concept to an inter-discursive relationship, does dialogism exceed its function as a metaphor or formal model and point the way toward not just a "rethinking" but a reformation of IR? Ultimately, it probably depends most on just how jealous each is of the right to the last word.

In sum, poststructuralism helps to disturb the convention upheld with such vigor in IR that theory and practice are distinct phenomena, or more fundamentally, that reality is independent of any language used to describe it. At a time when almost every other social as well as physical science has begun to consider how theory, practice, and language are inextricably linked through social constructions and representational practices, there is an added imperative for a poststructuralist approach (yes, among others) to IR. More specifically, the strange and estranging ways of writing and thinking by poststructuralists provide an intellectual method to reverse the acts of theoretical enclosure and political neutralization that have been instituted in North American IR theory, that assume rational choice, game theoretic, or formal modeling are sufficient representations of world politics. Finally, it is my belief that the accelerating, transparent, hypermediated practices of late modernity *exceed* the representational capabilities of traditional IR theory, and *require* new poststructuralist approaches.

Yet there remains a lingering criticism of poststructuralism, a criticism of criticism. However, poststructuralism is not simply a negative critique—although it has, by its more modish uses, been confused as such. In most cases—and certainly in the case of thinkers such as Michel Foucault—it clears but does not destroy or deny the existence of the ground for a constructive theory. Even in the more radical applications of deconstruction it takes aim at totalist, transcendentalist, closed theory—not *all* theory. If one ignores the disciplinary imprecations and drops the epistemological blinders of IR's modernist mandarins, a host of "constructive" or "applied" poststructuralist and critical theoretical research projects have been published and more can be spotted on the horizon. To name just a few:[28] books like Rob Walker's *Inside/Outside*, David Campbell's *Writing Security*, Bill Chaloupka's *Knowing Nukes*, Chris Hables Gray's *Post-modern War*, V. Spike Peterson's *Gendered States*, Christine Sylvester's *Feminist Theory and International Relations*, Cindy Weber's *Simulated Sovereignty*, and Roxanne Doty's *Imperial Encounters* as well as recent articles by Simon Dalby,

G. M. Dillon, Jerry Everard, Kate Manzo, Mark Neufeldt, Nicholas Rengger, Sandra Whitworth, and Michael Williams.

Semiology, genealogy, and dromology

What might the elements of a constructive poststructuralist theory look like? Here I can offer only the skeleton of three that have come to inform my work: genealogy, semiology, and dromology.

First, to reinterpret IR theory is to step backward, look wider, and dig deeper, not to excavate some reality that has been lost or lurks beneath the surface of things, but to lay bare persistent myths of a reality that can be transcribed by a school of thought and yet still claim to speak for itself. As I argued in my inquiry into the beginnings of diplomacy, a *genealogy* is the most appropriate way to begin such a task.[29] A genealogy calls into question the immaculate origins, essential identities, and deep structures of IR theory.

This is particularly true in the case of the strongest and most persistent form of IR theory, realism. A genealogy can reveal the metaphorical and mythical beginnings of a uniform realism while producing through interpretation several realisms that never "figure" in the IR official story. What Bertolt Brecht said of the study of realism in literature equally applies to our own field of inquiry: "Realism is an issue not only for literature: it is a major political, philosophical and practical issue and must be handled and explained as such—as a matter of general human interest."[30]

Second, a *semiology* is needed, in the sense of a study of IR theory as a symptom of a more general condition of late modernity, in which an old order is dying and a new one not yet constituted. To the ear of the other, this might have the sound of a Marxian dialectic, a linguistic structuralism, or a metaphysical eschatology. In intent if not in fact a semiology is an *anti-metaphysical*, pragmatic investigation of the reliance of realism in IR theory on an archaic sign-system in which words mirror objects and theory is independent of the reality it represents. The subsidiary purpose is to show how this paraphilosophical conceit has disabled IR theory's power to interpret as well as to manage the current disorder of things.[31]

A semiology, then, provides a method for a study of the interdependent mix of power, meaning and morality that makes up IR theory. In *The Twilight of the Idols*, Nietzsche exposes this link with a harsh clarity: "To this extent moral judgment is never to be taken literally: as such it never contains anything but nonsense. But as *semeiotics* it remains of incalculable value: it reveals, to the informed man at least, the most precious realities of cultures and inner worlds which did not *know* enough to 'understand' themselves. Morality is merely 'sign' language, merely symptomatology; one must already know *what* it is about to derive profit from it."[32]

He is equally blunt about the potentially radical effects of a semiological inquiry: "I fear we are not getting rid of God because we still believe in grammar."[33] His fear applies as well to poststructuralist theory: Disturbing the apodictic link between a positivist theory of IR and a correspondence philosophy of language, it cannot be construed as merely an academic exercise—which perhaps is one more reason why the IR academy has kept post-structuralism at a distance.[34] The dual imperative of securing a sovereign center for the state and IR theory, and protecting it from anything more threatening than incremental change, has placed a premium on "traditional" approaches. A semiology disturbs this naturalized order, not out of a faddish desire for innovation but out of a suspicion that there are high moral costs attached to the kinds of inertial systems of thought that become institutionalized in high politics and higher learning.[35]

Third, a *dromology* of IR is required, in Paul Virilio's sense of a study of the science or logic of speed, because the representational principle described earlier that underpins realism has itself increasingly become undermined by the ascendancy of temporality over spatiality in world politics.[36] Elsewhere I have identified this as the "(s)pace problematic" of IR, where the displacement of geopolitics by chronopolitics makes a nation-state security founded on the stasis of a fixed identity and impermeable territory increasingly difficult to maintain.[37] In turn, the multifarious effects of speed compound the need for a semiology of IR: The instantaneity of communication, the ubiquity of the image, the flow of capital, the videographic speed of war have made the reality of world politics a transitory, technologically contingent phenomenon.[38]

In a world in which speed is not just the measure but the end of progress, tendencies and flows, arrivals and departures, all forms of moment come to govern and devalue both the immobile object and objectivity itself. *Real* estate, in the dual sense of transparent and immovable property, loses out to *irreal* representations, which are infinitely transferable. In short, the dromocratic machine colonizes reality and its "reflective" mediation, realism. With a casual hyperbole Virilio freeze-frames this imperialism of movement: "It's clear that we are currently in a period of substitutions. One generation of reality is in the process of substituting itself for another and is still uncertain about how to represent itself. And we have to understand that it is very much connected to real-time images. It's not a problem of the configuration or the semiotics of the image, but a problem of the temporality of the image."[39]

In the current age of speed, surveillance, and simulation, genealogy, semiology, and dromology provide new deconstructive tools *and* antidiplomatic strategies to reinterpret IR.[40] Poststructuralism, then, is doubly prodomal for IR, a sign of both the heightened anxiety and trammeled hope that appear when the mirror of an old order cracks and we must remember, reimagine, and if possible, reconstruct a new image of our own self-identity.

A pre(post)erous provocation

Some years ago, when first invited to present this paper at Princeton, the speakers were asked to include an "empirical" account of how our first, stumbling efforts to rethink IR theory might yield new insights about world politics; in so many words, we were asked to "strut our stuff," Forgoing the easy out—declaiming this arbitrary separation of theory and practice—I spoke on the Gulf War as the first and certainly not our last hyperreal war of simulation, surveillance, and speed, and of how the poststructuralist writings of Baudrillard, Foucault, and Virilio should be gleaned for insights into these developments.[41] Five years on, while I do believe that my initial assessment still holds, I doubt whether the interest of the reader does. Hence, I would like to introduce a different event, one that might allow me to "strut" the theoretical, ethical, critical values of the poststructuralist approach that I have enumerated, without denying the importance of the "stuff" of world politics which so preoccupies IR today. I will do this *in extremis*, turning some of the criticisms of the critics back on them, to offer a reevaluation of the ethics and pragmatics of poststructuralism.

To be honest, I tire of this tactic. I look forward to pointed critiques of poststructuralism from both within and outside its ranks. But more often than not the range of criticisms have gone from simple to crude. Someone thumps on a table, and says, does this table not exist? Or worse, beats on their chest, and says, did the Holocaust not happen? I have become used to the caricature and vilification of relativism (of course the table exists—but that existence is conveyed by interpretive and discursive fields as well as perspectival action), but the ahistorical trivialization of genocide still stuns me. Of course the Holocaust happened, as did other genocides in the past, and as will others, I fear, in the future—especially if one thinks facts speak for themselves rather than through and for powerful discourses of memory and forgetting. Caught in this either/or logic—either a vulgar empirico-materialism or nothingness, either Enlightenment (i.e., rationalism, progressivism, foundationalism) or Barbarism—such inquisitors of postmodernism ignore or just cannot comprehend some of the most powerful "variables" of IR, like irony and contingency, accident and synchronicity, resentment and caring, alienation and recognition, ambiguity and paradox.

My response is to offer an empirico-postmodernist proof (more in the sense of a trial impression than the establishment of a truth) that poststructuralism can provide both pragmatic ways of thinking and ethical ways of being. Thinking and being are sundered when we "other" history, whether it takes the form of objective detachment, psychological denial, or political triumphalism. The very enjoinder "to rethink IR" reinforces this separation, presuming that history—especially a radical break in history—is something that happened, and that our task is merely to record what actually happened (*wie es eigentilich gewesen*), rather than to understand history as something perpetually under construction and reinterpretation. Where some find relativism, even nihilism in this perspective, Friedrich Nietzsche, nemesis of the Enlightenment project and one of the forefathers of postmodernist thought, locates the ethical imperative of the eternal return:

> Behold, we know what you teach: that all things recur eternally, and we ourselves too; and that we have already existed an eternal number of times, and all things with us. You teach that there is a great year of becoming, a monster of a great year, which must, like an hourglass, turn over again and again so that it may run down and run out again; and all of these years are

alike in what is greatest as in what is smallest; and we ourselves are like every great year, in what is greatest as in what is smallest.[42]

Nineteen eighty-nine was such a monster year, unleashing great changes, great hopes, and not a few conferences to rethink what it all meant. Yet there was no lingering sense of a great becoming. Too quickly the euphoria inspired by the twilight of totalitarianism faded in the morning-after of resurgent nationalisms. To be sure, decades of an intellectual inertia weighed heavily on a freshly minted idealism, which, once weakened by uncertainty and self-doubt, was soon invirallated in the West by an epidemic of endism, usually taking the graceless forms of triumphalist gloatings about what had been won (the Cold War) or nostalgic musings about what had been lost (again, the Cold War), rather than imaginative, globalist ideas about what now might be built. Before one could say "Henry Kissinger," realism, posing as superego comfort for a new global disorder, returned as the repressed. "Post's" and "pre's" proliferated—were we in a post–cold war, pre–cold peace, or post-imperial space?—attesting to the insecurity of living in flux-times, where accelerating flows of capital, goods, and information were force-multiplied by real-time media representations of spillover ethnic and civil conflicts that seemed beyond management by a balance or even a hegemony of power.

By now this story as well as the criticism has become overly familiar, too banal for serious scrutiny—one more reason, therefore, to defamiliarize it, to avoid the clichés of a folkloric common sense (*plus ça change ...*) but, more important, to reinterpret and possibly undermine the resurgence of yet another wave of realism in IR. This does not mean that we must refute realism's historical foundations (recurrence and repetition) but its pharmacological prescription (in the original Greek sense of *pharmakon* as both cure and poison, that is, power as the only antidote for the drug of power) posing as a philosophical conceit (that theory is independent of the reality it represents).

Nietzsche's genealogical approach and his idea of eternal return provides one way to go beyond rethinking and move toward a reliving of IR. As I stated earlier, a genealogy can be used to call into question the realist portrayal of immaculate origins, essential identities, and deep structures in IR, revealing, I believe, the metaphorical and mythical beginnings of a supposedly uniform statecraft while producing through interpretation dissident practices that never "figure" in the official story. Nietzsche's controversial idea of eternal return would then be seen not as some cosmological truth but as a practical guide for political practice in ambiguous and uncertain times. Both entail ethical considerations as well, for we live in conditions under which the Other is hard upon us and yet justice, in the sense of a mediated recognition for the Other, is hard to come by.

In my own work I have focused on this general and persistent condition of estrangement as it has been manifested and produced by diplomatic and antidiplomatic practices.[43] But it is a personal moment of synchronicity that prompts this particular deconstructive response: the invitation to write something new on IR, but also the discovery of a document that seemed to represent the eternal return of the old in the new, and the ethical obligation to respond in a critical way to this recurrence.

Writing of another "monster year," 1919, and eyeing only the "high politics" of diplomacy, participant and historian Harold Nicolson provided wise counsel for those who might think that the whole picture can be captured by traditional methods alone:

> Of all branches of human endeavor, diplomacy is the most protean. The historian and the jurist, relying upon the *procès verbal*, may seek to confine its lineaments within the strict outlines of a science. The essayist may hope to capture its colours in the vignettes of an art. The experts—and there have been many experts from Calliéres to Jusserand, from Machiavelli to Jules Cambon—may endeavour to record their own experience in manuals for the guidance of those that come after. The journalist may give to the picture the flashes and interpretation of the picturesque. Yet always there is some element in such accounts which escapes reality, always there is some aspect which refuses to be recorded or defined.[44]

From a somewhat lower perspective than the Paris peace conference, I found his view confirmed when I found a document referring to the same event. The document is yellowed-into-brown, well thumbed, and well traveled, having survived the journey from my grandfather's attic through the family archives maintained in a variety of basements by my father, and now to me. It is simply, if not naïvely titled in bold letters, "The Treaty." Reprinted from the *Boston Evening Transcript*, the forty-eight-page pamphlet contains the "Complete Text of the Treaty of Peace as Drawn by the Paris Conference and Issued by the United States Senate." It is signed and dated by my grandfather, June 20, 1919, less than a year after he had emigrated to America from Armenia.

A close reading reveals the reason why a straw boss of the coke ovens at Ford Motor Company would cherish "The Treaty." It was the first to give a legal, if provisional, standing to a country he had spent four years fighting for. Article 22 gave birth to the mandate system and, in the process, provided for the first, if brief, moment of the independence of Armenia. It reads:

> To those colonies and territories which as a consequence of the late war have ceased to be under the sovereignty of the states which formerly governed them and which are inhabited by peoples not yet able to stand by themselves under the strenuous conditions of the modern world, there should be applied the principle that the well-being and development of such peoples form a sacred trust of civilization and that securities for the performance of this trust should be embodied in this Covenant. … Certain communities formerly belonging to the Turkish Empire have reached a stage of development where their existence as independent nations can be provisionally recognized subject to the rendering of administrative advice and assistance by a mandatory until such time as they are able to stand alone.

The subsequent "treaties of the Paris suburbs" diplomatically inscribed the short life of Armenia as well as Kurdistan. The 1920 Treaty of Sèvres, in Articles 88–93, enshrined the independence of Armenia. However, the decline in Wilson's political and personal fortunes, differing views among the allies on what might assure security in conditions often described in the proceedings as "strenuous times," and, finally but not exhaustively, the need to enlist new allies from the associated powers against bolshevism in the Caucasus, all were key factors in the removal of the "self" from the determination of nationhood. Not three years later, in the 1923 Treaty of Lausanne, Armenia and Kurdistan simply disappear, unmentioned except as abstract "minorities" that Turkey committed itself to "protect" (Articles 37–45).

This is only one brief vignette from a recurring story of a nation's destiny determined by great-power diplomacy: 1648, 1815, 1871, 1919–1923, 1945–1948, and, still subject to debate, 1989 stand out as the "monster years." To be sure, and to a varying degree and duration, peace and order were secured in the aftermath of war and chaos. But for how long, and to what extent does injustice for the defeated or small powers come at the expense of a durable order? The dialogue between order and justice, most profoundly charted by Hedley Bull, is eternally renewed, and diplomacy seems eternally to get it wrong. I believe the most important question is not whether IR can be rethought or global politics renewed. It is whether IR can learn from the "monster years" and accept their eternal return not as bane or boon, but as Nietzsche did, as an ethical challenge to accept that one will relive the consequences of one's actions, in "greatness or smallness."

Will 1989, then, be what Nietzsche described as "a great year of becoming … which must, like an hourglass, turn over again and again so that it may run down and run out again"? Much depends on the philosophical as well as the practico-ethical response to great historic moments: Can we opt out of the either/or logic of Enlightenment or barbarism, idealism or realism, millenarianism or fatalism, and reinterpret the eternal return of history as an obligation to take every encounter with the Other as Nietzsche counsels, in the knowledge that in such encounters "we ourselves are like every great year, in what is greatest as in what is smallest."

If such questions are not to deteriorate into grand metaphysical musings, some historical sense is needed of *how* traditional interpretations of what is old, what is new, and what is recurrent in IR act to delimit the range of options not only for contemporary statecraft but also for individual ethical action. It is this constructive nature of theorizing that poststructuralism seeks to chart, reconstruct, and yes, deconstruct when violence, as it so often is, becomes naturalized in IR. Nowhere is this truer than in the motivation and justification of the genocidal act, whether it is considered necessitous to keep public order as the Ottoman Empire decays, to cleanse the body politic as the Hitlerite empire grows, or to define a Serbian identity out of a collapsing Yugoslavian one.[45]

The greatest Weight. What if some day or night a demon were to steal after you into your loneliest of loneliness and say to you: "This life as you now live it and have lived it, you will have to live once more and innumerable times more; and there will be nothing new in it, but every pain and every joy and every thought and everything unutterably small and great in your life will return to you, all in the same succession and sequence. ..."[46]

Between Nietzsche and Nicolson there can be found some common ground. Indeed, pararealist assumptions about the nature of humankind and the repetition of its errors are both on display. But where Nicolson (and traditional realists) would find in such a condition cause for the elevation of what he called the principle of *"sauve qui peut ... or security,"* Nietzsche would find one more reason for a transvaluation of all values.[47] Under such antidiplomatic conditions, in which no border is impermeable, no sovereignty absolute, no "people" without their internal Other, then security itself is predicated upon the insecurity of all values. Here Nietzsche is at home, and when he completes his thoughts on the "greatest weight" of the eternal return, we find an ethical imperative to revalue IR:

> If this thought [of the eternal return] were to gain possession of you, it would change you as you are, or perhaps crush you. The question in each and every thing: "Do you want this once more and innumerable times more?" would lie upon your actions as the greatest weight. Or how well-disposed would you have to become to yourself and life *to crave nothing more fervently* than this ultimate confirmation and seal?[48]

Post-script (not the last word)

The eternal return never stops. At a recent meeting on apocalyptic violence, I was asked to help organize and to sign a petition that was to appear in the *New York Times* and the *Chronicle of Higher Education;* it was to appear under the title, "Taking a Stand Against the Turkish Government's Denial of the Armenian Genocide and Scholarly Corruption in the Academy." It was prompted by a letter that Robert Jay Lifton had received in October 1990 from the Turkish ambassador, Nuzhet Kandemir, in which the ambassador criticizes references in Lifton's book, *The Nazi Doctors: Medical Killing and the Psychology of Genocide,* to the "so-called 'Armenian genocide,' allegedly perpetrated by the Ottoman Turk."[49] After dismissing Lifton's references because they were based on "questionable secondary sources," the ambassador applied the disciplinary whip: "It is particularly disturbing to see a major scholar on the Holocaust, a tragedy whose enormity and barbarity must never be forgotten, so careless in his reference to a field outside his area of expertise." Whence did the ambassador acquire his own scholarly expertise in the manner? By accident, or perhaps through a subversive act of solidarity, a memorandum and a draft letter had accompanied the official letter sent by the ambassador to Lifton. The memorandum is addressed to the ambassador. It includes excerpts and citations for each of Lifton's references to the Armenian genocide (there are seven in the 561 pages of the book). The memorandum ends with an offer from the author: "On the chance that you still wish to respond in writing to Lifton, I have drafted the following letter, which, due to the absence of an address for Lifton will have to be sent to him care of his publisher." The draft letter is virtually identical to the official letter.

The memorandum and letter are from "Dr. Heath W. Lowry." At the time that he wrote the letter and memorandum he was the head of the Institute of Turkish Studies in Washington, D.C., funded by grants from the Republic of Turkey. And from 1994 on, he has been the first incumbent of the Ataturk Chair in Turkish Studies at Princeton University, also funded by the Republic of Turkey.

Understandably, most studies on genocide have been undertaken to comprehend the act rather than the denial of genocide. Ideology, racism, and careerism are usually common to both. However, one study finds that scholars who deny the existence of genocide usually resort to "scientificism" (a lack of sufficient empirical evidence to prove genocide took place) and "definitionalism" (deaths are acknowledged but not as a result of "genocide" per se).[50]

One scholar's questionable actions do not besmirch a whole institution; nor does the dubious invocation of scientific method repudiate all positivist methodologies. Scholars and diplomats alike make choices and justify actions according to a given discursive field in which power is omnipresent. The denial of this relationship between power and knowledge is probably the surest sign of a pure congruence of the two at work. This means that when the stakes are high—and few come higher than the end of totalitarianism and the memory of genocide—one must do more than thump tables and evoke the Holocaust to have the last word. One must have recourse to a philosophical, reflexive, critical approach that helps us to understand how one's own identity is implicated in the study of the killing of others—for this remains the "greatest weight" of IR.

Notes

1 Hedley Bull endorsed the classical approach for similar reasons in his essay "International Theory: The Case for a Classical Approach," *World Politics*, vol. 18, no. 3 (April 1966):361–377. His criticism, leveled against the rise of behavioralism in IR theory, still holds for the wave of behavioralism by other means (such as rational-choice theory and game theory) that continues to dominate North American IR: "My seventh and final proposition is that the practitioners of the scientific approach, by cutting themselves off from history and philosophy, have deprived them selves of the means of self-criticism, and in consequence have a view of their subject and its possibilities that is callow and brash."

2 See J. Der Derian, "Introducing Philosophical Traditions in International Relations," *Millennium Journal of International Studies*, vol. 17, no. 2 (Summer 1988):189–194; "Preface" and "The Boundaries of Knowledge and Power in International Relations," in *Internationat/Intertextual Relations: Postmodern Readings of World Politics*, edited by J. Der Derian and M. Shapiro (Lexington, MA: Lexington Books, 1989), pp. ix–xi and 3–10; and J. Der Derian, "Introduction: A Case for a Poststructuralist Approach," in *Antidiplomacy: Spies, Terror, Speed, and War* (Oxford: Blackwell Publishers, 1992), pp. 1–15.

3 J. Der Derian, *On Diplomacy: A Genealogy of Western Estrangement* (Oxford: Blackwell, 1987).

4 See J. Der Derian, "Preface" in *International/Intertextual Relations*, pp. ix–x.

5 See *Antidiplomacy*, pp. 1–15.

6 John Ruggie, "Territoriality and Beyond: Problematizing Modernity in International Relations," *International Organization*, vol. 47, no. 1 (1993):139–174.

7 See Isaiah Berlin, *Four Essays on Liberty* (Oxford: Oxford University Press, 1969), p. 46; and Berlin, "Alleged Relativism in Eighteenth Century European Thought," in *The Crooked Timber of Humanity* (New York: Vintage, 1992), pp. 70–90.

8 F. Nietzsche, *Human, All Too Human* excerpted in *A Nietzsche Reader*, selected and translated by R. J. Hollingdale (Middlesex, UK: Penguin, 1977), p. 198.

9 J. S. Mill, *Principles of Political Economy*, in *Collected Works of John Stuart Mill* (London: 1981), p. 594, quoted by Berlin, *Crooked Timber of Humanity*, p. 90.

10 See William Connolly, *Identity/Difference: Democratic Negotiations of Political Paradox* (Ithaca: Cornell University Press, 1991), p. 174.

11 See Emmanuel Levinas, *Face to Face with Levinas*, edited by Richard A. Cohen (Albany: State University of New York Press, 1986). For an excellent elucidation and application of Levinas's ethical views, see David Campbell, *Politics Without Principle: Sovereignty, Ethics, and the Narratives of the Gulf War* (Boulder: Lynne Rienner, 1993).

12 A good example of how interpretation precedes facts with a political effect can be seen in the recent accusations that the journalist I. F. Stone was an agent of the KGB. When the original accuser, espionage "expert" Herbert Romerstein, was asked why he would now believe claims made by an unnamed source in the KGB (which were contradicted by another KGB agent, Oleg Kalugin), he replied "I disbelieved them when they said what I knew to be false. I believe those things that either can be confirmed or cannot be proved to be lies." See Andrew Brown, "The Attack on I. F. Stone," *New York Review of Books*, October 8, 1992, p. 21.

13 On semio-criticism, see R. Barthes, "To Write: An Intransitive Verb?" in *The Rustle of Language*, translated by R. Howard (New York: Hill and Wang, 1986), pp. 11–12. On the *"problematiques"* approach, see M. Foucault, "On the Genealogy of Ethics: An Overview of Work in Progress," *Foucault Reader*, ed. Paul Rabinow (New York: Pantheon, 1984), p. 343.

14 An infrequently noted pedigree of "postmodern" might temper this response. The writer credited by the Merriam-Webster dictionary with coining the term postmodern in 1947 (to describe the period of history since 1875) is Arnold Toynbee, the highly respected historian who influenced "classical realism" most notably through his collaboration with Martin Wight on parts of his multivolume A *Study of History* (Oxford: Oxford University Press, 1935–1959).

15 L. Wittgenstein, *Tractatus Logico-Philosophicus* (1922), 4.116.

16 F. Engels, "Preface to the English Edition," in K. Marx, *Capital*, vol. 1 (Moscow: Progress Publishers, 1974), p. 14.

17 G. Hegel, *Phenomenology of Spirit* (Oxford: Oxford University Press, 1977), p. 18.

18 An Anglo-Saxon intolerance for new words, which I witnessed firsthand at a British International Studies Association conference, might also be at work. At a panel organized by John Vincent on Hedley Bull's influence in IR theory, a voice from the audience cried out "Shame!" when I used the word "heterologue" to describe Bull's style—to which I felt compelled to reply that probably some of Bentham's peers took offense when he coined the word "international" in 1789.

19 See J. Derrida, "Spurs: Nietzsche's Styles," *A Derrida Reader*, edited by P. Kamuf (New York: Columbia University Press, 1991), pp. 355–377.

20 On the political implications of "plainspeak," see R. Barthes, *Criticism and Truth* (Minneapolis: University of Minnesota Press, 1987), and Henry Giroux and Stanley Aronowitz, "The Politics of Clarity," *Afterimage*, October 1991, pp. 4–5.

21 R. Barthes, *Criticism and Truth*, translated by K. Keuneman (Minneapolis: University of Minnesota Press, 1987), pp. 32–33.

22 Writing about Bakhtin, Paul de Man makes this point with more sophistication than I can muster: "On the other hand, dialogism also functions ... as a principle of radical otherness. ... [F]ar from aspiring to the telos of a synthesis or a resolution, as could be said to be the case in dialectical systems, the function of dialogism is to sustain and think through the radical exteriority or heterogeneity of one voice with regard to any other. ... The self-reflexive, autotelic or, if you wish, narcissistic structure of form, as a definitional description enclosed with specific borderlines, is hereby replaced by an *assertion* of the otherness of the other, preliminary to even the possibility of a *recognition* of his otherness." ("Dialogue and Dialogism," in *The Resistance to Theory* [Minneapolis; University of Minnesota Press, 1986], p. 109).

23 M. Bakhtin, *Problems of Dostoevsky's Poetics*, translated by Caryl Emerson (Minneapolis: University of Minnesota Press, 1984), p. 318.

24 M. Bakhtin, "Concerning Methodology in the Human Sciences," quoted by Tzvetan Todorov, *Mikhail Bakhtin: The Dialogical Principle* (Minneapolis: University of Minnesota Press, 1984), p. 110.

25 For a fuller understanding of how identity is not internally but rather dialogically constructed in a verbal community, see Mikhail Bakhtin, *The Dialogic Imagination: Four Essays by M. M. Bakhtin*, edited by Michael Holquist (Austin: University of Texas Press, 1981); Todorov, *Mikhail Bakhtin: The Dialogical Principle*; and Paul de Man, "Dialogue and Dialogism."

26 M. Bakhtin, *Marxism and the Philosophy of Language* (New York: Seminar Press, 1973), p. 39.

27 See William Connolly, "Global Political Discourse," in *Identity/Difference*, pp. 36–63, for an incisive study of the impact of the "globalization of contingency" on public identities.

28 For the first wave, see: David Campbell, *Writing Security: United States Foreign Policy and the Politics of Identity* (Minneapolis: University of Minnesota Press, 1992); James Der Derian, *Antidiplomacy;* Jim George, *Discourses of Global Politics: A Critical (Re)Introduction to International Relations* (Boulder: Lynne Rienner, 1993); Bradley Klein, *Strategic Studies and World Order* (Cambridge: Cambridge University Press, 1994); Christine Sylvester, *Feminist Theory and International Relations in a Postmodern Era* (Cambridge: Cambridge University Press, 1994); R.B.J. Walker, *Inside/Outside: International Relations as Political Theory* (Cambridge: Cambridge University Press, 1993). Of the IR journals, *Millennium, Alternatives, Review of International Studies,* and *European Journal of International Relations* are most likely to have articles on or applying poststructuralist approaches.

29 See J. Der Derian, *On Diplomacy: A Genealogy of Western Estrangement* (Oxford: Blackwell, 1987), and "A Genealogy of Security," in *The Political Subject of Violence*, edited by D. Campbell and M. Dillon (Manchester, UK: Manchester University Press, 1993).

30 Bertolt Brecht, quoted by Sandy Petrey, *Realism and Revolution: Balzac, Stendhal, Zola, and the Performances of History* (Ithaca: Cornell University Press, 1988), p. xii.

31 I characterize the current assumptions of realism in IR as "paraphilosophical" because they take on the dress (say, as Serbian paramilitary forces pose as a legitimate army) of a uniform realism without any intellectual engagement with the debates (especially of the last two decades) that have surrounded a mitotic body of thought. My particular point of purchase against the tradition is extrinsic and poststructuralist and can be tracked from Wittgenstein and Austin to Barthes and Derrida (see later). But there has been another tributary (among others) of thought closer to the mainstream of philosophical realism that poses just as serious an internal challenge to many of the positivist as well as political assumptions of IR realism—one, I might add, that has suffered just as serious neglect in the field. I refer to post-Marxist theorizing about the relationship of realism to idealism, materialism, and empiricism. For instance, the

interwar period produced a series of rich, aesthetic antinomies, most notably between Bertolt Brecht's agitprop expressionism and Georg Lukács's essentialist formalism, and Walter Benjamin's romantic subjectivism and Theodor Adorno's psychoanalytic modernism, all of which in one form or another held up realism as a means to cut through false consciousness, "defetishize" a reified reality, and provide a commonality of purpose and action. The emergence of the Frankfurt School as well as the post-Marxist phenomenological and structuralist critiques of Jean-Paul Sartre and Louis Althusser attest to a diversity of realisms that have been ignored until quite recently by IR theory. For a review of how some of these thinkers influenced debates over realism, see Frederic Jameson, *Marxism and Form: Twentieth-Century Dialectical Theories of Literature* (Princeton: Princeton University Press, 1971), and Roy Bashkar, *Reclaiming Reality: A Critical Introduction to Contemporary Philosophy* (London: Verso, 1989). For arguments endorsing their significance for IR, see V. Kubalkova and A. A. Cruickshank, *Marxism and International Relations* (London: Routledge, 1985); Mark Hoffman, "Critical Theory and the Inter-paradigm: Debate," *Millennium*, vol. 16, no. 2 (Summer 1987):231–250; John Maclean, "Marxism and International Relations: A Strange Case of Mutual Neglect," *Millennium*, vol. 17, no. 2 (Summer 1988): 295–320; and Jim George and David Campbell, "Patterns of Dissent and the Celebration of Difference: Critical Social Theory and International Relations, *International Studies Quarterly*, vol. 34 (1990):269–293.

32 F. Nietzsche, *Twilight of the Idols*, translated by R. J. Hollingdale (Middlesex, UK: Penguin, 1968), pp. 55.

33 Ibid., p. 38.

34 I cite Nietzsche and use the term "semiology" here to provide a broad description of the "linguistic turn," that is, the various theoretical reactions to the loss of a pivotal center of meaning that has taken the form of structuralism, structurationism, or poststructuralism. Although they remain in the shadows (largely because their visage—not to mention verbiage—is not overly appreciated in IR discourse), two thinkers along with Nietzsche guide this semiology: Roland Barthes and Jacques Derrida. Particularly useful are two essays that engage historical and linguistic forms of realism: Barthes's *S/Z* (New York; Farrar, Straus and Giroux, 1974), which takes apart line by line Balzac's *Sarrasine*—and many of the tenets of representational realism with it; and Derrida's *Limited, Inc a b c …* (Baltimore: Johns Hopkins University Press, 1977), which pushes beyond the limit the radical implications of J. L. Austin's speech-act theory through a critical, often polemical engagement with the philosopher of language, John Searle. An especially useful bridging text between speech-act theory and later applications of structuralist and poststructuralist theories of representation is Petrey's *Realism and Revolution*.

35 Semiology may be more resistant than other approaches to this inertia, but it is not immune, as Roland Barthes, whose own career moved from a structural semiotics to an artful semiology, makes amply clear in an interview: "[I] could say, however, that the present problem consists in disengaging semiology from the repetition to which it is has already fallen prey. We must produce something *new* in semiology, not merely to be original, but because it is necessary to consider the theoretical problem of repetition … to pursue a general and systematic enterprise, polyvalent, multidimensional, the fissuration of the symbolic and its discourse in the West." See "Interview: A Conversation with Roland Barthes," *Signs of the Times* (1971), reprinted in *The Grain of the Voice* (New York: Hill and Wang, 1985), p. 129.

36 See Paul Virilio, *Pure War* (New York: Semiotext(e), 1983); *Speed and Politics* (New York: Semiotext(e), 1986); *War and Cinema: The Logistics of Perception* (New York: Verso, 1989). A trivial but telling recent example of the primacy of time over space (and what fills that space) is the lead-in commentary on President Bill Clinton's 1993 inaugural address: The three major networks and PBS put the emphasis on its fourteen-minute brevity.

37 See J. Der Derian, "The (S)pace of International Relations: Speed, Simulation, and Surveillance," *International Studies Quarterly* 34 (1990), pp. 295–310.

38 This mood and need was captured in a remark by Tom Brokaw, quoted in Michael Kelly, "Being Whatever It Takes to Win Election," *New York Times*, August 23, 1992: "The news cycle has become a 24-hour-a-day thing, and it moves very fast all the time now. What happens is that a fragment of information, true or false, gets sucked into the cycle early in the morning, and once it gets into the cycle it gets whipped around to the point that it has gravitas by the end of the day. And, unfortunately, people are so busy chasing that fragment of information that they treat it as a fact, forgetting about whether it is true or not."

39 Virilio, interview, from *Art and Philosophy* (Milan: Giancarlo Politi Editore, 1991), p. 142.

40 For an explanation of the dangers and opportunities presented by the new "antidiplomacy," see Der Derian, *Antidiplomacy*.

41 For a full account, see Der Derian, "Cyberwar, Videogames, and the Gulf War Syndrome," in *Antidiplomacy*, pp. 173–202.

42 F. Nietzsche, *Thus Spoke Zarathustra*, translated by R. J. Hollingdale (Harmondsworth, UK: Penguin, 1969), p. 237.

43 See *On Diplomacy; Antidiplomacy;* and the entry "Diplomacy" in *The Oxford Companion to the Politics of the World*, ed. Joel Krieger (New York: Oxford University Press, 1993).

44 Harold Nicolson, *Peacemaking* (London: 1933), p. 3.

45 In spite of a contrary opinion in IR—often based on secondary accounts— postmodernism from Nietzsche to Derrida and after has been informed and compelled by ethical questions about violence and genocide. See Emmanuel Levinas, *The Levinas Reader*, edited by Sean Hand (Oxford: Blackwell Publishers, 1989); Zygmunt Bauman, *Modernity and the Holocaust* (Ithaca: Cornell University Press, 1990); and Jacques Derrida, *The Other Heading: Reflections on Today's Europe*, translated by Pascale-Anne Brault and Michael B. Naas (Bloomington: Indiana University Press, 1992).

46 Friedrich Nietzsche, *The Gay Science*, translated by Walter Kaufmann (New York: Vintage, 1974), p. 273.

47 Nicolson, *Peacemaking*, p. 70. With the meaning of 1989 at stake, the entire quote is worth repeating: "Paris was something very different from Delphi, and when pressed to explain himself our Oracle ended all too frequently by explaining himself away. It is no exaggeration to attribute the sudden 'slump in idealism,' which overwhelmed the Conference towards the middle of March, to the horrorstruck suspicion that Wilsonism was leaking badly, that the vessel upon which we had all embarked so confidently was foundering by the head. Our eyes shifted uneasily in the direction of the most contiguous life-belt. The end of the Conference became a *sauve qui peut:* we called it '*security*': it was almost with a panic rush that we scrambled for the boats; and when we reached them we found our colleagues of the Italian Delegation already comfortably installed. They made us very welcome."

48 Nietzsche, *The Gay Science*, p. 274.

49 See Roger W. Smith, Eric Markusen, and Robert Jay Lifton, "Professional Ethics and the Denial of the Armenian Genocide," *Holocaust and Genocide Studies*, vol. 9, no. 1 (Spring 1995): 1–22.

50 Israel Charny and Daphna Fromer, "A Follow-up of the Sixty-nine Scholars Who Signed an Advertisement Questioning the Armenian Genocide," *Internet on the Holocaust and Genocide*, special double issue, no. 25/26 (April 1990):6–7, quoted in Smith, Markusen, and Lifton, "Professional Ethics," p. 15.

13 Cyber-deterrence

Source: *Wired* (September 1994), 2.09., p. 116 (plus 7 pages).

Wired visits the digital battlefield of Desert Hammer VI to see whether the US Army can win the next war without firing another shot.

I missed the first yellow warning sign. It was dark, I was on a 40-mile, dead-end road into the heart of the high Mojave Desert, and I was running late. Not wanting to give the public affairs officer another opportunity to explain what o-five-hundred meant, I pushed the rental car up to 90. A few miles later there was a second sign. This time I put on the high beams and slowed down. On it was a black silhouette of a tank, and underneath, "Tank Xing."

I had reached Fort Irwin, California, site of the US Army's National Training Center. Created in 1980, its purpose is to take the troops as close to the edge of war as the technology of simulation and the rigors of the environment will allow. For three weeks in the spring of 1994, this 635,052-acre military base served as the testing ground of the first fully digitized task force, one element of the 194th Separate Armored Brigade from Fort Knox, Kentucky.

Digitally enhanced, computer-accessorized, and budgetarily gold-plated from the bottom of their combat boots to the top of their kevlars, soldiers of the 194th Brigade were here for Desert Hammer VI. Also known as the "digital rotation," this experimental war game was developed to show the top brass, a host of junketing members of Congress, and an odd mix of journalists how, in the words of the press release, "digital technology can enhance lethality, operations tempo, and survivability." Combining real-time airborne and satellite surveillance, digitized battlefield communications, helmet-mounted displays, a 486 computer for every warrior, and an array of other high-tech weaponry, the brigade had come wired to move faster, kill better, and live longer than the enemy. If the old nuclear deterrent was to depend on the frightful force of mass destruction, the new digital strategy is to win the total information war.

Back when messages traveled at the speed of a horse, and overhead surveillance meant a view from a hilltop, Prussian strategist Carl von Clausewitz warned in *On War* against the arrogance of leaders who thought scripted battles would resemble the actual thing: "All action must, to a certain extent, be planned in a mere twilight, which in addition not infrequently – like the effect of fog or moonlight – gives to things exaggerated dimensions and an unnatural appearance." Would digitization render von Clausewitz's famous dictum obsolete? Would today's commanders be able to use satellite tracking and computer-equipped soldiers to dispel the fog of war? After three days, I thought I knew the answer, but by then the question had changed.

Almost every US unit that fights at Fort Irwin goes to battle against the "Krasnovians," American soldiers serving in a simulated Soviet brigade. When global crises dictate, the Krasnovians can also take on the role of "Sumarians" (Iraqis) or "Hamchuks" (North Koreans). On the first day of Desert Hammer VI, I chased black-bereted Krasnovians through the Whale Gap, into the Valley of Death, and watched them kick American desert khaki all the way to the John Wayne Hills.

On paper, the digitized army's combination of brute force and high tech appeared formidable. At the high end of the lethality spectrum, the Americans had top-of-the-line M1A2 Abrams main battle tanks, each carrying an information system that collected real-time battlefield data from airplanes, satellites, and unmanned aerial vehicles. At the low end were the "21st Century Land Warriors" (also called "warfighters" but never "soldiers" or "infantry") who came equipped with day- and night-vision scopes mounted on their M-16s, video cameras, and 1-inch LED screens attached to their kevlar helmets. The 486 computers in their rucksacks were wired to radios that could send voice or digital-burst communications to a battle command vehicle coordinating the attack through a customized Windows program.

Fort Irwin's public affairs officers were equally well armed. With budget cuts clearly on their minds, our voluble handlers, equipped with glossy brochures, informed us more than once that "smaller is not better: better is better." Other slogans sounded like a hybrid of Nick Machiavelli and Bill Gates, promising to "Win the Battlefield Information War" and "Project and Sustain the Force." One major went so far as to speculate, "If General Custer had digitization, he never would have had a last stand." Analogies proliferated like mad: digitization is the equivalent of the addition of the stirrup to the saddle or the integration of helicopters into the Army.

However, when the motto miasma met the fog of war on the first day of battle, the fog seemed to win out, especially since it came amply supplemented by sand, dust, and smoke. Our personable handler, a Major Franklin Childress, attempted to narrate the battle as it unfolded. After leading our small convoy of three humvees to a fine hillside perch, he provided a running commentary on what we could see and also on what we could hear as we eavesdropped on the radio traffic. We overheard accounts of confusion and fratricide or, "friendly fire." Although no one in the military would go on record about how the war game had commenced, a defense industry rep let me know later that the first blow had been delivered by an unarmed cruise missile launched off the California coast. Fortunately for the residents of Las Vegas, the missile had stayed on course and landed on the live-fire range.

Our first visible sign of the battle came when an array of Black Hawk and Apache helicopters flew by so low that we could look down on them from our hillside perch. Some were pretending to be Soviet Hinds, and my first thought was of the helicopters shot down over Iraq on April 14, the week before my visit, in a deadly, real-life case of "friendly fire." I filed away my question as an F-16 followed the helicopter, sweeping over our hill and dropping flares to confuse possible ground-to-air missiles. Had the pilots who shot down the helicopters been trained to attack American Blackhawks pretending to be Soviet Hinds?

The confusion increased as loud bangs joined the visuals. An M-22 simulator round the size of a fat shotgun shell exploded nearby as a Stinger missile crew fired at an F-16 fighter plane. White plumes from the blank Hoffman shells that simulate tank and artillery fire spread across the battlefield. The arrival of the main show was signaled by tracks of dust on the horizon. Tanks, humvees, and armored personnel carriers came out of the wadis in bursts of speed. As the Krasnovians mixed it up with the Americans, vehicles bearing the orange flags of the observer-controllers darted in and out of the battle, tallying the kills. Rather than loaded weapons, they depended on the MILES, or Multiple Integrated Laser Engagement System, first developed by Xerox Electro-Optical and now better known to civilians as laser tag. Hits and near-misses were recorded by the electronic sensors on the vests and belts that circled soldiers and vehicles alike, and transmitted via microwave back to computers at "Star Wars," the command center. From our hillside we could see the flashing yellow strobes of the MILES sensors spread across the battlefield as the Krasnovians cut through the American forces. Simulation-hardened and terrain-savvy, the Krasnovians rarely lose.

Suddenly we got an order to move: our position was about to be overrun. For a brief moment, as the Krasnovian tanks came down the ridge, I became separated from the other observers and stood within smelling distance of the tanks as they roared between us. With synapses firing and hormones mixing into a high-octane cocktail, I sensed the seductive rush that comes with simulated war. I was detached and yet connected to a dangerous situation through a kind of voyeurism, as if I were watching myself watch the tanks bear down. Perhaps therein lies the hidden appeal of simulation: it enables soldiers to espy death in a fictitious borderland where fear and fun, pain and pleasure, you and the enemy encounter one another. The simulated battlefield makes dying and killing less plausible, and therefore more possible.

Day two began like the first: late and in the dark. But this time I did catch the icon on the first yellow warning sign. It was of a tortoise. One more question for the major.

The main group had already left. A humvee was waiting and ready to catch up to the media convoy. The new driver, however, failed to inspire much confidence. He was unable to make radio contact with Major Childress and kept switching frequencies, until I suggested that he put up the antenna. He kept getting the radio messages wrong, at one point even slowing down to check for a flat tire because he heard the humvee ahead inform the major that it had one.

After a cross-country shortcut through a minefield (marked by round plastic bowls that looked like doggie dishes) and a couple of wrong turns, we caught up with the rest of the group at what appeared to be a desert rest stop for

21st century warfighters. I was first directed to a medical unit, simulating the latest in "tele-medicine." Each soldier in Desert Hammer carried a 3.5-inch computer disk in a breast pocket, not to stop a bullet but to store a digitized image of a predestined wound. In a real war in the near future a video camera would record the body damage. In this case the medic popped the disk into a portable PowerBook to discover that his victim had a sucking chest wound. The image was digitized and transferred via a radiolink to a triage unit in the rear, where a doctor talked the medic through the treatment of the wounded soldier. It seemed to work: the soldier got up and walked away from the stretcher as I moved on to another station.

Standing in the sand next to a Bradley was a Borg. He was made of flesh and metal and looked like he had just walked off the set of Star Trek: The Next Generation. He had his Sony minicam, his eyeball-sized display screen, his portable 486, and his global-positioning-system antenna on his helmet. When I asked him if he realized he was a dead ringer for one of the tough colonial marines in Aliens, he curtly answered: "I don't know about that, Sir." (When talking to soldiers, all journalists enjoy an instant field promotion to officer.) I was taken aback, but later surmised that I had transgressed rule Number One of the armed services: never, never confuse an Army grunt, especially a fully digitized grunt, with a Marine no-neck. It seemed that all the hype we were hearing about joint operations was only slowly making its way down the ranks.

Judging from some of the thousand-mile stares I got during this and other interviews, the simulated battle in the Mojave Desert had managed to replicate at least one of war's primary characteristics: fatigue. Surprisingly often, soldiers responded to my questions about the reality factor in simulations with the claim that the Persian Gulf War was much easier than this. Technology has advanced quite a bit in a few years. Keeping up with machines is dirty business.

The final stop on the digital tour was an M1A2 tank. I took a few pictures and started to walk away but was stopped by the hovering Major Childress, who asked, "Do you want to take a look inside?" He surely registered my surprise. Three years ago, just after the Gulf War had ended, I came out to the desert to look at the training that was said to have won the war. At the time I was told that I could take pictures of just about anything – except for the inside of an M1 tank, which remained classified. Now, I was invited to videotape a state-of-the-art model. A gunner walked me through the cyberspaces of the Inter-Vehicular Information System: "Here, your position is triangulated by satellite, an enemy targeted by laser range finding, and a friendly identified by a relay from a J-STAR flying overhead."

I was impressed but also confused. What was the reason for this new policy of access? I asked my standard stock of questions: Would the friction of war overheat a cybernetic battle plan? Would the surge of information overload the digital systems, especially the primary information node of the battle network, the warfighter? Would the new technology further distance the killer from the business of killing? In response I received off-the-shelf, by-the-book answers: perhaps, but not so far – and, besides, this is all in the experimental stage.

However at some point – I think it began with the tour of the tank – I began to suspect that I was asking the wrong set of questions. The Army has always prided itself on being grounded in reality. Now, like the Navy and the Air Force before it, the Army is leaping into a realm of hyperreality, where the enemy disappeared as flesh and blood, and reappeared, pixelated and digitized on computer screens in kill zones, as icons of opportunity. Was there a paradox operating here, that the closer the war game was able to technically reproduce the reality of war, the greater the danger of confusing one for the other? When soldiers begin to mutate into cyborgs, the old questions seem irrelevant.

The transitional moment was the Gulf War. Although General H. Norman Schwarzkopf has always referred to himself as a "mud soldier," in 1990 he sponsored a war game called Exercise Internal Look '90, which combined computer simulations with minimal troop movements to model an Iraqi invasion. During the final days of the exercise, reality caught up with the simulation and Iraq actually invaded Kuwait. In his autobiography Schwarzkopf recounts that his planners kept mixing up reports of the simulation and the war. It turns out that the mud soldier was our first cyberpunk general.

The blurring of war and simulation goes back even further in the history of Operation Desert Storm. In a 1990 *USA Today* interview, Schwarzkopf revealed that before the war, Iraq was running computer simulations and war games for an invasion of Kuwait. During the war, Schwarzkopf, according to his own account, was programming daily computer battles against Iraq.

Among the many causes of the Gulf War, what importance should we place on the proliferation of simulations? Have new improved simulations begun to precede and engender the reality of the wars they are intended to model?

Clearly the Army doesn't read French critics like Jean Baudrillard or Paul Virilio for answers about the potential hazards of global simulation at digital speed. But what do they read? The day before my departure I had received an air-express package from the Office of the Secretary of the Army. Officially it was identified as the press kit for the Advanced Warfighting Experiment (AWE). But "press kit" does not do this document justice. Collected in a large, three-ring binder with the triangle logo for "The Digital Battlefield" on the cover (satellite, helicopter, and tank in each corner, connected by lightning bolts to a warfighter in the middle) were more than 30 press releases, brochures, and articles on the Army of the future. Computer-generated images were mixed in with all kinds of fonts and graphics.

Leading the paper charge was a prolegomenon from the office of the Chief of staff that provides the best encapsulation of the rationale behind the 21st Century Army, Force XXI:

> Today the Industrial Age is being superseded by the Information Age, the Third Wave, hard on the heels of the agrarian and industrial eras. Our present army is well-configured to fight and win in the late Industrial Age, and we can handle Agrarian-Age foes as well. We have begun to move into Third Wave warfare, to evolve a new force for a new century.

In the slickest brochure, bearing the short yet pretentious title, "The Vision," I found a section called "Exploit Modeling and Simulation" that read like a good cyberpunk novel:

> Ten thousand linked simulators! Entire literal armies online, Global real-time, broadband, fiber-optic, satellite-assisted, military simulation networking. And not just connected, not just simulated. Seamless.

It gets better, and for good reason: it was written by Bruce Sterling for *Wired* (see "War is Virtual Hell," issue 1.1, page 46). What does it mean when *Wired* is appropriated for the Army's information war? Perhaps in the new era of simulation, Sterling's writing, as well as my own reportorial presence at Fort Irwin is just one more chip in the Army's motherboard.

As early as 1964, after reading a breathless promotional account of the "cyborg" under development by General Electric (from the photographs the cyborg looks like a robotic elephant), architect and social critic Lewis Mumford warned of the coming of a new "technological exhibitionism." Soon, he believed, this perverse display of military technology would pervade all of society.

Was I bearing witness to an even more powerful hybrid? What happens when you combine media voyeurism, technological exhibitionism, and strategic simulations? News flash: In the 21st century Army, you get the cyber-deterrent.

If this sounds far-fetched, consider the worst-case scenario that currently underlies strategic thinking. As CIA Director James Woolsey put it at his confirmation hearings, a "bewildering variety of poisonous snakes" has sprung forth from the slain dragon of communism. When the dragon expired, so did the mighty, if illusory, deterrence value of nuclear weapons. On a quest since Vietnam to fight only quick, popular, winnable wars, and imbued by the spirit of feudal Chinese strategist Sun Tzu, who wrote that "those skilled in war subdue the enemy's army without battle," the 21st century Army has perhaps found in the cyber-deterrent its Holy Grail. The cyber-deterrent is fast, digitized, and is as spectacular in simulation as it is global in effect. With the price of nukes falling and their availability increasing, the digitized option has the added advantage of being out of reach of all but the richest rogues. And it makes a hell of a photo-op.

Digitization, making ever more convincing simulations possible, seems destined to replace an increasingly irrelevant nuclear balance of terror with a simulation of superiority.

Moreover, the digitized deterrence machine bears an important similarity to its nuclear counterpart: it does not necessarily have to work to be effective. Its power lies in a symbolic exchange of signs – give or take the odd reality check in the desert to bring religion to the doubters. This is the purpose of spectacles like Desert Hammer VI: to render visible and plausible the cyber-deterrent for all those potential snakes that might not have sufficiently learned the lesson of the prototype of cyberwar, Desert Storm.

Here at Fort Irwin, the desert functions again as a backdrop for the melodrama of national security. The effect of Desert Hammer is to turn von Clausewitz on his head. Military maneuvers are no longer about dispersing the fog of war, but about stage-managing the special effects. Combining Disneyland, Hollywood, and Silicon Valley, the National Training Center, full of video cameras and computerized special effects, not to mention thrilling rides, has superseded Los Alamos and the Nevada Test Site to become the premiere production set for the next generation of strategic superiority.

Can one conduct a critical inquiry into the information war without becoming just another informant for it, material for the Army's sequel, "(Re)Visions?" Biologist-turned-social-critic Donna Haraway, more sanguine than Mumford about the technological turn, offers a possible escape pod from the dilemma. In her embryonic 1985 essay, "Manifesto for Cyborgs," she wrote: "From one perspective, a cyborg world is about the final imposition of a grid of control on the planet, about the final abstraction embodied in a Star Wars apocalypse waged in the name of defense, about the final appropriation of women's bodies in a masculinist orgy of war. From another perspective, a cyborg world might be about lived social and bodily realities in which people are not afraid of their joint kinship with animals and machines...."

There are cyborg alternatives to be found in the desert. Heading back at the usual hellbent speed from the battlefield on day two, I asked the major over wind and noise about the strange warning sign that had caught my attention early in the morning. "Desert tortoise," he shouted. "Fifty thousand dollars if you kill one." I had to wait until we returned to the base to find out whether that was the bounty or the penalty. In asking, I learned that the tortoise had been assigned threatened species status in 1990. And since Fort Irwin encompasses some of its main breeding grounds, a clash of armored vehicles and armored reptiles was inevitable.

What was the Army to do? It decided to go green, or at least a slightly muddy version of it. The following morning, I met with Fort Irwin's civilian environmental scientists, enlisted by the military to protect the tortoises. Judging from their intensive prep and genuine enthusiasm, they didn't get many opportunities to sell their eco-wares to the press. After all, how could a lumbering desert tortoise possibly match the media appeal of an M1 tank going flat-out?

After the briefing, the tortoises' appeal was evident. The slide show was informative ("Without our help, the survival rate of the tortoise is 1 percent"), moving ("To a raven, a freshly hatched tortoise looks like a walking ravioli"), and amusing ("Here we see several tortoises in parade formation after completing their training at Fort Irwin").

The scientists claimed to be matching the warfighters chip for chip in the information war. Tortoises were tagged with transmitters, tracked by radio telemetry, and graphed in grid locations by computers. Landsat satellites were used to identify good habitat areas, aerial mine detection technology to find tortoises moving on the ground, and electronic sensors to warn off vehicles that might endanger the creatures.

Surveillance and communications technology was binding humans and tortoises into an interdependent community. By the end of the briefing, I began to believe that I had just witnessed the telling of a postmodern fable. Perhaps, with a techno-ethical assist and a leap of faith, the tortoise might yet beat the tank.

I knew it was a stretch – and not quite Aesop – but what more can one expect when machines take the place of animals in the imagining of the human race?

14 Global swarming, virtual security, and Bosnia

Source: *The Washington Quarterly* (Summer 1996), vol. 19, no. 3., pp. 45–56.

This chapter has its origins in a fax that I received while in England. Would I be willing to give a *"Wired*-cyber-anarcho-futuristic" perspective on the impact of the information revolution on national security? Judging from the reputation that seemed to have preceded me, I was supposed to lend some futureshock-value to the proceedings. That very night I turned on the television to the BBC news to find a video clip of Speaker of the House Newt Gingrich doing his Toffler two-step on MTV, declaiming that we must move from brute force to brain force in Bosnia. If this was the scene from inside, I wondered how I could possibly top that from outside the Beltway.

Luckily I had just come back from the future, or as close as U.S. Armed Forces in Europe can simulate it in Hohenfels, Germany, where the 1st Armored Division was preparing to intervene in Bosnia. At first glance, Bosnia would appear to have little to do with the information revolution. This is not infowar, cyberwar, antiwar, postwar, or anything else remotely connected to the future. It barely makes it into the present. This is a dirty, atavistic war with static trench lines, wetware-to-wetware combat, and very intense—even if highly imaginary—ethno-confessional hatreds going back to centuries-old holy wars between Christendom and the "Anti-Christ" Ottoman Turks. Many commentators have bemoaned the resistance of the Balkans to "civilized" reason and modern technologies:

> The abstract humanitarian–moralistic way of looking at the process of history is the most barren of all. I know this very well. But the chaotic mass of material acquisitions, habits, customs and prejudices that we call civilization hypnotizes us all, inspiring the false confidence that the main thing in human progress has already been achieved—and then war comes, and reveals that we have not yet crept out on all fours from the barbaric period of our history. We have learned how to wear suspenders, to write clever leading articles, and to make milk chocolate, but when we need to reach a serious decision about how a few different tribes are to live together on a well-endowed European peninsula, we are incapable of finding any other method than mutual extermination on a mass scale.

So wrote the exiled, out-of-work revolutionary Leon Trotsky in 1912, killing time during the Balkan Wars as foreign correspondent for the *Kievan Thought*, seeking answers to the so-called "Eastern Question" of what next after the decline and fall of the Ottoman Empire.

History never repeats itself. Yet, with the information revolution it does seem at critical times to get caught in a feedback loop. Now, with the technical reproducibility of war (i.e., on television), we are witnessing a kind of *global swarming*, where workers (world leaders) and drones (voyeuristic viewers) chase after the queen-bees of TV ("This is Christiane Amanpour reporting for CNN from yet another war-torn region of the world"). Individually, they might be in search of a New World Order, a Global Village, or only an ephemeral fix of Virtual Community, but together, as the exceptional moment is rendered by real-time TV into permanent movement, they forgo the security of the hive for the free terror of the global swarm. States still matter and wars are still fought, but a new border has been built by the information revolution, between the real-life victims who get stung and the viewers who get the buzz.

Clearly the information revolution has given the Bosnia Question a political urgency and extraterritorial proximity that the first and second Balkan Wars never had. What Western leader would now be willing to say, as did nineteenth century German Chancellor Otto von Bismarck, that "the whole Balkan Peninsula is not worth the bones of a single Pomeranian grenadier?" Or at least be willing to say it on TV, before an election, or with a major military budget to pass? These are the modern imperatives of states working for that elusive "democratic peace," of which Immanuel Kant wrote and contemporary leaders now speak. With a new post-cold war transparency, transnational, non-ideological television was supposed to spread the democratic word and to preempt the totalitarian urge.

But technology always cuts both ways. Indeed, in the case of television, the technological edge is multifaceted and fractal in effect. And Bosnia is not the first war to prove resistant to the televisual fix. Instead, the ubiquity of the image seems to have produced a simulation of war, dirtier than the Persian Gulf War, yet just as simulated for the viewer as it is deadly real for the victims. "It is only television!" said French *agent provocateur* Jean Baudrillard of the Gulf war in a notorious series of articles in *Libération*:

> The United Nations has given the green light to a diluted kind of war—the right of war. It is a green light for all kinds of precautions and concessions, making a kind of extended contraceptive against the act of war. First safe sex, now safe war.

Ever hyperbolic to capture the diabolic nature of the image, what he said then informs us now about Bosnia:

> In our fear of the real, of anything that is too real, we have created a gigantic simulator. We prefer the virtual to the catastrophe of the real, of which television is the universal mirror. Indeed it is more than a mirror: Today television

and news have become the ground itself, television plays the same role as the card which is substituted for territory in the Borges fable.

Baudrillard's allusion to "On Rigor in Science," by Argentinean writer Jorge Luis Borges, is instructive. An emperor sends out his royal cartographers to make the perfect map of his empire, only to have them return years later with a map that dwarfs the now-shrunken empire; the emperor naturally prefers the model to reality. Like all Borges, not an entirely fabulous tale: Consider the initial reaction of Western leaders when the Berlin Wall took its first hits from the sledgehammers. U.S. President George Bush and Secretary of State James Baker, at a hastily organized press conference, kept pointing to a map on the table in front of them, assuring the public that all frontiers—sovereignty indelibly inscribed on paper—would survive such an historic event. As in the childhood game rock-paper-scissors, paper covers stone taken down by the hammer blows. In contrast, the atlases of Rand-McNally (more market-oriented than governments to the flux of the times) began to sprout peel-away labels promising replacements should there be any more border changes.

Are we not witnessing in Bosnia the fractal effects of a similar decline of empires, a denial of reality, a retreat into virtuality? A bid for a kind of "virtual security"? Does not television now play the role of the emperor's cartographers, electronically mapping an empire, a state, a history that no longer exists—if it ever did? Now TV adds a human dimension—if not historical depth—to the fable, anthropology to cartography, tales of ancient hatreds that brook comprehension by the "civilized" viewers. Westerners come to recognize the former Yugoslavia as that region at the edge of the map where the sea-monsters lurk: Do Not Go There. The Slovenian social theorist Slovoj Zizek believes this "evocation of the complexity of circumstances serves to deliver us from the responsibility to act ... that is, to avoid the bitter truth that, far from presenting the case of an eccentric ethnic conflict, the Bosnian War is a direct result of the West's failure to grasp the political dynamic of the disintegration of Yugoslavia, of the West's silent support of 'ethnic cleansing.'" The complexities of Yugoslavia had been lost in the bipolar interstices of the cold war. With its end came an explosion of multipolar truths and multicultural identities.

At the borders of the Bosnia Question, between the military terror inside and diplomatic error outside, truths bitter or otherwise are hard to find. Instead, one finds dissimulations of war and ethnic enmity up hard against simulations of peace and military intervention. On the one hand, the "dissim skills" of Bosnian Serb leader Radovan Karadzic and Serbian President Slobodan Milosevic, honed in the deceit of communism, retooled through the conceit of nationalism, revived—let's call it what it is—a national socialism for the '90s. On the other hand, western leaders and pundit–cartographers, whether utopic about a new world order of self-determined polities or nostalgic for the lost stability of the cold war, rely once again on the pretense of TV to keep and video-bombs to make what never was peace. At this borderline, mutations of past empires mate with images of perpetual war: Gibbons of *Decline and Fall* meets Gibson the *Neuromancer* in the Balkans. Bosnia as a looped sim/dissim war.

But in Germany, the U.S. 1st Armored Division was simulating a more forceful answer to the Bosnia Question. Would it work? In microchip times, is there still a role for the Big Green Machine?

The Bosnia Question took me to the Hohenfels Combat and Maneuver Training Center (CMTC). The U.S. Army owns—or more precisely, has "maneuver rights" over—a significant piece of real estate in southern Germany, 178 square kilometers in Hohenfels alone. Spread out over the State of Bavaria like an isosceles triangle are the three major sites of the U.S. Seventh Army Training Command, through which rotate the Europe-based U.S. troops, as well as some units from the British, Spanish, Canadian, and German armies and the Dutch marines, for some laser-simulated warfare as well as for live-fire exercises.

The centers have an interesting heritage. Grafenwoehr, the oldest, was set up by the Royal Bavarian Army in 1907 to "play" some of the earliest *Kriegspiele*, or war games. It served as the southern tactical arm of the northern Prussian head, most infamously represented by Count von Schlieffen, Chief of the General Staff, who in 1905 designed the famous Schlieffen Plan that was supposed to anticipate the next German conflict. Instead, its iron-clad "war by timetable" helped to precipitate World War I as one mobilization triggered a cascade of others throughout Europe. The two other training centers owe their origins to Hitler's rejection of the Treaty of Versailles, World War I's "peace of the victors," which included the humiliating 100,000 troop limitation for Germany. Rapidly filling up the ranks with new conscripts, the *Wehrmacht* (German Army) found itself short on training space. Grafenwoehr was expanded and two new sites were created: Wildflecken in 1937 for the IX German Corps, and Hohenfels in 1938 for the VII German Corps.

The morning I drove past the front gate and into the Hohenfels CMTC, I learned a lesser-known part of its history. The tank-crossing sign, resembling World War I lead toys more than the Ml behemoths that skidded up the hill ahead of me, momentarily caught my attention. But it was the more conventional warning sign for "Cobblestones: Slippery When Wet" that seemed out of place. I later asked my handler, the very smart, very affable Colonel Wallace, why the short strip of quaint cobblestone interrupted the finely graded modern asphalt road into the base. He thought it had been left intact as a tribute to the Polish construction workers. I later filled in the blanks: Hohenfels, begun in 1938 and finished in 1940, had evidently been built by Polish *Sklavenarbeiter*, slave laborers. "Slippery when wet" was to become something of a coda for me during my visit to Hohenfels. Wars, when gamed, tend to lose their history of blood and deception.

The reason I was there had taken on a special urgency. Two weeks before my arrival at Hohenfels, North Atlantic Treaty Organization (NATO) air strikes on Bosnian Serb ammunition dumps triggered the Serbs to take more than 300 United Nations (UN) peacekeepers hostage. The cold peace flared hot when French soldiers in Sarajevo fought back after Bosnian Serbs disguised in French uniforms and UN blue helmets tried to take the Vrbanja Bridge. Britain and France announced plans to send a rapid reaction force. It seemed like the right time to come to Hohenfels to observe an "Operation other than War."

Just what that meant was supposed to be the subject of the morning brief. But confusion reigned, not least because sometime between my first fax-barrage requesting a visit to the base and my arrival, a name-change had taken place. "Operations other than War" had been replaced by the more anodyne "Stability Operations." Word hadn't quite gotten through the ranks, though, and people kept shifting back and forth between the two. The confusion mounted as I sat in a darkened theater with my two handlers, Captain Fisher and Colonel Wallace, on either side, and listened to the beginning of Major Demike's multi-media, name-negating "brief." The major clearly had a take-no-prisoners attitude toward the English language: "Army units from USAREUR (troops in Europe) rotate through the CMTC (I got that one) at least once a year for 21 days of Force-on-Opfor training" (good guys versus bad guys), "situational training with MILES in the Box" (dial-a-scenario field exercises using lasers rather than bullets), "BBS training" (not bulletin-board systems, but networked computer battle simulations with units based elsewhere), and "after-action reviews" (video presentations of what went right or wrong on the battlefield).

Major Demike got into the technology with vigor: "We have at CMTC the most realistic battlefield. The instrumentation system is state of the art. It is the best in the world." He skipped through technology like the MILES (Multiple Integrated Laser Engagement System) for firing and recording laser hits, the microwave relays that allowed for near real-time production of the video after-action reviews, and the simulated mortar and artillery capability. To punctuate the point, Colonel Wallace stepped in: "Once a unit goes into the Box, with the exception that they're shooting laser bullets, and that a guy, instead of falling down with a gunshot wound, will read from a card he's carrying in his pocket how badly hurt he is, virtually everything we do is real. There's nothing simulated in the Box."

After a long slog through computer graphics on the organization and function of the CMTC, we finally got to the geopolitical gist of the next day's "Stability Operation." Up came a map of "Danubia," trisected into "Sowenia," "Vilslakia," "Juraland," and, looking very much like a small fiefdom among them, the CMTC. The major's pointer started to fly: "Three separate countries have split off from Danubia—Sowenia and Vilslakia are at odds with each other. When we want to transition into high-intensity conflict, we have Juraland, which has heavy forces, come in on the side of one or other of the parties." Prodded to utter the word "Bosnia" just once, he would go no further, except to say that the scenario was based on intelligence sources, CNN reports, and the "threat books." For my benefit he did add, "You don't have to be a rocket scientist to figure out what this is modeled on."

No rocket scientist, I resorted to a kind of semiotics to sort out the countries. The new countries of the disintegrating Danubia bore some obvious similarities to the region of Yugoslavia; to the former republic, now independent state of Slovenia, or perhaps the western enclave of Slavonia contested by the Croats and Serbs; and, of course, to the Jural mountain range. "Vilslakia" remained a mystery.

The countries surrounding Danubia were familiar enough that I sought out my own intelligence source, Microsoft's CD-ROM version of Cinemania '95. It was not needed for the country to the northwest: "Teutonia" referred to the early Germanic tribes. However, "Freedonia," to the northeast of Danubia, was clearly taken from the 1933 war satire *Duck Soup*, in which Groucho Marx so effectively played the power-hungry dictator of said-country that the real dictator Mussolini banned the film in Italy. And below Danubia was "Ruritania," the country in the clouds that provided the surreal setting for W. C. Fields's 1941 classic, "Never Give a Sucker an Even Break." What should one make of the Army's strange choice of simulated countries? Probably nothing much, except that some war-gamer had a sense of humor as well as history—and, perhaps, also something for Margaret Dumont, who plays in both comedies the great dame (or Great Dane, as Fields might have drolled). But I wondered whether Bosnians would get the joke.

The briefing ended with a short video of a "Stability Operation." By way of introduction, Colonel Wallace informed me that "none of this stuff is staged, it's all from live footage taken by the Viper video teams in the Box." Before I could fully enjoy the colonel's knack for paradox, the lights dimmed, the screen flickered, and Graham Nash was singing about "soldiers of peace just playing the game." The first clip was of a confrontation between partisans and soldiers that escalates into heated words; the last was in the same tent, with hand-shakes and professions of friendship being exchanged. In between, UN convoys are stopped by civilians; soldiers go down, wounded or dead; a body-bagged corpse is spat upon by a partisan; food supplies are hijacked by townspeople; a female member of the media gets shoved around; a bomb explodes and panic ensues in the town streets; a sniper fires on a humvee; dogs sniff for explosives; infiltrators are caught in a nightscope; a UN flag waves defiantly; and an old man drops to his knees in the mud in front of a humvee, begging for food. More in the sentimental aesthetic of an AT&T advertisement than a hyperreal MTV clip, it was strangely moving. I was disarmed by it.

But the mood shifted quickly when the major concluded the briefing by handing me a four-inch-thick pile of documents. The rest of the day was a whirlwind of briefs-to-go. First stop was the "Warlord Simulation Center," full of desktop computers and Sun Microsystem computers for planning, preparing, and running simulations in the Box, out of the Box, or through the cyber-Box—that is, simulation networking (SIMNET), "remoting via satellite in and out of the Box to anywhere in the world." Next stop was a cavernous warehouse full of MILES gear under the watchful eye of Sergeant Kraus, who probably gave the best brief of the day. A man who clearly loved his job—or was just eager for some human company—he was as articulate as his lasers ("instead of a bullet, it sends out 120 words on a laser beam; in the center are eight kill words; anything else is a wound or near miss") as he made his way through the various shapes, types, and generations of lasers and sensors, all set up on a variety of weapons and menacing mannequins. He was stumped only once, when I asked what would happen if a Danubian snuck up and hit one of his dummies on the head. Would any bells and lights go off? "Excuse me?" he said. "ROE?" Colonel Wallace intervened to explain: "Against the Rules of Engagement. One-meter rule. No physical contact in the Box." It seems that one conveys body-to-body harm with real words, not laser words, e.g., "I am butt-stroking you now, so fall down." I would later find out that in Operations other than War, the Rules of Engagement were there to be broken.

The day ended with an interview with the pugnacious commander of the base, Colonel Lenz, who made a persuasive case for Stability Operations as essential training for the increasing number of missions in that "gray area between war and peace." He would not, however, be drawn out on the relationship between Stability Operations and Bosnia, especially when I queried him about the possibility that some might find the notion of stability based on the status quo to be offensive, in both senses of word, when stabilization is perceived to be an enemy of justice, or simply just deserts. "That's above my pay-grade," was the colonel's reply. At the end of the interview he kindly suggested a debrief after my visit to the Box: "I've got people upstairs who can suck a guy's brain dry."

That was sufficient incentive to stay up that night and wade through the stack of papers that I had been given. The bulk of it was a 400-page document called the "Coordinating Draft of the Seventh Army Training Command White Paper of Mission Training Plan for Military Operations Other Than War." The introduction conveyed the philosophy of operations other than war and—after I waded through all the acronymic muck and bureaucratese ("Traditional MTP crosswalk matrixes for references and collective tasks are also included in this MTP")—the final paragraph emerged as a reasonably clear summary of the purpose of the plan:

> As we continue to maintain our proficiency in traditional wartime operations, our forces must also be ready to operate effectively in non-traditional roles. Units involved in conflicts anywhere within the full spectrum of operations will always face some elements of a complex battlefield. These elements include civilians in the area of operations, the press, local authorities, and private organizations. This White Paper is designed to assist leaders at all levels to more fully understand and prepare for these new challenges.

In post-modern terms, the "White Paper" was this year's model for the high-tech, post–cold war simulations and training exercises that would prepare U.S. armed forces for pre-peacekeeping non-interventions into those postimperial spaces where once- and wannabe-states were engaged in postwar warring. In terms of past experiences rather than future threats, Somalia, Haiti, Rwanda, and—judging from the many references to the *British Wider Peacekeeping Manual*—Northern Ireland lurked between the lines. But in this simulated shadowland between military combat, police action, and relief aid, other clouds of global swarming could be discerned; Bosnia, yes, but why not as the next "operation other than war" a counternarcotics operation in Mexico? Or a quarantine of a paramilitary survivalist camp in Idaho? Or checkpoints and convoy escorts through a persistently riotous Los Angeles? This week, however, the enemy at Hohenfels reflected the headlines.

Very early the next day I headed for the Box, where the warring ethnic groups of a disintegrating "Danubia" were about to make life very hard for the visiting 1st Armored Division. The morning began with a low fog—confirmed by the weather report at yet another brief, the "Battle Update for Rotation 95–10." The mission: "To provide humanitarian assistance and separate belligerent factions." It was broken down from the level of "UNDANFOR" (United Nations Danubian Force) commander to squadron tasks and included equipment lists, tactical rules of engagement, task force organization, and maps with vehicle and troop positions that were presented through a series of computer graphics. A schedule of major events followed, some of which required translation from the briefer, like "1100–SCUD Ambush of Convoy" (not the missile, but the "Sowenian Communist Urban Defenders"), or "2230–JERK Raid vs. Care Facility in Raversdorf" (again, not Steve Martin, but the "Jurische Ethnic Rights Korps," guerrilla forces operating in the south sector). By the end of the brief I was in bad need of a scorecard.

Finally we were on our way to the Box. During the short ride through a gently sloping open terrain with trees on most of the hilltops, Colonel Wallace did the eco-army routine—"there are more trees and grass growing now than when we got here"—and, as if on cue, a substantial herd of deer dashed across the road in front of us. The valleys and hillsides looked pretty chewed up by all the maneuvers, and portable toilets dotted the landscape, but the fauna seemed to appreciate the fact that the U.S. Army—unlike the Bavarian hunters outside the Box—were shooting blanks.

The first stop was a UN checkpoint, one of many where civilians were stopped and forced to do kind of "self-search" for weapons or explosives. Most of the Ml tanks and Bradleys had their turrets reversed, the universal symbol of nonaggression (or surrender). We arrived with a UN food convoy which was supposed to pass through the mock-town of Übingsdorf. The town came complete with the steep-roofed houses of Bavaria, a church with a steeple (no sniper in sight), a cemetery (no names on the gravestones), a mix of Vilslakian and Sowenian townspeople (dressed by a retired psychological operations sergeant in what he described as "the eastern European 'grunge' look," accessorized with the requisite MILES vest), and a mayor who wore a green-felt fedora and insisted that the food be off-loaded for his hungry people.

Language differences, a belligerent crowd, and an aggressive reporter with an intrusive cameraman all jacked up the tension level. "Lieutenant Colonel Vladimir," commander of the local Vilslakian garrison, was refusing to bring the rabble to order. Chants for food in a kind of pidgin German—"Essen, Essen"—made voice communication difficult. Suddenly the crowd began to move towards the trucks and a few rocks were thrown. The U.S. troops began to retreat but already some of the townspeople were clambering up onto the trucks. It was then that one of the soldiers broke the first rule of engagement by grabbing a civilian to toss him off. "One-meter rule, one-meter rule!" shouted the observer/controllers on the scene. Some tanks and Bradleys, probably called up by the besieged sergeant in charge of negotiating with the mayor, came roaring up to join the convoy. The situation died down when the townspeople were rounded up and put under guard. Negotiations resumed, resulting in something of a compromise: The Army would unload the food at the local UN headquarters. But after the troops pulled out, I watched as some of the townspeople pulled off the most realistic maneuver of the day: They scampered off with some of the large crates of food. Colonel Wallace later told me this was not in the script. I had witnessed some Box Improv.

The script-writers clearly had it in for this convoy. At just about every checkpoint, food had to be traded for safe passage. As we roared ahead in the colonel's humvee for high ground, I noticed an observer/controller crouched in the ruins of a building probably dating back to the *Wehrmacht* days. A bad sign. As the convoy descended down the hill all hell broke loose—machine-gun fire from the hills, smoke bombs marking hits, and the light-and-sound show of MILES sensors going off. The Ml tanks and Bradleys reacted sluggishly to the ambush, not moving, and worse, keeping their turrets reversed in the defensive posture, making it impossible to identify the enemy with thermal sights. Instead, someone from the convoy called in for a Cobra helicopter gunship, breaking another rule of engagement: Only "minimum" or proportional force should be used in a counterattack, to prevent a needless escalation of violence. From the last two engagements, it seemed apparent that the shift from simulated war to simulated peace was not going to be an easy one.

Other answers to the Bosnia Question cause in a deeper shade of gray. Plugging "operations other than war" into the new grid of information warfare and national security, I had hoped to gain some new insights into the difficult and often dangerous relationships Bosnia produced—between technology and violence, media and war, us and them—relationships now extant in the post–cold war disorder as well. In spite of the bayings of the Western triumphalists, the only empire to emerge victorious from the end of the cold war was what Edmund Burke after an earlier revolution in Europe called the "empire of circumstance." The peace that followed, cold or hot, became an especially bad war for peoples in the borderlands like the Balkans who emerged from the thaw of once-rigid bipolar powers and truths into a traumatized condition of ethnic as well as ethical insecurity. All kinds of politicians, pundits, and soldiers-as-diplomats, feeling what Nietzsche called "the breath of empty space," rushed into this geopolitical flux and moral void with electoral promises (from U.S. President Bill Clinton to French President Jacques Chirac) and nationalist propaganda (from Karadzic's hard-cop to Milosevic's soft-cop). Others created a parallel universe of computerized simulations ("Operations other than War") and dissimulations (genocide as "ethnic cleansing"). And the majority, I would say, have hung back and avoided the void. Whether they have maintained their angelic status is another question.

But the Bosnia Question, simulated, reported, agonized over, remains unanswered—and the possibility is high that it cannot be answered by traditional geopolitics and statecraft. Capital, information, technology, drug, and refugee flows are supplanting and in some cases subverting the powers of not just the international society but of the sovereign states themselves to manage the deleterious effects of global swarming. Contemporary world politics as a hiveless cloud of angry bees remains at best a metaphorical question, not a conclusive answer.

But I do think that Bosnia has produced a new set of questions about the future of warfare and peacemaking. Have we moved beyond that modernist moment— so aptly expressed by the poet William Butler Yeats—when the center no longer holds, to a kind of permanent postmodern movement of power? Does the West's self-identity—whether in terms of the sovereign state, the sovereign self, or a supra-sovereign European Union—then become dependent upon a non-European Other? In other words, does Europe actually *need* Bosnia, the danger it represents, the otherness it embodies, for its own, on-the-fly, identity formation? If we fail to solve the Bosnia Question, what balkanized, post-imperial parastate will become the next dumping ground for the West's violence?

In the fickle light of television, the information revolution began to look much less glorious and the future of sim/dissim wars more ominous. But after my accelerated travels, there was a final speed-bump at the National Strategy forum on "The Information Revolution and National Security," which caused some reflection. The setting, the First Division Museum, was eerily apt: It had been founded by the former editor and publisher of the *Chicago Tribune*, Col. Robert McCormick, who had fought at the battle of Cantigny in World War I with the 1st Division. Propaganda poster art from the period covered the conference room walls. One in dark sepia tones from 1917 stood out from the rest: "Save Serbia, Our Ally."

That evening, former Director of Central Intelligence James Woolsey gave the dinner address, "The Impact of New Information and Communications Technologies on National Security." The opening to his talk was pure cyberpunk, drawing from Neal Stephenson's *Snow Crash* to make the point that people were coming to prefer the cyberspatial order of the "Metaverse" to the chaos and instability of the real world. He punched the message home with a line that drew the most laughs: "The Internet may be anarchic—but then we look at Bosnia." Woolsey, who probably gave the end of the cold war its best if bleakest sound-bite—"The dragon has been slain but the jungle is filled with a bewildering variety of poisonous snakes"—mixed metaphors and captured paradoxes with a kind of blithe power. In Bosnia, the simulated swords of the dragon-slayers and the cartographic pens of the diplomats had failed, abysmally. Four years of war in the gut of Europe were soon to be stopped—but not yet resolved—by air strikes, a truce-conference in Dayton, Ohio, and the compellent power of the 1st Armored Division. But that night, the Internet took on a new and appealing light as the metaphor and medium, if not the manager, of the New Chaos.

Acknowledgements

The author would like to thank the MacArthur Foundation, McCormick Tribune Foundation, and St. Antony's College, Oxford, for their support on this project.

15 The simulation triangle

In the simulated battlefields of tomorrow, war has more in common with Disneyworld than the Pentagon

Source: *21C* (Issue 24, 1997), pp. 19–25.

This idea of the indirect approach is closely related to all problems of the influence of mind upon mind – the most influential factor in human history. Yet it is hard to reconcile with another lesson: that true conclusions can only be reached, or approached, by pursuing the truth without regard to where it may lead or what its effects may be – on different interests. ... In strategy, the longest way round is often the shortest way home.

B.H. Liddell Hart, *Strategy*

"All but war is simulation." The phrase kept popping up like a bad mantra, first in the presentations with their Web-inspired graphics, then on the Nam June Paik-like wall of monitors in the Marriot Hotel's exhibition halls, and now as a banderole on an otherwise standard-issue business card. I had ambushed a colonel for a hallway interview after he finished a briefing on the virtues of virtual simulations. He handed me the card at the end of the interview, and I asked what the phrase meant. Running late, he offered a staccato history.

It originated in 1992 with the activation of STRICOM (Simulation, Training and Instrumentation Command), the newest and – as I was to find out – the most unusual command post in the military. Given the task of providing the United States Army's "vision for the future." STRICOM chose a bold motto to go with the command-post logo of a "land warrior" bisected by a lightening bolt in the middle of a bull's-eye. What the phrase means, the colonel said, is "that everything short of war is simulation." But he hastily added, "we don't *really* look at it that way, because you can't manage that properly. ... When you think about it, well, it's kind of like your love life: Everything short of it is simulation."

An officer of lesser rank, someone who knew a dodgy soundbite when he heard one, cut in to remind the colonel that he had a plane to catch. I was left standing in the hallway with a frozen half-grin. What did he mean by "love life"? Who did he mean by "your" love life? Did this mean war was to simulation as love was to stimulation? Was STRICOM into some kind of William Gibson sim/stim thing? These were not the kind of questions that had originally brought me to the 18th Interservice/Industry Training Systems and Education Conference (I/ITSEC).

In one corner of Orlando, I/ITSEC '96 was occupying the Marriot World Center for three days, with over 60 panels, 180 exhibition booths, and enough uniforms and suits to gridlock the Beltway. Gathering under one convention roof for this year's theme, "Information Technologies: The World Tomorrow," was a who's who of industry CEOs. Defense Department higher-ups, officers from the military and, not least, Tom Clancy as the banquet speaker (a no-show, as it turned out).

Forty minutes up the Central Florida Greeneway. STRICOM was preparing for an award ceremony for the SUS69 million ISIMS (Joint Simulation System) contract. According to the press release, ISIMS is "a distributed computerized warfare simulation system that provides a joint synthetic battlespace ... to support the 21st century warfighter's preparation for real world contingencies." And a few miles down Orlando's International Drive, through the pink arches and under a pair of mouse ears, Disneyworld was celebrating its 25th Anniversary with a paroxysm of Imagineered (copyrighted) fun.

I entered this Orlando Triangle as one might enter a paradox, where slogans like "everything but war is simulation," "prepare for war if you want peace" and "the land where the fun always shines" quickly enhance the appeal of tour guides who don't rely on linear reasoning and conventional cartography. My intent was to ask a few questions, make some observations, and get in and out quick, with the help of some thinkers who well understood the seductive powers of simulations. To jump the monorails of spectacle, I borrowed from Guy Debord the subversive power of the drift to tour a world where "everything that was directly lived has moved away into a representation." To counter the hazards of hyperreal simulacra, I relied on the hyperbole of Jean Baudrillard, who could well have had in mind the military–industrial–entertainment complex when he warned of "a group which dreams of a miraculous correspondence of the real to their models, and therefore of an absolute manipulation." And to avoid becoming one more casualty of "the war of images," I planned to take seriously Paul Virilio's advice that "winning today, whether it's a market or a fight, is merely not losing sight of yourself."

> The problem of security, as we know, haunts our societies and long ago replaced the problem of liberty. This is not as much a moral or philosophical change as an evolution in the objective state of systems.
>
> Jean Baudrillard, *Fatal Strategies*

This indirect approach was prompted by my first pilgrimage to I/ITSEC five years earlier, in the wake of the Gulf War. Back then, there was a real Patriot missile in the lobby, flanked by two looped videos extolling its virtues. Many of the military still seemed to be shaking the sand out of their boots. This year, however, with the kill-ratio of the Patriot dramatically downgraded, Kurds in refugee camps in the no-fly zone, and Saddam Hussein still playing the rogue, the victorious aura of the Gulf War had somewhat faded. Moreover, the poisonous snakes that emerged from the belly of the dead dragon – a post-Cold War metaphor and prophesy of former CIA director Admiral Woolsey – had since morphed into multi-headed hydras in the former Yugoslavia, Somalia, Chechnya, Rwanda and other expanding pockets of the new chaos. The pride and patriotism of I/ITSEC '91 still flared on occasion into imperial hubris and technological hype, but this years model was more a meld of corporate steel and glass with infotainment show-and-tell. Envisioning the future was still the goal, but enriching yourself and entertaining the stockholders en route made for a burgeoning of concessions on the way to Tomorrowland.

Nowhere was this more apparent than in the war of signs itself, with the self-help vocabulary of management consultants giving the acronymic, ritualized language of the military a run for its fiscal allocations. "Synergy" was the conference buzzword. Synergy between the high-flyers in the military and top players in defense industries, to make those thinner and thinner slices of the budgetary pie go that much further. Synergy in the form of alliances or outright mergers among the major defense industries. But also synergy at the advanced technological level, to imagine and engineer a new form of virtual warfare out of networked computer simulation (SIMNET) and Distributed Interactive Simulation (DIS): a command, control, communication, computer and intelligence system of systems (C41). and complete inter-operability through a common high-level architecture (HLA). Perched at the top of this synergy pyramid was the endgame of all wargames: ISIMS, the macro, mega- meta-simulation of the 21st century. Or so they said.

When I arrived at the convention, the synergy wave was making its way through the Grand Ballroom, where the Flag and General Officer Panel was in full session. On a podium at one end of the vast room, against a projected backdrop of the American flag, multiplied and magnified by two oversized video screens, the top brass and officials from the Department of Defense presented their views on the role of information technologies for the military. Deputy Undersecretary of Defense Louis Finch warned of a return to a post-Vietnam "hollow army" if new information technologies were not harnessed "to manage a massive transition." Vice Admiral Mazach called for a post-Cold War strategy that could deal with more-complex, multiple threats in a time of military downsizing, declaring that: "We must walk down the information highway – or be run down." Vice Admiral Patricia Tracey endorsed the use of "infomercials" in boot camp to train troops in issues like drug and alcohol abuse as well as in new sensitive areas like gender relations: "Disney has used it for years, we're ready to use it now." Major General Thomas Chase of the Air Force, citing the displacement of traditional battlefields by a digitized "battlespace," endorsed a global linking up of "synthetic environments."

Not everyone was so eager to jump on the cyber-wagon. Wearing battle ribbons from two tours in Vietnam, and unaccompanied by snappy graphics or intricate flow charts. Major General Ray Smith of the Marine Corps took a more cautious approach to simulations. No Luddite, he acknowledged the need for new skills and training techniques for the soldier, offering the story of a lance corporal abroad, who in a single day might re-hydrate a starving child, mediate between members of warring clans, handle the media, and use a global positioning system with a satellite link-up to call in a gunship attack. Simulations, while useful, are not sufficient to train such a range of complex and compressed duties: only experience in the field would do. When asked from the floor what industry could do to help, he paused, then bluntly said: "Make it cheap." After the panel, I probed him for the source of his guarded skepticism. "In war you fight people, not machines. We're training to beat computers, instead of training to beat the enemy. You cannot model the effects of confusion and surprise, the friction and fog of war."

> This makes the decisive new importance of the "logistics of perception" clearer, as well as accounting for the secrecy that continues to surround it. It is a war of images and sounds, rather than objects and things, in which winning is simply a matter of not losing sight of the opposition. The will to see all, to know all, at every moment, everywhere, the will to universalized Illumination: a scientific permutation on the eye of God which would forever rule out the surprise, the accident, the irruption of the unforeseen.
>
> Paul Virilio, *The Vision Machine*

Smith's view ran against the grain of an emergent technological imperative to manage uncertainty, unpredictability and worst-case scenarios of chaos through superior simulation-power. All the major corporate players were making the pitch in force – Lockheed Martin, McDonnell Douglas, Boeing, Hughes, Evans and Sutherland, Raytheon and Northrop – along with the rising stars of the simulation business, like SAIC, Silicon Graphics, Reflectone and Viewpoint DataLabs. They had come to sell the hardware and software of the future. Human wetware was more problematic. Indulged as a consumer, it otherwise took on the look of an expensive add-on, or a plug-in with compatibility problems. In most instances, the human component added a bizarro effect to the synergy mix. Consider an excerpt from one of the papers presented in the Modeling and Simulation section, called "Human Immersion into the DIS Battlefield":

> Recent advances in human motion capture and head-mounted display technologies, coupled with Distributed Interactive Simulation capabilities, now allow for the implementation of an untethered, fully immersable, DIS-compliant, real-time Dismounted Soldier Simulation (DSS) System. The untethered soldier, outfitted with a set of optical markers and a wireless helmet-mounted display, can move about freely within a real-world motion-capture area, while position and orientation data are gathered and sent onto a DIS network via tracking cameras and image-processing computers. ...

Fortunately, for those who can't tell DIS from DSS, there was a demonstration on hand to cut through the techno-babble: The STRICOM booth was running a looped version of the "dismounted soldier" – the "dis" saying it all about the level of respect for a grunt without wheels. Tracy Jones, lead engineer of individual-combatant simulations at STRICOM, gave me the blow-by-blow:

> We are trying to prove the principal of immersing the individual soldier in a virtual environment and having him interact with other entities in realtime. What we've got is a wireless optical-reflective marker system developed by

the entertainment industry about 10 years ago in movies like *Batman* and *Aliens*. It consists of a series of four camera systems with spotlights, 16 markers on the soldier's body, and three on his M-16. These markers will pick up exactly where he is in real time and render it into a 3-D model for a virtual database. He's wearing a wireless virtual head display so he can see where he is in the virtual environment.

Lifting an edge of the camouflage netting at the back of the display, she revealed the *deus ex machina* of DSS. "This is a MODSAF SGI station." She translated for me: "Modulated Semi-Automated Forces, Silicon Graphics Images." It was a program developed by the Army to construct computer-generated forces, because, as she put it, "you're never going to have enough men – uh, *people* – in the loop to populate a simulated battlefield, so we have computer-generated forces that are smart and intelligent, that can fight against our men in the loop." When I asked why "*semi*-automated," she admitted that "they're not completely smart. You can't just push a button and let them go." I was going to ask her if she knew about SKYNET and the semi-automated sentinels in *Terminator* that synergized into a very nasty Arnold Schwarzenegger. But I feared she might find that condescending.

I asked the wired soldier instead, a big guy in camouflage who looked more like Sly with a 'stache than Arnie in shades. "Isn't this getting close to the *Terminator?* Aren't you afraid of the machines getting smarter than the soldiers and taking over?" He gave me the narrow-eyed Clint look – or maybe it was just the camera lights. "Uh ..." Tracy intervened: "They're not that smart yet." Not sure who wasn't that smart, I asked who usually wins in the simulations. No hesitation from Sly this time: "I do." Is that programmed in? "Well, they can't kill me. Otherwise we'd have to stop and re-start the program." So you're immortal? "No. I'm Rambo." Before I can get him to elaborate on this distinction, Tracy announces that it is time to start the demonstration.

At the front of the booth I recognized the new commander of STRICOM, Brigadier General Geis, from the front cover of the recently launched magazine *Military Training and Technology*. He is surrounded by some VIPs but he agrees to a quick interview. What I get is a verbal version of the press release on the cost-effectiveness of simulations in a period of military draw-down – which is understandable, given his short tenure on the job. But after I confess to continued confusion about ISIMS, he invites me to come out to the base the next day to witness the signing ceremony of the contract award. There I could get a first-hand account from the architects and builders of ISIMS.

> The spectacle is the map of this new world, a map which exactly covers its territory. The very powers which escaped us show themselves to us in all their force.
>
> Guy Debord. *Society of the Spectacle*

I left the STRICOM booth and plunged into the vast exhibition hall full of simulated gunfire, flashing computer monitors and reps who varied in style from barkers at a freak show to the zen-haiku of a Nissan ad. There were simulated cockpits of jets and helicopters, tanks and spaceships. You could fire a simulated M-16 at "terrorists" (all looking like cousins of Arafat), throw simulated grenades (you smell the post-traumatic stress with each flash-bang), tear up some turf in a simulated MlA2 tank (no German farmer to complain), take out a bad guy in a simulated drug raid (in a curious fashion-lag, the *Miami Vice* look prevails), or blow up a building with a simulated truck bomb (essential viewing for every militia member). In this electromagnetic maelstrom of simulation, patriotism and profit, I thought a seizure was more likely than synergy. I drift, heading nowhere, searching everywhere for a psychogeography that might provide a map of meaning for the sound-and-light show.

I found a familiar landmark immediately behind the STRICOM booth, where a small group of Marines was using synergy to make simulation fun. Compared to the surroundings, theirs was a low-tech operation. Cordoned off by a black curtain, there were four monitors with keyboards, a projection screen and a sound system, all hooked up to a mini-computer. On a tight budget, and always looking for off-the-shelf technology, the Marine Corps Modeling and Simulation Office had decided to appropriate rather than innovate, to simulate what Marines do best: to fight independently in squads with small arms. There wasn't a smart weapon in sight, just a computer-generated four-man fire team in a re-tooled game of *Doom*. The monsters had been replaced by distant, barely visible forces that kept popping up out of foxholes and from around bunker walls to lay down some lethal fire.

I had stumbled upon *Marine Doom*, "a mental exercise in command and control in a situation of chaos." The lieutenant wanted to know if I was ready to walk the walk. Having spent some time in the video arcade, I thought it couldn't be too tough, especially since I would be playing with the lieutenant and two kids barely in their teens who seemed to have acquired squatter rights. That was my first mistake. With mouse and keyboard strokes controlling speed and direction. we were to head out of our foxhole, traverse the road, go around some bunkers, and clear a building of bad guys. In eight attempts, I was killed seven times. The single time I made it all the way to the building, I killed the lieutenant in a burst of "friendly fire." I wasn't sure if you had to say you're sorry in simulations, but I apologized nonetheless. The high-quality graphics, sounds of gunfire and heavy breathing, and the sight of rounds kicking up in your face, as well as the constant patter of the lieutenant ("Save your ammo, Point man, take that bunker. You're taking rounds. I'm going up, cover me, Ahh, I'm down!"), gave the "game" a pretty high dose of realism, especially if accelerated heart-beat is any measure.

The appropriation of *Doom* by the Marine Corps was significant for another reason. Usually, the technology transfer goes in the other direction, with military applications leading the way in research and development; from the earliest incarnations of the computer in simulation projects like Whirlwind at MIT's Servomechanisms Laboratory during World War 2, to SAGE, the first centralized air-defense system of the Cold War, there has been a close "link" between military simulations, the development of the computer, and the entertainment industry. In 1931, the US Navy purchased the first aircraft simulator from its designer, Edward Link. By 1932, the military still had only one Link Trainer – the amusement parks had bought close to 50. Now, the developmental lag between the real thing and its simulation has just about disappeared. From the F-16 to the F-117A, the MIA2 tank to the Bradley armored vehicle, the Aegis cruiser to the latest nuclear aircraft carrier, the videogame version arrives on the shelves almost as soon as the weapon system first appears. Indeed, a Pentium chip and a joystick will get you into the Comanche helicopter, the F-22 and the newest Seawolf SSN-21 submarine – which is more than a real pilot or sailor can currently claim as these projects suffer delays and budget cuts.

> For it is with the same Imperialism that present-day simulators try to make the real, all the real, coincide with their simulation models. But it is no longer a question of either maps or territory. Something has disappeared: the sovereign difference between them that was the abstraction's charm.
>
> Jean Baudrillard, *The Precession of Simulacra*

My drift was interrupted by an invitation to attend a lunch laid on by Lockheed Martin. Over a catered meal in a hotel suite, Stephen Buzzard, vice-president for business development at Lockheed Martin, walked a group of journalists – mainly from the military and defense-industry journals – through a series of organization flow charts, which seemed to be in constant need of verbal revisions. Mergermania had outstripped the capabilities of the graphics and public-relations departments. Lockheed, having barely digested Martin Marietta, added Loral in July, and Quinitron in August, then reorganized 40 subsidiary companies into "virtual organizations" to "create a mix of cultures." And, Buzzard concluded, "We have alliances with various other companies." With journalists and corporate executives on a first-name basis trading inside jokes, the closest thing to investigative reporting appeared to be a vying for stock tips. It all combined to make "synergy" a continuation of monopoly capitalism by other means – only this time the highest stage was not Lenin's vaunted imperialism but Baudrillard's hyperbolized simulation. This suspicion was supported the following week by Boeing's announcement of a SUS13 billion takeover of McDonnell Douglas, creating one more aerospace colossus.

But the smaller industries weren't waving any white flags. Silicon Graphics, for some time the David among the simulation Goliaths, had developed the most powerful slingshot yet, the Onyx2, with a memory capacity of 256 GB, memory bandwidth of 800MB/sec/CPU and, most importantly for simulation graphics, the capability to generate 20K polygons at 60HZ/pipeline. Watching one of these generate a simulation of a helicopter on the deck, down to the details of its reflections in the water and cows stopping in mid-rumination as it passes overhead, was a reality check that everyone seemed eager to cash. A hierarchy could be drawn from those booths that did and those that did not have one or more of the sleek, black Onyx2; obviously from their placement, they were there not just to run displays but to be the display of the simulation edge. Other firms were compensating by making synergy work at the organizational level. Highly visible – and offering the best food and drink at its reception – was The Solution Group, a consortium of close to 20 industries formed by Paradigm Simulation in 1994 to integrate product, services and support for the simulation consumer. Judging from current trends one could imagine two, maybe three, enormous booths filling the hall at I/ITSEC 2000. If you're not part of the Solution, you're part of Lockheed Martin, or Boeing McDonnell. And even if there are no more enemies in sight by the year 2000, one could surmise that there would still be a Solution in search of a problem.

Niche synergy was another way to go. One member of The Solution Group was leading the way, infiltrating the military–industrial–entertainment nexus by creating an ever-expanding database of hyperreal, real-time 3-D simulations. Viewpoint DataLabs might not have high name recognition, but anyone who has viewed over the last year a commercial, a television show, a hit film, or a video game with computer-generated graphics has probably sampled Viewpoint's product. Their booth's promo video was riveting and revealing, for the eclecticism of the content as well as the monotony of the style. It opens with the memorable scene of the alien foo fighters swarming the F-18s in *Independence Day*, which buzz-cuts into a pair of attacking mosquitoes in a Cutter insect-repellent commercial, then to spaceships attacking in *Star Trek Voyager*, followed by some requisite mega-explosions, a simulation of a missile launch from two helicopters, the dropping of a fuel-air dispersal bomb from *Outbreak*, and a trio of Eurofighter 2000s doing maneuvers that are aerodynamically impossible (a case of wishful flying, since the problem-plagued real Eurofighter has yet to make it into the air). Interspersed is a whimsical scene of a museum-bound Trex doing a little chiropracty for a McDonald's ad and, to my émigré eye, an offensive ad of Lady Liberty plucking an Oldsmobile Aurora off the Staten Island Ferry Lady (give her your riches, your muddled mind, and she'll make the right car choice for you – that's freedom). Big Bang backed by Bang-Bang, especially when it comes in 3-D with a techno-rave soundtrack, is a big seller. That night I made the rounds of the receptions hosted mainly by the larger defense industries. I learned a lot about the field from ex-fighter jocks turned corporate VPs, ex-artists turned graphic designers, ex-hackers turned software developers. After a few drinks, nearly everyone was eager to let me know about their former lives. I suppose making a living making machines that help stop others from living doesn't make for cocktail chatter. Nonetheless, it was there, in all the stones about what they once did. And I too was implicated, collecting data to entertain/train others in the ways of war, making war fun for the consumer/reader. I took some notes on what was being said, but I lost the cocktail napkin on which they were written.

An idol capable of realizing exactly what men's faith has been unable to accomplish ... A utopia of technical fundamentalism that has nothing at all to do with the religious variety that still requires virtues of men instead of advantages to "machines"?

Paul Virilio, afterword to *Bunker Archeology*

The previous night was not the only reason I was late the next morning for the awards ceremony at STRICOM. I could not find the place. When you drive up to most military bases, there's a perimeter, guard booth, at the very least a recognizable headquarters with flags flying out front. Here, there were just row after row of sleek steel-and-glass buildings, interrupted by nicely landscaped parking lots. This was military base as corporate research park, with all of the major defense industries represented on the base. I finally located the right building and room, and joined a circle of dark suits and a mix of army khaki, air-force blue and navy white, standing around a large conference table. At the front, Naval Captain Drew Beasley, program manager of JSIMS, was just getting into the background of the program. It began with a Memorandum of Agreement among the leadership of the armed forces and the Department of Defense, signed in 1994, to develop "an inter-operable training simulation capable of combining warfighting doctrine; Command, Control, Communication, Computer and Intelligence (C4I); and logistics into a team event." It would replace, said Beasley, older war-games devised "for the dreaded threat of the great Russian hordes coming over the tundra." Thirty-two military operations since the end of the Cold War, ranging from famine relief to armed conflict, have demonstrated that "we need a different paradigm that allows us to work cooperatively and jointly."

ISIMS would make it possible to combine and distribute three forms of simulations: live simulations (conducted with soldiers and equipment in "real" environments); virtual simulations (conducted with electronic and mechanical replicas of weapons systems in computer-generated scenarios); and constructive simulations (the highest level of abstraction where computer-modeled war-games play multiple scenarios of conflict). Advances in microprocessor speed, interactive communication, and real-time, high-resolution video mean that military exercises will be able to mix and match live, virtual and constructive simulations not only in Synthetic Theaters of Wars (STOW) but also on commercially available computers and networks. Experiments have already been conducted in which a group of colonels at Fort Leavenworth in Kansas introduce an electronic OPFOR (enemy, or "opposing forces") battalion into an actual training exercise at the National Training Center in the Mojave Desert, while soldiers in Martin Marietta tank simulators at Fort Knox "ride along" in real-time with either side, as part of a distributed Battle Lab simulation. But by the year 2003, JSIMS would make it possible for "all the services to play together" with "just-in-time" mission rehearsal and "a worldwide terrain database."

With the flash of cameras and a round of applause, Captain Beasley and Lane Arbuthnot, program manager at TRW of JSIMS projects, put pen to the $US69 million contract. A very efficient public-affairs officer had arranged an interview for me with Beasley, Arbuthnot and Kurt Simon, also from TRW, who was actually in charge of the technical aspect of building of the simulation. The captain once more deployed his demise of the Russian-hordes metaphor to emphasize the external motivation for a new macro-simulation, but spent most of the time going over the internal factors, like the need to standardize the disparate models of the different services (some based on hex-systems, others on Cartesian coordinates) and to globalize our preparation for future threats. Sounding like a modern-day Francis Bacon ("knowledge is power"), he made JSIMS sound as glorious as the founding of the library of Alexandria: "We are building a synthetic environment that can be used to pull down objects and representations out of our electronic libraries, objects that other services have placed there … as part of an overall streamlining process to bring a joint focus, commonality and collaboration within government and with industry." The captain moved to a white marker board to draw a series of circles representing live and constructive simulations, which increasingly overlap as JSIMS goes through its stages of development. In his schema, the constructive had engulfed the live by the year 2003.

> The Disneyland Imaginary is neither true nor false; it is a deterrence machine set up in order to rejuvenate in reverse the fiction of the real.
>
> Jean Baudrillard, *The Precession of Simulacra*

Compared to Disneyworld, the military and industry were open laptops on the role of simulations. My efforts to set up interviews with the architects of Imagineering and Audio-Animatronics (always with superscripted trademarks affixed), or better yet, to get a glimpse behind the technology of simulators like Star Tours or Body Wars, were met by some very polite, very efficient stonewalling. People were in meetings, on vacation, in California. Getting into STRICOM was a piece of cake compared to the obstacles I faced at Team Disney's po-mo headquarters. A series of abstracted mouse-ear arches, a formidable defense-in-depth of receptionists, multiple mazes of cubicles, and a sun-dial atrium that looked like a nuclear cooling tower, did not invoke a sense that this was a place where the fun always shines. When I finally reached the right cubicle, I was told that my designated handler was in a meeting. Further efforts produced meager results. After a couple of phone calls, clearance was finally reached from higher up: I was given a copy of the "25th Anniversary Press Book and Media Guide" and sent on my way.

The guide was full of noteworthy information, like the fact that Eddie Fisher and Debbie Reynolds had a flat tire and showed up late for the 1955 opening of Disneyland and that Walt Disney did not live to see the opening of Disneyworld (but no mention that his vision of the future as a frozen past included a cryogenic funeral for himself). The chronology provided for the opening year of Disneyworld is even stranger. In the Disney version, in 1971 astronauts take the lunar buggy for a spin. George C. Scott wins an Oscar for *Patton,* 18-year-olds get the right to vote, and President Nixon fights inflation. And just about saying it all, "Everyone was wearing smile buttons," and, "Charles Manson was convicted of murder." Others might have different memories – President Nixon setting up the "Plumbers," 18-year-olds drafted to fight in Vietnam, the Pentagon Papers leaked to the *New York Times*, and 31 prisoners and nine hostages killed at

Attica State Prison. Simulations of the future sometimes require a re-imagineering of the past.

> The society signs a sort of peace treaty with its most outspoken enemies by giving them a spot in its spectacle.
>
> Guy Debord, *In girum imus nocte et consumimur* (We go around in circles in the night and are consumed by fire.)

My trip to Orlando probably yielded more anxieties than insights. If anything, STRICOM's motto, "all but war is simulation," had taken on an even denser, fractal ambiguity. Through technical reproduction, repetition and regression, proliferations of simulation nuked any sense of an original meaning to war – or fun. Indeed, with increasing orders of verisimilitude, the simulations displayed a capability to precede and replace reality itself. Design and desire partially explain the spread of simulation. At the abstracted level of deterrence, simulations can and have worked. Total transparency through surveillance (at the airport or by satellites) combined with the occasional direct application of simulations (COPS or the Gulf War) have proven to be powerful cyber-deterrents. And it is understandable why some might desire the virtual security of simulation (JSIMS or Main Street USA) to the risks of the real (conflict overseas and crime in the cities) – even if it puts liberty as well as the reality principle at risk.

But there is an irony – and a danger – lurking at the edge of simulation, where it comes up hard against the contingencies of life. As superior computing power and networking increase its representational power and global reach, simulation leaves little room to imagine the unpredictable, the unforeseeable, the unknowable – except as accident. Will God's will, nature's caprice and human error seem puny in effect, as simulation becomes more interactive, more complex, more synergistic? In the context of industrial accidents, organizational theorists have already identified a "negative synergism" in complex systems that can produce unpredictable, worst-case failures. In the technological drive to control our environment, to deter known threats through their simulation, are we unknowingly constructing new, more catastrophic dangers?

In spite of my three days adrift in the Simulation Triangle, and the feeling that a bad case of post-simulation stress lies ahead, I still had hope for humanity. But it was sorely tested when I went to catch my flight home at the Orlando airport and saw the sign above the Delta curbside check-in: "Toy weapons must be checked at the counter."

16 Virtuous war and Hollywood

The Pentagon wants what Hollywood's got

Source: *The Nation* (3 April 2000), pp. 41–44.

Last August prominent political leaders, military officers and representatives from the computer and entertainment industries gathered at the University of Southern California to announce the opening of a new "Institute for Creative Technologies" (ICT). The innocuous title concealed a remarkable joint project: to produce state-of-the-art military simulations by pooling expertise, financial resources and the tools of virtual reality. Onstage for the signing ceremony and press conference were Steven Sample, president of USC; Louis Caldera, Secretary of the Army; "Rocky" Delgadillo, deputy mayor of Los Angeles; Rick Belluzzo, CEO of Silicon Graphics; and Jack Valenti, president and CEO of the Motion Picture Association of America. Even Governor Gray Davis made an appearance, virtual and gargantuan onscreen via satellite link from the Capitol. The front rows of the auditorium were sprinkled with uniforms and suits, the military's top computer war-gamers swapping stories with executives from the entertainment industry. Toward the back of the room the major network and print media, including CNN, had installed themselves to broadcast this new alliance to the world.

After some opening remarks, USC president Sample introduced the featured speaker, the Army's Louis Caldera. Caldera mapped out the purpose and potential of a "very exciting partnership" that seemed to include just about every major LA player in high tech, higher education and high- as well as low-brow entertainment. "This $45 million contract will fund joint modeling and simulation research and has high-value applications for the Army as well for the entertainment, media, videogame, film, destination theme park and information-technology industries that are such a key part of the California economy … . This partnership will leverage the US national defense and the enormous talent and creativity of the entertainment industry and their tremendous investment in cutting-edge applications of new technology." Having stroked the local powers, Caldera addressed the needs of his own constituency, in the now-common military language that makes *Neuromancer* sound like an out-of-date Army field manual. "The ICT will significantly enhance complex interactive simulations for large-scale warfighting exercises and allow us to test new doctrines in synthetic environments that are populated with intelligent agents in future threat challenges." The speakers who followed parroted the press releases in simpler language. "Synergy" and "verisimilitude" popped up with cue-card frequency; everyone was keen to dance on the "cutting edge."

But while the soldiers and politicians vied for media attention, the guy who made it all happen hugged the auditorium wall. The only evidence of his affiliation was a government pay-scale suit, a loud haw-hawing at the speakers' jokes and a slight rolling of the eyes at questions asked by the press. The ICT is the brainchild of Mike Macedonia, son of one of the Army's best war-gamers, graduate of West Point and now chief scientist and technical director at STRICOM (Simulation, Training and Instrumentation Command), the newest and probably the most unusual command post in the military. Thirty miles northeast of the pink arches of Disneyworld in Orlando, Florida, STRICOM looks like a research park pretending to be a military base. Steel and glass corporate buildings, owned by Lockheed Martin, Silicon Graphics, Westing-house, SAIC and other military industries, encircle the various headquarters of the Army, Navy, Marine Corps and Air Force. Charged with providing the military with a "vision for the future," STRICOM leads a combined military and industry effort to create "a distributed computerized warfare simulation system" and to support "the 21st century warfighter's preparation for real world contingencies." Its motto is telling: "All But War is Simulation."

Under the auspices of his boss, Michael Andrews, deputy assistant secretary of the Army for research and technology, Macedonia brought STRICOM to LA after he realized that the commercial sector—in particular the film, computer and video-game industries—was outstripping the military in technological innovation. Where trickle-down from military research on mainframe computers once fueled progress in the field, civilian programmers working on PCs could now design video games and virtual environments that put military simulations to shame. Macedonia came to Hollywood to find the tools and skills for simulating and, if necessary, fighting wars of the future. As the blood and iron of traditional war gave way to the bits and bytes of infowar, netwar and cyberwar, he saw the ICT as a vehicle for integrating the simulation and entertainment industries into this much-heralded "Revolution in Military Affairs."

Macedonia's initiative draws on a long tradition. Ever since nineteenth-century chemists began to fix images on film made with the same nitrocelluloids found in explosives, the military and the movie industry have been in a technological relay race for seeing and killing the enemy while securing and seducing the citizen. Gun and camera became a single calibration with the mobilization of Hollywood during the Second World War. At the start of the war, military-preparedness documentaries were quickly re-edited to produce propaganda movies like *To the Shores of Tripoli*. Famous Hollywood directors soon joined the cause, contributing feature and training films like Howard Hawks's *Air Force* (1943), John Huston's *The Battle of San Pietro* (1945) and Frank Capra's series *Why We Fight* (1943–45). The War Department supplied manpower, equipment and funding, and Hollywood provided actors, directors and, for the most part, the talent. Between 1939 and 1945, close to 2,500 war movies were made.

After such extensive collaboration, the opening of the Institute for Creative Technologies might appear to be another case of incest, just further proof that LA has never had much of a purchase on reality, rather than a cause for alarm. But there is a difference. By its very task and potential power to create totally immersive environments where one can see, hear, perhaps even touch and emotionally interact with digitally created agents, the ICT is leading the way into a brave new world that threatens to breach the last firewalls between reality and virtuality.

Set in the larger technostrategic scheme of things, ICT matters—very much. The diplomatic and military policies of the United States have become increasingly dependent on technological and representational forms of discipline, deterrence and coercion that might be described as *Virtuous War*. At the cyborg heart of virtuous war is the technical capability and ethical imperative to threaten and, if necessary, actualize violence from a distance with virtually no casualties.

On the surface, virtuous war cleans up the discourse of conflict. Fought in the same manner as they are represented, by real-time surveillance and TV "live feeds," virtuous wars promote a vision of bloodless, humanitarian, hygienic wars. This is not to say—and this point requires emphasis—that virtuous war is any less destructive, deadly or bloody for those on the short end of the big technological stick. One needs only to note the skewed casualty rates of prototypical virtuous wars like the Gulf War (287 Americans lost their lives—many by accidents), the Mogadishu raid (eighteen Americans killed) and the Kosovo air campaign (a remarkable, casualty-free conflict for the NATO forces). We seldom hear about the other side of the casualty list, Post-Vietnam, the US military studiously avoids body counts of the enemy.

Unlike other forms of warfare, virtuous war has an unsurpassed power to commute death, to keep it out of sight, out of mind. In simulated preparations and virtual executions of war, one learns how to kill but not to take responsibility for it; one experiences "death" but not the tragic consequences of it. We now face the danger of a new kind of trauma without sight, drama without tragedy, where the lines between war and game, pain and pleasure, fact and fiction do not blur. They pixelate in hyperreal detail on the same screen. In this context, when the Pentagon and Hollywood announce a new collaboration, we best tune in.

At the closed luncheon following the press conference, the writer and director John Milius (*Apocalypse Now, Red Dawn*) told war stories to an audience dining on chicken breast and "whipped goat cheese yukons." He spoke, half-jokingly, of how he wanted to put an end to the alienation between the military and the movie industry by setting up a production team for the Army that would make *Wag the Dog* look tame. That brought to mind Eisenhower's famous 1961 farewell address, when he warned of the "danger that public policy could itself become the captive of a scientific-technological elite." What would he have made of this addition of new media and entertainment industries to his "military-industrial complex"? Of new technologies of simulation being built at universities to create a high fidelity between the representation and the reality of war? Of the human mimetic faculty for entertainment and gaming joining forces with new cyborg programs for killing and warring? He'd probably not have let it get in the way of his golf game. By the end of the visit, I was left wondering, *pace* Eisenhower, if the Military-Industrial-Media-Entertainment network had just gone online.

Six months after the fact, I'm not so sure. My effort to find out just what was in the works at ICT produced more promissory notes than any actual project developments. The reasons given for not going on record were ongoing negotiations and imminent signings, with "one of the best-known directors in Hollywood" and some of the "best computer graphics guys on the planet." The only names dropped were Randal Kleiser (director of *The Blue Lagoon* and *Honey, I Blew Up the Kid*) and 3D Realms, makers of the video game Duke Nukem (motto: "The only good alien bastard is a dead alien bastard").

One person willing to talk on the record was Mike Zyda, chairman of Modeling, Virtual Environments & Simulation at the Naval Postgraduate School, chairman of the original 1997 National Research Council report that gave cause and code for the establishment of the ICT (*Modeling and Simulation,* http://books.nap.edu/catalog/5830.html) and, not coincidentally, chairman of Mike Macedonia's 1995 computer science PhD dissertation committee. Zyda originally envisioned the ICT as a place that would act as coordinator and broker for the most imaginative and technically advanced modelers and simulators. "The Defense Department," he says, "has spent millions and still can't match SimCity." ICT shouldn't be chasing Hollywood, says Zyda. It should target off-the-shelf videogame technology, like Sony Playstation2: Capable of generating 66 million polygons per second, it leaves platforms like Silicon Graphics in the dust. Commercial video games could be redesigned to test the intellectual aptitude and psychological attitudes of potential military recruits. Spin-off technology would be used to help kids at risk explore potential career paths.

Richard Lindheim, who was eventually appointed director of ICT, has a different vision. After a long career at NBC, Lindheim went on to become executive vice president of the Paramount Television Group, producing *The Equalizer* and taking charge of the later *Star Trek* series, *Next Generation, Deep Space Nine* and *Voyager*. I caught up with him at STRICOM, where he was preparing for a series of Washington briefings. His previous employment probably best explains why *Star Trek's* total-immersion simulation, the Holodeck, kept popping up in our conversation (as well as how Herman Zimmerman, the art director of *Star Trek,* was procured to design the ICT's office space). "The ICT is on a quest to envision and prepare for the future," and, says Lindheim, "our Holy Grail is the Holodeck." Lindheim invoked writers like Jules Verne, who popularized the idea of the modern submarine and inspired scientists to turn unreality into reality; *Voyager* could do the same for ICT. By the end of our conversation, I realized that the Holodeck was not just a metaphor; it was the endgame for ICT.

The Holodeck and the Holy Grail not-withstanding, the Institute for Creative Technologies is unlikely to save (or destroy) the world. It is not yet evident that it can run a project or a battlefield simulation, let alone an intergalactic war. However, cutting edge or opening wedge, the ICT does look to be Hollywood's—and the Pentagon's—premier laboratory for virtuous war. Will this new alchemy of brass, celluloid and silicon produce a kinder, gentler, sexier cyborg, like *Voyager's* Seven of Nine? Or will the simulations of Creative Technology turn on their creators, like Frankenstein's monster? Either way, the ICT warrants public scrutiny.

17 Virtuous war/virtual theory

Source: *International Affairs* (Fall, 2000), pp. 771–788.

> The destructiveness of war furnishes proof that society has not been mature enough to incorporate technology as its organ, that technology has not been sufficiently developed to cope with the elemental forces of society.
>
> Walter Benjamin, *The work of art in the age of technical reproducibility*

My search for a virtual theory of war and peace began several years ago on a hilltop in the high Mojave Desert, watching the first digitized war game at the US army's National Training Center. According to the briefing papers for Desert Hammer VI, a new array of high technology was being tested 'to enhance lethality, operations tempo, and survivability'. It was hard to tell if it was working. I had spent most of the first morning trying and, for the most part, failing to discern the significance of distant dust trails of M1A2 Abrams tanks, Bradley armoured personnel carriers, and swarming humvees. The NTC at Fort Irwin might be a military base stuck in the middle of the Mojave Desert, but like nearby Las Vegas, it was a perfect stage for the evocation of past and future, hopes and fears. I had entered the theatre of war, not literally but *virtually*.

This was to be the first of several encounters with the virtual continuation of war by other means. The means were technological; the continuation was one of distance foreshortened by speed of bytes and bits, missives and missiles. Distance was afforded by the F-16s and A-10s flying overhead; the simulated launch of precision munitions; the remote video cameras perched on the hilltops; the laser-sensor arrays on every soldier and every weapon; the computer networks which controlled the battle space; and all the other digital technologies operating as 'force-multipliers'. To be sure, accident, friction, or miscalculation could, and at times did collapse this virtual distancing. However, the ultimate measure of distance in war, the difference between life and death, was nowhere in sight.

At first take, this represents a worrying—perhaps even shocking—but hardly revolutionary transformation of military and diplomatic affairs. After all, the telephone in the First World War provided generals with the means and the arrogance to send hundreds of thousands of soldiers to their deaths from the relative safety of their chateaux headquarters. The radio, the tank, and especially the airplane before the Second World War, and then thermonuclear weapons after, were all vaunted by one strategist or another as technologies that would radically transform if not end traditional warfare. Obviously, it takes more than technological innovation to make a revolution. However, unlike prior radical developments in means of transportation, communication and information, virtual innovation is driven more by software than hardware, and enabled by networks rather than agents, which means adaptation (and mutation) is not only easier, but much more rapid. Moreover, the 'Advanced Warfighting Experiment', as it and a series of subsequent war games are called, is taking place at a pivot-point in history. post-Ford, post-modern, or just post-Cold War, the political and economic as well as rhetorical and cultural forces that shape the international system have entered a state of flux.

So, is the virtualization of violence a revolution in diplomatic, military, let alone human affairs? On its own, no. However, deployed with a new ethical imperative for global democratic reform, it could well be so. In spite of, and perhaps soon because of, efforts to spread a democratic peace through globalization and humanitarian intervention, war is ascending to an even higher plane, from the virtual to the *virtuous*. At one time, the two words virtual and virtuous were hardly distinguishable (although the Latin *virtuosos* preceded *virtualis*). Both originated in the medieval notion of a power inherent in the supernatural, of a divine being endowed with natural virtue. And both carried a moral weight, from the Greek and Roman sense of virtue, of properties and qualities of right conduct. But their meanings diverged in modern usage, with 'virtual' taking a morally neutral, more technical tone, while 'virtuous' lost its sense of exerting influence by means of inherent qualities. Now they seem ready to be rejoined by current efforts to effect ethical change through technological and martial means.

The United States, as *deus ex machina* of global politics, is leading the way in this virtual revolution. Its diplomatic and military policies are increasingly based on technological and representational forms of discipline, deterrence, and compellence that could best be described as *virtuous war*. At the heart of virtuous war is the technical capability and ethical imperative to threaten and, if necessary, actualize violence from a distance—*with no or minimal casualties*. Using networked information and virtual technologies to bring 'there' here in near-real time and with near-verisimilitude, virtuous war exercises a comparative as well as strategic advantage for the digitally advanced. It has become the 'fifth dimension' of US global hegemony.

On the surface, virtuous war cleans up the political discourse as well as the battlefield. Fought in the same manner as they are represented, by real-time surveillance and TV 'live-feeds', virtuous wars promote a vision of bloodless, humanitarian, hygienic wars. We can rattle off casualty rates of prototypical virtuous conflicts like the Gulf war (270 Americans lost their lives—more than half through accidents), the Mogadishu raid (18 Americans killed), and the Kosovo air campaign (barring accidents, a remarkable zero casualty conflict for the NATO forces). Yet, in spite of valorous efforts by human rights organizations, most people would probably come up short on acceptable figures for the other side of the casualty list. Post-Vietnam, the United States has made many digital advances; public body counts of the enemy are not one of them.

Unlike other forms of warfare, virtuous war has an unsurpassed power to commute death, to keep it out of sight, out of mind. In simulated preparations and virtual executions of war, there is a high risk that one learns how to kill but not to take responsibility for it, one experiences 'death' but not the tragic consequences of it. In virtuous war we now face not just the confusion but the pixillation of war and game on the same screen.

The United States leads the way, but other countries are in hot pursuit of virtual solutions to long-running political conflicts. At the height of the Israeli withdrawal from Lebanon, the British *Daily Telegraph* newspaper pronounced from a safe distance on its 'real' meaning:

> [T]he Israeli dot-com generation seems not to have the stomach for mortal combat. They have started to ask why they should risk their lives when precision weapons can reduce war to a video game. For the pony-tailed youth of Tel Aviv's night spots, the war in Lebanon was becoming their Vietnam and they would rather their government fought it by remote control.[1]

However, the *Daily Telegraph* article conspicuously failed to note that virtuous war is anything *but* less destructive, deadly, or bloody for those on the short end of the big technological stick. And the newspaper is not alone in this sometimes blithe but often intentional oversight. Bloody ethnic and religious conflicts involving land mines, small arms, and even machetes persist. For the last few years I have been trying to comprehend how the sanitization of violence that began with the Gulf War has come to overpower the mortification of the body that continues to mark communal wars in Nagorno-Karabakh, Somalia, Bosnia, Rwanda, and elsewhere. A felicitous oxymoron, a growing paradox, an ominous sign of things to come, virtuous war is, in that final analysis it seeks to evade, still about killing.

In a sense, war has always been a virtual reality, too traumatic for immediate comprehension. Trauma, Freud tells us, can be re-enacted, even re-experienced, but cannot be understood at the moment of shock. This is what Michael Herr was getting at in *Dispatches*, when he wrote about his experiences in Vietnam: 'It took the war to teach it, that you were as responsible for everything you saw as you were for everything you did. The problem was that you didn't always know what you were seeing until later, maybe years later, that a lot of it never made it in at all, it just stayed stored there in your eyes'.[2] But now there is an added danger, a further distancing of understanding. When compared to the real trauma of war, the pseudo-trauma of simulation pales. But an insidious threat emerges from its shadowing of reality. In this high-tech rehearsal for war, one learns how to kill but not to take responsibility for it, one experiences 'death' but not the tragic consequences of it. In the extreme case, with the predisposed pathologies of a Milosevic in Serbia, a McVeigh in Oklahoma City, or a Harris in Littleton, Colorado, this can lead to a kind of doubling or splitting of the self that psychologists Robert Jay Lifton and Erik Markusen see as a source of the 'genocidal mentality'. But what

I have witnessed is more a closing than an opening of a schism, between how we see and live, represent and experience, simulate and fight war. New technologies of imitation and simulation as well as surveillance and speed have collapsed the geographical distance, chronological duration, the gap itself between the reality and virtuality of war. As the confusion of one for the other grows, we now face the danger of a new kind of trauma without sight, drama without tragedy, where television wars and video war games blur together.

From the 1950s cybernetic notion of the 'automaton', to William Gibson's 1987 coining of 'cyberspace' as a 'consensual hallucination', the virtual has shared an isomorphic relationship to the dream. And like the dream, it requires critical interpretations if we are not to sleepwalk through the manifold travesties of war, whether between states or tribes, classes or castes, genders or generations. Quoting Karl Marx—'The reform of consciousness consists *solely* in the awakening of the world from its dream about itself'—the Jewish-German literary critic Walter Benjamin wonders how the modern, seduced and traduced by radio, film, and other new forms of technological reproduction, can possibly awake from the interwar crisis. In *The arcades project*, he identifies two first steps, one virtuous the other not, to escape modernity's most pernicious effects:

> The genuine liberation from an epoch, that is, has the structure of awakening in this respect as well: is entirely ruled by cunning. Only with cunning, not without it, can we work free of the realm of dreams. But there is also a false liberation; its sign is violence.[3]

Virtuous war is much more than a new form of organized violence. Call it a dream-state, a symbolic realm, or an unreality: virtuous war projects a mythos as well as an ethos, a kind of collective unconscious for an epoch's greatest aspirations and greatest insecurities. Indeed, it is heroic if not Homeric in its practice and promise: on one side, the face of Achilles, a tragic figure who represents the *virtù* (as well as hubris) of the great warrior, of honour, loyalty, and violence, willing to sacrifice his life for others in a strange land; and on the other, Odysseus, a man of many devices *(polymechanos)* and many contrivances *(polymetis)*, who prefers *techné* to *virtù*, cunning (and punning) to warring and wandering, who just wants to come home. Again, Benjamin: 'Only a thoughtless observer can deny that correspondences come into play between the world of modern technology and the archaic symbol-world of mythology'.[4]

Any portrayal of war presents dangers for the chronicler, many obvious, some not so obvious; but virtuous war in particular poses some serious obstacles. One tactic is to record war from the bunker and the beaches, so close that the word on the page, the image on the film is imprinted by, practically drips with the carnage of war. We might call this approach, *pace* Spielberg, 'saving the reality principle'. Another, most often practised in IR theory, is to keep a distance, to extract or abstract the causes, structures, and patterns of war. Either way, the choice seems to be Hobbes or Hobson: the blood-drenched prose, the *cinéma vérité*, the permanent war-of-all-against-all of the realist; or the bloodless, value-free, hygienic wars of the social scientist. Some writers, like John Keegan and Stephen Ambrose, have managed to work effectively, even eloquently, the space between the trenches and the ivory tower. But the wars they wrote about, full of heroic figures caught in black-and-white representations, are not the wars that we face now and in the future. These wars are fought in the same manner as they are represented, by military simulations and public dissimulations, by real-time surveillance and TV 'live-feeds'.

Clearly, the problem of representation is compounded when the foxhole itself goes virtual. The nature of war is mutating, morphing, virtualizing with new technologies and strategies. New media, generally identified as digitized, interactive, networked forms of communication, now exercise a global effect if not ubiquitous presence through real time access. Moreover, with the magnification and dramatization of old ailments like nationalism, balkanization, and civil war by new media, virtuous war reaches not only into every living room but splashes onto every screen, TV, computer and cinema. People will live and die, figuratively and literally, by the power of images, previewed by the famine child that drew American troops into Somalia, and of the dead US Ranger dragged through the streets that hastened their departure.

Today, in war, diplomacy, and the media, the virtual proliferates. As war goes virtual, through infowar, netwar, cyberwar, through a convergence of the PC and the TV, its foundation as the ultimate reality-check of international politics begins to erode. Sovereignty, the primary means by which the supreme power and legitimate violence of the state is territorially fixed in international politics, declared once, many-times dead, now seems to regain its vigour virtually, through media spasms about new terrorist threats that never materialize, like States-of-Concern-formerly-known-as-Rogues (to invoke the other Prince) that warrant a $60 billion ballistic missile defence, or new strains of killer diseases that make the *X-Files* seem understated. The favourite virtual threat is the 'cyber-attack', ominously mooted by the media and anticipated by the Pentagon as the 'next Pearl Harbor'—which must amuse (and motivate) teenage hackers who make up the overwhelming bulk of such 'attacks'.[5]

With the virtualization of war comes the simulation of peace and perhaps even more obscure yet obdurate dangers. 'Virtual diplomacy'—from teleconferencing to preventive media—is presented at high-level Washington conferences and in beltway defence industries as the ultimate technical fix for intractable political problems. And, where virtual diplomacy fails, the virtual economy supposedly amends. According to the techno-wizards of the 'new economy', the global economy is on the verge of total virtualization.[6] Whereas many policy-makers, including the present and previous US presidents, view this as one more step towards a global, democratic peace, some specialists in the field fear otherwise. As the Asian financial crisis swept westward, the global economy verged further towards the viral and the virtual: one financial expert emphatically stated that 'the distinction between software and money is disappearing', to which a Citibank executive responded, 'it's revolutionary—and we should be scared as hell'.[7]

Questions go begging. Is virtualization, not globalization, turning the millennial tide? Is the sovereign state disappearing in all but legal form, soon to be a relic for the museum of modernity? Or has it virtually become the undead, haunting international politics like a spectre? Is virtualization the continuation of war (as well as politics) by other means? Is it repudiating, reversing, or merely updating Clausewitz? Is virtuality replacing the reality of war? Will real or just simulated peaces result? In short, is virtuous war and simulated peace the harbinger of a new world order, or a brave new world?

New technologies engender new questions, which require new approaches. Digitized, interactive, networked forms of communication now exercise a global presence: instant video-feeds, satellite link-ups, T1–T3 links, overhead surveillance, global mapping, distributed computer profiling, programmed trading, and movies with Arnold Schwarzenegger make up some of the most visible forms. Virtualization represents the most penetrating and sharpest—to the point of invisibility—edge of globalization. The power of virtuality lies in its ability to collapse distance, between here and there, near and far, fact and fiction. And so far, it has only widened the distance between those who have and those who have not.

We are in need of a *virtual theory* for the military strategies, philosophical questions, ethical issues, and political controversies surrounding the future of war and peace. All journeys entail rituals in which the end is prefigured by the negotiations and preparations that take place at the beginning. The choice of what to and not to believe, where to go and who to see, what to record on tape and finally to interpret in writing, always involves rituals of knowledge (*techné*) and negotiations of power (*virtù*). In search of the virtual, it is a struggle between the disappearing original and the infinitely reproducible. It is about interests: which interests matter most in an increasingly virtualized world; which interests obstruct, which interests facilitate the investigation; and, of course, what interests me versus what might interest the reader. Most fundamental is the negotiation at the root of interest itself (*inter-est*), between states of being, between the senses of self and reality with which one begins and one ends a journey.[8]

In search of a virtual theory, I travelled with a rather unconventional set of intellectual tools. To be sure, the who, when, where, and whatever did inform my interests, questions, and eventual conclusions. I had like many others in our field read the classic works on war: Sun Tzu, Machiavelli, Jomini, Clausewitz, Delbrück, Mahan, Hart, and others. Tutorials, seminars, and lectures from professors such as Charles Taylor, Hedley Bull, Michael Howard, and Adam Roberts provided a deeper historical and theoretical context, as well as an attitude of intellectual scepticism that tested the canon as it was taught. Moreover, a four-year stint at Oxford coincided with the most dangerous years of the second Cold War, when much of Europe was divided over NATO war fighting strategies and the stationing of SS-20, Cruise, and Pershing missiles. The anti-nuclear movement—especially the writings and remarkable public presentations by E. P. Thompson—also informed much of my thinking about war and peace. And I spent as much of my spare time as I could in Paris, where my French-Armenian relatives and a brilliant group of continental philosophers—Roland Barthes, Michel Foucault, Gilles Deleuze, Jean Baudrillard, and, at the head of the pack, Paul Virilio—provided valuable French antidotes to British weather, food and common sense.

Together it made for an eclectic group of travel companions; but when you're setting off for the belly of the beast, it's best to be diplomatically and theoretically over-equipped. On my research trips I made it a habit to take along one of the small, cheap Semiotext(e) books, with the excerpted quotes on the back cover that confuse many and provoke others. They included: Baudrillard's *Simulations* ('The very definition of the real has become: that of which it is possible to give an equivalent reproduction ... The real is not only what can be reproduced, but that which is always already reproduced: That is, the hyperreal ... which is entirely in simulation'); Deleuze's and Guattari's *Nomadology: the war machine* ('The war machine is exterior to the State apparatus ... It is the invention of the nomads ... The very conditions that make the State possible ... trace creative lines of escape'); and Virilio's *Pure war* ('We tried to reveal a number of important tendencies: the question of speed; speed as the essence of war; technology as the producer of speed; war as logistics, not strategy; endocolonization; deterrence; ultimate weapons; Pure War'). The books came along for inspiration, but also because they fit nicely in a back pocket; and, on more than one occasion, they triggered conversations with soldiers, sailors, and marines that went much deeper than the usual public affair's sound-bite.

At this point, one usually defends or apologizes for their choice of fellow travellers. I won't: whichever theorist helps me best understand the subject of my inquiry gets to the head of the class. For some time, it meant that post-modernists, post-structuralists, post-anything ruled. As a concept, 'post-modern', enjoyed from the outset the curious utility of transparent meaning for some and utter meaningless for others. Debates raged on the very existence of an epochal break ('post-modernity') and the explanatory value of such an incoherent body of intellectual attitudes ('post-modernism'). For me, it represented an interpretive struggle to comprehend how modern history never seemed fully to awake from the Enlightenment dream of linear progress; how cultures as advanced as the ones that produced Bach and Goethe, or Jefferson and Emerson could also produce an Auschwitz or Hiroshima; how the past was uprooted and the future predetermined by new technologies of representation; how every universal meta-narrative and foundational grand theory (be it Immanuel Kant or Karl Marx) was unravelling in the face of accelerated change in global politics; how talk-radio, reality-based TV, and webcams made everyday life a public spectacle above and beyond conventional means of comprehension.

At some point academic fatigue set in, and I grew weary of the theoretical debates surrounding post-modernism. I just couldn't see the point of writing (or refereeing) one more journal article on whether we are pre-, post- or just preposterously modern. And truth be told—never an easy task in post-modern circles—I had a problem with 'problematize', and all the other cant terms that have increasingly come to signify membership and little else. Taking pluralism seriously, I had little time for any academic approach—from rational choice to post-positivist theory—that prescribes one way of inquiry over and against another at a purely theoretical level. Besides, isn't it *time*— after the US President states in a court video that the truth of the matter depends on what you mean by 'is', the US War College publishes a book on 'Post-modern warfare', and Amazon.com heavily discounts *Postmodernism for beginners*—to move on?[9] Are we not 'always already', as Derrida wrote, what Devo sang (with no gender sensitivity) in their ironic sequel to their memorable hit, 'post-post-modern men'?

But where to next? As is so often the case, the destination was to be found in the journey. In my travels I discovered ample evidence that we had accelerated beyond a 'post-modern condition', first identified as such by philosopher François Lyotard in 1979, and that we were entering a digitally enhanced *virtual immersion*, in which instant scandals, catastrophic accidents, impending weather disasters, 'wag-the-dog' foreign policy, live-feed wars, and quick-in, quick-out interventions into still-born or moribund states are all available, not just prime time, real time but 24/7, on the TV, PC, and PDA. Both on and off the road, in search of supplemental modes of understanding, I began to see the need for a *virtual theory* of war and peace.

From the beginning right up to the end of my travels, I also held to what some call a given, others a belief, and a few an episteme: that global politics remains a place of power and identity, space and borders, legitimacy and meaning. But where I once trusted thinkers like Hobbes, Grotius and Kant to tell the complete story of security in the language of sovereignty, I increasingly came to rely on critical theorists like Nietzsche, Benjamin, Baudrillard, Deleuze and Virilio to interpret new mimetic codes of competing authorities and cultural clashes that had yet to be mapped let alone deciphered in global politics. Facing new hyper-realms of economic penetration, technological acceleration, and new media, the spatialist, materialist, positivist perspective that informs realism and other traditional approaches cannot begin fully to comprehend the temporal, representational, deterritorial and potentially dangerous powers of virtualism. By tracing the reconfiguration of power into new immaterial forms, post-modernists provide a starting point. They help us to understand how acts of inscription and the production of information, how metaphor, discourse, and language in general, can reify consciousness, rigidify concepts, predetermine the future. But they also provide the critical tools to float signifiers, dismantle binary hierarchies, free the imagination. As the realities of international politics increasingly are generated, mediated, simulated by new digital means of reproduction, as the globalization of new media further confuses actual and virtual forms; as there is not so much a distancing from some original, power-emitting, truth-bearing source as there is an implosion; as meaning is set adrift and then disappears into media black-holes of insignificance, a little po-mo can go a long way.

I took my bearings regularly, with interviews and archival research as well as strategic and diplomatic theory; but it would be an act of stupidity, arrogance, or, as is often the case, both, to think one could map this new virtual terrain by conventional means alone. I sought not to enclose but to encompass virtuous war, with a mix of new and old techniques and theories, ranging from maps that had sea monsters at the edge (humanitarian intervention must go no further than Bosnia—darkness lurks in Rwanda) and global positioning systems that made weapons smarter and diplomacy dumber ('We hit what we were aiming for ... But we did not mean to hit the Chinese Embassy').[10]

Obviously it wasn't just a love of the open air that spurred this virtual road trip. I must admit that I also saw it as a way to escape the disciplinary boundaries (and extensive border skirmishes) of the academic field of International Relations. In general, the social sciences, an intellectual laggard when it comes to technological change, are not the best vehicle for understanding the virtual. Highly complex in the philosophical idiom, yet practically ubiquitous in popular discourse, it understandably comes with an intellectual taboo in the social sciences. It just doesn't seem to fit into a disciplinary inquiry. I've never needed a reason, but I do think going off-road is about the only way to assess fully the benefits against the dangers of the virtual.

Some might place it further down on the ladder than theoretical inspiration, conceptual incentives, ethical imperatives, or disciplinary escapism, but there is as well a good etymological reason to undertake the virtual trip. 'Theory', from its Greek root of *theorein*, contains within it the notions of a journey or embassy (*theoria*), which involves an attentive contemplation (*horao*) of a spectacle (*theama*), like theatre (*theatron*) or oracular deity (*theon*).[11] 'Virtual', from the Latin *virtualis*, conveys a sense of inherent qualities that can exert influence, by will (the *virtù* of Machiavelli's Prince) or by potential (the virtual capacity of the computer). By this unification of the classical and the digital, virtual theory becomes both software and hardware: it has the potential to make meaning, produce presence, create the actual through a theatrical differentiation and technical vision. It constructs a world—not *ex nihilio* but *ex machina*—where there was none before.[12]

On the epistemological spectrum, this clearly places the virtualists nearer to the constructivists than the rationalists or realists. Virtual theory repudiates the philosophical realism and positivism underlying most social science theory, where words transparently mirror objects, facts reside apart from values, and theory is independent of the reality that it represents.[13] Yet, I have found little of intellectual or pragmatic utility in the metatheoretical, structuralist, and curiously amorphous forms (again, where are the bodies/agents?) that constructivism has taken in International Relations. To me it is a step backwards, from structuralism to bloburalism, to invoke that classic of the 1950s, 'The Blob', where misunderstood teenagers (something of a stretch for the star, Steve McQueen) took on an extra-terrestrial gooey blob that had emerged from a meteor. In spite of efforts to destroy it by conventional means (i.e. lots of firepower), it grows to gargantuan proportions by parasitically sucking the life out of humans.

This might be something of a dramatic exaggeration, but some hyperbole might be warranted, if we are not to awake one day in the future, to find where once regime theorists ruled, critical theorists critiqued, standpoint feminists stood, epistemic communities communed, and post-structuralists problematized, only a protoplasmic trace remains. Not even the 'English school' of international theory appears to have raised the Oxbridge in time against the constructivist onslaught. Only neo-realists and neo-liberals, occupying the higher reaches of the discipline, protected by positivism from non-observable phenomena like the Blob, have so far escaped its saprophytic attack.

Constructivism in International Relations has demonstrated a remarkable capability to absorb any approach that privileges epistemology over methodology, identity over interest, relativism over rationalism, social facts over empirical data. To be fair, there are less metaphorical, not quite so philosophically obtuse, more practical reasons for the growth of constructivism. It can be attributed to the quality of its scholarship, the proselytizing energy of its proponents, as well as the strategic if somewhat compromising position it strives to occupy between other 'post-modern', 'rigid', 'hardcore', 'radical' or 'strong' approaches.[14] It could be argued that constructivism is spreading because it provides new and valuable concepts for interpreting a rapidly changing world that older approaches in IR have not, and perhaps cannot provide.[15] Indeed, it could be argued that argumentation itself, now thriving in the increasingly pluralistic and fragmented subfields of IR and schools of the social sciences, favours constructivism, which at least theoretically practises (a pragmatic evaluation of competing truth-claims) what it preaches (the world is what we make of it).[16]

How, then, to link virtual theory to constructivism without falling prey to its blob-like qualities? There is the conventional approach, that would rest constructivist claims with precise definitions, comparative literature reviews, theoretical analysis, and the reductionist diagram *viz.*, the kind of professional activity that keeps us all busy and our journals in business. Following economic models, this primitive accumulation of knowledge might well result in a great leap forward to a new stage of intellectual development in International Relations. However, progress in history, as well as discontinuous, epistemic innovation in science, rarely takes the linear path of incrementalism. A less direct critique might be more effective. It need not be on the order of past polemics, like Hedley Bull's infamous frontal assault on behaviouralists, which, we should remember, was spurred by his belief that one should 'study their position until one could state their own arguments better than they could and then—when they were least suspecting—to turn on them and slaughter them in an academic massacre of Glencoe'.[17] Given the nature of the beast, it might be more appropriate to play down the minor differences, to *mimic* constructivism, say, as predators do their prey, and co-opt it from without. As Steve McQueen discovered the hard way, Blobs are pretty much immune to flaming or caging: direct confrontation is just more thought for food. Not wishing to escalate to the thermonuclear level (as they did, counter-productively, in the sequel, 'Beware the Blob!'), I suggest a different strategy for the de-blobbing of constructivism, one that is *empirical, historical*, and *political*, which refigures constructivism as a progenitor rather than pre-empter of virtual theory.

This would clearly require another article. But I can give three good reasons for undertaking such an investigation. First, constructivism in IR, for all its metatheoretical trappings, is a curiously *sui generis* creature; as conventionally told in IR theory, constructivism could just as well as come from outer space.[18] Originary conceits are not confined to constructivists, but one would think that, by stint of name and nature, they would be less inclined to contribute to the philosophical amnesia that seems to strike successive generations of IR theory. Some might venture only so far from the mainstream as the near-abroad, to the recently emergent 'schools' of constructivism clustered, not surprisingly, around a variety of universities which have expediently assembled over the last decade a critical mass of professors, graduate students, and fine scholarship, as demonstrated by the 'Minnesota', 'Copenhagen' and 'Aberystwyth' schools. Others have recognized the extra-disciplinary influence of social and political theorists such as Anthony Giddens and Jürgen Habermas. But we need to travel further afield, to avoid the internecine wars of taxonomy that pose as theoretical dialogue, but also to estrange through genealogy the parochial version of constructivism which currently prevails in IR. A genealogy of constructivism is long overdue, and doubly needed, to re-establish the disparate beginnings and multiple alternatives that have escaped the official story. A genealogy—what Nietzsche refers to as 'effective history' (*wirkliche Historie*) and Foucault as a 'history of the present'—functions as a theoretical intervention into the past that illuminates and seeks to transform present political practices.[19]

Second, a genealogy is needed because constructivism in IR has been bleached of politics as well as history. Although it might make constructivism more amenable to the disciplinary imperative of a value-free social science, this renders it less useful for a transformative and transvaluative period in contemporary International Relations. Third, constructivism, in its currently de-historicized and de-politicized adaptation of structuralism, is left incapable of responding to the most vexing ethical question that it first raised (if not then begged). If we do indeed construct the world we live in, if our theories are inextricably interdependent with our practices, why do we go on reproducing so much of its violence, criminality, and outright evil? Such political questions and hard ethical choices have become subsumed by the constructivist equivalent of a 'structural adjustment'.

Perhaps these last remarks are unfairly directed and overly righteous. After all, most constructivists are quick to claim that there is no *theory* of constructivism *per se:* it is only an 'approach', 'analysis', 'model' or, at best, a 'research programme' for IR, and as such should not be held to strict scientific, predictive, or prescriptive standards.[20] Nor do I—as someone close to the constructivist project (and identified by others as one[21])—wish to contribute to one of the least attractive pathologies of the academy, the narcissism of petty intellectual differences. Theory-bound and structurationally constrained, constructivists nonetheless should suffer from an ethical imperative that other approaches— or at least those on its epistemological right—do not. Post-structuralism has, from its beginnings outside and through its deliberations inside International Relations, wrestled with this issue.[22] 'Hardcore' realists, evincing material interests, amoral actors and repetitious history, need not bother with such 'idealist' concerns, thereby repudiating any responsibility for reproducing a world they claim only to record. Even 'softer' rationalist variants of neo-realism and neo-liberalism, focusing on the behaviour of given identities interacting at domestic and systemic levels, can offer explanatory, if not totally exculpatory answers based on game-theoretic issues like transaction cost and asymmetrical uncertainty that result in sub-optimal outcomes. Constructivists, operating in a more intersubjective, constitutive, normative model of the world, cannot so easily duck the ethical question. They might 'problematize' the subject of the question, by attacking the universalist and masculinist assumptions behind the use of a self-identical 'we' and a metaphysical sense of human nature.[23] They might 'disaggregate' the object of the question, by positing a more 'mediative' and scientific, rather than 'constitutive' and critical role for constructivism.[24] They might even 'interpellate' the answer, by arguing that a 'bounded' rationality delimits the constitutive options of the structurally 'embedded' agent.[25] However, demonstrations of epistemological correctness and ontological hair-splitting will not make the ethical question go away, and like the dead upon the living, the question will continue to haunt constructivism until it confronts its variegated past as well as its current abeyance of responsibility for the future.

Constructing a de-territorialized sense of being—neither here nor there as being but always as becoming different—virtually represents a paradoxical extra-reality that does not fit the dominant dyads of the social sciences, the real and the ideal, structure and agent, fact and value. It represents and provides an *interzone*, an interstice in which future possibilities are forged from the encounter between critical imagination and technological determinism. It offers a theoretical, historical and political mediation for International Relations. It is the first step towards the awakening, of which Benjamin wrote, from a perpetual state of interwar to a potential state of postwar.

The French philosopher Gilles Deleuze is most at home in this virtual interzone. He views the virtual as possessing a reality that is not yet actual, somewhat like Proust's remembrances, which are 'real without being actual, ideal without being abstract'.[26] Unlike the Aristotelian conception of the virtual as potential *(dynamis)*, the virtual now has a constitutive capacity of its own, creative of rather than dependent upon the actual. Deleuze traces this modern formulation of the virtual back to the coeval emergence of cinema and Bergson's concept of the *élan vital*. Just as images begin 'to move' in cinema, so too do our concepts need to incorporate mobility and time if they are to keep up with rapidly shifting events. The moving image/concept represents a kind of 'self-moving thought', which produces powerful effects of perception, affection, and action. Just as the simulacrum of the cinema has no 'real' identity, there is no natural 'there' to the virtual: its identity is based on pure difference, a difference-in-itself which privileges differentiation over resemblance, and the creative over the imitative—except, perhaps, in the case of the *Diehard* or *Lethal weapon* sequels. 'The virtual', says Deleuze, 'does not have to be realized, but rather actualized; and the rules of actualization are not those of resemblance and limitation, but those of difference or divergence and of creation'.[27]

Deleuze provides a complex model of the virtual as a problematic which is resolved through the interpretation of its eventual actualization. Organic examples—like the seed that carries the virtual code for but cannot control the circumstance of its actualization as a tree—do not adequately convey the power, ambiguity, and complexity of the virtual in a media-saturated environment.[28] Following Deleuze's dictum that 'the task of philosophy is to be worthy of the event', one is better advised to pick up the newspaper to find potential interzones in search of a worthy theory. Consider a single day in the *New York Times*. An Op-Ed piece by the economist Paul Krugman invokes the Wall Street crash of 1987 (which was virtually and literally programmed by computer trading) to demonstrate how the economic crisis in Asia and Russia will cease to be a 'real-economy non-event' and could be transformed into a global slump should the private sector succumb to 'a self-fulfilling pessimism'.[29] After the movie *Wag the dog* became the virtual standard by which President Clinton's foreign policy was framed, it is no surprise that in another article, this one on President Clinton's trip to Russia, former Secretary of State Lawrence Eagleberger says 'the trouble Clinton is going to have … is that we talk so much about him weakened that it becomes a self-fulfilling prophecy'.[30] And in perhaps the clearest if most metaphysical example of the prophetic powers of the virtual, the front page carries a story on Audrey Santo, a girl from Worcester, Massachusetts, 'inert and unspeaking' for 11 of her 14 years because of an accident, who is believed by thousands to have miraculous healing powers after blood appeared four times in her presence on the eucharistic hosts, the virtual body of Christ.[31]

Most traditional approaches in the social sciences, assuming the bifurcation rather than interaction of subjective mind and objective nature, are not philosophically equipped to explore this interzone of the virtual, where simulacra reverse causality, being is simultaneously here and there, and identity is deterritorialized by interconnectivity. Virtual theory posits that the retrieval of facts—empirical or social—is preceded by interpretation, conveyed by technical media, conducted through experimentation, and succeeded by the creation of new virtualities. War and peace both are still in need of approaches that study *what* is being represented. But it is also in need of a virtual theory that can explore *how* reality is seen, framed, read, and *generated* in the actualization of the event. Virtual theory does not, as vulgar realists would claim, deny the existence of 'reality'. Virtual theory seeks to understand how new technologies create the effects of reality, but it also begins with the premise, argued forcefully by philosophers from Leibniz and Nietzsche to Peirce and Putnam, that reality has always been inflected by the virtual.

This does not preclude a scientific investigation—unless one ignores the advances of Heisenberg, Einstein and quantum theory in general, and confines science (as is often the case in the social sciences) to the Baconian-Cartesian-Newtonian mechanistic model. Virtual theory relies on the scientific approach mapped out with clarity if not clairvoyance by Heisenberg:

> We can no longer speak of the behavior of the particle independently of the process of observation. As a final consequence, the natural laws formulated

mathematically in quantum theory no longer deal with the elementary particles themselves but with our knowledge of them .... The atomic physicist has had to resign himself to the fact that his science is but a link in the infinite chain of man's argument with nature, and that it cannot simply speak of nature 'in itself.' Science always presupposes the existence of man and, as Bohr has said, we must become conscious of the fact that we are not merely observers but also actors on the stage of life.[32]

Empirically, historically, and politically, a virtual theory of International Relations begins where General, turned President, Eisenhower left off in his famous (but now little debated) 1961 farewell address, warning of the 'danger that public policy could itself become the captive of a scientific-technological elite'. But with the addition of the media and entertainment industries to the mix, a seductive captivation now augments the powers of what he had labelled the 'military-industrial complex'. When the simulations used to train fighter pilots show up in the special effects of the film *Independence day*, four-person Marine fire-teams train with the videogame 'Doom', and Disney's former head-Imagineer, Bran Ferren shows up as the keynote speaker at an annual joint meeting of industry and military on high technology, reality becomes one more attraction at the Virtual Theme Park of War and Peace.

With apologies to Eisenhower, virtual theory takes aim at the cyborg heart of the 'Military-Industrial-Media-Entertainment' network (MIME-NET for short), not only to investigate its role in the production of war, but to study up close the mimetic power that travels along the hyphens. It would be historically specious to claim this relationship is wholly new. For instance, the Ford Motor Company's River Rouge plant at which my grandfather worked owed a great deal to Henry Ford's copying of the British Royal Navy's innovations in the mass production of cannon and ships; and in turn, Ford's assembly line production and hierarchical system of manufacturing became a mimetic model for the new Hollywood studio system of vertically controlling actors, movies, and theatres.[33] The feedback loop between military and civilian technology, particularly during and after the Second World War, from the cracking of German codes at Bletchley Park (the computer), to the early development of radar (the television), to the first semi-automated air defence systems (networks), has also been well documented.[34] What is qualitatively new is the power of the MIME-NET seamlessly to merge the production, representation and execution of war. The result is not merely the copy of a copy, or the creation of something new: it represents a convergence of the means by which we make the distinctions between the original and the new, the real and the reproduced.

Where once the study and practice of war began and ended with the black box of the state, new modes of production and networks of information have erased old and created new demarcations of power and identity, reality and virtuality. A virtual theory is needed to map these new developments: how new technologies and media of simulation create a fidelity between the representation and the reality of war; what are the political consequences when the human mimetic faculty for entertainment and gaming joins forces with new cyborg programmes for killing and warring; and what does it mean for peace and security, in an increasingly accelerated, highly contingent, uncertain global condition, when war goes virtuous.

In search of answers, and to separate the hype from the hyperreality of virtuous war, I decided early on to forego the public affairs machine of the Pentagon, to avoid the vices of academic abstraction as well as second-hand journalism, and to go where doctrine confronts reality (or, as my military handlers liked to put it, 'where the rubber meets the road'). I have spent the last seven years trying to get behind and beyond the images of modern warfare. My travels in virtuality have taken me to places not usually visited by scholars or pundits. My stops included Orlando, Florida, to see military officers and corporate leaders showcase their information technology at joint conferences on simulations; the East Mojave desert to chase after the 'Krasnovian Brigade' for two digitized war games at the Army National Training Center; to Central Command in Tampa to learn how computer gamers were busy programming the lessons of the Gulf war for the next war; to Fort Knox, Kentucky, to observe a distributed SimNet tank exercise in action; to the Combat and Maneuvering Training Center in Hohenfels, Germany, to watch the First Armored Division 'peacegame' their humanitarian intervention into Bosnia; to X-File territory at the Defense Advanced Research Projects Agency (DARPA) in Virginia, to learn how the Synthetic Theater of War (STOW) was being created to integrate virtual, live and constructive simulations of war in real time; back again to visit STRICOM (Simulation, Training, and Instrumentation Command), the newest, and probably the most unusual command post in the military; to the Bay area to observe its occupation by the Navy and Marines in the 'Urban Warrior' experiment; and finally to Vicenza, Italy, to compare the claims and the outcome of the air campaign in Kosovo. I did eventually make the pilgrimage to the Pentagon, interviewing, among others, Andrew Marshall, Director of the Office of Net Assessment, the Yoda of the 'Revolution in Military Affairs' (RMA), and General Wesley Clark, former Supreme Allied Commander in Europe, on the day before his retirement from the army.

My travels ended not far from where they started, in Los Angeles, where the Pentagon and Hollywood announced at the University of Southern California a new collaborative project. Over $40 million dollars will be spent to establish an 'Institute for Creative Technologies', where the best military gamers and studio artists will gather to prepare for the next war. From the desert to the laboratory to the studio, a virtual theory chronicles the successive stages—and staging—of virtuous warfare.

Inside and outside the military, the future of war is up for grabs. With lives and profits at stake, wars of position and manoeuvre are being fought on multiple fronts, within and among the military services, between Congress and the White House, in think-tanks and defence industries, at home and abroad. In my travels, I came across many other cases of open dissent and secret battles, where 'mud soldiers' were fighting a rearguard action against the 'virtuous warriors'. All are struggling with the uncertainties of the post-Cold War.

When critical thinking lags behind new technologies, as Albert Einstein famously remarked about the atom bomb, the results can be catastrophic.

My encounters in the field, interviews with experts, and research in the archives do suggest that the 'MIME', the 'RMA' and virtuous war are emerging as the preferred means to secure the United States in highly insecure times. Yet critical questions go unasked by the proponents, planners, and practitioners of virtuous war. Is this one more attempt to find a technological fix for what is clearly a political, even ontological problem? Will the tail of military strategy and virtual entertainment wag the dog of democratic choice and civilian policy? Most worrying, is there potential for catastrophe, as with all new complex systems, from what organizational theorists call *negative synergy*, 'normal accidents' of the sort that produced Three Mile Island, Chernobyl, Mogadishu? Or even a system-wide, networked accident?

In spite or because of virtuous war and democratic peace, global violence persists—and continues to resist both moral indictment and technological fixes. Virtual theory might not be the solution. But in a world where the virtual tail increasingly wags the body politic, it can point us in the right direction.

Notes

1 *Daily Telegraph*, 23 May 2000 (online).
2 See Michael Herr, *Dispatches* (New York: Avon Books, 1978), p. 20.
3 See Walter Benjamin, *The arcades project* (Cambridge, MA: Belknap Press, 1999), pp. 456 and 173.
4 Ibid., p. 461.
5 In March 1999, Air Force Major General John Campbell, then vice-director of the Defense Information Systems Agency (DISA is in charge of cybersecurity and provides worldwide communication, network and software support to the Defense Department), told Congress that there were a total of 22,144 'attacks' detected on Defense Department networks, an increase of 5,844 in 1998. From January to August 2000, there have been a total of 13,998 reported 'events', according to Betsy Flood, a spokeswoman at DISA (she defined 'events' as 'probes, scans, virus incidents and intrusions'). However, according to Richard Thieme, a technology consultant and one of the chairs of the annual 'DEF CON' computer hackers convention, all but 1,000 of last year's reported attacks were attributed to recreational hackers. See Jim Wolf, 'Hacking of Pentagon computers persists', *Washington Post*, 9 August 2000, p. 23.
6 See e.g. cover story of *Time Magazine* 151: 16, 27 April 1998.
7 Ibid.
8 In his 1994 Dewey Lectures at Columbia University, the philosopher Hilary Putnam provided the best word of caution for a virtual journey, warning against 'the common philosophical error of supposing that the term "reality" must refer to a single super thing, instead of looking at the ways in which we endlessly renegotiate and *are forced* to renegotiate our sense of reality as our language and our life develops'. 'Sense, nonsense, and the senses: an inquiry into the powers of the human mind, *The Journal of Philosophy*, vol. XCI, 1995, p. 452.
9 My last foray into the theory wars can be found in, 'Post-theory: the eternal return of ethics in international relations', in Michael Doyle and John Ikenberry, eds, *New thinking in international relations theory* (Boulder, CO: Westview Press, 1997), pp. 54–76. For my take on the superannuation of postmodernism, see James Der Derian, ed., *The Virilio reader* (Oxford: Blackwell Publishers, 1998). Introduction, pp. 1–15. See also Steven Metz, *Armed conflict in the 21st century: the information revolution and post-modern warfare* (Carlisle, PA: Strategic Studies Institute, 2000).

10 Unnamed NATO representative, quoted in Michael Gordon, 'NATO says it thought embassy was arms agency', *New York Times, 2* May 2000, p. 1.

11 This etymology is drawn from Martin Heidegger, *The question concerning technology and other essays*, trans. William Lovitt (New York: Harper, 1977); Costas Constantinou, *On the way to diplomacy* (Minneapolis, MN: University of Minnesota Press, 1996); and the always insightful suggestions of Michael Degener.

12 This definition and the description of the virtual which follows is a shorthand, highly condensed interpretation drawn from the work of Martin Heidegger, Gilles Deleuze, Félix Guattari, Jacques Derrida, Pierre Lévy and Paul Virilio. See Heidegger, *The question concerning technology*; Gilles Deleuze, *Bergsonism*, trans. Hugh Tomlinson and Barbara Habberjam (New York: Zone Books, 1988), *Différence et répétition* (Paris: PUF, 1968); Gilles Deleuze and Félix Guattari, *A thousand plateaus: capitalism and schizophrenia*, trans. Brian Massumi (Minneapolis, MN: University of Minnesota Press, 1987); Jacques Derrida, *Specters of Marx*, trans. Peggy Kamuf (New York and London: Routledge, 1994); Pierre Lévy, *Becoming virtual: reality in the digital age*, trans. Robert Bononno (New York and London: Plenum, 1998); Paul Virilio, *The Virilio reader*, trans. Michael Degener, Lauren Osepchuk and James Der Derian (Oxford: Blackwell Publishers, 1998). I have found the best philosophical synopsis to be Wolfgang Welsch's, 'Virtual anyway?', in Candido Mendes and Enrique Larreta, eds, *Media and social perception* (Rio de Janeiro, Brazil: UNESCO, 1999), pp. 242–85.

13 See James Der Derian, 'A reinterpretation of realism: genealogy, semiology, and dromology', in Der Derian, ed., *International theory: critical investigations* (New York: New York University Press, 1995), pp. 363–96.

14 These are terms used by many constructivists to self-differentiate from similar approaches, as well as to claim the 'modern', 'soft' and 'mediative'; 'milder'; or more 'conventional' middle ground in IR theory. See respectively Alexander Wendt, 'Anarchy is what states make of it: the social construction of power polities', in James Der Derian, ed., *International theory: critical investigations* (New York: New York University Press, 1995), pp. 131–3, 153–5; Emanuel Adler, 'Seizing the middle ground: constructivism in world polities', *European Journal of International Relations* 3: 3, September 1997, pp. 321–3, 333–7; Ronald Jepperson, Alexander Wendt and Peter Katzenstein, 'Norms, identity, and culture in national security', in Peter Katzenstein, ed., *The culture of national security* (New York: Columbia University Press, 1996), pp. 33—75; Daniel Deudney, 'Binding sovereigns: authorities, structures, and geopolitics in Philadelphian systems', in Thomas Biersteker and Cynthia Weber, eds, *State sovereignty as social construct* (Cambridge: Cambridge University Press, 1996), pp. 192–5; and Ted Hopf 'The promise of constructivism in International Relations theory', *International Security* 23: 1, summer 1998, pp. 171–200.

Dating back at least to Aristotle, the *via media* is hardly a novel move. However, earlier practitioners of it in the so-called 'English school' of IR, such as Martin Wight and Hedley Bull who advocated a 'Grotian' approach against 'Kantian' or 'Machiavellian' ones, recognized and advertized this gambit as an ethical preference, especially when one takes into account the cultural, social, and economic diversity in typological classification. See Hedley Bull (pp. xiv, xxi) and Martin Wight (pp. 259, and esp. 265, where he also distinguishes 'soft' from 'hard' versions of realism, rationalism, and revolution, in Gabriele Wight and Brian Porter, eds, *International theory: the three traditions* (Leicester: Leicester University Press, 1991).

15 As for testing constructivism by its ability to interpret or explain international politics, there is another obstacle: the singular tendency in IR to confuse causal links between theory and practice with the food chain of disciplinary schools of thought and proximity to powerful institutions (for *prima facie* evidence, see the ingratiating notes of acknowledgement which grace most *IO* or *ISQ* articles).

16 Two recent articles stand out in this regard: Ted Hopf, in one of the best overviews to date of constructivism, makes a virtue of its 'heterogamous research approach: that is, it readily combines with different fields and disciplines', (see 'The promise of constructivism', p. 196); and Neta Crawford presents a persuasive case for a constructivist ethics in post-modern times (see 'Postmodern ethics and the critical challenge', *Ethics and International Affairs* 12, 1998).

17 Wight and Porter, eds, *International theory*, p. xi.

18 The two early exceptions, by Nicholas Onuf and Friedrich Kratochwil, provide extensive, critical expositions of the precursors of constructivism in IR. The fact that they rely for the most part on legal philosophers and speech-act theorists, not a favoured analytic in North American IR, helps to explain their limited impact on the development of constructivism. See Onuf, *World of our making* (Columbia. SC: University of South Carolina Press 1989); and Kratochwil, *Rules, norms, and decisions* (Cambridge: Cambridge University Press, 1989).

19 If one takes a strictly nominalist approach, constructivism first appears in Russian in the early 1920s to describe the revolutionary effort 'to create a new world' out of new technology and politics by artists like Valdimir Tatlin, El Lissitzky, Naum Gabo, Antoine Pevsner, and most prominently, Aleksandr Rodchenko. From the outset, the concept is a site of great semantic, artistic and political contestation. One of its earliest invocations, 'The realistic manifesto', written by Gabo and Pevsner for an open-air exhibition and posted all over Moscow in 1920, calls for 'the construction of the new Great Style' which would succeed where the Futurists ('clad in the tatters of worn-out words like "Patriotism", "militarism", "contempt for the female" ') and Cubists ('broken in shards by their logical anarchy') had failed: 'We construct our work as the universe constructs its own, as the engineer constructs his bridges, as the mathematician his formula of the orbits … We affirm in these arts a new element, the kinetic rhythms as the basic forms of our perception of real time. We assert that the shouts about the future are for us the same as the tears about the past: a renovated day-dream of the romantics'. See Naum Gabo and Antoine Pevsner, 'The realistic manifesto', in Stephen Bann, ed., *The tradition of constructivism* (New York: Da Capo Press, 1974), pp. 3–10.

20 See respectively Adler (1997), pp. 321–3; Wendt (1995), pp. 153–6; Wendt (1996), pp. 242–5; and Hopf (1998), pp. 196–7.

21 See Hopf (1998), p. 182.

22 There has been a continuing debate in post-structuralism on subjectivity and ethics, based on the work of Nietzche, Bakhtin, Foucault, Levinas, Derrida, Rorty and others, in the political theory of Judith Butler, Wendy Brown and William Connolly; and in the international theory of David Campbell. Daniel Warner and Jim George, among others. For a synopsis, see Der Derian, 'Post-theory', pp. 54–76.

23 See Ann Tickner, 'Identity in International Relations theory: feminist perspectives', in Yosef Lapid and Friedrich Kratochwil, *The return of culture and identity in IR theory* (Boulder, CO: Lynne Rienner, 1996), pp. 147–62; and *Gender in International Relations* (New York: Columbia University Press, 1992), pp. 22–66.

24 See Adler, 'Seizing the middle ground', pp. 330–6.

25 See Alexander Wendt and Daniel Friedheim, 'Hierarchy under anarchy: informal empire and the East German state', in *State sovereignty as social construct*, pp. 245–53.

26 See Deleuze, *Bergsonism*, pp. 96–7. See also Constantin Boundas, 'Deleuze-Bergson: an ontology of the virtual', in Paul Patton, ed., *Deleuze: a critical reader* (Blackwell Publishers, 1996), pp. 81–106.

27 See Deleuze, *Bergsonism*, p. 97.

28 See Lévy, *Becoming virtual*, p. 24.

29 See Paul Krugman, 'Let's not panic—yet', *New York Times*, 30 August 1998, p. 13.

30 See Elaine Sciolino, 'Dear Mr President: what to do in Moscow', *New York Times*, 30 Aug. 1998, p. 11.

31 See Gustav Niehbur, 'Unconscious girl inspires stream of pilgrims', *New York Times*, 30 Aug. 1998, p. 24.

32 See Werner Heisenberg, *The physicist's conception of Nature*, trans. Arnold J. Pomerans (New York: Hutchinson, 1958), pp. 12–16, 28–9, 33–41.

33 See Martin Walker, *America reborn* (New York: Knopf, 2000).

34 See Paul Edwards, *Closed Worlds: Computers and the politics of discourse in Cold War America* (Cambridge, MA: MIT Press, 1996); and Friedrich Kittler, *Literature, media, information system* (Amsterdam: OPA, 1997).

18 The illusion of a grand strategy

Source: Op-ed, *The New York Times*, May 25, 2001.

Today President Bush will deliver what has been billed as a major defense policy statement. Coming on the heels of a Pentagon "top-to-bottom" defense review – the result of two dozen panels of experts meeting for several months behind closed doors – his speech has been preceded by high expectations and not a small amount of controversy. Will he come to the Naval Academy armed with a revolutionary plan to transform the military, as his earlier statements have suggested? In the end, it may not matter. No plan, said Clausewitz, the Prussian strategist, survives the first battle; and the counterattacks have already begun.

On Capitol Hill, military reform has the unpleasant ring of bases being closed and pet weapons projects getting axed. Largely excluded from the planning process, Congress is likely to put up a fight – a prospect that Secretary of Defense Donald Rumsfeld has belatedly recognized this week in his trips to the Hill.

Fearing the loss of a division, carrier group or fighter program, each of the armed services has launched both public and private protests. In the defense industry, cracks will further widen between the heavy-metal advocates (those who favor tanks, ships and planes) and the electronica faction (who prefer precision munitions, remote sensors and robotics).

Public debates are already heating up over readiness to fight simultaneously one, one and a half, or two major regional conflicts. The power and vulnerability of aircraft carriers are being contrasted to the speed and cost of "streetfighter" ships, and the advantages of piloted aircraft against those of precision strike weapons and unmanned aerial vehicles.

Whatever the outcome, much of the credit, or blame, is likely to be laid at the doorstep of one man: Andrew Marshall. He was handpicked by Mr. Rumsfeld to guide the strategic review. Yet Mr. Marshall and his views remain enigmatic. Well-known if not adored by a tight circle of civilian and military strategists – the so-called "church of St. Andrew" – Mr. Marshall has been nearly invisible outside the defense establishment. A RAND Corporation nuclear expert beginning in 1949, he was brought by Henry Kissinger onto the National Security Council then appointed by President Nixon to direct the Pentagon's Office of Net Assessment.

He has been there ever since, despite efforts by some defense secretaries to get rid of him. His innocuous-sounding office comes with a big brief: to "assess" regional and global military balances and to determine long-term trends and threats.

Insiders say Mr. Marshall was behind some of the key strategic decisions of the Reagan years. His strategy for a protracted nuclear war – based on weapons modernization, protection of governmental leaders from a first strike and an early version of Star Wars – effectively beggared the Soviet war machine. He advocated providing Afghan resistance fighters with the highly effective Stinger missiles. He tagged AIDS as a national security issue.

Supporters call Mr. Marshall "iconoclastic" and "delphic"; his detractors prefer "paranoiac" or worse. No one has ever called him prolix. At a future-war seminar that he sponsored, Mr. Marshall mumbled a few introductory words and then sat in silence, eyebrows arched, arms folded, for the remaining two days. His only intervention came at the end. He suggested that when it came to the future, it would be better to err on the side of being unimaginative. After that experience, I better understood why he has been called the Pentagon's Yoda.

Five years ago, I sought him out because of his legendary seven-page memo, "Some Thoughts on Military Revolutions." First circulated in August 1993, it promoted the "revolution in military affairs," a new movement in military analysis, in which information technologies combined with innovative military doctrine transform the nature of war.

My interview with Mr. Marshall took place in his paper-strewn Pentagon office. With one eye on the primitive rocket that stood between our chairs, I asked him about his current concerns. Even then Mr. Marshall saw Asia looming on the horizon. But his gaze was also directed backward, to Europe between the world wars. He had teams analyzing the failure of Great Britain, the leading power of the day, to formulate effective strategies of defense and deterrence from new technologies like the tank, airplane and radio. Relying on past glories, antiquated doctrine and international institutions like the League of Nations, Britain missed the revolution in military affairs of its day. Germany did not, and subdued most of Europe by blitzkrieg.

The rest may be history, but not for Andrew Marshall. In a time of great transformations, the interwar period shows what might happen if a "peer competitor" gets the technological jump on a complacent United States. "The 20's," he told me, "turned out to be a period of illusion."

Andrew Marshall is unusual in that he may have the power to make his vision of our enemies – whether illusionary or true – into reality. However, the horse-trading, pork-barreling, balkanizing process called "defense policy making" has a way of chewing up grand visions, even when they are proclaimed by presidents.

19 *In terrorem*

Before and after 9/11[1]

Source: *Worlds in Collision*, eds. Ken Booth and Tim Dunne (New York: Palgrave Macmillan, 2002), pp. 101–116.

Before 9/11 and after 9/11: it is as if the history and future of international relations were disappeared by this temporal rift. Old rules of statecraft, diplomacy and warfare have been thrown out by terrorist and anti-terrorist alike, and in this interregnum – best described by Chris Patten, the last governor of Hong Kong and current European Union Commissioner for External Affairs, as one of 'unilateralist overdrive' – critical enquiry is threatened by a global *in terrorem*.[2]

Obviously, the sheer scale, scope and shock of the events themselves are partially to blame for the paucity as well as the poverty of the response by the field of International Relations. Perhaps we witness once again what happened at academic conferences after the fall of the Berlin Wall, when social scientists were reluctant to posit cause and effect from a single data point. Or perhaps something more is at work, a great deal more. After terrorist hijackers transformed three commercial jetliners into highly explosive kinetic weapons, toppled the Twin Towers of the World Trade Center, substantially damaged the Pentagon, killed over 3000 people and triggered a state of emergency – and before the dead are fully grieved, Osama bin Laden's head brought on a platter, justice perceived as done, and information no longer considered a subsidiary of war – there is very little about 9/11 that is *safe* to say. Unless one was firmly situated in a patriotic, ideological, or religious position (which at home and abroad drew uncomfortably close), it is intellectually difficult and even politically dangerous to assess the meaning of a conflict that phase-shifted with every news cycle, from 'Terror Attack' to 'America Fights Back'; from a 'crusade' to a 'counter-terror campaign'; from 'the first war of the twenty-first century' to a now familiar combination of humanitarian intervention and remote killing; from kinetic terror to bioterror; from the spectacle of war to a war of spectacles.

Under such conditions, I believe the task is to uncover what is *dangerous* to think and say. Or as Walter Benjamin put it best in an earlier interim of violence and uncertainty, 'in times of terror, when everyone is something of a conspirator, everybody will be in a situation where he has to play detective'.[3]

Detective work and some courage are needed because questions about the root causes or political intentions of the terrorist acts have been either silenced by charges of 'moral equivalency' or rendered moot by claims that the exceptional nature of the act placed it outside political discourse: explanation is identified as exoneration.[4] Reflecting the nature of the attacks, as well as the chaos and confusion which followed, the conventional boundaries of the infosphere expanded during the first week to include political, historical and ethical analysis by some voices not usually heard on primetime. However, as the flow of information became practically entropic, there was a willingness (as judged by the unholy trinity of polls, pols and programming) to accept as wisdom President Bush's early declaration that evil – which expanded from a person to a network to the now notorious 'axis of evil' – was to blame. From that moment, policy debate and political action downshifted to a simple declarative with an impossible performative: to eradicate evil. Binary narratives displaced any complex or critical analysis of what happened and why. Retribution required certainty, and certainty was produced as salve for the actually as well as symbolically injured.

More sophisticated analysts like Michael Ignatieff also downplayed the significance of social or political enquiry by declaiming the exceptionality of the act:

> What we are up against is apocalyptic nihilism. The nihilism of their means – the indifference to human costs – takes their actions not only out of the realm of politics, but even out of the realm of war itself. The apocalyptic nature of their goals makes it absurd to believe they are making political demands at all. They are seeking the violent transformation of an irremediably sinful and unjust world. Terror does not express a politics, but a metaphysics, a desire to give ultimate meaning to time and history through ever-escalating acts of violence which culminate in a final battle between good and evil.[5]

By funnelling the experience through the image of American exceptionalism, 9/11 quickly took on an *exceptional ahistoricity*. For the most part, history was only invoked – mainly in the sepia tones of the Second World War – to prepare the US for the sacrifice and suffering that lay ahead. The influential conservative George Will wrote that there were now only two time zones left for the United States:

> America, whose birth was mid-wived by a war and whose history has been punctuated by many more, is the bearer of great responsibilities and the focus of myriad resentments. Which is why for America, there are only two kinds of years, the war years and the interwar years.[6]

Under such forced circumstances, of being beyond experience, outside of history and between wars, 9/11 does not easily yield to philosophical, political or social enquiry. The best one can do is to thickly describe, robustly interrogate and directly challenge the authorized truths and official actions of all parties who posit a world view of absolute differences in need of final solutions. I do so here by first challenging the now common assumption that 9/11 is an exceptional event beyond history and theory, especially those theories tainted, as Edward Rothstein claimed in the *New York Times*, by 'postmodernism' and 'post-colonialism'.[7] Second, I examine the representations, technologies and strategies of network wars that have eluded mainstream journalism and 'traditional' social science. I conclude by uncovering what I consider to be the main dangers that emerged from the counter/terror of 9/11.

An exceptional act?

On the question of exceptionalism, consider a few testimonials; the first from an editorial in the *New York Times*:

> If the attack against the World Trade Center proves anything it is that our offices, factories, transportation and communication networks and infrastructures are relatively vulnerable to skilled terrorists ... Among the rewards for our attempts to provide the leadership needed in a fragmented, crisis-prone world will be as yet unimagined terrorists and other socio-paths determined to settle scores with us.[8]

Another from a cover story of *Newsweek*:

> The explosion shook more than the building: it rattled the smug illusion that Americans were immune, somehow, to the plague of terrorism that torments so many countries.[9]

And finally, one from the *Sunday Times*:

> He began the day as a clerk working for the Dean Witter brokerage on the 74th floor of the World Trade Center in New York and ended it as an extra in a real-life sequel to *Towering Inferno* ...[10]

It might surprise some to learn that these are all quotes taken from 1993, the first and much less deadly terrorist attack on the World Trade Center. They are presented here as a caution, against reading terrorism only in the light – the often-blinding light – of the events of September 11. Obviously the two WTC events differ in the scale of the devastation as well as the nature of the attack. 9/11 defied the public imagination of the real – not to mention, as just about every public official and media authority is loath to admit, the official imagination and pre-emptive capacity of the intelligence community, federal law enforcement, airport security, military and other governmental agencies. Shock and surprise produced an immediate and nearly uniform reading of the event that was limited in official discourse to condemnation, retribution and counter-terror. But there is a professional as well as a public responsibility to place 9/11 in a historical context and interpretive field that reaches beyond the immediacy of personal tragedy and official injury. Otherwise 9/11 will be remembered not for the attack itself but for the increasing cycles of violence that follow.

If 9/11 is not wholly new, what is it? As we have seen too well, the official response was a struggle of evil against good – of which, given the rhetorical excess deemed necessary by our leaders to mobilize the public to action, there have been more than a few cases in American history. As an actual practice of warfare we again received a better picture of what 9/11 is not than what it is: from the President and Secretary of Defense and on down the food chain of the national security hierarchy, we heard that this would not be the Gulf War or Kosovo, and it most definitely would not be Vietnam or Mogadishu. And they were partially right – certainly more so than commentators from the kneejerk factions of both the right and left, who flooded the airwaves with sloppy historical analogies from the Second World War (Pearl Harbor and the Reichstag fire being most prominent) and convergent conspiracy theories (the Israeli Mossad and Big Oil pulling all the strings).

From my perspective, new and old forms of representation and violence synergized on 9/11. The neo-medieval rhetoric of holy war reverberated from the minaret to the television and, at an unprecedented level, to the internet. A hypermodern war of simulation and surveillance was played out at flight schools, airports and in practically every nook, cranny and cave of Afghanistan. A remote aerial war was directed from Central Command in Tampa, Florida, 7750 miles away from targets that were surveyed by drone aircraft like the Predator and Global Hawk, and destroyed by smart GPS-guided JDAMs (Joint Direct Attack Munitions with a circular error probability of about 10 feet), CBU-87 and CBU-103 'cluster bombs' (Combined Effects Munitions containing over 200 bomblets that have anti-tank, anti-personnel as well as an incendiary capability), and dumb bombs, topped by the 15,000 pound 'Daisy-cutter' (BLU-82) that explodes 3 feet above the ground and incinerates anything within 600 yards. And in a dirty war of blood and bluff, special operations forces led an anti-Taliban coalition in a limited and, by early reports, highly successful land campaign.

This strange new hybrid of conflict fully qualifies, perverse as it might sound, as a *virtuous war*. Post-Vietnam, post-Cold War, post-modern, virtuous war emerged prior to 9/11, from the battlespace of the Gulf War and the aerial campaigns of Bosnia and Kosovo in which the killing was kept, as much as it was technologically and ethically possible, virtual and virtuous. Virtuous war relies on computer simulation, media manipulation, global surveillance and networked warfare to deter, discipline and, if need be, destroy potential enemies. It draws on just war doctrine (when possible) and holy war (when necessary). Post-9/11, virtuous war now looks to be the ultimate means by which the US intends to re-secure its borders, maintain its hegemony and bring a modicum of order if not justice back to international politics. The difference from pre-9/11 is that the virtual enemy – at least at home – now comes with a face (indeed, 22 faces; all of them displayed on the FBI's new website of most-wanted terrorists[11]).

In the name of the holy trinity of international order – global free markets, democratic sovereign states and limited humanitarian interventions – the US has led the way in a revolution in military affairs (RMA) which underlies virtuous war. At the heart as well as the muscle of this transformation is the technical capability and ethical imperative to threaten and, if necessary, actualize violence from a distance – but again, with minimal casualties when possible.

This is not to claim that people do not die in virtuous wars, but rather that new technologies of killing skew the casualty rates, both off and on the battlefield. In the 9/11 attack, 19 terrorist hijackers killed over 3000 people in the United States. By the end of January, 20 American military personnel were killed overseas in the line of duty, the majority of whom died in accidents or by friendly fire: only one soldier, Sergeant First Class Nathan Chapman, was actually killed by hostile fire.[12] As was the case in the Kosovo campaign, more journalists *covering* the war were killed by hostile fire (ten by the end of January) than American military fighting the war. The high incidence of friendly-fire deaths (as well as ratio to hostile fire deaths) reflects the increased lethality of precision munitions when they are mistargeted: three members of the US Army 5th Special Forces Group team were killed and 19 soldiers wounded after they mistakenly gave their own geocoordinates for satellite-guided JDAMs. It also reflects a 'low risk, low yield' military strategy that some see as a lingering legacy of the 'Vietnam Syndrome' (the erosion of public support if body bags come home in high numbers) which resurfaced at the beginning and then was declared 'kicked' at the end of the Gulf War by the first President Bush in 1991.[13] On the other side of virtuous war, enemy casualties are increasingly hard to come by. As the war was winding down in December, estimates of enemy combatant deaths ranged wildly, from 3000 to 10,000. And when a lone economics professor, Marc Herold at the University of New Hampshire, researched the number of Afghan non-combatant casualties at 3767, a maelstrom of controversy erupted.[14]

Network wars

From the start, it was apparent that 9/11 was and would continue to be a war of networks. Whether terrorist, internet or primetime, most of the networks were linked by a push/pull propagation of violence, fear and dis/mis/information. For a prolonged moment, in the first week of confusion and chaos where there was no detached point of observation, these networks seemed almost neurally attached, immersing viewers in a 24/7 cycle of tragic images of destruction and loss. A national state of emergency and trauma reached into all levels of society. It was as if the American political culture experienced a collective Freudian trauma, which could be re-enacted (endlessly on cable and the internet) but not understood at the moment of shock. And in a state of emergency, as in war, the first images stick. There was an initial attempt by the media to transform these images of horror into responsible discourses of reflection and action, but the blame game kicked in with a fury. Moving at the speed of the news cycle and in the rush to judgement, there was little time for deliberation, for understanding the motivations of the attackers, or for assessing the potential consequences, intended as well as unintended, of a military response.

It quickly became apparent that the war networks were not merely nodes connected by wiring of one sort of another. They conveyed, mimicked and in some cases generated human attributes and intentions, as suggested by *Wired* founding editor Kevin Kelly, who defined a network as 'organic behavior in a technological matrix'. But 9/11 knocked akilter this always problematical relationship between meat and wire. Technologically driven events outpaced organic modes of comprehension, and human actions, whether out of trauma or information overload, seemed increasingly to resemble machinic reflexes. Indeed, the first reaction by most onlookers and television reporters was to deem the event an accident. The attack on the second tower destroyed the accidental thesis, and also, it seemed, our ability to map cognitively the devastating aftermath. Instead, into the void left by the collapse of the WTC towers and the absence of detached analysis, there rushed a host of metaphors, analogies and metonyms, dominated by denial ('It's a movie'), history ('It's Pearl Harbor') and non-specific horror ('It's the end of the world as we have known it').

In our public culture, the media networks rather than the family, the community or the government provide the first and, by its very speed and pervasiveness, most powerful response to a crisis. Questions of utility, responsibility and accountability inevitably arose, and as one would expect, the media's pull-down menu was not mapped for the twin-towered collapse of American invulnerability. Primetime networks did their best (Peter Jennings of ABC better than the rest) to keep up with the real-time crises. But fear, white noise and technical glitches kept intruding, creating a cognitive lag so profound between event and interpretation that I wondered if superstring theory had not been proven right, that one of the ten other dimensions that make up the universe had suddenly intruded upon our own, formerly ordered, one, exposing the chaos beneath.

Indeed, after the looped footage of the collapse of the towers began to take on the feeling of *déjà vu*, I seriously wondered if the reality principle, as in nothing so much as *The Matrix*, had not taken a fatal blow. Like Ignatieff, I discerned a nihilism at work, but of a different kind, of the sort vividly on display in the movie. It first appears when some punky-looking customers in search of bootleg virtual reality software come to see Neo, the protagonist played by Keanu Reeves. He pulls from a shelf a green leather-bound book, the title of which is briefly identifiable as Jean Baudrillard's *Simulacra and Simulation*. When he opens the hollowed-out book to retrieve the software, the first page of the last chapter appears: 'On Nihilism'. Clearly a homage by the two directors, the Wachowski brothers, it all happens very quickly; too quickly to read the original words of Baudrillard, but here they are:

> Nihilism no longer wears the dark, Wagnerian, Spenglerian, fuliginous colors of the end of the century. It no longer comes from a Weltanschauung of decadence nor from a metaphysical radicality born of the death of God and of all the consequences that must be taken from this death. Today's nihilism is one of transparency, this irresolution is indissolubly that of the system, and that of all the theory that still pretends to analyze it.[15]

With the toppling of the WTC a core belief was destroyed: it could not happen here. Into this void the networks rushed, to provide transparency without depth, a simulacrum of horror, a much purer form of nihilism than imagined by moralist commentators like Ignatieff or Rothstein. In official circles, there was a concerted effort to fence off the void: the critical use of language, imagination, even humour, was tightly delimited by moral sanctions and government warnings. This first strike against critical thought took the peculiar form of a semantic debate over the meaning of 'coward'. In the *New Yorker* and on *Politically Incorrect*, the question was raised of whether it is more cowardly to commandeer a commercial airliner and pilot it into the World Trade Center, to bomb Serbians from 15,000 feet, or to direct a cruise missile attack against bin Laden from several thousand miles away. The official response was swift, with advertisements yanked, talk show condemnations, and Ari Fleischer, White House Press Secretary, saying that people like Bill Maher of *Politically Incorrect* 'should watch what they say, watch what they do'.

Other protected zones of language began to take shape. When Reuters news agency questioned the abuse-into-meaningless of the term 'terrorism', George Will, on a Sunday morning news programme, retaliated by advocating a boycott of Reuters.[16] Irony and laughter were permitted in some places, not in others. At a Defense Department press conference Secretary of Defense Rumsfeld could ridicule, and effectively disarm, a reporter who dared to ask if anyone in the Department of Defense would be authorized to lie to the news media.[17] President Bush was given room to joke in a morale-boosting visit to the CIA, saying that he had been 'spending a lot of quality time lately' with George Tenet, the director of the CIA.[18] And then there was *New York Times* reporter Edward Rothstein, taking his opportunistic shot at postmodernists and post-colonialists, claiming that their irony and relativism was 'ethically perverse' and produced a 'guilty passivity'.[19] Some of us were left wondering where that view would place fervent truth-seekers and serious enemies of relativism and irony like Osama bin Laden: terrorist foe but epistemological ally?

The mimetic war of images

The air war started on October 7, 2001, with a split-screen war of images: in one box, a desolate Kabul seen through a nightscope camera lens, in grainy-green pixels except for the occasional white arc of anti-aircraft fire followed by the flash of an explosion; in the other, a rotating cast of characters, beginning with President Bush, followed over the course of that day and the next by Secretary of Defense Rumsfeld, Chairman of the Joint Chiefs General Meyers and Attorney-General John Ashcroft, then progressively down the media food chain of war reporters, beltway pundits and recently retired generals. On the one side we witnessed images of embodied resolve in high resolution; on the other, nighttime shadows with nobody in sight.

Strategic and narrative binaries cropped up in President Bush's war statement, incongruously delivered from the Treaty Room of the White House: 'as we strike military targets, we will also drop food'; the United States is 'a friend to the Afghan people' and 'an enemy of those who aid terrorists'; 'the only way to pursue peace is to pursue those who threaten it'. And once more, the ultimate either/or was issued: 'Every nation has a choice to make. In this conflict there is no neutral ground.'[20]

However, the war programming was interrupted by the media-savvy bin Laden. Shortly after the air strikes began, he appeared on Qatar's al-Jazeera television network ('the Arab world's CNN') in a pre-taped statement that was cannily delivered as a counter air-strike to the US. Kitted out in turban and battle fatigues, bin Laden presented his own bipolar view of the world: 'These events have divided the world into two camps, the camp of the faithful and the camp of infidels.' But if opposition constituted his world view, it was a historical mimic battle that sanctioned the counter-violence: 'America has been filled with horror from north to south and east to west, and thanks be to God what America is tasting now is only a copy of what we have tasted.'[21]

Without falling into the trap of 'moral equivalency', one can discern striking similarities. Secretary of Defense Rumsfeld and others have made much of the 'asymmetrical' war being waged by the terrorists. And it is indeed a canny and even diabolical use of asymmetrical tactics as well as strategies when terrorists commandeer commercial aircraft and transform them into kinetic weapons of indiscriminate violence – and then deploy commercial media to counter the military strikes that follow. Yet a fearful symmetry is also at work at an unconscious, possibly pathological level; a war of escalating and competing and imitative oppositions, a *mimetic war of images*.

A mimetic war is a battle of imitation and representation, in which the relationship of who we are and who they are is played out along a wide spectrum of familiarity and friendliness, indifference and tolerance, estrangement and hostility. It can result in appreciation or denigration, accommodation or separation, assimilation or extermination. It draws physical boundaries between peoples, as well as metaphysical boundaries between life and the most radical other of life, death. It separates human from god. It builds the fence that makes good neighbours; it builds the wall that confines a whole people. And it sanctions just about every kind of violence. President Bush announces that Iran is now part of the 'axis of evil'; Iran complies by staging the first large-scale anti-American demonstration since the moderate Khatami regime came to power.

More than a rational calculation of interests takes us to war. People go to war because of how they see, perceive, picture, imagine and speak of others; that is, how they construct the difference of others as well as the sameness of themselves through representations. From Greek tragedy and Roman gladiatorial spectacles to futurist art and fascist rallies, the mimetic mix of image and violence has proven to be more powerful than the most rational discourse. Indeed, the medical definition of mimesis is 'the appearance, often caused by hysteria, of symptoms of a disease not actually present'. Before one can find a cure, one must study the symptoms – or, as it was once known in medical science, practise *semiology*.

Mime-net

It was not long before morbid symptoms began to surface from an array of terror and counter-terror networks. Al-Qaeda members reportedly used encrypted email to communicate; steganography to hide encoded messages in web images (including pornography); Kinko's and public library computers to send messages; underground banking networks called *hawala* to transfer untraceable funds; 24/7 cable networks like al-Jazeera and CNN to get the word out; and, in their preparations for 9/11, a host of other information technologies like rented cell phones, online travel agencies, and flight simulators.

In general, networks – from television primetime to internet real-time – delivered events with an alacrity and celerity that left not only viewers but also decision makers racing to keep up. With information as the life-blood and speed as the killer variable of networks, getting inside the decision making as well the image making loop of the opponent became the central strategy of network warfare. This was not lost on the American national security team as it struggled after the initial attack to get ahead of the network curve. Sluggish reactions were followed by quicker pre-emptive actions on multiple networks. Congress passed the 'Uniting and Strengthening America by Providing Appropriate Tools Required to Intercept and Obstruct Terrorism (USA PATRIOT) Act', which allowed for 'roving wiretaps' of multiple telephones, easier surveillance of email and internet traffic, more sharing between foreign and domestic intelligence, and the divulgence of grand jury and wiretap transcripts to intelligence agencies.[22] National Security adviser Condoleeza Rice made personal calls to heads of the television networks, asking them to pre-screen and to consider editing al-Qaeda videos for possible coded messages.[23] Information about the air campaign as well as the unfolding ground interventions was heavily filtered by the Pentagon, which set up an Office of Strategic Influence' to correct unfavourable news reports and, supposedly, to plant favourable ones in the foreign press. Open information flows slowed to a trickle from the White House and the Defense Department after tough restrictions were imposed against leaks. Psychological operations were piggy-backed on to humanitarian interventions by the dropping of propaganda leaflets and food packs. The Voice of America began broadcasting anti-Taliban messages in Pashto. After the 22 'Most Wanted Terrorists' were featured on the FBI's website, the popular TV programme *America's Most Wanted* ran an extended program on their individual cases. The infowar was on.

Some of the most powerful networks are often the least visible, but it was hard to keep a secret when Hollywood was added to the mix. The entertainment industry journal *Variety* first broke the news about a meeting between White House officials and Hollywood executives. The stated intention was ominous enough, to 'enlist Hollywood in the war effort':

> The White House is asking Hollywood to rally round the flag in a style reminiscent of the early days of World War II. Network heads and studio chiefs heard that message Wednesday in a closed-door meeting with emissaries from the Bush administration in Beverly Hills, and committed themselves to new initiatives in support of the war on terrorism. These initiatives would stress efforts to enhance the perception of America around the world, to 'get out the message' on the fight against terrorism and to mobilize existing resources, such as satellites and cable, to foster better global understanding.[24]

Although some big media picked up this aspect of the story, none except for *Newsweek* took note of an earlier meeting organized by the military and the University of Southern California's Institute for Creative Technology.[25] I knew about the ICT because I had covered its opening for *Wired* and *The Nation* back in 1999, when the army ponied up $43 million to bring together the simulation talents of Hollywood, Silicon Valley and the US military.[26] Now it seemed that they were gathering top talent to help coordinate a new virtual war effort:

> In a reversal of roles, government intelligence specialists have been secretly soliciting terrorist scenarios from top Hollywood filmmakers and writers. A unique ad hoc working group convened at USC just last week at the behest of the US Army. The goal was to brainstorm about possible terrorist targets and schemes in America and to offer solutions to those threats, in light of the twin assaults on the Pentagon and the World Trade Center. Among those in the working group based at USC's Institute for Creative Technology are those with obvious connections to the terrorist pic milieu, like 'Die Hard' screenwriter Steven E. De Souza, TV writer David Engelbach ('MacGyver') and Joseph Zito, who directed the features 'Delta Force One,' 'Missing in Action' and 'The Abduction.' But the list also includes more mainstream suspense helmers like David Fincher ('Fight Club'), Spike Jonze ('Being John Malkovich'), Randal Kleiser ('Grease') and Mary Lambert ('The In Crowd') as well as feature screenwriters Paul De Meo and Danny Bilson ('The Rocketeer').[27]

It would appear that 9/11 christened a new network: the military-industrial-media-entertainment network (MIME-NET). If Vietnam was a war waged in the living rooms of the United States, the first and most likely the last battles of the counter/terror war are going to be waged on global networks that reach much more widely and deeply into our everyday lives.

Counter/terror dangers

Terror came to America on 9/11 not by rogue state or ballistic missile or high-tech biological, chemical and nuclear weapons of mass destruction – as presaged by the intelligence and national security experts – but by an unholy network, hijacked airliners and the terrorist's favourite 'force-multiplier', primetime, cable and internet weapons of mass distraction and disruption. Have we learned the right lessons since then? Or will the 'evil' regimes, missiles and high-tech create more blindspots from which new threats will emerge with devastating effects? What lies ahead?

My greatest concern is not so much the future as how past futures become reproduced; that is, how we seem unable to escape the feedback loops of bad intelligence, bureaucratic thinking and failed imagination. From my own experience, when confronted by the complexity and speed of networked conflicts, the fields of political science and international relations are too slow to respond when it matters most. This leaves another intellectual void into which policy makers, military planners and media pundits are always ready to rush. Currently the RMA-mantra among the techno-optimists in the Pentagon is to swiftly implement 'network-centric warfare'. As first formulated by Vice Admiral Arthur Cebrowski (formerly President of the Naval War College and hand-picked by Defense Secretary Rumsfeld to head the Pentagon's new Office of Force Transformation), network-centric war is fought by getting inside the decision making loop of the adversary's network and disrupting or destroying it before it can do the same to yours. The basic idea is that people make war as they make wealth, and, in the information age, networked technology has become the enabler of both (probably not a view currently shared by Enron stockholders). Information and speed are now the key variables in warfare: whoever has the fastest network wins.

I interviewed Cebrowski about network war while he was still President of the Naval War College. He came across as very smart, highly articulate, deeply religious and quirky.[28] His comments were laced with quotes from an unusual cast of characters, such as former head of Disney's Imagineering, Bran Ferren ('The advent of interconnectivity is comparable to the advent of fire'), and Executive Editor of *Wired*, Kevin Kelly ('The first thing you need for innovation is a well-nurtured network'). In light of 9/11, one answer stood out from the rest. I asked him about the implications of network wars, where the goal is always to be faster than the opponent: Would this not squeeze out deliberation time? Did he really want machine-time to replace human-time? He replied, 'As soon as you can.' The goal was 'to relieve humanity of a lower level decision making process'.

The shift from state-centric to network-centric modes of deterring and defeating new threats makes sense within a rational framework. However, diminishing the role of human decisions, *especially* ones in which emotion plays such a significant part, might not be the best way to confront future threats of terrorism. Furthermore, after the Pentagon released the bin Laden home video in December, where dreams and theology mix with strategies of destruction and slaughter, there was little evidence of any kind of rational purchase for a network-centric deterrence to work.[29] And after witnessing that same day the revival of missile defence as the *deus ex machina* cure for American vulnerability, the consignment of 'lower levels of decision making' to networked technology seems practically (rather than as it had been in the past, mutually) suicidal.

It is clear that the allure of technological solutions reaches across cultures and often beyond rationality. Bandwidth as well as bombs might offer short-term fixes for the immediate threats posed by terrorism. But no matter how weak the flesh, neural networks, human spirit and political will are still needed to make the future safe again. In the rush to harden and to accelerate networks, all kinds of checks and balances are being left behind. There seems to be little concern for what organizational theorists see as the negative synergy operating in tightly coupled systems, in which unintended consequences produce cascading effects and normal accidents, in which the very complexity and supposed redundancy of the network produce unforeseen but built-in disasters. Think Three Mile Island in a pre-1914 diplomatic-military milieu. Think Pentagon *and* Enron when Paul Virilio writes of the 'integral accident':

> The proliferation of atomic weapons, freshly boosted by India, Pakistan and probably other destabilized countries on the Asian continent, is prompting the United States – the last great world power – to accelerate the famous 'revolution in military affairs' by developing that emergent strategy known as 'information war', which consists in using electronics as a hegemonic technology: a role it now takes over from nuclear physics … It is in this context of financial instability and military uncertainty, in which it is impossible to differentiate between information and disinformation, that the question of the *integral accident* arises once again …[30]

My second concern is as much political as it is theoretical: are the social sciences intrinsically unsuited for the kind of investigation demanded by the emergence of a military–industrial–media–entertainment network? President Eisenhower in his 1961 farewell address famously warned the US of the emergence of a 'military–industrial complex', and of what might happen should 'public policy be captured by a scientific and technological elite'. Now that Silicon Valley and Hollywood have been added to the mix, the dangers have morphed and multiplied. Think *Wag the Dog* meets *The Matrix*. Think of C. Wright Mills' power elite with much better gear to reproduce reality:

> The media provide much information and news about what is happening in the world, but they do not often enable the listener or the viewer truly to connect his daily life with these larger realities. On the contrary, they distract him and obscure his chance to understand himself or his world, by fastening his attention upon artificial frenzies that are resolved within the program framework, usually by violent action or by what is called humor … There is almost always the general tone of animated distraction, of suspended agitation, but it is going nowhere and it has nowhere to go.[31]

So, for the near future, virtuous war as played out by the military-industrial-media-entertainment network will be our daily bread and nightly circus. Some would see us staying there, suspended perpetually, in between wars of terror and counter-terror. How do we break out of the distractive, often self-prophesying circles? Are there theoretical approaches that can respond critically without falling into the trap of the interwar? One that can escape the nullity of thought which equates the desire to comprehend with a willingness to condone terrorism? The use of sloppy analogies of resistance as well as petty infighting among critics does not give one much hope. We need to acknowledge that the majority of Americans, whether out of patriotism, trauma, apathy or sheer reasonableness, think it best to leave matters in the hands of the experts. That will not change, the cycle will not be broken, until a public rather than expert assessment is made of what distinguishes new from old dangers, real from virtual effects, terror from counter-terror – and whether we are then ready to live with new levels of uncertainty about those very distinctions.

Otherwise, the last word might well come from the first words I heard of the last war the US fought. Circling ten years ago over Chicago O'Hare airport, the captain came on the PA to inform us that the bombing of Iraq had just begun. In the taxi on the way to my hotel, I heard the first radio reports of stealth aircraft, smart bombs and incredibly low casualty rates. But what stuck from that evening were the last and only words of my cab driver. In the thickest Russian accent, in a terribly war-weary voice, without the benefit of any context but the overexcitement of the radio reports, he said: 'They told us we would be in Afghanistan for ten weeks. We were there for ten years.'

Notes

1 This chapter draws from earlier postings at <www.infopeace.org>, <http://www. ssrc.org/sept11/essays/der_derian.htm> and <http://muse.jhu.edu/journals/theory_&_ event>.
2 '*in terrorem*, as a warning, in order to terrify or deter others' (*Oxford English Dictionary*).
3 Walter Benjamin, *A Lyric Poet in the Era of High Capitalism* (London: Verso, 1997).
4 For an earlier discussion of the ideological, epistemological and ontological obstacles facing any enquiry into terrorism, see my 'The Terrorist Discourse: Signs, States, and Systems of Global Political Violence', *Antidiplomacy: Spies, Terror, Speed, and War* (Cambridge, MA, and Oxford: Blackwell, 1992), pp. 92–126.
5 Michael Ignatieff, 'It's War – But It Doesn't Have to Be Dirty', *Guardian*, October 1, 2001.
6 George Will, 'On the Health of the State', *Newsweek*, October 1, 2001, p. 70.
7 Edward Rothstein, 'Attacks on US Challenge the Perspectives of Postmodern True Believers', *New York Times*, September 22, 2001, p. A17.
8 Mark Edington, *New York Times*, March 2, 1993.
9 *Newsweek*, March 8, 1993, p. 22.
10 *Sunday Times*, February 28, 1993, p. 10.
11 See <http://www.fb.gov/mostwant/terrorists/fugitives.htm>.
12 See <http://abcnews.go.com/sections/us/DailyNews/STRIKE_Casualties.html>, and *New York Times*, February 9, 2002, p. A7.
13 By comparison, 35 of 148 US troops killed in action in the Gulf War were hit by US fire, with 11 killed by accidental US air strikes; and of 467 US military personnel wounded, 72 were hit by friendly fire.
14 See <http://www.media-alliance.org/mediafile/20-5/dossier/herold12-6.html>. *On the difficulty of assessing civilian casualties in Afghanistan, see <http://www.washington post.com/ac2/wp-dyn?pagename=article&node=&contentId=A59457-2002Jan3> and <http://www.arizonarepublic.com/news/articles/0125attacks-civilian25.html>. More recently, the Project on Defense Alternatives, using mainly media sources, has put the number of Afghanistan civilian casualties at between 1000 and 1300. See 'Uncertain Toll in the Fog of War: Civilian Deaths in Afghanistan', *New York Times*, February 10, 2002, p. A1.
15 Jean Baudrillard, *Simulacra and Simulation*, trans. Sheila Glaser (Ann Arbor, MI: University of Michigan Press, 1994), p. 159.
16 *ABC Sunday News*, September 30, 2001.
17 See <http://www.defenselink.mil/news/Sep2001/t09252001_t0925sd.html>.

18 See <http://www.washingtonpost.com/wp-srv/nation/specials/attacked/transcripts/bushtext-092601.html>.

19 See *New York Times*, September 22, 2001 (<http://query.nytimes.com/search/abstract?res=FA091FF6355F0C718EDDA00894D9404482>).

20 See <http://www.whitehouse.gov/news/releases/200l/10/20011007-8.html>.

21 See <http://www.cnn.com/2002/US/01/31/gen.binladen.interview/index.html>.

22 See <http://www.eff.org/Privacy/Surveillance/Terrorism_militias/20011025_hr3162_usa_patriot_bill.html>.

23 In a videotape interview with the Arabic cable network, al-Jazeera (which they never aired but was partially seen on January 31 on CNN), bin Laden displayed his affinity for information technology while scoffing at the White House 'request' that American television networks not broadcast his statements: 'They made hilarious claims. They said that Osama's messages have codes in them to the terrorists. It's as if we were living in the time of mail by carrier pigeon, when there are no phones, no travelers, no Internet, no regular mail, no express mail and no electronic mail.'
    See <http://www.washingtonpost.com/wp-dyn/articles/A5371-2002Jan31.html>.

24 See *Washington Post*, September 26, 2001 (<http://www.variety.com/index.asp?layout=story&articleid=VR1117854476&categoryid=10(&query=H%27wood+enlists+in+ war>).

25 Disclaimer: I provided the information to them. See <http://www.msnbc.com/news/642434.asp>.

26 See my 'Virtuous War Goes to Hollywood', *Virtuous War: Mapping the Military-Industrial-Media-Entertainment Network* (Boulder, CO, and Oxford: Westview Press/Perseus, 2001), pp. 153–78.

27 See <http://www.variety.com/index.asp?layout=story&articleid=VR1117853841&categoryid =10&query=Institute+for+Creative+Technology>.

28 See my *Virtuous War*, pp. 123–51.

29 See <http://www.defenselink.mil/news/Dec2001/b12132001_bt630-01.html>.

30 Paul Virilio, *The Information Bomb*, trans. Chris Turner (London and New York: Verso, 2000), p. 132.

31 C. Wright Mills, *The Power Elite* (New York: Oxford University Press, 1957), pp. 314–15.

20 The question of information technology in international relations

Source: *Millennium Journal of International Studies* (vol. 32, no. 3, 2003), pp. 441–456.

Against the backdrop of events produced by the InfoTechWarPeace Project at Brown University, including internet interventions, videoconferences, symposia, public forums, multi-media exhibitions and video documentaries, this chapter seeks to understand through information technology (IT) how the 'Digital Age' and an 'Age of Terror' converged on 9/11. As an inquiry into the impact of IT on International Relations (IR), it mobilizes the key concepts of 'infowar' and 'infopeace' to trace the development of network-centric forms of conflict and peacemaking. Two short case studies of 11/9 and 9/11 are presented to assess the dual capacity of IT in IR. Trapped in a new interwar of technological and theological fundamentalisms, we need to tap into the surplus capacity of information networks to awaken a global critical consciousness.

Becoming digital

It is an honour as well as a challenge to speak at this *Millennium* conference, for the topic invokes what I believe to be one of the most important issues facing us today: the question of Information Technology (IT) in International Relations (IR). Let us call it the 'IT/IR Question', and begin first by asking whether IR, as suggested by your title, has entered a 'Digital Age'. We need to pose the question because historic moments are supposed to speak for themselves, yet they bear different meanings for different observers. Think of the 'Middle Ages', the 'American Century', the '60's'. Consider 2001, a year that signified awe for an extraterrestrial future in Kubrick's film; that is, until kamikaze airplanes piloted by al-Qaeda terrorists brought the year, and the World Trade Center (WTC), crashing to earth.

We must question how the Digital Age came to enjoy a natural hegemony over other descriptors of modernity, and whether, after 9/11 and subsequent crises, it will continue to dominate all other challengers. Fuelled by a revolution in the digitisation and networking of information, the forces driving the Digital Age show no sign of abating. From its embryonic moments in the 1940's (when Claude Shannon wrote the first paper on information theory, transistors were invented, and ENIAC, the first computer, was built) to its accelerated take-off in the 1990's (when packet-switching, personal computers, html, and the Internet produced a world wide web), the information revolution has outpaced, outlasted and outperformed all commensurable comers.

However, it might not only be premature but simply wrong to assign the Digital Age the status of a *longue durée*. Although the Digital Age might stretch in the United States from Silicon Valley to Alley and globally from Bangalore to Singapore, the distinguishing characteristic of the Digital Age is a spatio-temporal *intensivity* rather than a geopolitical extensivity; that is, a capacity to intensify global effects through a collapse of time and distance. Developing unevenly within and across nation-states, and beset by rapid cycles of dot-com booms and busts, the Digital Age is short on universality and long on instability. When a revolution stops auguring change and begins signifying an age, it usually means that a regime has been stabilised, a cultural shift codified and predictability restored. Not so with the information revolution at the palpitating heart of the Digital Age. The only constant is fast, repetitious, and highly reproducible change: a kind of hyper-speed Nietzschean 'eternal recurrence' that defies—in spite of efforts by democratic peace theorists (with Thomas Friedman leading the pundit's charge)—the predetermined logic of progressivist teleologies. Modernity in a Digital Age manifests itself not as a more advanced era succeeding an earlier backward one, but as rapid oscillations of message and medium (signal-to-noise ratio), regressive repetitions of images (feed-back loops), and phase-shifts between order and disorder (complexity).

The conceit of a discrete and uniform Digital Age further breaks down when we zoom in from a general conception of extensive time to the singularity of intensive global events. Consider the relatively small scale of a decade, from the first to the second President Bush and between the two Gulf Wars, during which we witnessed the rise and fall and rise again of a New World Order. How does the notion of a Digital Age hold up against the crusading character, fundamentalist beliefs, and overlapping authorities of this sordid decade? Does it not emerge first fully formed from war, as industrial war between states gives way to network-centric conflicts among a variety of digitally enhanced combatants? What if we zoom in closer, to that fateful day, 9/11?[1] Has what little was left of the teleological promise of a 'Digital Age' now morphed into the repetitive horror of an endless 'Age of Terror'? Are we now condemned, like Bill Murray in *Groundhog Day*, to wake up every day, not to the horrors of Sonny and Cher on the radio but to O'Reilly, Matthews, and King on cable TV, always the same, unable to change ourselves, the future or even the channel? Or can we learn, as Murray eventually discovers, that this eternal recurrence comes with a highly individuated ethical imperative, that makes every decision, small or large, count, for each one will be revisited with profound consequences.

It should be clear that a revolution's coming of age is not the same as *becoming* an age. Hegel, Murray, and other philosophers of history argue that it takes a crisis to bring self-consciousness to an individual as well as to an era. My second question, then: after 9/11, has the owl of Minerva taken wing? If so, is it signalling the arrival of wisdom, or simply leaving the scene of a heinous crime? Obviously, the meaning of modernity cannot be reduced deterministically to a revolution in information technology; nor can it be understood in the context of terror alone. There are powerful political interests working hard to define the age for their own ends. Through 9/11, both President Bush and Osama Bin Laden are intent on establishing a world that brooks no ambiguity in meaning nor negotiation of politics. As we have seen, President Bush was quick to link the remembrance of 9/11 to the necessity of an Iraqi intervention:

> We also must never forget the most vivid events of recent history. On September the 11th, 2001, America felt its vulnerability—even to threats that gather on the other side of the earth. We resolved then, and we are resolved today, to confront every threat, from any source, that could bring sudden terror and suffering to America. Members of the Congress of both political parties, and members of the United Nations Security Council, agree that Saddam Hussein is a threat to peace and must disarm. We agree that the Iraqi dictator must not be permitted to threaten America and the world with horrible poisons and diseases and gases and atomic weapons. Since we all agree on this goal, the issue is: how can we best achieve it?[2]

This manipulation of fear by the White House prompted Maja Zehfuss and other revisionists to declare emphatically that we must repudiate all political efforts to forestall the interpretation of events through a selective memorialisation of time: 'We must forget 9/11.'[3]

Can we forget the day of terror and reclaim the Digital Age? It is a valiant rallying cry, but not one to assure the fearful or appease the vengeful. Rather than forget, let us try to understand *through* information technology how the 'Digital Age' and the 'Age of Terror' converged on 9/11. I do not invest much time or hope in some edenic, pastoral, pre-digital state of nature in which sweet reason and enlightened thought win out over our dark times. Nor do I think, in our media-saturated world, that a realist unveiling of the truth, whether by Huntington on the right or Chomsky on the left, is preferable or even possible. The best I can provide, and the best that I believe the world can support, are critical questions and counter-visions that challenge the ubiquitous surveillance, instrumental rationality, real-time coverage, and fundamentalist beliefs that have transformed IT into weapons of mass distraction, deception, and destruction. We must begin by questioning this totalising tendency of IT, the 'system of systems', as the military calls it, that would envelope public ways of being from within and from without. But critique is only a start. We must use micro-, crypto-, and other counter-technologies, as does the CitizenLab in Toronto, InfoWar Monitor in Cambridge, and as we try to with the InfoTechWarPeace Project at Brown University, to provide alternative imaginings of America and visions for global security.

Interrogating IT

The first step is to ask what's new and most transformative about IT in IR. Aside from the familiar technological innovations already recounted, I believe that IT has given rise to a new digital media based on a *moving* image of the world. In both senses of the word, this multi-media is *e*-motive, a transient electronic affect conveyed at speed. At the emotional level, this means image-based sentiments of fear, hate, and empathy now dominate word-based discourses of ideas, interests, and power. At the electronic level, the speed of the transmission—with real-time currently the gold standard of media—matters as much as the content of the message. Paul Virilio, urban architect and social critic, has spent a lifetime demonstrating how this media-driven acceleration has produced what he calls an 'aesthetics of disappearance', in which the political subject, be it the accountable leader, participatory citizen, the deliberative process itself, is diminished and quickly engulfed by a growing 'infosphere'.[4]

Secondly, we need to question how IT, increasingly, repetitively, unavoidably, acts not only as trigger and transmitter of the global event, but determines whether or not we respond to the event by diplomatic action or military intervention.[5] From the actual moment to the eventual interpretation—for better or worse—IT records, relays, represents and informs our response to global events. IT also shapes how we remember or forget their significance: we are back to chronology. We are all familiar with the contemporary production and transformation of multimedia by networked information technologies, from increased CPU speeds and broadband access, to realtime cable news and CNN effects, to embedded journalists and network-centric warfare. The global networking of multi-media has become unstoppable, and I believe that its effects may well have accelerated beyond our political as well as theoretical grasp. A public attention deficit disorder leaves little time for critical inquiry and political action by a permanently distracted audience.

Thirdly, we must interrogate as critical pluralists (rather than corroborate as social scientists) the extant knowledge of how IT operates in IR. Questions insist on a down-shifting, from authoritative, incremental, sequential statements to reflective, critical, and—I hope—consequential deliberations about many of the fundamental assumptions of IT. My predilection for multi-media montage over parsimonious rationalist approaches is as much a response to these technological changes as it is a reflection of my earlier critiques of IR theory's failure to keep up with the pace of these changes. This is not an anti-theoretical position. Rather, it shifts our intellectual priorities from the slow, incremental development of theory to the more supple and strategic application of concepts. Put pragmatically, theory informs, concepts perform.

In the case of IT in IR, I rely on the theoretical interventions of two German thinkers who politically straddle yet philosophically converge on the question of technology in art, politics, and war: in particular, Martin Heidegger's *Destruktion* ('dismantling') critique of modernity, and Walter Benjamin's *Jetzeit* ('now-time') analysis of war aesthetics.[6] In the spirit (if not by the letter) of their investigations into the ontotheological foundations of modern technologies, I consider *techne* not as a mere tool but as a way of knowing that 'enframes' for better or worse (and often simultaneously) our image of the world (to use Heidegger's language). Their theoretical orientations inform my adaptations of two of their most performative concepts: *mimesis* and *poeisis*. Over the last few years I have developed Benjamin's concept of the 'mimetic faculty' to interpret how IT in an age of terror reproduces, anticipates, and, if necessary, violently preempts the contingencies, uncertainties and threats that are reduced to a nominal 'enemy' that challenges our ways of being. And I have adapted, by montage technique as well as by textual argument, Heidegger's concept of creative *poeisis* over and against the mimetic and technological fundamentalisms that have plunged global politics into a bipolar disorder.[7]

In the new and alarming Anglo-American tradition of the preemptive strike, let me address those who might be sharpening their knives at my reliance on two thinkers, one a jack-booted philosopher and the other a hashish-smoking literary critic, who are known more for their metaphysics than for a pragmatic approach to global issues. First, although no two times are the same, I do believe that we have entered a period of perpetual crisis that has produced more than a few similarities with their own disturbing experiences in the interwar period.[8] Secondly, metaphysics enjoys a comparative advantage over methodology when ways of being precede and dominate our ways of knowing in IR. William Connolly, who has taken good measure of this development, persuasively argues for a metaphysical strategy:

> Let me put it this way: a particular orientation to method is apt to express in some way or other a set of metaphysical commitments to which the methodist is deeply attached; and a close definition of a political problem is apt to be infiltrated by similar attachments. I do not mean anything technical by 'metaphysical commitment' in this context. It is merely the most profound image of being or the world in which your thinking is set. Differences in world image between Plato, Sophocles, Augustine, Epicurus, Spinoza, Kant, Nietzsche, Freud, James, Charles Taylor, Bertrand Russell, Jon Elster and Merleau-Ponty might all be taken to be metaphysical in this sense. Freud, James and Merleau-Ponty diverge not only in the method of dream analysis each pursues, but also in their faiths about the shape of the world in which dreaming occurs. If, however, you flinch at the heavy term 'metaphysical', I will drop it in favor of another phrase. Indeed, 'existential faith' highlights something that the cold term 'metaphysic' downplays.[9]

What I wish to question is how information technology has come to dominate, in Connolly's words, our most profound image of being in the world. This is not to deny the power of fundamentalism; it is to acknowledge not only the dependency of a religious fundamentalism on IT for the projection and magnification of its power, but also to recognise the rise of a new techno-fundamentalism, in which secularists seek security, salvation, and transcendence through the fetishisation of technology. The stakes now are very high: as Benjamin said (and I like to repeat), 'in times of terror, when everyone is something of a conspirator, everybody will be in a situation where he has to play detective.'[10] We have entered a new convergence of ages, less Aquarian than Orwellian: let us call it the 'Age of Infoterror'. Just as the invention of scientific genocide and the management of a nuclear balance of terror weapons became the key issues of the twentieth century, so too shall the new nexus of terror, information, and technology become the most pressing question of the twenty-first.

To put it as simply as possible, the central question considering information technology is how a revolution in networked forms of digital media has transformed the way advanced societies conduct war and make peace. Obviously such a question warrants not one but multiple approaches. I will not spend much time engaging with the usual rituals of IR, in which the virtues of one approach are measured against another. Instead, I will try to provide some strategic concepts and historical context for assessing the most dangerous against the most promising elements of the information revolution in international relations; a cost-benefit analysis, if you will. In that spirit, and in keeping with our desire to fix a fluid age, I would like to begin with two contrasting stories of potential and peril in IT that took place on a set of singularly inverted dates: 11/9 and 9/11.[11]

The inversion of ages

After the November 9, 1989 opening of the Berlin Wall, which marked the beginning of the end of the Soviet Union, political dissident and playwright Vaclav Havel famously stated (he was actually quoting the historian, Timothy Garton Ash) that what took years in Poland, months in Hungary, weeks in Germany, would probably take days in Czechoslovakia.[12] This compression of time has many causes, but in the context of our topic, one bears further scrutiny. In the spring of 1990 I received a small grant to study the role of the media on the transformation of the Soviet bloc. After stops in Berlin and Budapest, I arrived in Prague to cover the first free elections in over 50 years. I quickly realised that the best place to find the press was in the hotel bars, and over drinks at the Palace Hotel, Claude Adams, foreign correspondent for the Canadian Broadcast Corporation (CBC), told me a remarkable story.

On 7 October 1989, the fortieth anniversary of the founding of the GDR, a small protest demonstration in Berlin was violently broken up by the police. However, two days later, 100,000 people in Leipzig staged a peaceful demonstration. Many might remember the grainy images of the incredible night-time, candle-lit procession. That video was taken by Claude Adams. While other Western camera crews travelled by car and were detained at the border, Adams travelled alone by train as a tourist, carrying only a brand new Sony mini-camcorder that fit nicely under his overcoat. He managed to get the images out to the networks, images that then spilled over the borders into Czechoslovakia at a key moment: the November 17th anniversary demonstration for the Czech student martyr Jan Opletal, who died at the hands of the country's Nazi occupiers 50 years earlier on November 17th. Bolstered by the broadcast of images that had been smuggled out from the Leipzig demonstrations, 15,000 people showed up that day in Prague, followed by a march of 200,000 a week later, and the resignation of the Communist Party leadership in December 1989.

Now fast-forward to 9/11: to the use of the Internet, mobile phones, flight simulators, hawala fund transfers, and other information technologies that made it possible to convert three commercial airliners into kinetic weapons of mass destruction—all, according to intelligence estimates, for less than US$500,000; to the 18-minute gap between the first and second strike on the WTC, which allowed video cameras in a global feedback loop of shock and horror to transform a local catastrophe originally perceived as an accident into a global event that was unmistakably an intentional attack; to Bin Laden's own strategic use of videotape, like the November tape in which he recounted the need to stop the sharing of dreams before 9/11 because it was threatening operational secrecy within al-Qaeda; to the wars of counter-terror, in which informational, technological, and ethical superiority was used to deadly efficient effect by Great Britain and the United States.

9/11 and 11/9. One date speaks of toppling towers, terror, and trauma; the other a falling wall, joy, and hope. Viewed in tandem, we see how the repetitive images and patriotic stories of 9/11 effectively trumped the diverse perspectives and cosmopolitan promise of 11/9. These dates exemplify yet exceed conventional categorisations of information technology as a neutral tool of human agency. IT aesthetically and strategically produced these dates, transforming them from local into global events. IT is not only the means by which we grasp the significance of the events; it determines our way of being in the wake of them. In an age of infoterror, the question of IT in IR cannot help but be metaphysical.

Conceptualising the question

Much of my analysis, based on a montage of images, ideas, and technology, is drawn from web interventions, videoteleconferences, symposia, public forums, art exhibitions, and video documentaries produced over the last few years by the InfoTechWarPeace Project. Central to this effort has been the refinement of terms and the development of new concepts for understanding the power of IT in IR. Our goal has been to produce the kind of networked knowledge, critical thinking, and ethical sensibility that can raise public awareness and inform new policies on global technological issues in war and peace. We seek to open the blackbox of technology and decodify the information by which it operates.

The first step to take, as long as we recognise it as the beginning rather than the end of an argument, is one of definition: what do we mean by information technology? Max Weber once remarked that academics are as proprietary about their definitions as they are of their toothbrushes. When one considers that the electric toothbrush now comes with 300 lines of proprietary code etched in a microchip, the problem of definition becomes much more complicated. Although IT is currently and most commonly identified with binary software, computer hardware, and networked systems, the need to access and communicate information has a long and rich pre-digital history. The rise and fall of just about every civilisation follows a narrative of innovative as well as destructive applications of information technologies. From the gods' messengers to the diplomats' notes, from the telegraph and typewriter to the satellite and computer, power has been organised and instituted by the ability to collect information, convey messages, and secure a knowledge base. Ultimately, IT is defined by the interaction of power, knowledge, and technique, in which archives are created, knowledge is codified, information is transmitted, and effects are produced by remote control.

Advances in microprocessing power and software functionality, coupled with a general decline in cost, have made information technology much more widely available and accessible. Areas of computation and communication have been bridged by the advent of network technologies, primarily in the form of Internet access. A global (if uneven) spread of networked technologies accelerates the pace of cultural, political, economic, and military transformations.

In the twenty-first century, information technology has become essential for the global circulation of power, the waging of war, and the imagining of peace. Information technology is now an unparalleled force in the organisation, execution, justification, and representation of global violence, as witnessed in the first Gulf War, the Kosovo air campaign, and the terrorist attacks on 11 September. After the recent war in Iraq, the global effects of IT in IR became inescapable. We witnessed how anti-war organisers used the Internet globally to muster millions of protesters in large metropolitan areas; US military commanders leveraged technological superiority to wage network-centric warfare; and embedded journalists provided influential battlefield reports by satellite videophones in realtime. A glut of information (if a dearth of knowledge) drew viewers by the millions, not only to primetime TV and cable news, but also to instantly updated online press sites and unofficial war blogs. We witnessed the first, but certainly not the last, networked war.

Moreover, the darker side of networks, although freighted in the occasional media spasm, continues to evade the sustained attention of IR theory as well as the concern of international institutions.[13] Networked terror, network-centric warfare, network attacks by the Blaster, Nachi, and SoBig viruses, and a hot summer of electrical network failures had a tremendous transnational impact.[14] Networked technologies merged issues of national, corporate, and personal security (and liberty) into an interconnected global problem. Yet the new global risks of interconnectivity, including negative synergies, unintended consequences, and the pathologies of networks like viruses, worms, and Trojan horses, often fail to make the global political agenda at all.

Based on these recent events, I offer three general propositions about how IT is changing IR. First, the most obvious: IT is producing new networks of power in IR. By now there should be no need to rehearse the fall-of-the-Wall and rise-of-the-Internet story. Yet the social sciences have been slow to take into account how the coeval devolution of the Soviet Union into Russia and of ARPANET into the Internet has produced new constellations of power and security. Many scholars saw the end of the Cold War as an occasion to consider the loss of bipolar stability and to argue the merits of multipolar over unipolar state-systems. Though these perspectives on world order are vital debates, they continue to be circumscribed by state-centric as well as realist interpretations of how power works.

I take and advocate a different worldview, in which networks, best defined by Kevin Kelly as 'Organic behavior in a technological matrix', are challenging and changing the nature of state power through new lattices of relatedness and responsiveness.[15] Obviously, the United States has emerged as the dominant military and economic power, and even in the worst-case nightmares of global realists, it is difficult to identify a potential 'peer competitor' on the horizon. However, post-Cold War, post-9/11, we have witnessed the emergence of competing sources and mediations of power: what I call a *global heteropolar matrix*, in which different actors are able to produce profound global effects through interconnectivity. Varying in identity, interests, and strength, ranging from fundamentalist terrorists to peace activists, new global actors gain advantage through the broad bandwidth of information technology rather than through the narrow stovepipe of territorially-based sovereign governments. Enhanced by IT, non-state actors have become super-empowered players in international politics. Traditional forms of statecraft have become transformed and in some cases undermined by infowar, cyberwar and netwar. The technologies of weapons of mass destruction, networked terror, accidental crises, and global media have transformed the meaning and discourse of national security.

Networked IT provides new global actors the means to traverse political, economic, religious, and cultural boundaries, changing not only how war is fought and peace is made, but making it ever more difficult to maintain the very distinction of war and peace. The 'West' might enjoy an advantage in surveillance, media, and military technologies; but the 'Rest', including fundamentalist terrorist groups, non-governmental organisations, and anti-globalisation activists, have tapped the political potential of networked technologies of information collection, transmission, and storage. We need to undertake a full-scale investigation of how global political actors force-multiply their influence in IR through networked IT.

Secondly, if we are to challenge as well as understand the role of IT in IR, we must use networked knowledge. New informational and technological networks of power in IR require new modes of comprehension and instruction, and the social sciences have not been quick to take up the challenge. The virtual nature and accelerating pace of IT is partly responsible: actualising global events in realtime across traditional political, social, and cultural boundaries, IT resists the social-scientific emphasis on discerning rational behaviour, applying static models, and conducting incremental research projects. Moreover, the study of IT requires a dialogue among technological, scientific, military and other non-academic circles that has been notably lacking in discipline-bounded university programs and politically oriented think tanks. Taking into account the heteropolar as well as multicultural nature of global politics, we need a strategy that endorses plural, conceptual and multidisciplinary approaches to investigate what we consider to be the most challenging issue of the twenty-first century: the global application and management of IT in war and peace. We need a strategy that produces, sustains, and extends global networks of knowledge and authority that will help raise public awareness and inform new policies on IT in IR.

Thirdly, the information transformation of IR requires new conceptual approaches. The signs of rapid change are in the system: information, to paraphrase William Burroughs, has become a virus, and the immune response is often worse than the original contagion; densely networked systems produce negative as well as positive synergies with cascading effects; and everywhere global institutions of governance are failing to keep up with the new global risks of interconnectivity. We must adopt new strategies, concepts, and polices for the new dangers and opportunities presented by IT. Again, as a preliminary step, I adapt and update a pair of concepts from the interwar, *mimesis* and *poeisis*, to understand the dual capability of IT to enable the continuation of violence through infowar, as well as to provide the means to prevent, mediate and resolve conflicts through infopeace.

Information warfare, or infowar, has become the umbrella concept for understanding cyberwar, hackerwar, netwar, virtual war, and other network-centric conflicts. It has a history that goes back at least as far as Sun Tzu, who considered defeating an enemy without violence to be the 'acme of skill' in warfare. From its earliest application in the beating of gongs and drums, to more sophisticated uses of propaganda and psychological operations, infowar has traditionally been deployed by the military as a 'force-multiplier' of other, more conventional forms of violence. In this sense, infowar is an adjunct of conventional war, in which command and control of the battlefield is augmented by computers, communications, and intelligence. With the development of mass and multiple media, infowar has taken on new forms and greater significance. As the infosphere engulfs the biosphere, as the global struggle for 'full spectrum dominance' supplants discrete battlefields, as transnational business, criminal, and terrorist networks challenge the supremacy and sovereignty of the territorial state, information warfare has ascended to a significant site for the struggle of power and knowledge. Infowar wages an epistemic battle for reality in which opinions, beliefs, and decisions are created and destroyed by a contest of networked information and communication systems.

Infowar couples sign-systems and weapons-systems. Command and control, simulation and dissimulation, deception and destruction, virtual reality and hyper-reality: all are binary functions—sometimes symbiotic, other times antagonistic. Networks of remote sensing and iconic representation enable the targeting, demonisation, and, if necessary, killing of the enemy. In its 'hard' form, infowar provides 'battlespace domination' by violent (GPS-guided missiles and bombs) as well non-lethal (pulse weapons and psychological operations) applications of technology. In its 'soft' form, infowar includes a virus attack on a computer network or the wiping out of terrorist organisations' bank accounts. In its most virtualised form, infowar can generate simulated battlefields or even create *Wag the Dog* versions of a terrorist event. In any of these three forms, information warfare can be offensive (network-centric war, Trojan horse virus, or intelligence dissimulations) or defensive (ballistic missile defence, network firewall, or preventive media).

In spite of the official spin, infowar is not a precision munition. It might seek to discriminate in its targeting of enemies, but it is as broadcast forms of media that it is likely to produce all kinds of collateral damage, blowback, and newly resentful enemies.

At the other end of the IT spectrum lies infopeace: the production, application, and analysis of information by peaceful means for peaceful ends. Starting with Gregory Bateson's definition of information as 'a difference that makes a difference'[16]—this is war, that is peace, this war is here, that war is over there, this war is now, that war was then—infopeace seeks to make a difference through a difference in the quality of thinking about the global contest of will, goods, and might. Measuring information in terms of quality rather than quantity, and assessing quality by the difference it makes in the reduction of personal and structural violence, infopeace opens up possibilities of alternative thought and action in global politics. Unabashedly utopian yet pragmatic, it counters a 'natural' state of war with an historicised state of peace.

Infopeace seeks to prevent, mediate, and resolve states of war by the actualisation of a mindful state of peace. Positing the eventual abolition of violence as a global political option, peace-mindedness ranges from the prevention, admonition and mediation of violence, to the outright disavowal of violence to resolve problems in the international arena. It draws on a long tradition of peace-thinking, exemplified in early Christian pacifism and Eastern philosophies, in which the need for peace begins internally and proceeds outwardly. It starts by embracing a wholeness of the individual, and expands to families, communities, countries, and beyond. The notion of Gaia as a self-regulating biosphere contributes to the rhetoric of peace thinking, but it is the networked reality of an expanding infosphere that makes peace an attainable and ever more vital necessity.

Infopeace stresses the actualisation of peace through the creative application of information and technology. As a form of critical imagination, infopeace resists a technological determinism that increasingly circumscribes human choices. Further, infopeace integrates a strategy in which difference, conflict, and antagonism are recognised as essential aspects of human relations. It aims to develop an awareness of how these aspects can be addressed by non-violent means.

From mimesis to poeisis

We must not stop asking the question of IT; but at some point wheels begin to spin, critique runs out of gas, and the world moves on, unaffected by our inquiry. My strategy has been to fight fire with fire, concept with concept, media with media. Against the imitative, repetitive, regressive practices of infowar, I have posited the imaginative, creative, visionary strategies of infopeace. But how do we get from mimesis to poeisis in an age of infoterror?

It would seem that the deck is stacked against us. We have moved from an aesthetic to a pathological condition of mimesis, medically defined as 'the appearance, often caused by hysteria, of symptoms of a disease not actually present.' In such an atmosphere of pervasive terror, virtuous war, and mimetic politics, one seeks the counsel of thinkers who have faced similar hazards in a different, yet increasingly familiar, interwar. On the nature and dangers of mimesis, Walter Benjamin has no rival. Consider when Benjamin warns in 'The Work of Art in the Age of its Technical Reproducibility' of new forms of technologised war in which self-alienated humans become 'their own showpiece, enjoying their own self-destruction as an aesthetic pleasure of the highest order'[17]; when he writes in 'On Aesthetics' that mimesis and violence have a linked origin going back to 'the human from the stone-age' who 'sketches the elk so incomparably, only because the hand which leads the crayon still recalls the bow with which it shot the animal[18]; or when he states in 'Theories of German Fascism' that 'the harshest, most disastrous aspects of imperialist war are in part the result of the gaping discrepancy between the gigantic power of technology and the minuscule moral illumination it affords', concluding that 'any future war will also be a slave revolt of technology.'[19] Do we not hear our own latter-day crusaders and jihadists at work?

For Benjamin, the first essential step one must take to escape the mimetic trap of the interwar was an awakening of critical consciousness. Citing Marx, he says we must 'awaken the world from its dream about itself, seeking not the 'false liberation of violence' but the way of 'cunning'.[20] Benjamin refutes not only a Rankean realism that would reduce history to a narcotising story of how it 'really was' and ever shall be; he also rejects the mimetic homogenisation of humanity into self-maximising units.[21] The challenge is to confront the alterity, contingency, and paradox—meaning, fundamentally, the terror—of the human condition, and to have the courage to make our choices in the face of those who would want necessity to decide for us.

It might seem tendentious to invoke thinkers and concepts drawn from an earlier period of war, totalitarianism, and genocide. But after my own travels into the cyborg heart of the Military-Industrial-Media-Entertainment Network, I have come to realise that the interwar is not so much a demarcation of past history and future peril as an invocation of a bad dream—all in the guise of a virtual and inevitable reality.[22] Hence, the dream's long and intimate relationship to the ultimate necessity, war. Benjamin writes:

> Dreams have started wars, and wars, from the very earliest times, have determined the propriety and impropriety—indeed, the range—of dreams. No longer does the dream reveal a blue horizon … Dreams are now a shortcut to banality. Technology consigns the outer image of things to a long farewell, like banknotes that are bound to lose their value.[23]

In our period of interwar, in which the Bush Administration and al-Qaeda have produced a pathological bipolarity that goes beyond the ideological binaries of the Cold War, we must revitalise the power of poeisis in the service of infopeace. This might have a utopian ring to it, were it not for the tool at hand, the networked computer. We have seen first hand how networks enable anti-war movements as well as acts of war. Unlike other dual-use technologies, the networked computer has an excess capacity; or, as simply put by Bruno Latour (reducing Alan Turing's more complex idea): 'you get out of it much more than you put in.'[24] In the Digital Age, power devolves upon those who best understand and channel the surplus value operating in networks.

Under the weight of states of emergency and conspiracies of terror, cunning becomes not a choice but a new necessity. We must tap into the powers of IT and find new ways to network cunning into a collective awakening from our current nightmare.

Notes

1 After 9/11, epochs were reduced not only to a single day but to hours, as chronicled by none other than one of LSE's own, Fred Halliday: *Two Hours That Shook the World. September 11, 2001: Causes and Consequences* (London: Saqi, 2002). Indeed, I considered titling my talk '60 Minutes that Shook the Millennium', but thought 'The Question of Information Technology in International Relations' was pretentious enough.

2 President Bush, Cincinnati, Ohio address, 7 October 2002, http://www.whitehouse.gov/news/releases/2002/10/20021007-8.html.

3 Maja Zefuss, *After 9/11* videodocumentary, from a presentation at the 'Technologies of Anti/Counter/Terror' symposium held at the Watson Institute in June 2002.

4 See Paul Virilio, *The Aesthetics of Disappearance*, trans. Philip Beitchman (New York: Semiotext(e), 1991), and James Der Derian, 'Introduction', *The Paul Virilio Reader* (Oxford: Blackwell Publishers, 1998), 1–15.

5 See *Philosophy in a Time of Terror: Dialogues with Jurgen Habermas and Jacques Derrida*, ed. Giovanna Borradori (Chicago, IL and London: University of Chicago Press, 2003), 85–90.

6 See Martin Heidegger, *The Question Concerning Technology and Other Essays*, trans. William Lovitt (New York: Harper & Row, 1977); Walter Benjamin, 'On the Mimetic Faculty', in *Reflections*, ed. Edmund Jephcott (New York: Schocken, 1978); Philip Rosen, 'Introduction 'Benjamin Now: Critical Encounters with the Arcades Project', *Boundary 2* (Spring 2003): 1–4.

7 This conceptual and pragmatic application of Heidegger and Benjamin builds on an earlier theoretical exposition of their work, first outlined in James Der Derian, 'A Virtual Theory of Global Politics, Mimetic War, and the Spectral State', *Angelaki: Journal of Theoretical Humanities* 4, no 2 (1999): 53–67.

8 For instance, shortly after the 9/11 attack, columnist George Will wrote that there were now only two time zones left for the United States: 'America, whose birth was mid-wived by a war and whose history has been punctuated by many more, is the bearer of great responsibilities and the focus of myriad resentments. Which is why for America, there are only two kinds of years, the war years and the interwar years.' George Will, 'On the Health of the State', *Newsweek*, 1 October 2001, 70. See also James Der Derian, 'Between Wars', in *Virtuous War: Mapping the Military-Industrial-Media-Entertainment Network* (Boulder, CO and Oxford: Westview Press, 2001), 23–47.

9 William E. Connolly, 'Method, Problem, Faith', (unpublished paper, Fall 2002).

10 Walter Benjamin, *Charles Baudelaire: A Lyric Poet in the Era of High Capitalism* (London and New York: Verso, 1973).

11 I would like to thank Thomas Risse for inspiring this inversion of dates, during a plenary session of the German Political Science Association on the significance of 9/11 for the IR discipline, 24 September 2003, Mainz, Germany.

12 Timothy Garton Ash, 'The Revolution of the Magic Lantern', *New York Review of Books* (18 January 1990), 42.

13 This was born out at the December 2003 World Summit on the Information Society recently held in Geneva, at which the techno-optimists, vamping the political, cultural, and developmental promise of technological interconnectivity, had centre stage while critics—especially American ones—were marginalised and kept out of the main planning sessions.

14 These global viral attacks were surpassed by the Mydoom virus, which targeted the SCO Group (which is in a legal fight for control of the Unix operating system) and Microsoft (every hacker's favorite bad guy), and managed to infect over 1 million computers and 40 per cent of all email.

15 Kevin Kelly, *New Rules for the New Economy* (London: Fourth Estate, 1999), 31.

16 Gregory Bateson, *Steps to an Ecology of Mind* (Chicago: University of Chicago Press, 2000), 459.

17 Walter Benjamin, 'Das Kustwek im Zeitalter seiner technischen Reproduzierbarkeit', in *Gesammelte Schriften* 1.2, eds. Rolf Teidemann and Hermann Schweppenhauser (Frankfurt am Main: Suhrkamp, 1974–89). I rely here on Jeneen Hobby's translation and interpretation of the 'second version' of the essay (discovered by Gary Smith in the Max Horkheimer Archive in the 1980s and included in the collected works), as it includes the epilogue as well as material on mimetic theory that is missing from other versions. See Jeneen Hobby, 'Raising Consciousness in the Writings of Walter Benjamin', Ph.D. dissertation (Amherst, MA: University of Massachusetts, 1996), 254, fn 1.

18 Teidemann and Schweppenhauser (eds.), *Gesammelte Schriften*, VI, 127, quoted by Jeneen Hobby, 270.

19 'Theories of German Fascism: *On the Collection of Essays War and Warrior*, ed. Ernst Jüinger (1930), *Gesammelte Schriften*, III, 238–50.

20 Walter Benjamin, *The Arcades Project* (Cambridge, MA: Belknap Press, 1999), 456, 173.

21 Benjamin, *The Arcades Project*, 463.

22 See Der Derian, *Virtuous War.*

23 Ibid.

24 Bruno Latour, 'Why Has Critique Ruin Out of Steam?', *Critical Inquiry* (Winter 2004).

21 Hedley Bull and the case for a post-classical approach

Source: *International Relations at LSE: A History of 75 Years* (London: Millennium Publishing Group, 2003), pp. 61–87.

'An institution is the lengthened shadow of one man'.[1]

No single event defines a life, but from my first to my last encounter with Hedley Bull, the compass of my academic life was set. Even when our paths diverged, Bull's antipodal nature—the Oxford robes barely cloaked an Australian nonconformism—would continue to influence my future choices.

The first encounter took place in his Balliol College study. Barely into the first term of a political philosophy graduate degree at Oxford, I had already managed to burn my way through two tutors; one was interested only in John Rawls, the other in dry sherry. The word in the dining hall was that the Montague Burton Professor was revamping the International Relations (IR) programme for the better, that not only was he a good tutor and lecturer, but unlike most Oxford dons he actually knew how to run a graduate seminar. I requested a meeting. After a few pleasantries, Bull got down to it: what IR courses had I taken as an undergraduate in North America? To this day I believe that my acceptance into the IR program hinged on my response. After pausing to consider how I might inflate the actual truth of the matter, I hesitantly answered: 'only one'. After a couple of wheezy puffs, he asked me why. I confessed to boredom and a chronic inability to distinguish a dependent from an independent variable. One chortle later, Bull took me on as a student, sealing the decision with an invitation to the drink's party that he hosted each year for new graduate students in IR.

At the drink's party, I got my first glimpse of the idiosyncratic side of Bull. The IR program had not yet been colonised by North American students, and all twenty of us along with the odd, some quite odd, assortment of dons could fit into the Master's Garden. A new student acquired Bull's ear, and confidently expounded on the general neglect of Leon Trotsky's writings in the field of IR. Bull listened, rocking from heel to toe. I learned later to decipher this pendular motion as a kind of physical wind-up to an imminent verbal salvo. However, the fan of Trotsky took Bull's bemused silence as an opportunity to dig himself a deeper hole, into which he stacked concepts for the rescue of bourgeois IR, like the 'law of uneven and combined development', 'permanent revolution', and 'dual power'. Just as the widening arc of Bull's rocking threatened to plant a Liverpool kiss on Trotsky's young acolyte, Bull spoke: 'Hmmm, yes, yes, and when I was an undergraduate, we thought the divine light shone forth from Stalin's arse'.

My last encounter came as a letter, a mixed signal that would have a powerful and lasting impact. Dated 17 January 1985, the letter was a response to an earlier request that he read a new draft introduction of my Oxford dissertation that I was then revising for publication. He wrote:

> Do finish your revised thesis and publish it before you become bored with it. I am very suspicious of your 'post-classical approach to International Relations theory'. It seems rather pretentious and likely to get you into trouble. Does your thesis really need this? I have always felt that it would be better standing on its own as an orthodox account of the evolution of diplomacy than as an exercise in some mysterious new methodology which will have to be shot down in due course by some sceptical critic as all the previous methodologies have been. If you would like me to read it, however, I should be delighted.

He then informed me of the bad news: 'To cut a long story short, I have had a malign tumour lodged in my spine'. At the bottom of the typewritten letter, he penned in his barely readable script a final message, one that I interpreted not as an afterthought but as a supplement, the excess of writing that undoes the coherency of the given text. He wrote: 'Stick to your guns, and do what *you* think is important, not what others want you to do'.

Bull died three months later. He never read the introduction but it didn't matter; weighing his advice, I jettisoned the 'post-classical approach'. A small portion of it did, however, see the light of day as part of an introduction to the 1988 special issue of *Millennium: Journal of International Studies* on *Philosophical Traditions in International Relations.*[2] When the *Millennium* editors came calling again for a Special Edition on the Department's anniversary, I tried to consider the options as Bull might have. The editors specifically asked for my 'impressions, recollections and thoughts on his mentorship, and the way it did or did not influence your take on the field of IR'. From my encounters with Bull it should be obvious that he had little use for sycophants of any stripe. However, the editors' *coda* to the request gave me an opening: 'the more unconventional and innovative the piece, the better'. I detected an echo of Bull's take-it-and-leave-it advice to me; indeed, it was not unlike waving a red flag in front of a bull. I decided there could be no better way to honour Bull as well as the editors' needs than to make my case for a post-classical approach.[3]

My strategy is simple: I first present a synopsis of the classical approach as the 'lengthened shadow of an individual'; that is, as I learned it from Hedley Bull in four years of tutorials, lectures, seminars, and dissertational supervision, and as I subsequently compared that knowledge to future surveys of the 'English School'. Second, I introduce what I consider to be the shortcomings of the classical approach, which entail a post-classical supplement of *identity, representation,* and *epistemes.* Third, I consider three historical and philosophical questions that distinguish the post-classical from the classical approach. How does the formation and interaction of identity and difference, among self and groups, define international relations? Second, how do written, visual, and other forms of representation act as both constructive and destructive forces in international relations? Third, what new post-classical thinkers might guide us from the present to the past and back again, and provide us in the interpretive process some wisdom about future dangers and opportunities?

The classical approach to international relations

Hedley Bull brought to the classical approach an appreciation of theory. Whereas Martin Wight, Herbert Butterfield and others thought historical reasoning and empirical techniques were sufficient for their diplomatic investigations, Bull plunged headfirst in the theoretical debates of the day. His definition of IR theory was deceptively simple: 'the leading ideas that have governed and do govern our thinking about International Relations'.[4] And the three goals of IR theory were plainly laid out: 'to expound what those ideas are, to relate them to their historical context, and to examine their truth and their bearing on our present political concerns, in relation to past practice and to present practice'.[5] But it was in the theoretical historicisation—and hence differentiation from the behaviouralists—that the depth of the classical approach emerges. Bull clearly thought the philosophical-historical investigations of the classical approach superior to methodological-behavioural proofs because they were time-tested, self-reflecting, and judgmental.

The classical character of his version of IR theory can be traced back to the origins of theory itself. People once travelled to Delphi, one of the most sacred sites in ancient Greece, to pursue knowledge of the truth, an act that came to be described by the joining of the Greek terms *theoria* and *horao* for journey and an attentive contemplation.[6] We should not make too much of linguistic origins, but it would appear from time immemorial that theory required a journey, to seek out a distant truth, to look outside oneself, to reach for (if never entirely achieve) a balance between one's own world and the world beyond. From my first tutorials with Bull, I have come to identify theory with travelling, often to very strange places, in pursuit of highly elusive truths, and with the greatest insights coming from the journey itself rather than the final destination.

Second, Bull took culture seriously. Culture is as old as the first attempt to cultivate a seed, a germ, or an idea. Matthew Arnold placed the concept on a pedestal, writing in 1866 in his influential *Culture and Anarchy*, that culture is 'a pursuit of our total perfection by means of getting to know ... the best which has been thought and said in the world'.[7] In a realm so imperfect as IR, it is not surprising that culture long suffered from neglect. It has, however, enjoyed a resurgence of attention in both the theoretical and policy sides of IR.[8] Bull construed culture as the glue as well as the proof of his key concept, the international society.[9] Contrary to the realist view that states are engaged in a perpetual struggle for power in an international anarchy, the classical approach upholds a belief in an international society composed of states tied together by a common set of values, rules, and institutions. According to this view, an underlying 'international system' or 'states system' provides a level of interaction such that one state's actions will impinge upon another's. But something more than the contiguity of physical action is at work in an international society: a common culture. The formation of an international society has been dependent upon the expansion—sometimes peaceful, more often not—of predominately Western cultural values, codes, and symbols.

Bull identifies three primary cultures at work in the international society.[10] He distinguishes the elite 'international political culture'—the formative and reflective attitude of international society—and 'diplomatic culture'—the ideas and beliefs held in common by official representatives of states—from a more universal, cosmopolitan 'world culture', which is identified by modernity. World culture is still a 'culture of the dominant Western powers' but one that is moving to absorb non-Western elements and values. In turn, all three of these cultures could be sub-divided into 'a common intellectual culture—such as a common language, a common philosophical or epistemological outlook, a common literary or artistic tradition—the presence of which served to facilitate communication between the member states of the society'; and 'common values—such as a common religion or a common code—the presence of which served to reinforce the sense of common interests that united the states in question by a sense of common obligation'.

Third, before the study of norms became the norm of IR theory, Bull was doing ethics, in both the most general sense of investigating the principles and rules of conduct which guide international relations, but also as an a priori critical attitude that must attend all theoretical inquiry. Ethics has suffered from neglect in IR, but the subject has recently reappeared in the liberal/constructivist analysis of norms as an influential set of principles, rules or values, as well as in the critical/post-structuralist study of ethics as part of a normative process by which theory helps to construct the world through acts of perception, narration, and inscription.[11] Bull was speaking both languages before they had become theorised into opposing camps. He advocated objectivity but openly declared it unattainable. Bull thought it a laudable but unlikely prospect that we might be able to separate how we see, tell stories, and write about the world, from how we judge what is right or wrong, possible or not in that world. Ethics is as much the product of *how* as it is the object of *what* we study in IR. Moreover, ethics tightens the bond between theory and practice, making us partially, if not individually, responsible for what we make of the world. Bull's radical view on this in the preface to *Anarchical Society* bears repeating: 'inquiry has its own morality, and is necessarily subversive of political institutions and movements of all kinds, good as well as bad'.[12]

Bull's classical triangulation of theory, culture, and ethics work as a kind of Global Positioning System for his wide-ranging historical and empirical investigations of international relations. They help the reader position themselves in the text, in the complexities of history, and in the rapidly changing present. More broadly, they also help us to understand how our own positions, as scholars and students, writers and readers, are influenced and fixed by how we study the world. Bull was very aware of the pull of power on knowledge, and of how the key questions in IR of objectivity (the where, what, and when) are inflected by subjectivity (the who, why, and how). Bull contributed a philosophical self-consciousness to the classical approach, but he stopped at the edge of the Enlightenment map. If we are to find and begin to understand the sea monsters that lurk beyond the edge, however, more is needed: a post-classical approach that understands how the representational powers of the maps themselves help to determine who is friend or foe, when and how wars will be fought or ended, and whether or not just the West but the rest of the world constitutes the international society.

Identity

A post-classical approach reopens the question of identity. A dictionary definition might emphasise the distinguishing characteristics of an individual, or the essential sameness of a group. Everyday events can give us a good sense of the importance of identity. Some identities we choose, while many seem to choose us: one needs state identity to vote, photo identity to get on a plane, national identity to go from one country to another, and for some unfortunates, proof-of-age identity to buy an alcoholic beverage. Identities come with benefits and costs: differences in gender and racial identities show up in disparate income levels, rates of incarceration, even probabilities of execution. The focus on identity shifts in different fields of knowledge: a psychologist might focus on the attitudes and the perceptions of the individual; a sociologist on the formation and behaviour of group identity; an anthropologist on the rituals and ceremonies of a tribal or communal group; a linguist on the common sign-system of a language group; and a political theorist on the legitimacy of a governmental identity. Long before constructivists in IR caught on to the question of identity, British philosopher David Hume wrote of its pertinence in 1739: 'Of all relations the most universal is that of identity, being common to every being whose existence has any duration'.[13] In other words, identity is fundamental to all.

The identity question in international relations raises the ante. The most general function is the relationship between those we identify as us and those we identify as them, as self and as other, as identity and as difference. Identity is a constitutive part of international relations, unifying as well as dividing whole peoples. The effects of identity can range from familiarity and friendliness, to indifference and tolerance, to estrangement and hostility. Understanding or not understanding others' identities can result in appreciation or denigration, accommodation or separation, assimilation or extermination. Together, the formations, functions, and effects of identity can draw physical boundaries between peoples, as well as metaphysical boundaries between life and the most radical other of life, death. They can separate humans from God. And they can build the fence that makes good neighbours, as well as the wall that confines a whole people.

The ultimate reason to study the concept of identity in international relations is that 'we' make war and make peace with 'others'. These others might be newly encountered people from across an ocean or over a mountain range. They might be all-too-familiar people, who once were fellow humans, reliable allies, friendly neighbours, or even likeable kin. They might be a projection of some aspect of ourselves. But for one reason or many—or, as we seem forced to relearn in every generation, for no reason at all—they come to be recognised as the 'other': barbarian, infidel, heretic, savage, revolutionary, traitor, racist, sexist, lunatic, alien, cyborg. In turn, the collective identity of 'us'—the citizen, the patriot, the believer—becomes dependent upon these differences. These historic encounters of identity and difference have created fundamental physical, metaphysical, and representational boundaries in and of international relations.

Representation

Identities do not form in a vacuum. Social, political and historical factors are important influences. But in every case there is at work a formative relationship between identity and representation. Representation generally refers to an action or a symbol that stands for or expresses something else. In traditional textbooks on politics, representation usually refers to the process in which an elected or appointed person expresses the interests of a greater number of persons. We need to expand that notion to include the study of symbolic and metaphorical representations, which like identity itself are formed out of a relationship to something different. We need to examine how representation and identity are mutually constitutive, in the sense that both are defined by an interaction of differences: we become who we are by how we represent ourselves as different from others. This is the second arena in which a post-classical approach is required.

This becomes clearer when we get more deeply into the similarities and differences between political and linguistic uses of representation. Just as representatives in a democracy 'stand for' others who are not present in a parliament or legislature, words, images, symbols, signs, and other representations stand for the complex realities of the world. There are similar difficulties with the realities of war and peace: they cannot all 'fit' into a single representation. Ambiguities and uncertainties can arise from acts of perception and interpretation. To paraphrase a past President of the United States, one person's freedom fighter is another person's terrorist. But how do we know what distinguishes one from the other? How, for that matter, do we know that freedom fighters, unlike fire fighters, fight *for* rather than *against* freedom?

Whether representations say what they mean and mean what they say is a key question (a question that might also be raised about some political 'representatives'). Some philosophers of language claim that reality is transparently reproduced by representations: representations reflect reality. When I write 'mouse', these philosophers would say that I have clearly indicated a furry rodent with four legs and a tail. Others believe that reality can be distorted or obscured by the context, intentions, and method of representation: representations refract reality. When I write mouse, such a philosopher would say that I could have meant a rodent, a timid person, or, perhaps because I mis-clicked with a different kind of mouse, a louse. And the most radical interpreters of language go so far as to say that reality is entirely created by representations: representations construct reality. When I write mouse, they see a relationship of signs which produce an image of a rodent rather than, say, that of a house, because of internally governed linguistic conventions which generate meaning without any reference to an external material reality.

Representations can do all three things: reflect, refract, and construct reality. As well, a powerful synergy between representations and identity is often in operation. They both are produced and sustained by difference. To put it simply, representations and identities are informed and constructed by a relationship to something different. Understanding the nature of this mutually constitutive relationship is fundamental to understanding international relations. This is especially true in the context of war and peace, where the representation and constitution of identity are all too often accompanied by a rigidifying violence that often defies purely rational explanations.

War, as an organised form of violence, is age-old. So too are efforts to end, prevent, and outlaw war. Yet, as Geoffrey Blainey remarks in the opening lines of *The Cause of War*, 'For every thousand pages published on the causes of wars there is less than one page directly on the causes of peace'.[14] After discussing a host of other explanations, Blainey speculates that war is simply more interesting, more newsworthy than peace. War is simply more difficult to ignore than peace. Probably even Hedley Bull would have agreed with Leon Trotsky, when he stated that 'You may not be interested in war, but war is interested in you'. We could go further, and say that war is not only more newsworthy and interesting than peace: it is more representative of the long history of violence and conflict in international relations. The story of war must be told, but with an awareness that in the constant telling and retelling of war we also delimit and ignore the possibilities of peace.

No politics, especially international politics, stands above or outside of representation. The role of representation is a matter of philosophical controversy, from the early dialogues in ancient Greece between Socrates and the Sophists to more modern debates between different schools in IR theory. But there would probably be wide agreement that the number and pace of critical representations in international politics are rapidly outstripping human comprehension: microprocessor speeds double every year, ubiquitous surveillance intrudes into our public and private lives, 500 channels are available on television sets that now outnumber toilets in American households.

We can see how the introduction of identity and representations raises concerns and questions to which the classical approach has not and probably cannot respond. What roles have national, religious, cultural, social, racial, gendered, political and other identities played in the preparation, execution, and termination of war? How, in turn, have new forms of representation, from mass newspapers to radio speeches to popular films to video and the Internet, created new identities? Who controls representations and identities? Are they freely chosen, or chosen for us? Is peace possible without some deeper understanding of how we produce, in the very act of understanding of who 'we' are and what we are not, the conditions for war or peace, of fear, hate, and resentment, or accommodation, mediation, and reconciliation? Can there ever be a truly secure identity? Can there ever be a peace that is not merely a temporary absence of war? At what cost? These are the type of questions that the classical traditions of IR can hardly understand, let alone answer.

The classical traditions

History involves a dialogue of the living with the dead, or rather the 'undead', those representatives of the past who haunt the present with invocations of tradition. Tradition can be a collection of doctrines, a type of behaviour, or even a way of regarding others. From its Latin origins in Roman law, *tradere* (meaning to 'hand over' or 'pass on', to its invocation by the powers that be, tradition has been the means by which the continuity, the authority, and—one hopes—the wisdom of the past is transmitted or handed down to the present.

In IR, the classical approach bears the cross of tradition more so than any other IR theory. From Martin Wight on, it has located three powerful traditions in international relations: the Realist, Rationalist, and Revolutionist traditions. Following the names of their respective seminal thinkers, Niccolò Machiavelli (although Bull preferred the more 'modern' Thomas Hobbes), Hugo Grotius, and Immanuel Kant, they are also identified as 'Machiavellian' (Realist), 'Grotian' (Rationalist), and 'Kantian' (Revolutionist).[15] Although rooted in particular moments in history, these traditions acquire a 'classical' status because they transcend the constraints of time and place to provide transhistorical insights about the theory and practice of international relations. They continue to shape not only how scholars think about the world, but also how leaders and diplomats practice international politics according to the principles embodied by the traditions. Before challenging the traditions, it is important to understand, if even in shorthand, their analytical value.

The Machiavellians (or Realists) were described by Martin Wight as the 'blood and iron men'.[16] In their ranks were thinkers like Thomas Hobbes and Georg Friedrich Hegel, and leaders like Frederick the Great and Otto von Bismarck, whose ideas and lives became the source for twentieth century realist theorists like E.H. Carr and Hans Morgenthau. Their view of human nature was starkly pessimistic; consequently, human relations were full of 'sin, suffering, and conflict'. In *Leviathan*, Hobbes famously extrapolated from human nature the causes of conflict: competition, diffidence, and glory that give rise to wars of gain, safety, and reputation. This meant that international politics, without a 'common power to keep all in awe', was indistinguishable from a state of nature or anarchy: men are in a 'condition called war', *Bellum omnium contra omnes*— 'every man against every man'.[17] International society was, at best, a convenient fiction to cloak the naked pursuit of power in legal niceties and diplomatic formality. Justice was whatever was in the interests of the strongest party. Foreign policy consisted of cunning and coercion. The endless struggle for power assured a history marked by repetition and recurrence. The 'other' had no rights, except to be conquered if weak. In short, might makes right.

The Grotians (or Rationalists) are the 'law and order men'. Some of the more influential Grotian thinkers were John Locke and Edmund Burke; famous leaders were Franklin Roosevelt and Winston Churchill. They took a more moderate view of human nature than the Machiavellians, and saw good as well as bad, in a state of constant tension. Unlike Hobbes, Locke discerned evidence of comity and goodwill in a state of nature. Property rights and contract law were expanding from the domestic to the international realm. Human and international relations, improved through reason (by great men) and paternal vigilance (by great powers), could produce some sense of historical progress. Most importantly, the innate nature of humans for sociability provided the germ for an international society, to be nurtured and protected by institutions like a balance of power, diplomacy and international law which might mitigate the excesses of sovereign states pursuing national interests. Conflict among states would still arise, but in the Rationalist perspective social and economic intercourse elevated the value of cooperation. Without a world government, wars break out, but they were 'just wars', fought according to shared principles of legitimate authority and proportionality. Foreign policy was best served by honesty and trust in negotiation. The 'other' had some rights under tenuous universals like natural jaw, but not the right to obstruct trade or to limit the expansion of 'civilisation', for these are the forces bringing peace to international society. In short, reciprocity rules.

The Kantians (or Revolutionists) are the 'subversion and liberation men'. Their view of human nature as redeemable by education and acculturation was optimistic, and the source of a conviction that the anarchy of independent states was an obstacle for the progressive movement towards a community of mankind. Composed of thinkers who wrote of the world as it ought to be, the pantheon of Kantians was small but influential, and came with a wide range of views on how to change an unjust system of states. At one end there were evolutionists like Woodrow Wilson who advocated constitutionalist reforms for the states system, and at the other revolutionists like Vladimir Lenin who called for its eradication. The Kantian perceived a Manichaean international politics, of a world divided between good and evil, the saved and the damned, the oppressed and the oppressors. The ends of foreign policy was to end the state itself, so as to replace national interests with the interests of humanity. Therefore, propaganda and subversion were preferable to negotiation and compromise for the goal of human perfectibility. The only just war was holy war, leading to total victory. The right of the 'other' was to assimilate—or risk extermination. In short, right makes might.

Classical international theorists are well aware that there are risks as well as benefits to a theoretical approach based on traditions. In both the original formulation by Martin Wight and in the reassessment by Hedley Bull, caveats accompany the traditions of international theory.[18] They are both aware that traditions work because they reduce the complexities of the past in order to transmit it in a comprehensible form to the next generation of thinkers. The traditions are not to be construed as some magic key to open the door of history, or a pigeon-hole into which contemporary events and figures should be stuffed. Wight and Bull view them as general paradigms inspired and embodied by seminal thinkers who provided a useful set of historical *descriptions* (of what happened), political *prescriptions* (of what ought to be), and, in some instances, theoretical *inscriptions* (of what can be thought and written). As Hedley Bull noted in his lectures, not even Machiavelli was a Machiavellian. These representative thinkers were much deeper, more reflective observers of their respective times than any synoptic tradition can possibly convey. Their status as 'classical' thinkers reflects an ability to transcend their own time, to offer some timeless wisdom for world politics. But it also reflects a certain openness, even ambiguity to their thought, that allows for transhistorical interpretation. This is why these traditions remain useful analytical and interpretive tools for understanding present as well as past practices and principles of IR.

Nonetheless, there remain theoretical hazards. The traditions can be abused to distort the past into expedient justifications of the present. They can make the present a mirror image of the past. This would impoverish international relations theory by a 'presentism', where the past neatly adds up, like a mathematical formula, to the present. Moreover, with the accretions of time and power, traditions can also fossilise into 'natural histories' that weigh heavily on the living, and provide fewer as well as thinner insights as contemporary IR goes through radical transformations. At such moments, counter-traditions take on an appealing form.

The post-classical epistemes

As well as providing a new set of historical guides, a post-classical approach adopts stricter philosophical guidelines for defining the classical traditions. It takes the traditions seriously, perhaps even more so than the classical international theorists, because the traditions are treated as constitutive rather than merely reflective forces in international politics. According to this approach, the traditions do not simply record and transmit the history of world politics: they are part of a constant making and unmaking of history through interrogation, interpretation, and narration. The traditions act as narratives, or stories of the past that limit as well as enable a set of interpretations for the present. Traditions are used to interrogate rather than confirm current conventions and assumptions in IR, by setting up dialogues with alternative, counter-traditional perspectives. It is a first step towards the kind of critical, historical reasoning that makes the reader an ethical producer rather than a neutral consumer of knowledge.

Traditions and counter-traditions in the post-classical approach serve as historical markers for the emergence of particular discourses, or authoritative statements that shape international politics, which are then further reduced to pithy aphorisms, like 'prepare for war if you desire peace', or 'might is right'. Discourses, narratives, and traditions determine what can be said, who can say it, and when it can be said with power and persuasion, legitimacy and authority. When they are elevated into dominant paradigms that explain events to the exclusion of all other explanations—one story is naturalised into the truth—we can, and shall in this case, call them *epistemes* (from the Greek term for 'knowledge'). Drawn from the work of Michel Foucault, the French philosopher of systems of thought, *epistemes* are defined as the foundational discourses that establish the origins, methods, and limits of systems of understanding.[19] For a traditional or counter-traditional discourse to take on an epistemic power, it must be debated by powerful figures, spread by new technologies of communication, routinised by custom and habit, institutionalised by formal practices, and finally (but not necessarily sequentially), philosophically and consciously rendered by criticism, sometimes even outright opposition, into a (counter-)tradition.[20]

The enduring concepts and institutions of international relations, from power and sovereignty to international law and diplomacy, took shape during the time Machiavelli, Grotius, and Kant were writing. But innovations in transportation (railroad and steamship), communication (telegraph and radio), and production (assembly line and machines) ushered in an industrial age that forever altered how humans make war and peace. Moreover, the realities of world politics are increasingly generated, mediated, and even simulated by new means of representation, further distancing them from some original historical moment or original meaning. Moving at speed from the industrial to the informational to the virtual age, the classical traditions are hard-pressed to keep up. How can we expect Machiavelli, Grotius or Kant to further our understanding of permanent states of neither war nor peace (cold war), new technological forms of warfare (information war, cyber-war, net-war), para-wars that rely as much on the metaphor as the reality of war (trade war, drug war), and the whole array of wars that do not fit into the traditional categories and explanations (race war, class war, gender war, culture wars)? New forms and multiple sources of conflict often seem to resist comprehension through the traditional paradigms, not least because they all place a premium on the value of reason and the secular to explain international politics. The failure to anticipate the end of the cold war—as well as the lack of a vision after it—is the most recent and notable testimony to this resistance. Alternative security regimes, feminisms, the accelerated flows of information, capital, refugees, critical social movements, trans-national crime, environmentalism, media politics, and fundamentalism are just some of the more powerful challenges which have suffered from theoretical neglect by traditional approaches.

To enhance the critical pluralism needed to comprehend newly multipolar and multicultural times, I offer a new *troika* of post-classical counter-traditions: the Nietzschean (Friedrich Nietzsche); the Gandhian (Mahatma Gandhi); and the Beauvoirian (Simone de Beauvoir).[21] In keeping with Wight's penchant for alliteration, they will also be called the Relativists, Revelationists, and Irenists.

The Nietzscheans, or Relativists, are the 'will to power men'.[22] Like the Realists, they view the world as a site of permanent contestation of the will, the most vital of life forces: 'life is a consequence of war, society itself a means to war'.[23] But the will to power cannot be reduced, as the Realist would, to self-preservation: 'Life itself is will to power; self-preservation is only one of the indirect and most frequent results'.[24] Therefore, the will to power should not be confused with a Machiavellian lust for power. When repressed, the will to power can produce a reactive and resentful longing for only power, leading to the triumph of nihilism.

But under conditions of freedom, will to power is an active and affirmative force which revalues all imposed values. It pits individuals against themselves, not others, in an act of self-overcoming. Neither human nature nor the state of nature can be defined as a given, or a timeless fixity; only something that has no history can be defined. Nor can they be seen as existing as some kind of prior condition or permanent cause of strife. They are powerful effects of the 'death of God',[25] like the end of first principles and the rise of modernity, all of which have led to the construction of new systems of faith based on rationality as well as systems of politics based on sovereignty. Nietzsche attacks these and all other demonstrations of a 'will to a system'. Life is a contest of wills and a desire for recognition. Systems might promise protection but they also corrupt life, leading to the decadence of mass society and mastery over others rather than a self-becoming and mastery over oneself. Adolf Hitler is the arch-example of the former; Vaclav Havel, the latter. The will to power is repressed, domesticated, and bureaucratised by the dominant system of modernity, the nation-state, producing all kinds of pathologies: 'madness is rare among individuals; in entire nations it is common'.[26] In foreign policy, the will to power is projected as the desire for security, producing a collective resentment of others and the uncertainty they represent. This, in turn, triggers further insecurities. Real peace only comes when states stop preparing for war, even if done in the name of self-defence. Real security only comes when one recognises and learns to live with a multitude of perspectives and the insecurity of all values. Like the Realist, the Relativist views history as discontinuous yet recurrent, an endless cycle. This does not, however, lead to despair or amorality. Rather, the 'eternal recurrence' entails an ethical challenge to accept that one will relive the consequences of one's actions, either in smallness or greatness. From God to Rational Man, from Empire to Republic, from King to the People, the history of IR has been an effort to resecure the centre, to keep at bay anarchy, chaos, and difference. Rather than substitute a new foundational centre, the Nietzscheans offer a philosophy of relativism and perspectivism, an ethics of revaluation, and a politics of pluralism to negotiate the ambiguities and paradoxes of a life in which the only certainty is death. In sum, right is always relative to might.

The Gandhians (or Revelationists) are the 'truth and faith men'. Founding father of India, leading proponent of non-violence, and ardent believer in the revealed truth, Gandhi is the name-sake of the Revelationist counter-tradition. He has earned emblematic status to represent what often goes under-represented in the study of war and peace: the profound role of faith, love, and truth in struggles of national liberation and anti-imperialism as well as in the non-violent resolution of conflict and the reconciliation of belligerents. All too often religion is studied in the social sciences as the enemy of reason and a threat to peace. In its most extreme fundamentalist forms this has been and continues to be the case for some religious movements. But there is another story to be told— one that gets lost in the exhibitionism of fundamentalist violence. Testifying to the cross-cultural as well as cross-faith power of the Revelationists, Tolstoy in Russia, Martin Luther King in the US, and the Dalai Lama in Tibet share an alternative vision to the pervasive violence at the core of the international system. The aim of the Revelationists is to end conflict through non-violent, persuasive, empathetic means. The means matter as much as the ends. The Gandhian idea of *satyagraha* (literally, 'truth in firmness') best captures this sense of means as ends-in-the-making. Truth is not to be found in reason, a state, or a culture but in the revelation of the will of God. The Revelationists do not, however, call for holy war. The force of truth cannot be used to inflict pain or punishment upon others because humans are incapable of absolute knowledge of the truth: 'what appears to be truth to the one may appear to be error to the other'.[27] One cannot be sure enough to impose one's views upon. Moreover, truth is tempered by love for the whole of humanity; Gandhi refers to *satyagraha* as the force which is born of truth and love. In the Revelationists' struggles against conditions of injustice and oppression, symbolic power levels the playing field, and gives this counter-tradition a pragmatic power. The symbolic powers of ritual of sacrifice, catharsis through tragedy, and purification through suffering (*tapasya*) are augmented by the reciprocal powers of forgiveness, tolerance, and compassion. Together, these powers of the Revelationists are practically applied through a range of political actions: civil disobedience, non-violent strikes hunger strikes, occupations, demonstrations, amnesties and commissions of truth and reconciliation. A world without war—defined as political, economic, and religious violence—is the goal, but this means one must endure rather than inflict pain, be ready to lay down your life rather than to take others. In short, righteousness makes non-violent might.

The Beauvoirians (or Irenists) are the 'gender and peace' women. Simone de Beauvoir's book, *The Second Sex*, was the first to offer a systematic feminist critique which linked the perpetuation of inequality and violence to masculine *cultures* and *representations*, rather than to fixed human natures or biological differences.[28] Two of her most famous epitaphs are: 'One is not born but rather becomes a woman'; and 'Representation of the world, like the world itself, is the work of men; they describe it from their own point of view, which they confuse with absolute truth'.[29] Since Beauvoir, feminist counter-traditions have been fruitful and multiplied, ranging from existentialist to essentialist, standpoint to empirical, psychoanalytic to post-structuralist, liberal to backlash. Each of these feminisms differ on how gender is viewed, as natural, constructed, or just androgynously irrelevant. But most strands of feminism continue to share, more or less, a critique of masculinity which links patriarchy to war; hence the emblematic tag of 'Irenists', from Irene, the Greek goddess of peace. In this counter-tradition, men are not necessarily the 'bad' warriors, and women the 'good' peacemakers, although some essentialist feminists do blame testosterone and credit motherhood to imply such a position. More often, Irenists represent a theoretically sophisticated attempt to understand how certain representations and constructions of gendered identities, both male and female, have perpetuated conditions of injustice and violence. Historically, patriarchy has enforced such conditions through a politics of exclusion (public space is for men, private space for women); theories of psychoanalysis (men are enabled by the penis, women disabled by envy and hysteria); discriminatory legal codes (the 'law of the father' keeping wealth and power in the hands of the men); and privileging one side of a binary opposition over another (mind over body, strong over weak, rational over emotional as natural conditions of gender). The Irenists expose, so to speak, masculinist values posing as universalist principles. In IR, the autonomous self, the sovereign state, the principle of self-help are all interpreted as masculine values, in contrast to feminine ones of interdependence, cooperation, and caring. Irenist foreign policy revalues neglected issues like reproductive rights and equality for women as well as disarmament and peace-making. The Irenists subvert the hierarchy of war when they take a set of gendered identities and values that appear biologically fixed, and reveal its historical, cultural, and representational contingency. In short, care makes might.

Identity through dialogue

A post-classical approach does not construe epistemes as frozen artefacts of the past. This approach treats the present itself as a continuous dialogue, between a past that is open to interpretation and a future that is open to construction. Moreover, in this dialogue, where neither the past nor the future is a given, the question of identity is always present and pressing. The identity of the subject—that is, the self, the sovereign state, or international society—is constituted through this dialogue. The subject is made 'real' by the meaning that is conferred upon it by the dialogue between past and present. This post-classical approach, which recognises that identity is always under construction, grants a greater role to history. But it also suggests that there might be a wider range of options for the future than is usually presented in international relations.

The Russian linguist Mikhail Bakhtin used the model of language to raise the importance of dialogue in the formation of identity. He suggested, as Hume did of identity, that a 'dialogism' is at work in all human relations. He challenged the closed Marxist orthodoxy of 'dialectics' with the open concept of the 'dialogic', using language as the model for how we recognise the very necessity of difference for understanding ourselves and others:

> There is no first or last discourse, and dialogical context knows no limits (it disappears into an unlimited past and in our unlimited future). Even past meanings, that is those that have arisen in the dialogue of past centuries, can never be stable (completed once and for all, finished), they will always change (renewing themselves) in the course of the dialogue's subsequent development, and yet to come. At every moment of the dialogue, there are immense and unlimited masses of forgotten meanings, but, in some subsequent moments, as the dialogue moves forward, they will return to memory and live

in renewed form (in a new context). Nothing is absolutely dead: every meaning will celebrate its rebirth.[30]

In the act of communicating and negotiating meaning with others, we constitute the self. This entails forward as well as backward perspectives: every responsive act depends upon prior as well as anticipates future discourses.[31] This means that identity is not just some internal, psychological creation: identity requires difference. We are dialogically constructed in discursive communities, whether it is a group of people debating one version of their past over another, historians arguing over the rise of Nazism, or IR theorists engaged in a variety of specialised languages. In other words, we are more dependent upon discourse with others for our own identity than we tend to realise. In Bakhtin's words, 'The psyche enjoys extraterritorial status'.[32] Yet, in world politics, the state continues to 'enjoy' the status of a highly territorial, sovereign identity. Bakhtin would respond that when the monologue of one tradition dominates a dialogue among many traditions, hard, fixed, conflictive identities tend to follow.

These insights on dialogues between the present and past, the self and other, as well as between and among the traditions, might take us one step closer to my earlier call in *Millennium* for a post-classical approach that can help us to understand '*why a* particular tradition develops in a specific historical moment, *how* it makes the world intelligible, the *source* of its persuasive power, and the *cost* of a tradition which outlives its heuristic value'.[33]

We can see how these theoretical questions might have a variety of pragmatic implications. Consider the first (amidst the mess of the second) Gulf War. Was it fought to keep the US strong and our gas tanks full? Was it an effort to counter an illegal intervention by Iraq into Kuwait, which required a re-establishment of a regional balance of power best achieved through a coalition of forces? Was it a struggle of good against evil, Western civilisation and democracy against the barbarism and dictatorship of Saddam Hussein? Or was it fought, as the first President Bush declared, 'to kick the Vietnam syndrome': to renew, in other words, a collective identity of Americans willing to intervene in distant conflicts? Each of these questions represents a tradition, and it is in the dialogue between them, rather than the imposition of any single one, that might yield the best explanation of the Gulf War. Moreover, the philosophical as well as pragmatic aim of a dialogue is to provide what a monologue cannot: an informed plurality of perspectives which might then produce both public and ethical support for the toughest policy decisions faced by national leaders of when to and not to go to war.

Studying war and peace as a dialogue leads inevitably to the question of identity. A dialogical approach means that we do not treat history and meaning as 'other', as something to conquer, transcend or end, but as something with which we continually engage in the process of forming our own identity. The extent to which we make history or history makes us is a critical question for our identity as a citizen of a particular country. Does the identification of one belief with the truth define particular identities? In times of war and terror, do we choose the identity of patriot, or is it chosen for us? Does the very creation of a collective identity require war? Why would it? Just how free are 'we' to make peace?

The devolution of Hedley Bull

I often find myself wondering, what would Hedley Bull now make of a post-classical approach? Or of IR in general? Difficult to say, but past encounters might again provide some clues. I can still see his eyebrow raised in scepticism when I first outlined a master's thesis in 1980 that appropriated alienation theory for an inquiry into diplomacy. A couple of years later I escalated my original misdemeanour into a major felony, by proposing to use the ideas of the French thinkers Sartre, Barthes, and Foucault for a doctoral dissertation on diplomacy as a system of estrangement. But by then Bull was more than an accomplice to the crime. He anticipated Huntington's clash of civilisations by over a decade, lecturing on historic encounters of identity in his 1981 Trinity Term lectures on 'Ideas of the Unity of Mankind'.[34] As supervisor of my doctoral dissertation, 'On Diplomacy: From States of Alienation to the Alienation of States', he combined muted praise with benign neglect, until it came down to the wire, when he hosted at home evening-long sessions of sentence-by-sentence critiques, softened by the consumption of fine Riesling wines. He picked up the pieces after a parlous viva defence, at which my examiners, Michael Howard and Adam Watson, so rattled my cage that I failed to hear them announce that I had passed, but figured out as much when they invited me to Bull's house for a celebratory garden party (how this invitation was conveyed in advance of the viva, given the strict Oxford guidelines that there be no communication between the examiners and the supervisor, remains a mystery). Based on past experience, I suspect that Bull would have carried on as before, slightly out of step and yet always one step ahead, because he knew the old paths better than just about everyone else, and because he was not about to waste much time trying to break new ones.

References

1. Ralph Waldo Emerson, 'Self-Reliance', in *Essays and English Traits, The Harvard Classics*, vol. 5, ed. Charles W. Eliot (New York: P.F. Collier and Son, 1909–14[1841]), 17.

2. James Der Derian, 'Introducing Philosophical Traditions in International Relations', *Millennium: Journal of International Studies* 17, no. 2 (1988): 189–93. In this essay I marked the arrival of post-structuralist and post-marxist as well as post-classical approaches in IR. I have since made the case for a post-structuralist approach. History has rendered a verdict, an unjust one that will come back to haunt IR (yes, like a spectre), on the viability of a post-marxist approach.

3. I wish to emphasise that this essay outlines an 'approach' rather than attempts to develop a full blown theory or a school of thought—at a time when Bull is commonly identified as a fully-paid up member of the 'English School' now being touted as a 'globally recognized brand name'; Barry Buzan, 'The English School as a Research Program: An Overview, and A Proposal for Reconvening' (paper presented at the BISA Conference, Manchester, December 1999) http://www.leeds.ac.uk/polis/englishschool/buzan99.htm (21 September 2003). It might be useful to remember that Bull dismissed the notion of IR

as a disciplinary 'school' and thought, at best, that it represented a subject-matter. Equally, my focus on Bull is delimiting: many thinkers shaped the classical as well as post-classical approaches. However, based on my marching orders from the *Millennium* editors as well as my own view that the English School is a 'pseudo-institution' (as Hedley Bull, following Martin Wight, called the United Nations), i.e., laudable aspirations without commensurate powers, my interpretation adopts the Emersonian view that all institutions are the 'the lengthened shadow of one man'.

4.   Wight coined the term 'international theory', which Bull also used but came to prefer 'theory of international relations' as he put it, for reasons of precision since it is the relations that are international rather than the theory. It might still be an ambiguous term, but what Martin Wight says about the language of Grotius equally applies to 'international theory': that a 'fruitful imprecision' better reflects the subject under scrutiny. See Martin Wight, *International Theory: The Three Traditions*, eds. Gabriele Wight and Brian Porter (London: Leicester University Press, 1994), xii and 1; and Hedley Bull, Lecture Notes to Theory and Practice of International Relations 1648–1789, author's files.

5.   Ibid.

6.   This etymology of theory is drawn from James Der Derian, *On Dipomacy: A Genealogy of Western Estrangement* (Oxford: Blackwell, 1987); Martin Heidegger, *The Question Concerning Technology and Other Essays*, trans. William Lovitt (New York: Harper, 1977); Costas Constantinou, *On the Way to Diplomacy* (Minneapolis, MN: University of Minnesota Press, 1996); and the always insightful suggestions of Michael Degener.

7.   Matthew Arnold, *Culture and Anarchy* (Cambridge: Cambridge University Press, 1932), 6.

8.   On the theory side, see Friedrich Kratochwil and Yosef Lapid, *The Return of Culture and Identity in IR Theory* (London: Lynne Rienner, 1996); on the policy implications of culture, see Samuel Huntington, 'The Clash of Civilizations?', *Foreign Affairs* 72, no. 3 (1993): 22–49.

9.   See James Der Derian, 'Hedley Bull and the Idea of Diplomatic Culture', in *International Society after the Cold War*, eds. Rick Fawn and Jeremy Larkins (London: Macmillan, 1996).

10.   Hedley Bull, *Anarchical Society: A Study of Order in World Politics* (New York: Columbia University Press, 1977), 303–35 and Hedley Bull and Adam Watson, eds., *The Expansion of International Society* (Oxford: Clarendon Press, 1984).

11.   For liberal and constructivist approaches, see Peter Katzenstein, ed., *The Culture of National Security: Norms and Identity in World Politics*, (New York: Columbia University Press, 1996); Andrew Moravcsik, 'Explaining International Human Rights Regimes: Liberal Theory and Western Europe', *European Journal of International Relations* 1, no. 3 (1995): 157–89; and Jeffrey Checkel, 'International Norms and Domestic Politics: Bridging the Rationalist-Constructivist Divide', *European Journal of International Relations* 3, no. 4 (1997): 473–95. For examples of critical and post-structural approaches, see David Campbell, *National Deconstruction: Violence, Identity, and Justice in Bosnia* (Minneapolis, MN: Minnesota University Press, 1998) and Neta Crawford, *Argument and Change in World Politics: Ethics, Decolonization, and Humanitarian Intervention* (Cambridge: Cambridge University Press, 2002).

12.   Bull, *Anarchical Society*, xviii.

13.   David Hume, *A Treatise of Human Nature*, vol. 1, 1874, 323.

14.   Geoffrey Blainey, *The Causes of War* (New York: Free Press, 1973), 3.

15.   Wight, *International Theory*.

16.   These forensic composites are mainly drawn from the lectures and writings of Martin Wight and Hedley Bull, and, as can be discerned from the casual use of 'men' for all actors in IR, they were not much touched by feminist thinking.

17.   Thomas Hobbes, *Leviathan*, ed. Richard Tuck (Cambridge: Cambridge University Press, 1991 [1651]), Chapter 13.

18.   Hedley Bull, 'Martin Wight and the Theory of International Relations', in Martin Wight, *International Theory*, ix–xxvii; Brian Porter, 'Patterns of Thought and Practice: Martin Wight's "International Theory"', in *Reason of States: A Study in International Political Theory*, ed. Michael Donelan (London: Allen and Unwin, 1978), 64–74; and Michael Donelan, *Elements of International Political Theory* (Oxford: Clarendon Press, 1990).

19.   'By episteme, we mean, in fact, the total set of relations that unite, at a given period, the discursive practices that give rise to epistemological figures, sciences, and possibly formalized systems'; Michel Foucault, *The Archeology of Knowledge and the Discourse on Language*, trans. A. M. Sheridan Smith (New York: Harper & Row, 1976), 191. See also Michel Foucault, *The Order of Things: An Archeology of the Human Sciences* (New York: Vintage, 1973).

20.   It might be somewhat romantic but useful nonetheless to note that Machiavelli was banished from public life (after a short spell of torture and imprisonment), and only achieved political notoriety after a barrage of anti-Machiavellian tracts. Grotius wrote some of his best work while in prison for high crimes against the state. And even the relatively timid Kant once suffered censure from the Prussian King Frederick for his writings on religion. It is important to remember the often insurgent origins of traditions that come to dominate international politics.

21.   Just as there are other candidates for the traditions (e.g., Thomas Hobbes, who Bull preferred over Machiavelli, Adam Smith or Karl Marx), so too with the counter-traditions (e.g., Frantz Fanon, Simone Weil, or Hannah Arendt). The choices I have made should be judged by their ability to help us navigate through the issues, complexities and dilemmas of contemporary international politics.

22.   Friedrich Nietzsche, *Will to Power*, #53.

23.   Friedrich Nietzsche, *Beyond Good and Evil*, trans. Walter Kaufmann (New York: Vintage, 1989), 21.

24.   Friedrich Nietzsche, *Twilight of the Idols*, trans. R.J. Hollingdale (Harmondsworth: Penguin Books, 1968), 25.

25.   Friedrich Nietzsche, *The Wanderer and His Shadow*.

26.   Walter Kaufmann ed., *The Portable Nietzsche* (New York: Viking Press, 1954), 71–72.

27.   Mohandas Karamchand Gandhi, *Teachings of Mahatma Gandhi*, ed. Jag Parvesh Chander (Lahore: The Indian Printing Works, 1947), 494.

28.   Simone de Beauvoir, *The Second Sex* (New York: Knopf, 1952).

29.   Ibid., 301,161.

30.   Mikhail Bakhtin as quoted in Tzvetan Todorov, *Mikhail Bakhtin: The Dialogical Principle* (Minneapolis, MN: University of Minnesota Press, 1984), 110.

31.   Mikhail Bakhtin, *The Dialogic Imagination: Four Essays by M.M. Bakhtin*, ed. Michael Holquist (Austin, TX: University of Texas Press, 1981); Todorov, *Mikhail Bakhtin;* and Paul de Man, 'Dialogue and Dialogism', in *The Resistance to Theory* (Minneapolis, MN: University of Minnesota Press, 1986), 106–15.

32.   Mikhail Bakhtin, *Marxism and the Philosophy of Language* (New York: Seminar Press, 1973), 39.

33.   Der Derian, 'Introducing Philosophical Traditions', 190.

34.   On several occasions, the last in a letter of 7 February 1984, Bull suggested that we cooperate in a study of how such encounters shaped IR. Inspired by his 1981 lectures, I have been teaching a course and updating a textbook for the last ten years, 'Representations of War, Peace and Identity', which begins, as Bull did, with the Greeks and Barbarians and ends with the Humans and Cyborgs.

Index